✹ CREDITS

LEAD WRITER: David F. Chapman
WRITING: Will Brooks, Walt Ciechanowski, Steve Darlington, Morgan Davie, Robin Farndon, Nick Huggins, Derek Johnston, Andrew Kenrick, Mark Lawford, Charles Meigh, Andrew Peregrine, Jacqueline Rayner, Gareth-Michael Skarka, Alasdair Stuart and Nathaniel Torson.
EDITING: Andrew Kenrick
COVER: Paul Bourne
GRAPHIC DESIGN AND LAYOUT: Paul Bourne
CREATIVE DIRECTOR: Jon Hodgson
ART DIRECTOR: Jon Hodgson
PUBLISHER: Dominic McDowall
PROOFREADERS: Jim Blanas, Ian Finney, Karl Fordham, Peter Gilham and Brian Swift.
SPECIAL THANKS: Ross McGlinchey and the BBC team for all their help.

The **Doctor Who Roleplaying Game** uses the Vortex system, designed by David F. Chapman.

Published by Cubicle 7 Entertainment Ltd
Suite D3 Unit 4 Gemini House, Hargreaves Road, Groundwell Industrial Estate, Swindon, SN25 5AZ, UK. (UK reg. no.6036414).

Find out more about us and our games at www.cubicle7.co.uk

Printed by: Standartų Spaustuvė www.standart.lt, Vilnius, Lithuania.

⚙ CONTENTS

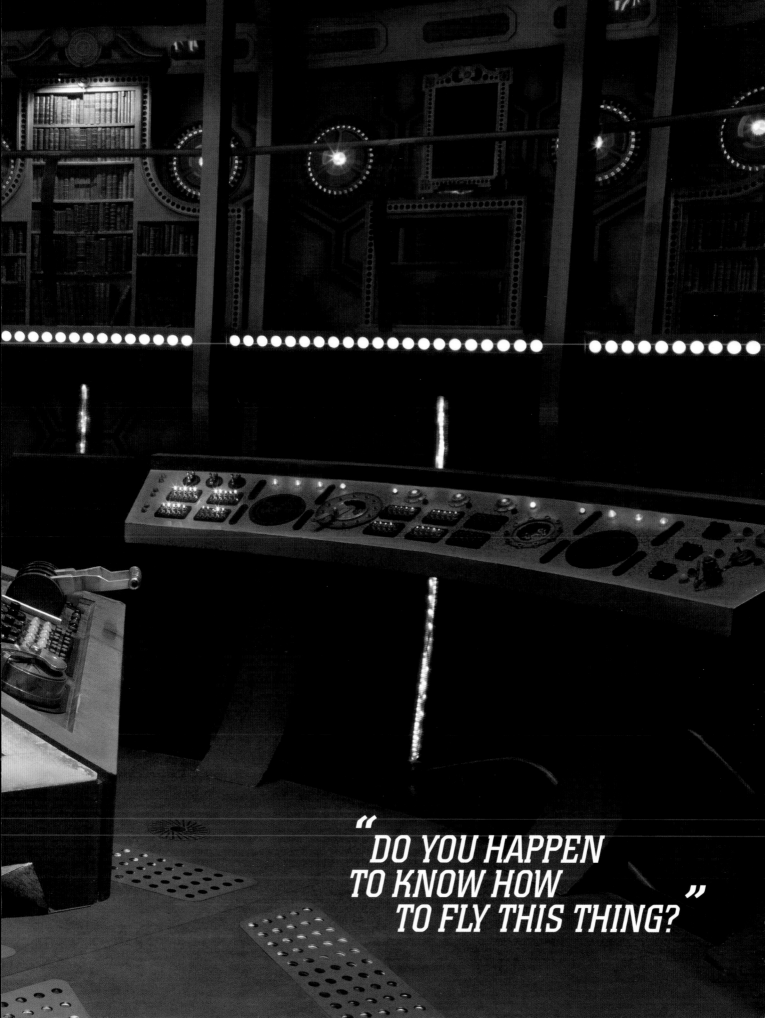

"DO YOU HAPPEN
TO KNOW HOW
TO FLY THIS THING?"

CHAPTER ONE:
THE TRIP OF A LIFETIME

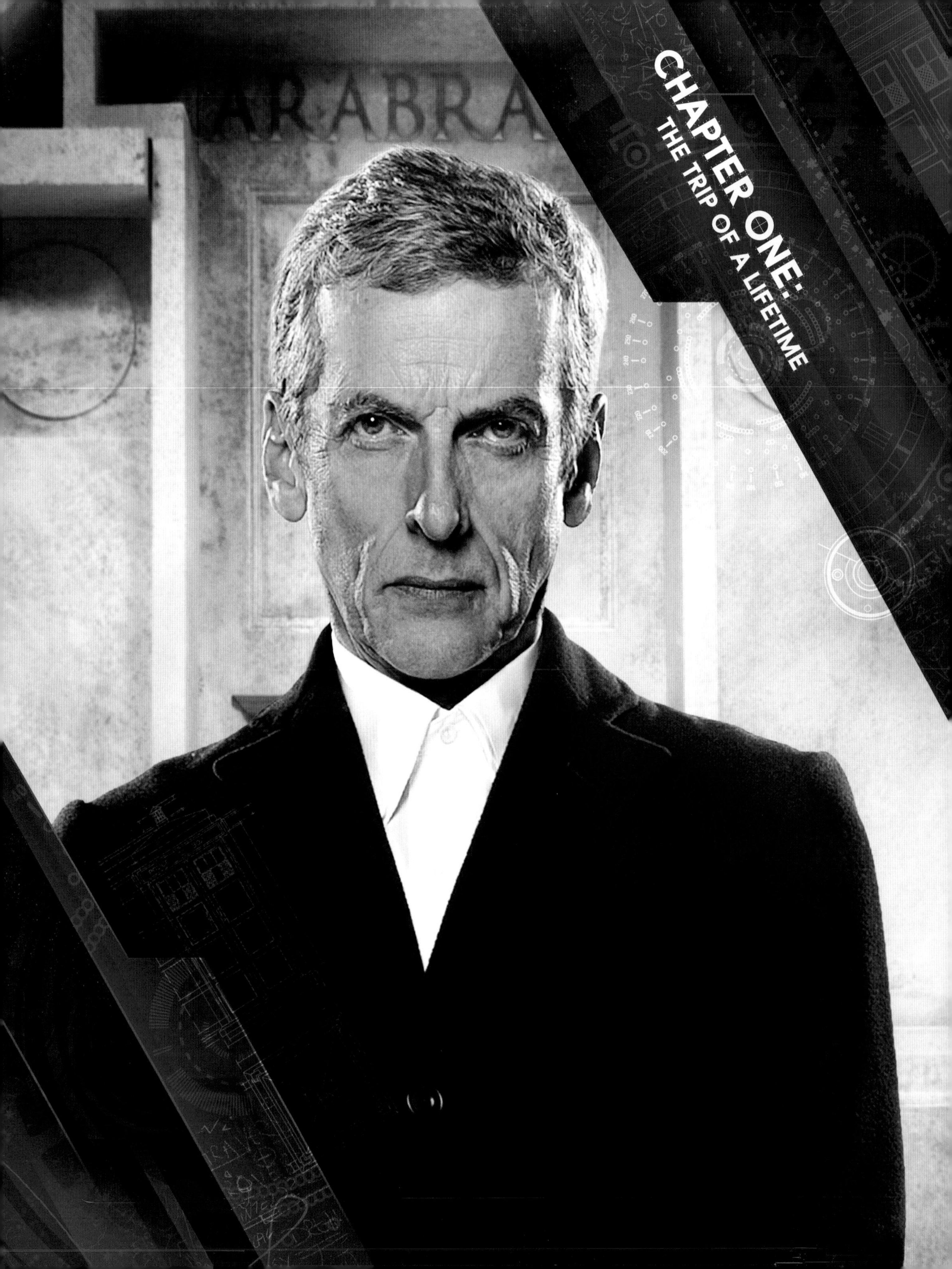

THE TRIP OF A LIFETIME

✲ IMAGINE YOU COULD GO ANYWHERE...

...Not just a nice trip to Lanzarote on your summer holiday, imagine you could go **anywhere**. This world or countless others, encountering strange alien races, new cultures or hostile environments. Now imagine you could travel to any time. Meet Robin Hood (and duel him with a spoon!), discover what terrible monster lives under your bed, journey *inside* a Dalek or travel to the last planet in the universe. Where would you go?

The power is in your hands. You can go anywhere or any**when** in the universe, the only thing you need is the power of imagination and a key to the TARDIS. It's not going to be easy. It'll probably be dangerous. The universe is a hostile place, full of Daleks, Zygons, Sontarans, the Boneless, Cybermen, Clockwork Robots, Silurians and worse. There will be fear, heartbreak and excitement, but above all, it'll be the trip of a lifetime.

The Doctor has this tendency to assume you know what he's talking about, but we don't want to lose you on the way, so we'll take a second to explain

everything. The **Doctor Who Roleplaying Game** is made up of two elements: the first is **Doctor Who**, the second is **Roleplaying**.

✲ WHO IS THE DOCTOR?

We imagine that you are already familiar with the Doctor. He looks human, but has two hearts and is a complete genius. He travels through time and space in his ship called the TARDIS, which stands for Time And Relative Dimension In Space. It's complicated, but from the outside it looks like an old 1960s police public call box. Inside it is vast and alive.

The Doctor travels the galaxy and history, doing good, stopping villainous aliens who try to take over the Earth (if not the universe), and showing the wonders of time and space to various companions who join him on his adventures. The Doctor's travels are usually more than a little dangerous, and he's had to employ one of his alien abilities to survive: the ability to regenerate every part of his body into a new Doctor.

You don't need to know all of the Doctor's adventures from his 2000 and more years of travelling through time and space to play this game, and we'll give you a brief summary of his epic story later in this chapter (see pg.11).

Similarly, even if you're aware of the Doctor's adventures it doesn't mean that you'll have experienced roleplaying before. If you're familiar with roleplaying games, you may want to skip ahead; however, if you've come to this new you may be wondering how you actually play.

⚙ WHAT IS ROLEPLAYING?

Roleplaying games (sometimes called RPGs or adventure games) are shared storytelling. You play the part of your character, but you don't need to dress up and leap about (well, not if you don't want to). You get together with a group of friends and create your own **Doctor Who** adventure, taking the heroes to any location in the universe, at any time. The action takes place in your imaginations, and the story is told through your interaction. You're in control and you can do anything, go anywhere, **be** anything. All that limits you is the power of your mind... and, if you're a Time Lord, that's a lot of power!

Let's show you the basics of how this 'roleplaying' thing works. It's not as scary as it sounds, and once you get started we're sure you'll have many years of exciting adventures ahead of you. The first element you need to know about is **Characters**.

THE CHARACTERS

Each player creates a character, an alternative persona that they will play as in the game. During the course of the game, you make this character's decisions, speak for them and describe their actions.

Each character has a character sheet that describes what they are like, what they are good at and other details. If you like, you can play the Doctor, or any of his companions that have accompanied him during his adventures. This is the easiest option, as we have provided you with ready-made character sheets for them.

You might take on another role, perhaps one you've seen in a movie or read in a book, or you could just get creative and make up a character of your own. In this case, you choose the character's strengths and weaknesses, abilities and limitations, and – in particular – personality. They can look like anyone, dress in anything you choose, or they can even be you.

You could decide to have a game with or without the Doctor in it. Perhaps a UNIT Task Force operating alone somewhere in the world, or maybe one of the Doctor's previous companions continuing their struggle to protect the Earth from alien invaders. Possibly a game set before the last Time War, when there were a number of Time Lords travelling the universe. Anything is possible.

With us so far? Good. So we've established that the players all adopt the roles of their characters. But one of the players is different; they're going to be the **Gamemaster**.

THE GAMEMASTER

All the players and their characters are important, but one of you is in charge, the one who makes it all work. That key player is called the Gamemaster. The Gamemaster starts the story by deciding the plot for the adventure, sets the scene by describing to the other players what is going on, interprets the outcomes of the players' actions and has the final decision on how the rules of the game are applied.

The Gamemaster speaks for the other people in the story: anyone that the characters meet in their adventures. They can be helpful, informative or just witnesses to the events. As they don't have a player (other than the Gamemaster) they're usually called Non-Player Characters, or NPCs. NPCs could be the friends of one of the player characters, such as Robin Hood and his Merry Men, or for added firepower for that climactic battle against the Robot Knights, or even just a nosey policeman wondering why there's a 1960s police box on his beat. They can help, hinder or just be a great source of information.

If the Gamemaster-controlled characters are out for universal domination or worse, they are called Villains. These include the aliens, critters, and other nasties. They are the evil that pervades the universe, trying to dominate, destroy or corrupt the peace-loving civilisations, and their schemes usually result in some much-needed intervention from our time-travelling heroes.

GAME SESSIONS

Game sessions in the **Doctor Who Roleplaying Game** can take anywhere from a couple hours to an entire weekend (depends on how into it you get!). There is no formal start or end – that's up to the Gamemaster and players to decide. Also, in roleplaying, there are no winners or losers. The objective is to create a story, engage in some spontaneous and often hilarious conversations, and have a good time with friends. And no, no electronics of any kind are necessary. It's a social activity and doesn't involve computers. It has even been shown to aid team building, social and problem solving skills!

It all sounds a little chaotic, but it is far more logical than it seems. The game is divided into Adventures, resolved in one or more gaming sessions that play just like the Doctor's adventures you're familiar with. Adventures, and their related story arcs, may be connected in some way with their own undercurrent plot like 'the Impossible Girl' or 'The Nethersphere', created purely by the interaction between the players' characters and the Gamemaster.

⚙ THE BASICS

The example of play (see pg.13) introduces just about everything you'll need to know as a player in the **Doctor Who Roleplaying Game**. You talk, describe your actions and, any time you want to do something that you may or may not succeed at, you need to roll some dice.

When you roll dice, you also add some numbers from your character sheet that define how good you are at certain things. To succeed, you have to beat a number defined by the Gamemaster. The harder the thing you are trying to do, the higher the number. If you beat the number you succeed and can perform the task, whether it's jumping a gap, winning an argument or dodging a gun blast. If you don't beat the number, you fail to accomplish the task. This could have severe effects on your character and change the course of the game, but it makes for an interesting story! Either way, rolling dice and adding some numbers is about all you'll have to do when it comes to rules. So you're going to need some dice.

You'll need a handful of traditional six-sided dice, like those you'd find in Monopoly or Risk. People who game a lot with other roleplaying games call them D6s, so they don't get confused with other dice with different numbers of sides on them. We don't need to worry about those here, as we'll be sticking to normal six-sided dice as they're pretty easy to come by. You can pick up dice in many different colours and styles from hobby game stores, some department stores and bookstores, and places where they sell those fantasy tabletop wargames.

Besides dice, you need something to keep track of Story Points during the fast and furious exchanges that'll occur during the average game. You can use poker chips, markers, pennies, tiddlywinks or even jelly babies. These Story Points could save your character's life at some point, so it's vital to keep track of how many you have. We'll explain Story Points in **Chapter Three: I Can Fight Monsters, I Can't Fight Physics**.

You'll also need some pencils, paper, an eraser or two and you're good to go. Have fun, and don't forget your Sonic Screwdriver!

⚙ HOW TO USE THIS BOOK

You'll already have noticed there's a lot of information here – to make it a little easier, here is what you need to look for.

This book will provide players with all the information needed to play the game, create new characters, as well as some guidance to help make game the best experience possible, and provides the Gamemaster with additional information on time travel and how to create new Adventures.

The Appendix also has loads of photocopiable character sheets. Some give details about characters

you'll be familiar with from the Doctor's adventures and some are new, almost complete characters, that we call 'Archetypes'.

These characters can be used straight away so you don't need to create your own. You just need to supply some background and a name, or you can customise them to suit your own design. You can find more about characters in **Chapter Two: Old-Fashioned Heroes from Old-Fashioned Storybooks**.

However (and here's the important bit), so you don't get too lost with all this text, we've made all the type look different if something special is going on.

TEXT

The text in the book looks different depending on what's going on. When the words change their look, something important just happened. The text you are reading now is standard text. It covers general explanations and narrative sections.

> Some information is presented in a box like this, which usually contains optional rules, further detail on existing rules and examples of play.

TITLE

Boxes like these contain details of NPCs or Villains that can be used in your adventures

GENDER

We don't want use 'he or she' in every sentence, but we also don't want to appear sexist in any way. Most games like this use 'he' all the time and assume you understand that they're talking about the player or character regardless of whether they are male or female. While the Doctor is male, his companions are often (though not exclusively) female. So, we'll reach the happy medium and use the more generic 'they'.

MEASUREMENTS AND LANGUAGE

The metric system is predominant in much of the world, though the US (and Torchwood) still uses the old Imperial system. As **Doctor Who** is quintessentially British, we'll be using the metric system. Though, as shown in the classic series, travelling before 1970 will mean you may have to convert to Imperial. Rough conversions may be found by halving miles to get kilometres, equating metres with yards, doubling pounds to get

kilograms, and so on. It's not 100% accurate, but it keeps things simple.

Being British, there may be the odd word or spelling here and there that may stand out in some of the many other countries familiar with the Doctor's adventures. Most of the time, this won't be too jarring, but you'll probably notice a few extra 'u's and fewer 'z's.

PAGE REFERENCES

As the **Doctor Who Roleplaying Game** already has a number of supplements, you may have to refer to another book rather than the one you're holding. If the text tells you to "see pg.27", then it's letting you know that additional information can be found on that page within the book you're currently holding. If it says "see pg.27 of **The Time Traveller's Companion**", then the page can be found in that supplement.

✷ THE DOCTOR'S UNIVERSE

There's a slim chance that you may be unaware of the living legend that is the Doctor. He has thwarted many alien invasions and has saved the universe so many times without waiting around for thanks or recognition. Before getting into the details of the rules, it's a good idea to familiarise yourself with the Doctor, his companions and his most recent adventures.

THE DOCTOR

Just who is the Doctor? The Doctor may look human, but he certainly isn't. He's over 2000 years old and from a planet called Gallifrey. He has two hearts, is incredibly intelligent (as well as being mildly telepathic) and can 'cheat death' by regenerating into a completely new body. The Doctor is a Time Lord, a race all-but-extinct now. He was on the front lines of the last great Time War against the Daleks, where both races appeared to have perished in the conflict.

TIME LORDS

The Time Lords were an ancient civilisation that mastered the art of travelling through time and space long before humanity had even discovered fire. They harnessed the power of a black hole and created time-ships often nicknamed TARDISes that allowed them to travel anywhere or anywhen in the universe (except into their own planet's past or future). They became rather judgmental guardians of the universe. This superiority complex led to their downfall when they tried to remove the militaristic Daleks from history. They didn't all die, as most of the universe believes; the Doctor 'saved' them by locking Gallifrey away in a parallel pocket universe. And at least one other Time Lord - his arch-enemy Missy - escaped.

THE TARDIS

The Doctor didn't see eye to eye with the Time Lords and fled Gallifrey early in his life, taking one of their TARDISes for his own. TARDIS stands for Time And Relative Dimension In Space, and its interior and exterior exist in different dimensions – that is, the relatively small outside houses a vast interior. The Doctor's TARDIS is an old Type 40 and its Chameleon Circuit – the device that allows it to blend into its surroundings – has become stuck in the shape of an old 1960s Police Call Box. The TARDIS is a living thing with a mind of its own – and it can be particularly temperamental at times...

THE DOCTOR'S COMPANIONS

Travelling time and space can be lonely, especially when you're the last of your race. The Doctor likes to share the wonders of the universe with someone, and he has developed a real affection for the peoples of Earth. He brings someone aboard the TARDIS to share his adventures, and sometimes just to keep himself under control. These companions come and go, have adventures, help to save the universe many times over, and then they leave. Whether this is through their own choice, circumstances or constant danger, they leave the Doctor to his lonely existence until he finds someone to share his adventures with again.

THE DOCTOR'S ENEMIES

The universe is full of wonder and excitement, but there are also many alien races and people who wish to usurp, to dominate and control for their own ends. The Doctor is usually there to stop them, and over the hundreds of years he has been travelling, he's accumulated many enemies by halting their evil plans. The militaristic Daleks in their heavy armour casing, the Cybermen and their desire to make everyone like them, the Sontarans bred for a war that has raged for thousands of years, and countless more. They keep trying to dominate, integrate, upgrade, destroy or plunder the universe, and the Doctor is there to stop them.

When he travelled to meet his fate on the planet of Trenzalore, the Doctor thought that he would die - truly die - there. But the Time Lords, sealed away in a parallel pocket universe, granted him a new set of regenerations. Changed by his brush with death, the Doctor set off to put right his past mistakes and discover who he was once more.

EXAMPLE OF PLAY

Still not sure what's going on? It'll all become clear soon, honest. Many gamers get their start by joining an existing group or taking part in a demo. Obviously, that's not possible for everyone, so let's give you a taste of what's to come by looking at a sample game. As the game is mostly conversation, imagine that we're listening to the players. There are three people, sitting around a table: Peter, Jenna and Samuel. Peter is our Gamemaster. They're just starting...

Peter: OK, here we go! Jenna, you're playing the Doctor?

Jenna: Shut up! Shuttity up! Just warming up.

Samuel: Well I'm playing Clara. So careful who you tell to shut up.

Peter: Great. Let's jump right in. You open your eyes, and you're in a bad situation already. You're strapped down in a box, like a transparent plastic box roughly the size of a coffin.

Jenna: Wait, who's strapped down? Both of us?

Peter: You're both strapped down and alone. But you look to the side and you can see another box, similar to yours. Except strapped down inside that box is a big lizard. It's wiggling its fingers and waggling its snout.

Samuel: How did we get here?

Peter: You don't know. Last thing you remember, you were in the TARDIS, roaming through time and space. And now – waking up in a box.

Jenna (as the Doctor): What? No no no. Clara, what have you done?

Samuel (as Clara): Nothing to do with me!

Peter: Remember, you can't see each other, or hear each other.

Samuel (as Clara): I know just what he'd be saying if he was here, "Clara, what have you done"?

Jenna (as the Doctor): She must have done something, this can't be my fault.

Peter: One more thing about the box - there's this little metal widget above your bellybutton, a bit like a penlight.

Outside is a classroom! Just like a typical Year 10 class you might have, Clara. And a teacher – but he's right out of a comic book, mortarboard and cane and big black robe. He's writing on the chalkboard.

Samuel: So it looks like we're pre-World War One?

Peter: The teacher looks that way. But the kids are contemporary, they look completely normal to you. They're reading the chalkboard, which says "goatasaurs, dumb animals, feel no pain. Today's lesson: dissect the goatasaur and remove three major internal organs."

Jenna: Have I ever heard of a goatasaur? Is that what the lizard is?

Peter: Let's find out. Make an Ingenuity + Knowledge roll. Let's make it difficulty fifteen.

Jenna: The Doctor's Ingenuity is 9, his Knowledge is 6, so that's 15 already, do I even need to roll?

Peter: Right now you just have a bare success, which means something will go a bit wrong too. So roll!

Jenna takes two dice, rolls and gets a 5 and a 4, which adds to 9. She adds this to the 15 from Ingenuity + Knowledge: 15+9=24.

Jenna: That's 24!

Peter: There's no such thing as a goatasaur. 9 more than the difficulty is a Fantastic result, so you also know this: that lizard in the other box is a very unconvincing lizard. It's Clara. The box is somehow making Clara look just like a lizard.

Jenna: I probably don't even notice she looks like a lizard.

Samuel: Well thanks very much.

Peter: Anyway, you can't hear what the teacher is saying but suddenly all the pupils come out of their seats and, pushing and shoving, they come up surround the boxes. Some of them grab little control devices and that little metal pen above your bellybutton starts wiggling in response...

Samuel: Uh oh. Can I headbutt the box?

Peter: You can't quite reach.

Jenna: Do I have the Sonic Screwdriver?

Peter: Not in your hand, no. The little lasers are starting to light up...

Samuel: Argh! Um, OK. These kids could be from a London school, right? Can I spend a Story Point to say I know one of them? Maybe he transferred out from Coal Hill or he was a friend of those kids I nannied?

Peter: Yeah, why not.

Samuel spends a Story Point from his pool.

Samuel: OK, he sees me as a lizard? And he can't hear me, and I'm tied down? Right. I'm going to make eye contact with him, try and catch his eye, and then I want to use my eyes to indicate my hands. And I'm going to be using my finger to draw the shape of the letters of his name. Steve!

Peter: Genius! OK, let's see how this goes. Um, this is a Convince skill, but I'm not sure what Attribute fits. Presence I guess? Call it Presence. Normal difficulty, which is 12.

Samuel rolls two dice, getting two and five which adds up to 7. He adds Clara's Presence (3) and Convince (4), getting a total of 14.

Samuel: I make it by 2. That's a "Yes, But" result, right?

Peter: It is! So Clara catches Steve's attention and makes him notice she's spelling out his name - but instead of stopping the other pupils he just sort of freezes up...

Jenna: Say something Steve!

Peter: The other pupils are about to use the laser...

Jenna: I haven't acted yet! OK, can I wiggle out of the restraints Harry Houdini style?

Peter: Go for it, Coordination + Subterfuge, difficulty is 18 though.

Jenna: I'm going to spend a Story Point in advance for the two extra dice.

Jenna spends a Story Point from her pool, and rolls 4 dice with a result of 15. She adds the Doctor's

Coordination (5) and Subterfuge (3), giving a final total of 23.

Peter: That succeeds by 5, a Good success. You wriggle out your arms and legs somehow. You're still stuck in the box!

Jenna: I grab the laser and point it at the side of the box, and generally make it known that I will not be dissected without protest! I'm hoping my kerfuffle will distract the ones at Clara's box too.

Peter: That's exactly what happens. Clara, the laser above your bellybutton dims as the pupils there all turn to stare at the other box, where the lizard person has climbed out of the restraints and is making its displeasure known.

Samuel: Ha, and Clara finally works out it's the Doctor! She recognises his bad temper!

Peter: And this moment gives Steve a chance to gather his wits, too. You can't hear him, but you see him pointing at you and saying something, and the other pupils start looking to see what he's saying.

Samuel: I keep finger-writing his name! Steve Steve!

Jenna: OK, now that they're doing that, I'm trying to use the laser housing to send a shockwave through the boxes so it stops making us look like lizards.

Peter: OK Jenna, roll Ingenuity + Technology, difficulty 12. Breaking stuff is easier than making stuff, I guess.

Jenna: Do I get to add my Technically Adept trait?

Peter: You do! That gives you a +2.

Jenna rolls 6, and after adding the Doctor's Ingenuity (9) and Technology (5), and another 2 for the trait, she has a grand total of 22, beating the difficulty by 10.

Peter: Another "Yes, And" result! So there's a wave of energy that rushes across the boxes, and after it passes you both look like yourselves from the outside. For the first time you can look and see each other instead of just seeing lizards.

Jenna: I have an idea for the "And"! Can I make words appear on the box?

Peter: Yes you can.

Jenna: So the Doctor gives the teacher his most furious eyebrows possible, and these words come up on the box: "I am very very grumpy with you".

Peter: The teacher stares at you. Then he jerks his eyes away and strides around the boxes. You still can't hear him but he's yelling, and the pupils are all hurrying back to their seats. As he's yelling he's pointing with his cane and you can see he's pointing at a large door on the side of the room, and there's a sign on it saying "Expulsion".

Jenna: Don't I get a chance to intimidate him into letting us out?

Peter: You don't. Something is odd about this teacher. Give me an Awareness + Ingenuity roll.

Jenna rolls, getting a Good result.

Peter: Yes, something definitely odd. This teacher doesn't move like a living being. More like a robot. Anyway, not all the pupils go back to their desks. A few stay in front, in open defiance of the teacher. The teacher is threatening them with his cane, which itself starts to glow and spark...

Samuel: Time to get out of here! I try and catch Steve's eye again and hope he can lip-read: "use the lasers! Cut us free!"

Peter: Fine, don't even bother rolling there. Steve grabs the little joystick control and he aims the laser at the side of the box, and starts cutting open a hole for you. It smells like melting plastic but it's working!

Jenna: I put more words on my box, this time so Clara can see. "What did you do this time?"

Samuel: (as Clara) This isn't my fault!

Jenna: The words change to "Oh really."

Peter: The hole is big enough for you to slide out now. You hear the teacher, "Sit down you brats or I'll see you expelled!" And the pupils are shouting, "Leave them alone, you can't cut up people!"

Samuel: (as Clara) Thank you very much Steve.

Peter (as Steve): You're welcome Miss Oswald.

Samuel (as Clara): How's the new school working out?

Peter (as Steve): A bit confusing Miss Oswald.

Samuel (as Clara): Let's get my friend out too, shall we?

Peter: Steve goes to the controls for the Doctor's laser, but the teacher has seen enough. (As the teacher:) "Hickey! Get back to your desk this instant or you'll get six of the best!"

Samuel (as Clara): You need a cane to keep control in the classroom? You're a rubbish teacher.

Peter: OK, three things happen. First, Steve operates the Doctor's laser to punch open a small hole – not quite big enough to climb out yet. Second, Clara, your eyes are really stinging. At first you thought it was the melting plastic but now you think something is seriously wrong and you're about to lose your vision entirely. Third, one of the last things you see clearly is the teacher firing a bolt of energy from his cane to strike Steve in the back. Steve goes limp. What do you both do?

Jenna: I reach my arm through the hole, grab the controls from Steve, and finish the job.

Samuel: Clara is disgusted. She's going to grab the cane out of the teacher's hand and snap it.

Peter: Well the teacher's going to try and zap you with the cane first. Let's do this as an extended conflict. Talkers go first but we have no talkers, or Movers. The Doctor is a Doer, though, so you go first Jenna. Roll Coordination and, um, how about Subterfuge? Difficulty 15?

Jenna rolls a 15, which means she gets a bare minimum Success.

Peter: That's a Yes, But...

Jenna: How about I get out, but the laser is ruined? If it isn't ruined I'm totally going to use it on the teacher.

Peter: Sounds good to me. The Doctor grabs the controls through the hole, points the laser to finish opening the hole, then slides out as the laser melts into slag. Ta da! Doc, your eyes instantly start hurting too.

Samuel: My turn, am I a Doer as well? I'm not really fighting, I'm trying to disarm him.

Peter: No, I'm going to call that fighting. So you both go at the same time. I'll say your actions oppose each other, OK? So you roll Strength + Fighting, and he rolls Coordination + Marksman. If you win, you get the cane before he can fire it, if he wins, he zaps you before you get it.

Samuel: Strength and Fighting! I am so bad at both those things! Um, I have a total of 4. And I'll roll... I roll 5. 9! I fail!

Peter: Hang on! He only has a total of 3 in his Coordination and Marksman! He rolls... 4. That's 9 as well!

Samuel: What happens on a tie?

Peter: I think you both succeed. He zaps you – but you strip him of the cane.

Jenna: I can totally see that. Clara just takes it because she's so angry at this awful teacher.

Peter: Clara gets zapped for 2 levels of damage. It hits your Resolve.

Samuel notes that Clara's Resolve is reduced by 2 for the time being.

Jenna: That's the end of the round, right? Hey, I have another suggestion. I think Clara stepping up to the teacher like that is a reflection of her Obligation bad trait, even though the kids aren't from Coal Hill. She put herself in harm's way to keep them safe. Maybe she should get a Story Point for that?

Peter: That's a great suggestion, yes, you get a Story Point for that Samuel.

Samuel adds a Story Point to his pool.

Peter: Right, new round. The teacher is caneless now. Clara, you're zapped and angry and your eyes are really messed up but you can still just barely

see. The Doctor is free but he's noticing his eyes are starting to water too.

Jenna: Where's my Sonic Screwdriver?

Samuel: Movers can go, right? I go to the teacher's desk and pull open the drawer. Is the Sonic Screwdriver in there?

Peter decides this is such a perfect revelation that it won't even cost a Story Point.

Peter: It sure is.

Samuel: I throw it to the Doctor.

Jenna: I catch it and deactivate the robot teacher!

Peter: The teacher is ranting, "You must learn to dissect! Silence, boys and girls!"

Jenna: I roll Ingenuity + Technology again? Bonus for the same trait? And for the Sonic Screwdriver too?

Jenna rolls and gets a Good success.

Jenna (as the Doctor): Shuttity up.

Peter: The teacher robot goes still. And that, I'm afraid, is the last thing you see. Both of you are now completely blind...

[You can continue the story yourself by playing the adventure *Seeing Eyes*, on pg. 217.]

OLD-FASHIONED HEROES FROM OLD-FASHIONED STORYBOOKS

This chapter will provide everything you need to know about creating a character for you to play in the **Doctor Who Roleplaying Game**. If you don't want to go through the process of creating a new character, you can simply play as the Doctor and some of his companions, or even use some of the ready-made characters we've provided for you in the Appendix.

Before you leap ahead and use them, though, you'll need to know what all the numbers mean, so it will still be worth reading on. This chapter will allow you to play exciting new companions, or even your own Time Lord for very different adventures. The only limitation is your imagination, and whatever characters will work best for your Gamemaster.

✿ CHARACTERS

Deciding on the types of characters to be used is one of the most important steps towards a good game. The characters are vital to the story and the more interesting the characters are, the better the story will be. Don't worry though, we'll go through it all stage by stage and it's not as daunting as it sounds.

The Gamemaster will guide the players through the character creation process, starting with giving

the players an idea of what sort of companions are suitable and what type of story is planned. This may be as simple as "the game is the Twelfth Doctor and his new companions, set after he rescues Clara from the Dream Crabs." Or it could be as detailed and different as "the game is about Torchwood operatives working in London at the time of the Second World War. I need all human characters. No time travellers and no aliens are allowed." As long as you don't choose something too over the top or conflicting, like trying to play Missy or a human-sympathetic Cyberman, you'll be fine.

If this is your first game, or you want to get started quickly, the easiest thing to do is play as the Doctor and his companions, using the ready-made characters provided.

✿ WHO CAN YOU PLAY?

This is where roleplaying games really come into their own – you can play anybody you like. The options are endless, but there are probably going to be a few choices you'll need to make initially about what sort of game you're going to play. Is it going to be the Doctor and Clara, the Doctor with a new companion, or something else entirely? Here are some suggestions.

THE DOCTOR AND COMPANIONS

In this option, you and your fellow gamers take on the roles of the Doctor and the companions we're familiar with, whether this is Clara, Danny, Osgood or even Robin Hood. The characters have their own sheets already prepared (see the Appendix) and the Gamemaster just photocopies the character sheets, hands them out and runs through the explanation of the numbers so everyone knows what they all mean. This is certainly the easiest option as everyone knows the characters, assuming you're familiar with the Doctor's adventures. It's quick – you'll be up and playing faster than you can say "Did I mention it also travels in time?" On the downside, the options are a little limited. There will always be that "you can't all play the Doctor" problem (see sidebar), though if you're lucky everyone will be happy with their characters.

This is really the default setting of the game. After all, it's what we've come to expect from the Doctor's adventures. The Doctor is obvious, but what do the companions bring? Usually, they're there to ground the Doctor, but each brings something different to the mix. Rose was initially about fun, adventure and companionship, though this developed into a deeper friendship until she eventually had the chance to be with 'a' Doctor. Martha brought something different; the Doctor's equal in her smarts and drive, capable of looking after herself. Donna brought a different type of equality into the mix: a more human and 'normal' person to humanise the Doctor a little. Amy brought a new level of fun and adventure to the Doctor's life as he was recovering from his latest regeneration, providing the Doctor not only with companionship but also a mystery that would follow them through time and space. River brought a hint of romance and a glimpse into the Doctor's future, while Clara was not only an enigma but also tied to the very fabric of the Doctor's timeline. So what does your companion provide the Doctor? Just friendship? An intellectual foil to bounce radical ideas off of? Someone to steer him in the right directions, to remind him what's right and wrong? Of course, you could opt to play a game using one of the Doctor's earlier incarnations and either the companions that he associated with at that time, or new companions.

THE DOCTOR AND NEW COMPANIONS

The Doctor has travelled with many, many passengers in the TARDIS and there have been a few instances when the Doctor has travelled alone. In many cases, the Doctor has said goodbye to one companion, and has found a new companion somewhere else soon afterwards. That doesn't mean that he hasn't had a passenger or two in the TARDIS for a few adventures in between

"YOU CAN'T ALL PLAY THE DOCTOR"

There may be a time when the players argue over who gets to play everyone's favourite Time Lord. The final call should always be with the Gamemaster, and short of being bribed with chocolate, the decision should be based upon who can bring the most fun and excitement to the role of the Doctor and who can play him well. Will the player be able to take control during desperate situations? Will they be able to talk down a mass of advancing Cybermen?

If players are still unhappy about who gets to play the Doctor, it could be that everyone takes a turn, shifting to the next player with every adventure. Or you could change players with each regeneration - after all the Doctor's appearance and personality changes dramatically during the regeneration process, so it's only fitting that a different player takes the part.

Most of the time players will be happy to take part in the adventures, no matter what role they play. Just remember, the Doctor may be important, but his companions are just as important to the story and have been known to save the world on more than one occasion. Every character will have their chance to shine.

Advice for Gamemasters about making sure everyone is involved can be found on pg. 187.

the companions we're familiar with. In this option, the Doctor has the character sheet we've provided (which you can adjust for any of his earlier incarnations), and the other players take the part of new characters. Whether these are freshly created ones of your own making, or a selection based on the Archetypes we've provided (see the sheets in the Appendix), that's up to you.

NO TIME LORD AT ALL

It's not entirely necessary for the Doctor to actually appear in the game; after all UNIT and Sarah Jane Smith have proved that they can defend the Earth without the Doctor's help. Sure, they mention him from time to time – after all, an encounter with the Doctor is a life-changing event – but he's not the focus of the story, and he doesn't have to be in yours either. The characters could be rogue Time Agents, members of UNIT (see below), alien explorers or plucky humans, robots or colonists, rebels or soldiers; the possibilities are endless in the vast universe. If you want the game to travel to different worlds, they'll need access to a ship or possibly just hop from place to place with a Transmat. If you want time travel, you'll need access to some means of travelling the Vortex, be it a TARDIS, a recovered Vortex Manipulator or other time travel device. None of these need to be out of the reach of the characters, so long is it makes a great story. You could start with all human characters from present-day Earth who are scooped up by an alien ship. They could bumble from one adventure to another in the depths of space without transport of their own, catching a ride where they can. Anything you can imagine is possible.

UNIT SQUAD / TORCHWOOD TEAM

The Unified Intelligence Taskforce is the United Nation's first line of defence against alien invasion. As such, they have divisions worldwide with many different task forces and operations running to investigate, research, experiment and protect. A UNIT squad could be a great basis for a group of player characters: it could include scientific advisors, diplomatic negotiators, archaeologists and technicians, as well as the expected military firepower. Each member would be assigned due to their unique set of skills, allowing them to complement each other and creating a good, balanced team. You could even equip them with experimental time travel or teleportation equipment like Project Indigo to get them moving around the universe or through history. More information and guidance for running a UNIT campaign can be found in **Defending the Earth: The UNIT Sourcebook**.

A similar approach could be used to create an independent Torchwood team, allowing the players to create a secret base (like the Hub, before it was destroyed) to investigate the strange and mysterious, and protect the Earth from alien incursion.

✷ CREATING A NEW CHARACTER

It's a big universe out there with plenty of room for new characters. It takes a little more time to set up, but this allows you to bring something of your own to the game. You get the character you'd like to play, and you can take the stories in different directions with unique characters of your own.

As long as the Gamemaster approves, you can try anything. The Doctor's companions in the past have been very varied to say the least – a highlander, an air stewardess, a shop assistant, a journalist, more than a few school teachers, a robot, a doctor, a librarian and a primitive. All have joined the Doctor aboard the TARDIS, so if you think they'll be interesting, give it a try. Above all, most (though not all of them) have their hearts in the right place and are on the side of good.

If this all seems too complicated, instead of creating a character from scratch you can use one of the ready-made Archetypes: these character sheets can be found in the Appendix. These are pre-generated companions that can be customised or used just as they are, thrown into the adventure almost instantly. Just come up with a background and a name, and you're good to go, or you can tweak the numbers a little to better suit your tastes. Just check what all the terms and numbers mean and you're ready to travel the stars.

Characters are defined by **Attributes**, **Skills** and **Traits**.

Attributes are what your character is like: how strong they are, how clever they are, how perceptive, and so on.

Skills are what your character knows: can they drive a car, hack into computers, apply a bandage, how to ski, how to fight or how to bluff their way out of a situation?

Finally, **traits** detail what your character can do or, in some cases, cannot do: are they ambidextrous, have a particular knack for fixing things, do they heal unnaturally quickly, are they rich, famous or have a family that keeps getting them into trouble?

Attributes and skills have numerical ratings, the higher the rating the better they are at something.

You are given a number of points to purchase your attributes, skills and traits, but these points are limited, so you may have to think it through a little before assigning numbers. You'll have to decide if the character is stronger than they are smart, wittier than they are agile, and what their particular areas of expertise are. For example, Clara may be brave and curious, the Doctor's trusted friend who would sacrifice herself for him, but she's not as ruthless as the Doctor. She might be 'just' a teacher, but that never stopped her from trying to save the world.

Points and scores are only part of it. Most of what makes your character special is the player. How you play them, the voice you give them, the decisions you make for them – all of this shapes the character into a living, breathing person with a history and a personality.

WHO ARE THEY?

First of all, the player should think about what the character is like. Meddling investigator, curious scientist, or something else entirely? This will not only define what the character is capable of doing, but also where they spend the points to build them. Are they a companion? A civilian or soldier, heroic or just a normal average guy or girl? Luckily, everyone is created equal in this game. We'll take it one stage at a time, and guide you through.

This method of character creation works the same for everyone from Clara and Danny, to Robin Hood and Santa Claus. Everyone starts with a number of points to spend on attributes, skills and traits. You're also assigned a number of Story Points: make a note of these as they'll come in handy later.

Creating someone with a special ability, like Saibra and her ability to shapeshift, should be worked out closely between players and Gamemaster. The Gamemaster has to be sure that the character will fit into the game, after all.

HOW DO THEY FIT IN?

An important element to consider is each character's role in the 'team'. The Doctor may be able to do almost anything – he's smart, quick and charismatic – but he needs his companions for a reason. They ground him, because sometimes he doesn't know when to stop. His companions also provide him with knowledge of his 'second home' – Earth. They also provide companionship. Being the last of his kind is a lonely place to be and his companions help keep him active, happy and enthusiastic, rather than slipping into aimless, depressed wandering.

So what does each character bring? Are they a specialist in a particular field? A doctor, a soldier or a computer genius? Think of the team as a complete person and maybe assign each character a part – the brains, the heart, the muscles or the soul. The players should bear this in mind when they are creating characters, and they should discuss what kind of role each person will play in the group.

The types of characters and the group dynamic will depend on what the Gamemaster, has in mind for the game.

⚙ ATTRIBUTES

Attributes give you an indication of what a character is capable of doing. How strong they are, how smart, how charming, how clever, all these are defined by attributes ranked from 1 to 6.

Players use Character Points to purchase the attributes of the character, limited to a maximum of six in each. 6 is the human maximum, and no character may have an attribute above 6 (unless they're something seriously special or alien). It is very rare for a character to start with an attribute at 6. At the other extreme, you must put at least one point into each attribute. You can't have an attribute of 0 – when attributes reach 0 due to injury or other effects, the character becomes incapacitated, so you can't start in that state!

You could put more points into the character's Strength, and less into their Ingenuity, meaning that they're more of an athlete. On the other hand, you could put more into Ingenuity and Awareness, and less into Coordination, making your character a slightly clumsy brain-box! Or you could make all of the attributes the same, making them equally good (or bad) at everything, though that may not be very realistic – nobody is equally good at everything.

CHARACTER CREATION POINTS

Character Points: 24
Character Points are used to purchase attributes and traits. We recommend you spend 18 points on Attributes and save 6 for traits. You'll gain additional Character Points by taking some Bad traits. If you have any Character Points left over, you can convert them into Skill Points.

Skill Points: 18
Skill Points are used purely to purchase skills. You can get extra Skill Points from any leftover Character Points.

Story Points: 12
Story Points are important as they allow you to do extraordinary things in the game, like avoid fatal injury, do special things or get out of a pickle. You don't spend them during character creation, though this figure (12) is the maximum Story Point pool between adventures. Purchasing particularly powerful abilities and traits (such as being a Time Lord, or having a power like Immortality) can reduce this maximum.

These Character Points will also be used to purchase traits later, so we'd recommend that players spend 18 of their Character Points on attributes and save 6 for later, for buying cool traits. If they don't spend them, or if they gain more points later on by taking Bad traits, they can always 'top up' their attributes.

The six attributes are:

AWARENESS

Travelling the universe is a dangerous occupation, and you've really got to be aware of your surroundings. Whether it is spotting the object that has been disguised with a perception filter, or the Dalek Antibody that's just appearing round the corner, both use Awareness. Awareness takes into account anything that uses the five senses (sight, hearing, touch, smell or taste), or even that indefinable sixth sense of just knowing that something is coming, sensing someone is looking at you or talking behind your back. Awareness can be used to notice an enemy or to look for clues.

Awareness 1 – oblivious to the goings on around them. Their friends frequently have to stop them from stepping out into busy traffic, and they usually miss important clues or signs.
Awareness 2 – still lower than average, but this could be that they are preoccupied with something or easily distracted.
Awareness 3 – average person, fairly aware of their surroundings, likely to spot some hidden clues, notice the approaching enemy or hear the strange happenings going on in the flat upstairs.
Awareness 4 – above average, quick to notice when there is something wrong.

Awareness 5 – perceptive, aware of everything going on, can read others like a book, gut feelings are rarely wrong.
Awareness 6 – human maximum, incredibly rare. Takes in everything around them subconsciously, uncannily good at spotting clues. Able to read what people are really intending just by fluctuations in their voice, or notice the most minuscule details
Awareness 7+ – superhuman, possessing enhanced senses.

COORDINATION

Some people are just better at controlling what their bodies do, rather than flailing wildly or falling over constantly. Characters with a higher Coordination can twirl batons, juggle, are pretty good at aiming weapons, and are great at paintball or laser-tag.

Coordination is a combination of physical dexterity and hand-eye coordination (hence the name). You may not think it, but playing your average video game will need good Coordination just as much as healthier options like basketball or football. Doesn't mean the video gaming couch potato isn't lacking in the other attributes though!

Coordination 1 – a lot lower than your average person. They may have very poor control over their bodily movements, possibly due to being ungainly or a very slow reaction time.

Coordination 2 – still less than average, they're sometimes clumsy, not brilliant shots and don't get the best scores on video games.

Coordination 3 – human average, meaning they're able and coordinated.

Coordination 4 – above average, with an almost athletic ability with good reflexes and hand-eye coordination.

Coordination 5 – instinctive reactions, superior reflexes and best suited to professions where such abilities are key, such as pilots or racing drivers.

Coordination 6 – human maximum, the quickest and most agile people on Earth.

Coordination 7+ – superhuman, special characters or aliens who move and aim with pinpoint accuracy.

INGENUITY

The Doctor is all about brains over brawn, he can think (and usually talk) his way out of any situation. Knowledge is power, quite literally in most cases.

Ingenuity is a measure of how smart a character is, their basic reasoning ability, lateral thinking and overall intellectual capability, coupled with general knowledge and practical experience. This doesn't cover a specific knowledge (that's what skills are for), or their aptitudes (those are covered with traits), merely the flexibility of mind and the general knowledge they have gathered. Ingenuity is all about how inventive they are, their lateral thinking as well as their overall intelligence.

Ingenuity 1 – someone who's not exactly quick witted. They may not necessarily be stupid, but it takes them a little longer than your average person to work things out (if at all), or they may be from a primitive culture that doesn't respect reasoning or learning.

Ingenuity 2 – still lower than average, and they are unlikely to have continued their studies (unless they got their qualification from Mrs Golightly's Happy Travelling University and Dry Cleaners). They may just not be interested and they certainly aren't so hot when it comes to computer programming.

Ingenuity 3 – human average – they understand mortgages and current affairs and have a good general education, grasps the basics of computers and technology and can come up with solutions to simple problems that get in their way.

Ingenuity 4 – above average – you're talking University graduates (from a real University that is) with a flexible

mind that can adapt itself to many circumstances and capable of deducing whodunnit from a few clues, possibly due to some natural talent.

Ingenuity 5 – well above average for a human, having a keen and penetrating mind that is full of useful general wisdom gained through a pursuit of knowledge, hard-earned practical experience and a natural gift towards applying their brains in novel ways.

Ingenuity 6 – the human maximum and one of the keenest intellects on the planet, with truly open minds able to make incredible leaps of reason.

Ingenuity 7+ – superhuman intelligence or alien characters, and remarkable minds such as the Doctor.

PRESENCE

Some characters are impressive because of their actions, others are charming and highly charismatic by nature, still others are intimidating and a rare few are all of these things at once. Characters with a low Presence are either easily ignored or unable to get dates, whereas characters with a high Presence can charm, carouse and persuade their way out of trouble. Presence 1 is the lowest humanly possible, lower than this is purely for the bestial monsters of the galaxy.

Presence 1 – socially inept or just plain rude (usually unintentionally). People can find it hard to get along with them and they may get ignored a little.

Presence 2 – off-putting, they could be arrogant and selfish, incredibly shy or just a little creepy.

Presence 3 – human average, generally likeable and easy to get on with but not necessarily a strong leader.

Presence 4 – charming and commanding, people pay attention to them and take notice of what they're saying.

Presence 5 – silver-tongued or commanding, someone who can charm or boss their way through almost anything.

Presence 6 – awe-inspiring, regarded with respect, people want to be with them.

Presence 7+ – alien or superhuman characters, whose commanding and charismatic presence can sway minds and influence thoughts.

RESOLVE

Resolve is a measure of the character's determination and willpower. Whether it's something simple like resisting the urge to eat those chips even though you're on a diet, or keeping your mind clear of guilty thoughts in the presence of the Teller. It also shows your determination to do something, how convincing you can be and how resolved to your cause you are. This determination can make an enemy pause before opening fire, change someone's mind or instill confidence in your colleagues.

Resolve 1 – weak-willed and easily persuaded, or possibly lazy, crumbling quickly in the face of terror and adversity.

Resolve 2 – less than your average human, failing to keep their New Year's Resolution beyond mid January, and quick to succumb to mind control.

Resolve 3 – human average, moderately strong willed, able to control themselves, though they'll freeze under gunfire just like any normal person would.

Resolve 4 – a strength of will above your average person, enduring hardships and willing to face injury or death for their personal convictions and beliefs.

Resolve 5 – determined and resolute, at the peak of personal discipline and control, showing much stronger willpower than most people.

Resolve 6 – paragon of virtue, morally immovable and able to resist almost any temptation or fear.

Resolve 7+ – alien resolve, the most iron willed and unstoppable of aliens or superhuman characters.

STRENGTH

Strength, just like the Defrabricator, does exactly what it says on the tin – it is a measure of how strong your character is. Stronger characters pack more of a punch when they have to resort to physical violence, are able to lift heavy objects or people, and can carry all that scientific equipment a lot further before having to take a rest. Stronger characters are usually physically active, sportsmen or women, or in the armed forces. Your average checkout girl at the supermarket may not be exactly feeble, but she's not going to be able to hold their own in an arm-wrestling contest with a weight lifter!

Strength is also used to determine physical damage inflicted on others. The stronger the character is, the more damage they will do when they throw a punch. Every level of Strength relates to one point of damage inflicted from a punch or kick. More information on fighting and damage can be found in **Chapter Three: I Can Fight Monsters, I Can't Fight Physics.**

On average, a character can comfortably lift around 15kgs for every level of Strength they have. They can carry this around for a while without too much of a strain, but in dire circumstances (and for short periods of time) they can lift twice this amount. So a character with Strength 3 can comfortably carry around 45kgs, or lift 90kgs for a short period. In times of great stress, and with a suitable roll characters may lift even more than this when the adrenaline kicks in.

Strength 1 – your typical weakling, winded answering the door, has difficulty opening a packet of crisps.

Strength 2 – weaker than normal, struggles changing a car tyre, gets out of breath running for the bus.

Strength 3 – average human, able to hold their own in a fight, open the toughest of jar lids, and can carry someone on a stretcher for a good distance.

Strength 4 – stronger than the average human.

Strength 5 – the toughest athletes, sportsmen and women.

Strength 6 – human peak, capable of picking people up and throwing them over their heads. This sort of Strength is usually seen in professional weightlifters or bodybuilders.

Strength 7+ – only for the specially enhanced characters or more-powerful aliens.

ASSIGNING ATTRIBUTES FOR YOUR CHARACTER'S STRENGTHS AND WEAKNESSES

If you're unsure how to begin assigning the Character Points, imagine what the character is going to be like - are they stronger than they are smart, more determined than they are observant? Have a look at the six attributes and pick one that they are most known for. Make a note on the character sheet next to that attribute, and put a 4 in that one. Next, think of where the character is weakest. Are they a little weak when it comes to physical strength, or do they crumble in the face of terror or mind-control? Whichever attribute you choose as your weakest, give it a value of 2. The remaining four attributes are just average, so put 3s in them all.

SHAKE IT UP!

Now you have the numbers next to your attributes, you can change them a little if you like. You can increase an attribute by a point, but you'll have to reduce a different one by a point to compensate. If you lose track, just add up the attributes and they should come to 18. Just remember, no attribute can be higher than 6 or lower than 1. This will leave you with 6 points for purchasing Good traits. Feel free to play about with the numbers to best suit the character.

HIGHER ATTRIBUTES

Superhuman or alien attributes that go higher than 6 are handled in exactly the same way as normal attributes, but they're certainly not for normal characters. These are reserved for special characters. Of course, aliens and Villains often have attributes higher than the human norm, but they are treated in the same way. These characters are often stronger and more powerful than others and should only be created under the watchful eye of the Gamemaster.

Attributes above 6 cost the same (thought it's going to be expensive to buy an attribute that high). However, you cannot purchase attributes above level 6 without being enhanced or alien in some way. You'll need to purchase a trait (such as Cyborg, or Alien) to allow you to do this (see Special traits, pg. 49).

CHARACTER CREATION EXAMPLE

Edward ponders the sort of character he'd like to play. He wants to be smart and quirky, something of a boffin. He decides this is what people think of first when describing his character. Smart is the key, so he decides that Ingenuity is going to be his most important attribute, and puts 4 next to it on the character sheet. He also decides that all this time spent becoming smart has meant that his character isn't particularly physically strong, so he puts 2 into Strength. That leaves Awareness, Coordination, Presence and Resolve so he puts 3s into all of those. It's still not quite how he'd like, so he bumps Ingenuity up to 5, but he has to take a point off of something else to balance. He figures that he is somewhat clumsy, so drops his Coordination by a point. Edward wants to be able to pick up on things others might miss, so increases his character's Awareness to 4, and drops Presence to 2 (he's planning on being a bit shy, to start with).

His Attributes are therefore: Awareness 4, Coordination 2, Ingenuity 5, Presence 2, Resolve 3, Strength 2. He's neither strong nor agile, but there's not much that will get past him.

UNDER-BUYING ATTRIBUTES

The 24 Character Points you have to play with when it comes to assigning attributes will still create an above-average companion – after all, they may appear to have average lives but come into their own when the Earth or themselves are in danger.

Your average person on the street will have attributes ranging from 2-3, with 3 being the normal. If you'd prefer a character that is **really** normal, and not slightly above-average like the Doctor's usual companions, you can opt to save more of the points for later, and spend them on Traits.

Careful purchasing of attributes and using your points in creative ways will reflect what your character is like. For example, playing a slightly older character than your average companion, you could spend less on physical attributes such as Strength and Coordination, increase Ingenuity and save points for more skills.

⚙ TRAITS

Everyone is different and everyone has their own unique mix of mental and physical peculiarities. In the **Doctor Who Roleplaying Game** we call these traits. Traits can be good or bad, but further help to define the character. Are they brave, pretty or particularly cool with gadgets? Are they cruel at times, boring or likely to trip over their own feet? All of these can be traits.

For example, being able to calculate the square root of Pi is a Good trait (though don't try it at parties), whereas having an irrational fear of crabs is a Bad trait (especially if you come across any Macra).

When the characters are in a situation where a trait may come into play, it can aid or hinder their actions. If the player thinks that the situation could involve one of their traits, they should mention it to the Gamemaster, even if it's a Bad Trait and will make things harder for the character. If it's in keeping with the character by bringing a Bad Trait into play, the player may be rewarded with Story Points (more on this later).

For example, when the Doctor is piloting the TARDIS, he uses his Ingenuity and the Technology skill. The Vortex trait means that he's familiar with using the TARDIS and piloting the time streams in general, and the Doctor's player mentions this. It's a Good Trait, so it'll make things easier for the Doctor, giving him a bonus to his dice rolls.

Sometimes, a trait can affect game play without you having to roll any dice. Some traits simply help or hinder the character all of the time. For example, Phobia can hinder your actions if you face the object of your fears, or Code of Conduct can limit your choices in any given situation, just as Tough can save your life in a fight without any dice needing to be rolled. The trait's description will give you an idea of how each of the specific traits work, but if the player and the Gamemaster think the trait is apt to the situation, then it comes into play.

Some Good Traits are very powerful and require the expenditure of a Story Point (or more) to 'activate'. Actively playing in character and using Bad Traits during the game to make it more dramatic, like running into the unknown because you have the Impulsive trait, can often earn you Story Points.

BUYING TRAITS

Traits are purchased with Character Points, like attributes. If you've already spent all your Character Points, don't worry. If you want to go back and lower an attribute so you can use the Character Point for a trait, feel free. Or you can choose to take a Bad Trait to give you an extra Character Point to play with to buy a Good Trait.

Traits come in different sizes too. Let's face it, being able to recite the alphabet backwards isn't going to be as useful as being able to regenerate your wounds. To reflect this, traits are split into three types.

Minor Traits cost 1 Character Point to purchase (or provide the character with 1 point if they're Bad).

Major Traits cost 2 Character Points to purchase (or provide 2 points if they're bad for the character).

Special Traits are the big guns of the traits world, they cover the ability to do superhuman things and cost Character Points and sometimes some of your Story Points as well... yes, they're that expensive! Some of these Special Traits are not really for your average character or companion, so the Gamemaster will have final say whether the player should have any of these Special Traits, and players should discuss having these special characters with them before purchasing them. Many of these traits are for aliens and alien characters.

EARNING CHARACTER POINTS WITH BAD TRAITS

Giving the character a Bad Trait will give you more Character Points that can be either spent on attributes, additional Good Traits or even spent on skills if you think the character is lacking in a particular area. Taking a lot of Bad Traits may give you a wealth of Character Points to spend elsewhere, but it can be very limiting to the character.

It is recommended that the Gamemaster limits the number of Bad Traits to 6 points per character. However, some of the Special Traits cost so many points that they require some Bad Traits to even begin to be able to purchase them.

PURCHASING TRAITS MORE THAN ONCE

Traits can only be purchased once, unless the Gamemaster approves. In these rare cases, it is only with traits that can relate to multiple things – for example a phobia of rats and spiders (two different Phobia Traits, but woe betide if they meet a rat-spider hybrid!). As a guide, traits that can be purchased multiple times are marked with an asterisk (*), but multiple purchases must be approved by the Gamemaster.

OPPOSING TRAITS

Also, opposing traits shouldn't be purchased as they simply cancel each other out. You cannot be both Technically Adept and Technically Inept, and you cannot be Distinctive and have Face in the Crowd. Some opposing traits may be purchased if the

Gamemaster allows – for example, a character could be both Lucky and Unlucky, meaning that their luck is extreme in both cases. Brave can be purchased with Phobia, as you can be brave in the face of everything except the thing you're secretly scared of. If the player can rationalise it sensibly, and the Gamemaster approves, they can purchase almost any trait they wish. We'll point out some of these restrictions in the trait's descriptive text.

⚙ LIST OF TRAITS

Below is a list of traits that can be purchased or taken by the character. Each trait describes its effects upon the character or how it can be used, along with the trait's value (whether it is a Minor or Major Trait), either Good or Bad.

The list is by no means exhaustive. The Gamemaster can create new traits from scratch. They will have to assign the new trait a value (Minor or Major, Good or Bad) and define any features, working with the players to create something cool and interesting. Use the existing traits as a guide.

Traits should effectively follow the character through time and space. Ones that are relative to their own planet or time zone may only be worthwhile if your adventurers intend to repeatedly return home. Creating traits such as Wealthy or Famous are fine if you're going to stay on Earth, but the moment you leave these traits become worthless.

The following list of traits is split into Good Traits (first), then Bad Traits, and finally Special Traits.

⚙ GOOD TRAITS

ANIMAL FRIENDSHIP (Minor Good Trait)

Some people just have a natural affinity for animals – creatures seem to like them for no apparent reason. Maybe they just smell friendly or give off the right signals, but animals are put at ease and may even go against their training to greet their new friend.

Effects: When encountering an animal for the first time, the character may attempt to show it that they mean no harm and calm any aggressive tendencies. This trait gives them a +2 modifier to a Presence and Convince skill roll to calm an animal. With a Fantastic result, the animal, even a trained guard dog, may adopt the character as their new master!

ARROGANT (Minor Good Trait)

While it doesn't make them very easy to get along with, some individuals have a powerful confidence that allow them to deal with any situation.

Effects: The character gains +2 to resisting fear and feelings of hopelessness, but suffer –1 to social interactions with those they consider to be inferior.

ATTRACTIVE (Minor Good Trait)

For every horrible beastie the Doctor encounters, there's a pretty face. Of course, a lot of this is subjective, and can depend upon personal taste or even species! After all, Chantho was kinda pretty for a big bug lady, even to us humans, so imagine how pretty she would be to another of the Malmooth on Malcassairo. Having the Attractive trait means the character is attractive and pleasant on the eye.

Effects: The Attractive trait comes into play whenever the character is doing something that their looks can influence. As a Good Trait, the character will get a +2 bonus to any rolls that involve their stunning good looks, from charming their way past guards to getting information out of someone.

Note: Cannot be taken with the Unattractive Bad trait.

BIOCHEMICAL GENIUS (Major Good Trait)

Some people are a dab hand with chemistry and biology and have a natural 'feel' for the way the two combine.

Effects: The character gains Areas of Expertise for the Science skill in Biology and Chemistry and may create biological or chemical 'Gadgets' using the Jiggery-Pokery rules, using the Science skill instead of Technology for all relevant rolls.

BOFFIN (Major Good Trait)

Boffin is a term that originated in WWII to describe those who constantly tinkered and experimented with equipment and technology to create futuristic devices. Having the Boffin trait means that you're a genius when it comes to tweaking with electronics and machinery to cobble together the most useful gadgets and gizmos.

Effects: This trait allows the character to create Gadgets through the fine art of 'Jiggery-Pokery'. Your average Joe can try to open their household appliances and wire them together to try to make something – though they'll probably only gain an electric shock or worse. Only a Boffin can create a useful device that can scan DNA, crack a safe or disable Dalek forcefields. More details on creating Gadgets can be found in the Jiggery-Pokery rules on pg. 113.

Note: Cannot be taken with the Technically Inept Bad trait.

BRAVE (Minor Good Trait)
Facing the invading monsters, bloodthirsty aliens and the many threats that companions encounter will mean that the characters are usually fairly courageous to even get involved. However, some people are more fearless, and can stare down a Sontaran in the face without flinching or shout at the Cybermen without worrying about the imminent reprisal.

Effects: The Brave trait provides a +2 bonus to any Resolve roll when the character could get scared or need to show their courage.

Note: Cannot be taken with the Cowardly Bad Trait, though individual Phobia Bad Traits can still be purchased.

CHARMING (Minor Good Trait)
Robin Hood could probably charm his way through an entire adventure, just by smiling at the people he meets and carousing his way. Some people are naturally charming, and can make people swoon; very handy if you need to get people to do something

for you, or to let you into a facility. The Charming trait reflects this additional seductive quality, and gives them an edge when trying to schmooze their way through any situation.

Effects: Charming is a Minor Good Trait, and when the character is trying to charm their way through an encounter, they receive a +2 bonus to the roll. Useful for talking your way out of being killed, but not always suitable for every social situation.

EMPATHIC (Minor Good Trait)
People naturally hide their true emotions unless they are really upset or stressed, and it takes training or a natural gift to be able to read the tiny signals that give away what they're really thinking or feeling. Some people have an empathy with how others are feeling and can use this gift to aid them when trying to get information or to calm someone down.

Effects: Empathic is a Minor Good Trait that provides the character with a +2 bonus on any rolls when they are trying to empathise or read another person. This could be a simple Presence + Convince roll to reassure someone who's panicking in the middle of a battle, or an Awareness + Ingenuity roll to try to read another's actions and speech to see if they're lying.

FACE IN THE CROWD (Minor Good Trait)
Some people can be unremarkable in manner or appearance, or are so comfortable in foreign places and with alien creatures that they can fade into the

background and not be too noticeable. This means that despite wearing something that might not be authentic to the time period, you fit in and people seem to ignore your 'alien-ness'.

Effects: As long as they're not dressing like a clown or anything too weird, and not doing anything that'll attract their attention, people will leave the character to go about what they're doing. If the Gamemaster asks for a roll to 'blend in', the trait provides a bonus of +2 to any Subterfuge skill roll when they're trying to sneak about and not get noticed when in a crowd of people.

Note: Cannot be taken with the Distinctive Bad Trait.

FAST HEALING (Major/Special Good Trait)

The ability to recover quickly from an injury is bound to be useful in your daily attempts to fend off alien invasion. Some people simply recover quicker than others, halting the bleeding and managing to carry on. Some very special individuals can heal major injuries, even regrowing limbs, within moments! This doesn't make them immortal (they can still be killed if they receive too much damage) but if they survive, the injuries they sustain heal themselves at a remarkable rate.

Effects: Fast Healing is either a Major Trait or a Special Trait, depending upon the speed of recovery. As a Major Good Trait, the character will heal any damage they have sustained quicker than a normal person. Any Attribute Points they have lost due to injury are regained at a rate of 1 point per hour, though the Gamemaster may decide that broken bones will take longer to heal. They might not be able to regrow lost limbs or compete in athletic events with a gunshot wound, but they'll still be up on their feet faster than most. The player may still have to rationalise why the character can heal quickly with the Gamemaster before taking this trait.

However, as a **Special Good Trait**, the Attribute Points lost are recovered at a rate of 1 point per minute! Bullet wounds heal over before your eyes and lost limbs are regrown. This is a very rare trait, though some creatures have been known to recover this quickly thanks to healing nanobots or a fast alien metabolism. They can still be killed as normal if three or more of their attributes are reduced to zero or lower, or if they are hit by a Lethal attack, but they will quickly recover from most damage that isn't fatal. As a Special Trait, this costs 6 Character Points as well as 6 Story Points. Having a character recover this quickly is certainly not natural, and the reason for their ability should be discussed with the Gamemaster before players are allowed to purchase this trait.

FRIENDS (Minor or Major Good Trait)

The character has people they can call upon for information or help. They may have reliable friends who can help them out (maybe they know someone who has some political pull or is well respected in the

community), contacts within an institution (do they know someone who works in UNIT, Torchwood or even the White House?), or someone who can supply information (a shady guy who keeps finding out things that the public aren't meant to know). Friends can be either a Minor or a Major Trait, depending upon how informative or helpful the friend in question is!

The trait will not replace investigating something yourself. After all, where's the fun if you get other people to do all the sneaking around and research for you? However, these friends are a great source of information on the background of a place or person that may otherwise take a while to uncover, while your character is busy doing something else. This can also be an excellent source of fresh and new adventures as the friend tips you off when something is happening.

Effects: As a Minor Trait, they know someone who knows someone – a 'friend of a friend', but the source (and their information) is usually reliable. It may be that they know a friend who works in the local newspaper or council office who hears things as they're reported and can steer the character in the direction of strange events. As a Major Trait, the person in the know is far more reliable, the information is accurate, or their contact may be leaking information from somewhere like UNIT or may even be someone of some power like Winston Churchill or the Queen of England!

Their contact may be putting themselves at risk to get the information to the character, but it's unlikely to be discovered. It should be noted that away from their home planet, unless their Friends are time and space travellers, this trait cannot be used where the friends cannot help them.

HOT SHOT (Minor Good Trait)
Some people are a natural when it comes to most forms of transport. They can fly planes through the harshest of thunderstorms or drive cars at high speeds without crashing. They are the best of the best when it comes to piloting vehicles.

Effect: Hot Shot is a Minor Good Trait providing the character with a +2 bonus to all Transport rolls. This bonus is especially effective when used to push the speed of a vehicle, as they can get the best performance from the craft.

HYPNOSIS (Minor/Major/Special Good Trait)
The Doctor has been known to use a bit of hypnotism to calm a savage beast and to help people to remember things, putting them in a calm and relaxed state. Hypnosis as a Minor Good Trait means the character can put people into a mild hypnotic state. We're not talking mind control here, just some basic hypnotic techniques – a tone of voice, a calm way of talking – that can calm people down and possibly influence them to do what you want. The Major Good Trait verges on mind control, and not the sort of thing a companion would do. The Special version of this trait allows complete possession, and is best left to the Master and other Villains.

Effects: As a Minor Trait, Hypnosis adds a +2 bonus to any social interaction where you're trying to either calm someone down or to get them to do what you'd like. It's dependent upon the situation of course; the Gamemaster may not allow in the middle of a battlefield, for instance. Usually, there should be few distractions, and the target and the hypnotist should be able to hear and see each other, unless there is some advanced or alien technology involved. The target can resist using Ingenuity + Resolve (see 'Being Possessed', p.97).

The Major Trait works the same way, but if the character succeeds in hypnotising the subject (using Presence + Convince), they can make them do anything not intrinsically against their nature (such as harm a friend or themselves) – in this case, the target can make another roll to resist (with a +3 bonus) to snap out of their hypnotic state, waking to wonder what they were doing. No matter what, they cannot be hypnotised into killing themselves – their survival instinct is too strong.

The Special version of this trait costs 3 points and effectively allows the character to possess another person. This can be full-on mind control, or actually leaving their body to inhabit someone else's. This level is reserved for alien or special characters, not for normal player characters.

INDOMITABLE (Major Good Trait)

That's the human race all round... indomitable. The character has determination and an iron will, meaning they are better at resisting mind control and hypnosis. They have something that grounds them, reassures them of who they are and protects their minds against invasion or hypnotic control.

Effects: The Indomitable trait gives the character a +4 bonus to any rolls to resist becoming possessed, hypnotised, psychically controlled or similar. In many ways, this trait can also be used to avoid being dissuaded from their course of action – for example, River Song is usually determined to go off by herself despite the Doctor's warnings. If the Doctor tried to convince her to stay, her Indomitable nature would help her to remain single-minded and determined to do as she wants, even if it isn't the best idea in the world.

KEEN SENSES (Minor/Major Good Trait)

The character is very aware of their surroundings. Whether they have a keen eye for detail and noticing when something is wrong, or a nose for a particular scent, they are particularly perceptive – always a good thing when tracking or encountering alien intruders.

Effects: As a Minor Trait you should specify which of the character's senses is particularly keen. A +2 bonus only applies to Awareness rolls that use that sense, whether it is sight, hearing, smell, touch, taste or that elusive sixth sense. Only one sense can be chosen – more than one, and it's a Major Trait. The Major Trait, a +2 bonus applies in any instance when using Awareness to notice or spot something, no matter what sense is being used.

Note: Cannot be taken with the Impaired Senses Bad Trait in the same sense, although different ones can be taken. For example, you could have keen vision, but be hard of hearing. The Impaired Senses Bad Trait should not be taken with the Keen Senses Major Trait, unless all of the character's other senses are compensating for a single impaired sense.

LUCKY (Minor Good Trait)

Lady Luck is on their side. Call it a fluke, call it chance, but fortune is smiling on the character. The traffic lights changed just at the right moment to give them a chance to get through, they just managed to roll under the blast doors before they closed and they flicked the right switch to restart the ship's engines. Every day is their lucky day!

Effects: The character is lucky! Simple as that. If you roll two '1's on your dice – 'snake-eyes' as they call 'em in Vegas – you're probably going to fail. At least normally. Characters with the Lucky trait get a second chance when double '1's are rolled, and you can re-roll both dice, trying for something better. If you get double '1's again, well, your luck obviously doesn't run that far, and you must keep the second result.

MILITARY RANK*
(Minor, Major or Special Good Trait)

The character has a military rank, with all the privileges and responsibilities that entails. If they belong to UNIT but do not have this trait they are considered to be regular enlisted soldiers (Privates or Corporals).

Effects: As a Minor Trait, the character is a Sergeant. As a Major Trait, they are a Lieutenant. With the permission of the Gamemaster, a player may begin higher than a Lieutenant, with good back story justification and by purchasing the trait additional times. The table below summarises ranks. The Special version of this trait also gives the Friends (Government and Military) trait to represent the officer's political and military connections.

RANK TRAIT	RANKS
None	Private or Corporal (player's choice)
Minor	Sergeant
Major	Lieutenant
Major x 2	Captain
Major x 3	Lieutenant Colonel or Major

NOBLE (Minor Good Trait)

Some people are born into the highest levels of society and are used to entertaining dignitaries, ambassadors and even kings and queens.

Effects: The character's experience gives them a +2 bonus whenever they deal socially with the cream of society, especially when you are in a formal environment.

OWED FAVOUR* (Minor/Major Good Trait)

Someone out there owes the character a favour. It can be anything from a sum of money, repayment for introducing them to their future wife or even saving their life. Whatever it was, they're not going to forget it, and in the character's moment of need they can be called upon to help out in a dire situation.

Effects: As a Minor Trait, the favour is something relatively small – a small amount of money (only £1000 or so), introducing someone to them at a party who later became a valuable business client or romantic partner, or you bailed them out when they were in trouble. As a Major Trait, the favour is more important, from a large amount of money (over £10,000) to saving their life. If appropriate, you may opt to call in the favour and seek assistance in the current adventure. Of course, if you ask for a favour bigger than the original debt, they may walk off afterwards saying "we're quits, don't call on me again", or you could even end up owing them a favour, and gain the Owes Favour Bad Trait (see pg. 46).

PERCUSSIVE MAINTENANCE
(Minor Good Trait)

There are some people (mad scientists, leather jacketed greasers from the 1950s, etc.) who have a rather peculiar innate understanding of machines that allows them to activate malfunctioning machinery with a single well placed blow to the appropriate area.

Effects: Whenever the character fails a roll to repair some sort of technology, they may immediately whack it with their fist or some other object and may roll again, replacing Ingenuity with Strength. They may only attempt this once per repair.

In addition, if they don't have time to make a proper repair, they may use Percussive Maintenance to get a piece of technology temporarily working by making a Strength + Technology roll. On a Success, the tech will work for one use, on a Good Success, it will work for D6 uses, and on a Fantastic Success it will continue to function until the Gamemaster decides otherwise.

PHOTOGRAPHIC MEMORY (Major Good Trait)

With just a few seconds of concentration, the character can commit something to memory to be instantly recalled when needed. People with this trait rarely have problems passing exams, and can remember exact lines from books.

Effects: The Photographic Memory trait can be used in a couple of different ways. If the character knows they're going to have to remember something at a later time, such as the combination to a lock or the instructions to program a computer, they can spend a moment to take the information in and commit it to memory. If they want to recall the information, they can without having to roll, but they must have declared that they've taken the time to concentrate and remember it at the time. Similarly, if they want to remember something that they haven't actively committed to memory, there's a chance it may be stored in there somewhere along with last week's shopping list or what time that film is on they wanted to watch. To recall something vital that they may have only glanced at or possibly missed altogether, you can spend a Story Point.

Note: Cannot be taken with the Forgetful Bad Trait.

PSYCHIC TRAINING (Minor Good Trait)

Don't you just hate it when you wave your Psychic Paper at someone and they don't see anything? Psychic Training means they are able to protect themselves from mental coercion or deception and are aware of psychic attack or memory alteration. They can put up basic defences to protect themselves, which can be as simple as imagining a plain white wall to repeating a Beatles tune in their head.

Effects: This Minor Trait gives the character a +2 bonus to Resolve rolls when trying to resist psychic attack or deception. It doesn't always work, but it is strong enough to resist a low level telepathic field such as that of Psychic Paper.

QUICK REFLEXES (Minor Good Trait)

The character is fast to act when things happen, reacting to situations almost instinctively. It doesn't mean they cannot be surprised – if they don't know something's coming they can't react to it – but when something attacks or bad happens, they're often the first to react to it.

Effects: In a conflict situation, when they haven't been taken completely by surprise, the character is assumed to always go first when acting at the same time as

others. They won't always go first in a round, but if two or more people are acting in a single phase (such as Talkers, Runners, etc.), the person with Quick Reflexes goes first. If more than one person in a phase has the Quick Reflexes trait, the character with the higher relative attribute goes first. For more information on Conflicts, Actions and Rounds, see pg. 80.

Note: Cannot be taken with the Slow Reflexes Bad Trait.

RESOURCEFUL POCKETS (Minor Good Trait)

The Doctor has said that he has pockets like the TARDIS, and he does seem to carry some strange things around in them. Sometimes people just have that knack of accumulating things – nothing terribly important or bulky, but little things that can be useful when you have to MacGyver something together at a time of peril. If you have the Resourceful Pockets trait there's a chance, albeit a slim one, that you may have something useful in them that could get you out of a sticky situation. Remember, Resourceful Pockets doesn't have to mean 'pockets' – you could have an excellent utility belt, and who knows what can be found in a handbag.

Effects: The player can either spend a Story Point and find the thing they need, or roll a couple of dice. If they get a 'double', for example rolling two '1's or two '3's, then they find something helpful in their pocket, from a cricket ball to a clockwork mouse. Of course it may not be exactly what you were expecting, but it may still be useful in some way.

REVERSE THE POLARITY OF THE NEUTRON FLOW (Major Good Trait)

Those with a particular genius for science have an innate understanding of the ebb and flow of energy and can make intuitive leaps that allow them to solve scientific and technological problems through unusual applications of that energy.

Effects: This trait may be used once per adventure. After the character has failed a roll using the Science or Technology skill, the player may declare they are "Reversing the polarity of the neutron flow" and turn the result into an automatic Fantastic Success.

RUN FOR YOUR LIFE! (Minor Good Trait)

There are many times when the opposing forces are too numerous or just too powerful to take down. The best thing you can do is to flee, run for your life and regroup to plan a new angle of attack. The character

with this trait has obviously got this running thing down to a fine art and when danger is close behind there is that extra motivation to simply scarper!

Effects: The character is better at running away from danger, usually due to all the practice they've had! When being chased (see pg. 98), you receive a +1 bonus to your Speed when fleeing.

SCREAMER! (Minor Good Trait)

The character has been known to scream in the face of terror on many occasion, and this ear-splitting sound will penetrate miles of corridor to alert others to their location and the imminent threat.

Effects: At times when they are scared or threatened, the character can scream their lungs out. No roll is necessary, though using this trait will cost a Story Point. Anything or anyone else in the room will be stunned and will be unable to act for their next action. The Screamer should take their next action running away while the enemy is stunned – they are rarely brave enough to do anything else. The scream also alerts their companions, and the rest of the group will automatically know the direction they are in.

Note: Screamers usually gain this trait from being easily scared. The Screamer trait cannot be taken with Brave and the character will never receive any bonuses when trying resist getting scared (see 'Getting Scared' on pg. 94).

SENSE OF DIRECTION (Minor Good Trait)

There are some people who instinctively know the easiest way to get from one place to the next. It may be a labyrinthine maze of streets and identical houses, but characters with the Sense of Direction trait rarely seem to get lost, or can usually find their bearings if they do.

Effects: This trait gives the character a +2 bonus to any roll (usually Awareness and Ingenuity) to regain their direction when lost, or to simply work out how to get from A to B. This can be map reading, running through a miles of similar corridors, or simply knowing which way is up while spinning in zero gravity.

TECHNICALLY ADEPT (Minor Good Trait)

The character has an innate connection to technology, and can sometimes fix things just by hitting them! They're skilled enough to operate and repair most things with limited tools, taking half the time it normally takes. Often, if the device stopped working within thirty minutes, it can be restarted just by thumping it. It may not last long, but long enough...

Effects: The Technically Adept trait provides the character with +2 to any Technology roll to fix a broken or faulty device, and to use complex gadgets or equipment. The bonus also applies to any gadget-creating jiggery-pokery, and can be combined with the Boffin trait.

Note: Cannot be taken with the Technically Inept Bad Trait.

TIME TRAVELLER* (Minor/Major Good Trait)

The character is experienced with the technology and society of time periods different to their own.

The Time Traveller trait also reflects how much travelling in time the character has done, and can be used as a rough indicator of how much background Artron Radiation they have picked up from travelling the Vortex. While this isn't actually harmful, some alien races have been known to target individuals that have high Artron levels to fuel or activate their technology.

Effects: Players define the character's home Technology Level (see pg. 66), and using technology from outside of the character's experience may impose penalties as they're unfamiliar with the way it works. The Time Traveller trait means that they're used to some time periods and can operate the technology with little or no penalty.

The character automatically has a familiarity with their home Tech Level, but the Time Traveller

trait records additional Tech Levels levels they're comfortable with. Lower Technology Levels to their home are Minor Good Traits, whereas more advanced Technology Levels are Major Good Traits. Technology Levels do not come into play all of the time – after all a gun is a gun and a socket wrench is a socket wrench, but there are times when technology is so advanced or primitive that your character may feel out of place or unable to recognise the technology for what it is. More information on interacting with technology out of the character's experience can be found on pg. 110. This trait can be purchased more than once, and the Gamemaster may award this trait during play if the character becomes particularly familiar with a certain Tech Level.

TOUGH (Minor Good Trait)

Not everyone can take a punch on the nose and brush it off as if nothing had happened. Few people can take getting shot or starved, tortured or wounded in the course of their everyday lives. However, people with the Tough trait are used to the adventure, can take the knocks and brush them off.

Effects: Tough reduces the amount of damage that would normally be deducted from the character's attributes by 2. This is after any other effects, such as armour, are taken into account.

For example, Danny Pink had to face many hostiles when he was a soldier, which has made him more resilient. He fails during a Conflict with a Dalek, but not badly enough to kill him. He'd normally be told to knock 4 points off one or more of his attributes to reflect his injury, but his Tough trait reduces the damage by 2. Now he only has to take 2 points off his attributes. A wound all the same, but not as bad as it could have been.

VOICE OF AUTHORITY (Minor Good Trait)

The character has the air of command about them, possibly from being a figure of authority – a doctor, politician, military commander or a police constable – or they may have an aura of intelligence or experience that inspires people to listen and trust their judgement. This is especially handy when trying to clear an area because of some approaching danger, to order people about or simply try to gain their trust.

Effects: This trait provides a +2 bonus to Presence and Convince rolls to try to get people to do as you wish or to gain their trust. The Gamemaster may modify this to suit the situation.

⚙ BAD TRAITS

ADVERSARY* (Minor/Major Bad Trait)

The Doctor has made many enemies in his travels, but a few of them recur enough to warrant a whole trait to themselves. The Adversary trait means that the character has made an enemy in the past who is actively trying to hinder them whenever possible. The key word here is 'actively'. For example, the Daleks have gone to great lengths to battle the Doctor, chasing him through time and space, laying traps, and even luring him to WWII London to trick him into aiding the rebirth of their race.

Effects: Adversary can be a Minor or a Major Bad Trait depending upon the power and frequency of the Adversary's appearance. For example, the Doctor scuppered the plans of Fenric and the Haemovores, but they haven't resurfaced. If another colony of the Haemovores heard of the fate of their Northumbrian counterparts and decided to try to track down the Doctor for revenge, they'd count as a Minor Adversary Trait. They're not too powerful, unlikely to appear in every campaign, but may appear as recurring villains. A fairly powerful Villain that makes an appearance every campaign such as the Daleks would count as a Major Adversary. They just keep surviving and coming back again and again, and consider the Doctor their greatest enemy.

AMNESIA (Minor/Major Bad Trait)

Memory is a fragile thing that can easily be manipulated or lost entirely. The Amnesia trait means that some or even all of the character's memories are missing and they have 'holes' in their past.

These memories may return in time, with the right triggers, but for the time being there are periods in their past that they know nothing about. This could be deliberate, the result of mind-wiping technology, psychic powers or Torchwood's amnesia drug Retcon, or due to mental or physical damage.

Effects: As a Minor Bad Trait, the character has lost a portion of their memory. It could be as small as a couple of days, weeks or even a couple of years, but the character will have no idea of what happened to them in that time. As a Major Bad Trait, this Amnesia is total, the character having no memory of their past, or even who they really are. Events, sights, sounds or even smells can trigger memories of their lost time, and this is a great source of adventure ideas for the Gamemaster – over many adventures the character can uncover more and more of their 'lost time'.

Of course, this adds to the work the Gamemaster has to do, coming up with the character's lost memories, so the Amnesia trait should be approved by the Gamemaster before purchasing it.

ARGUMENTATIVE (Minor Bad Trait)

Some people just think they're right all the time, even when they're not. Some even provoke an argument just for arguing's sake. Characters with the Argumentative trait are like this and will argue their point of view even if it is with their teammates or with the leader of an invading alien fleet.

However, they don't start arguments all the time – that would make the character impossible to be around, but when someone contradicts their opinion or knowledge, they will actively try to correct them.

Effects: Argumentative is a Minor Trait, so it shouldn't get in the way too much of their normal behaviour. However, they will find it difficult to hold their tongue when their opinion or knowledge is contradicted. If this situation arises, the Gamemaster will reward 'playing in character' with Story Points. If the argument may end in a fight, the character may try to back down for their own safety, but the player will have to make an Ingenuity and Resolve roll, with a -2 modifier, to try to hold their tongue.

BY THE BOOK (Minor Bad Trait)
I'm sorry, I can't let you do that. Protocol clearly states that you must follow the correct procedure when you are opening a dialogue with a potentially hostile species. I really shouldn't let you do that at all. Look, if you want to go that way and ignore the signs, then be my guest. I, however, will be following the arrows to the nearest escape hatch while putting on my lifejacket.

Effects: The character will follow instructions, advice or correct procedure to the letter without deviating. Soldiers with intensive military training often have this trait, following the orders of the commanding officer without question. It doesn't mean the character is a mindless drone, but it does mean that it may take some serious convincing to get them to go against their training or orders. If someone tries to convince them otherwise, they will usually make an Ingenuity and Resolve roll, and the trait gives them a +2 bonus to the roll.

This is a bonus, despite it being a Bad Trait, as most of the time failing to show initiative and going against orders will result in putting themselves in danger or annoying their teammates. The bonus does, however, also apply when trying to resist Hypnosis or Possession if the mental control is trying to get them to do something they'd normally refuse to do.

CLUMSY (Minor Bad Trait)
It seems as if the character is unable to keep hold of things, keeps tripping over the smallest hazard, and shouldn't be trusted with that pocket universe suspended in a glass chamber.

Effect: Clumsy is a Minor Bad Trait, but it doesn't mean the character will pratfall every five minutes. It does mean that in times of stress, especially when being chased, the player will have to make additional Awareness and Coordination rolls to avoid knocking vital things over, dropping the vial of toxic chemicals or tripping up and landing on their face.

CODE OF CONDUCT (Minor/Major Bad Trait)

The Code of Conduct trait means that the character adheres to a strict moral standing or self-imposed set of rules they follow at all times. Depending upon whether it's a Minor or Major rait, this can be purely guidelines or a deep-seated way of life. The Doctor has a strict Major Code of Conduct, as he believes all life is precious and would even offer his hand of forgiveness and help to a Dalek or Missy.

While this is listed as a Bad Trait, it doesn't mean that having a code is bad; just that it can restrict your actions and limit your choices. Being good is often the harder option, but it means you're a better person for it.

Effects: As a Minor Trait, Code of Conduct means that the character should try to do good at most times, and are unable to harm another being unless it is absolutely necessary and for the greater good.

As a Major Trait, their limits their actions dramatically, meaning they need to strive to do their best at every moment, almost verging on the saintly! Discuss the character's own unique Code of Conduct with the Gamemaster when you take this trait. Breaking it may be very costly, resulting in the loss of Story Points!

COWARDLY (Minor Bad Trait)

Facing those monsters, some people become nervous wrecks rather than becoming hardened to it. Cowardly is a Bad Trait reflecting the character's lack of natural courage, and means they will usually avoid dangerous situations unless it means that staying where they are is even more life-threatening!

Effects: The Cowardly Trait reduces the character's chance to resist getting scared, suffering a -2 penalty to any roll when they need to resist running away screaming! (See "Getting Scared" on pg. 94).

Note: Cannot be taken with the Brave Good Trait.

DARK SECRET (Minor/Major Bad Trait)

The character has a skeleton in the closet and if it's revealed it could change the way people think about them. It could be something mundane, such as a criminal record that they're trying to gloss over after turning their back on a life of crime. Or it could be something more extreme, that the character is actually an alien (though the Alien trait should be taken as well, see pg. 49) or the result of some strange genetic experiments conducted by the US Government. It's probably best to discuss with the Gamemaster what the Dark Secret actually is,

possibly before creating the character with your friends, just so you really do have a secret to keep from the other players.

Effects: Dark Secret can be either a Minor or a Major Bad Trait, depending upon the severity of the reaction should the secret be revealed. Something that would change the way people think about you is a Minor Trait.

For example, having a criminal record would usually be a Minor Trait. If people found out about it, they might not like you any more, or certainly act more cautiously around you.

If a more hostile reaction would result, not necessarily from your companions but certainly from others, it would be a Major Trait – for example, being an escaped criminal like River Song has been during many of her encounters with the Doctor. If people discovered the secret the character could be arrested and imprisoned again, or shot at by law enforcement agents. Your companions may be sympathetic, knowing you've changed your ways, but it doesn't stop the Judoon or the local police from hunting you once you've been discovered. Remember, for it to warrant being a Major Bad Trait, the secret should still have some ramifications even away from your home planet.

DEPENDENCY (Minor/Major Bad Trait)
Sometimes you just rely on others. It could be said that the Doctor's companions are all dependent upon him, but there have been many times when they've shown that they are easily his equals, so they're far from dependent. Having the Dependency trait means they are dependent upon something or someone to survive. Maybe this is blood like a Plasmavore or the support of others, like Lady Cassandra. The level of the trait determines how desperate they will get, and how bad the effects will be, if they can't get their fix. Players should be careful not to take such a high Dependency that their character becomes too difficult to play.

Effect: As a Minor Bad Trait, they can go for extended periods without their dependency getting in the way. If the Gamemaster decides their need is urgent, the character may suffer a -2 penalty to their actions until they fulfil their need. As a Major Trait, they are unable to survive without their dependency. It could be that they need something to survive like blood or moisture. If they go without it for any period of time (defined by the Gamemaster and the player) they suffer a -4 penalty to every action. This could be

because they're unable to think of anything else, or because they're unable to act properly without help.

DISTINCTIVE (Minor Bad Trait)
There is something very striking or obvious about your character that makes them stand out in the crowd. Whether they are just tall, short, have coloured hair or are striking in the way they dress or act, they get noticed and people seem to remember them. They're not going to provoke people pointing and staring, but they'll certainly be remembered and recognised if encountered again. This doesn't mean 'Alien' in appearance – for example, if Bannakaffalatta walked around on modern Earth he'd provoke a far more extreme reaction than the Distinctive trait; he'd have the Alien Appearance Trait (see pg. 49).

Effect: This trait works in a couple of ways. If the character is trying to 'blend in' or go unnoticed in a crowd, they suffer a -2 penalty to the roll. Also, if they're seen doing something, or if another character or NPC is asked to describe or remember the distinctive character, they will receive a +2 bonus to remember or recognise them after their initial encounter.

Note: Cannot be taken with the Face in the Crowd trait.

ECCENTRIC (Minor/Major Bad Trait)

Some people behave rather oddly. The Doctor acts in ways that baffles his companions and throws his opponents off their game, switching from excited schoolboy to dark and imposing in a moment. The Eccentric trait means the character has a behaviour that makes them stand out, or sometimes makes it more difficult when interacting with others.

As a Minor Bad trait, their behaviour isn't too upsetting. It could be an odd mannerism during times of stress, out-of-place reactions to everyday events, or even talking to themselves.

The Major Bad Trait, is probably too unpredictable to be purchased by a player character. We're getting into seriously wacky territory, sometimes a little dangerous to be around. Missy is a prime example of someone with the Major Eccentric Trait, straying into unpredictable behaviour with little provocation. But just because the character has a Major Eccentric Trait, it doesn't mean they're homicidal (except it does in Missy's case, of course).

Effects: The specifics of the character's Eccentric trait should be discussed with the Gamemaster at character creation. Just how does this behaviour manifest? Are they aloof, a loner, irrational, tangential, a natural clown, a sour-puss? Once their odd behaviour is defined, the Gamemaster will help to decide how this behaviour is triggered. Is it when they're stressed, cross, happy, jealous, or tired? It is then down to the player to act in character when the situation arises, which will gain them Story Points for good roleplaying.

FORGETFUL (Minor Bad Trait)

The character's memory is less than reliable. It usually isn't too drastic if they don't remember everything on the shopping list when they're standing in the supermarket, but if they've got to they're which wire to cut to stop a bomb, or the precise words to use to halt a curse, there's a good chance you're going to forget and cause a disaster.

Effects: When the character needs to remember something vital, an Ingenuity + Resolve roll is required

with a -2 penalty. If the information is particularly complicated, such as an entire monologue from Shakespeare, the Gamemaster may increase the penalty.

Note: Cannot be taken with the Photographic Memory trait.

IMPAIRED SENSES* (Minor/Major Bad Trait)

The Impaired Senses trait means that one of the character's senses is not at its best. Whether this is the need for glasses, a hearing aid or being colour blind, the sense is less sensitive than the average person's. When selecting this trait, the player should choose which sense is affected.

Effect: Players should discuss with the Gamemaster which sense is affected, as well as the severity of the impairment. Minor Bad Traits would be: no sense of smell, colour blind, no sense of taste, needing to wear glasses or needing a hearing aid. Awareness rolls using these senses suffer a -2 penalty if the sense isn't aided. The penalties don't affect the character all of the time, only when there's something to detect such as a strange gas leak, needing to rewire a device with different-coloured wires or losing their glasses. Major Bad Traits would be losing a sense that impacts on their everyday actions, such as blindness or deafness.

Note: Cannot be taken with Keen Senses, unless the Keen Sense is Minor and then in a Sense that isn't Impaired.

IMPULSIVE (Minor Bad Trait)

"Why worry, it'll be fine, let's go!" Impulsive people do not think things through before acting and are likely to leap before they look. It doesn't mean they have a death wish – far from it – it's just that they do things on a whim and sometimes come to regret it.

Effect: There are no penalties or modifiers for this Minor Bad Trait, but the player should remember the impulsive nature of the character and bring it into play when possible. It doesn't force them to take unnecessary risks, but they will leap into a situation before they have all of the facts, thinking they're doing good. Playing up to the trait should be rewarded by the Gamemaster if the situation and roleplaying is suitable for the plot and the game. At times the Gamemaster can make it a dramatic struggle, trying to resist the urge to be impulsive (in which case, a -2 modifier is applied to Ingenuity and Resolve).

INSATIABLE CURIOSITY (Minor Bad Trait)

The character has a thirst for knowing what's going on and investigating, even when it may not be good for them to do so. What was that down that hole? Where does that corridor go, and what are those aliens up to? In many cases, Insatiable Curiosity has been the cause of many adventures (especially in Clara's case).

Effect: This is a Minor Bad Trait that rewards playing in character and remembering their curious nature. It is usually unhelpful, but the character simply **has** to know what is going on, why something is happening or how it works. It may put their life at risk, but it doesn't make them suicidal. If the character tries to fight the urge to press that button or open that door, the player can make an Ingenuity + Resolve roll, with a -2 modifier to resist.

Note: Cannot be taken with the Unadventurous Bad Trait. If the character gains the Unadventurous trait (see pg. 46), the character loses the Insatiable Curiosity trait.

OBLIGATION (Minor/Major Bad Trait)

The character has a duty to a group or organisation and responsibilities that need to be upheld. They may be member of a government agency, such as UNIT, Torchwood, part of the government, a teacher at a school or even a secret order.

Effect: Obligation is a Minor or Major Bad Trait, depending upon the responsibilities and the size of the organisation the character is associated with. As a Minor Trait, Obligation means the character belongs to a 'normal' organisation. They will not betray their allies and other members, and will be willing to risk a lot for what they believe in.

As a Major Trait, Obligation means the organisation is more important than the character. They are always 'on call' and may not have time for a personal life. Their dedication is such that they'd be willing to lay down their life for the organisation, and penalties for disobedience or betrayal are severe. The Gamemaster should determine the ramifications of betraying their obligation - from disciplinary action to making a dangerous enemy (see the Adversary trait, pg. 39).

OBSESSION (Minor/Major Bad Trait)

Someone, something, or some goal constantly weighs on the character's mind. It may be just keeping track of time, doing things in threes, or it could be something as strong as the need for revenge or the love of a special someone. Having the Obsession trait is rarely something helpful, and this Bad Trait is uncommon in player characters. This sort of fanaticism is best suited to people like Missy or the Half-Face Man.

Effect: As a Minor Bad Trait, it means the character has a mild obsession, a bit like Clive and his investigation into the Doctor. It doesn't creep into every part of their lives, but it's always there, itching at the back of their minds. Their obsession isn't strong enough to be too troublesome, but there are times when they simply have to do something because of their compulsion. Often, this isn't anything too drastic, like switching the gas on and off again before leaving a house, checking their emails every hour or needing to wear a certain pair of underwear on Wednesdays. They can try to resist acting upon their obsessive nature with an Ingenuity and Resolve roll, suffering a -2 penalty.

As a Major Bad Trait, the character is crazed with determination to do something. Almost every action or plan is designed to get them closer to achieving their aim, whether this is galactic domination or acquiring vast amounts of wealth. At this level, it is not usually suitable for player characters.

OUTCAST (Minor Bad Trait)

The character has done something that has led to a section of society, or an entire race or planet, shunning them or viewing them with fear, dread or loathing. It could be that they've offended someone's beliefs, or committed a crime, or even just made such a fool of themselves that people regard them with complete disdain. They could have spoken out about their extreme scientific belief in aliens and been ridiculed in academic circles, or shunned by the government agency they work for and given an office in the basement.

Effect: Players should discuss with the Gamemaster what the character has done and who regards them with such dislike or dismissal. When anyone that would react negatively to their presence encounters the character, they should make an Awareness + Ingenuity roll to recognise them. If the character is recognised, they'll suffer a -2 penalty on all social rolls (such as trying to Convince or to even share their knowledge). If the 'something' they've done is more severe than this, they should take a Major Dark Secret Bad Trait instead.

OUTSIDER (Minor Bad Trait)

You aren't very good at making friends and fitting in with groups. Somehow you just don't seem to connect to other people very well.

Effects: You suffer a -2 penalty to social rolls with strangers and may not take the 'Friends' trait at character creation.

OWES FAVOUR* (Minor/Major Bad Trait)

In the past, someone did the character a favour. It could be anything from a sum of money, repaying them for getting a great job, or even saving the character's life. Whatever it was, they're not going to forget it, and they can call on the character to repay the favour.

Effect: As a Minor Trait, the favour is something relatively small – a small amount of money (up to £1000 or so), an introduction to someone important, or bailed the character out when in trouble. As a Major Trait, the favour is more important, a large amount of money (over £10,000) to saving the character's life. If the Gamemaster chooses, and if it suits the plot, they may opt to call in the favour, possibly even becoming an adventure in itself. Of course, if the favour called in is bigger than the first debt, it may be quits and this trait may be lost, or even gain the Owed Favour Good Trait!

PHOBIA* (Minor Bad Trait)

Some people just don't like spiders. Others, it's cats. Or heights, flying, llamas or cheese. Having a Phobia trait means that there is something (that the player will define, usually with the Gamemaster's help) that they are afraid of. A Phobia ignores the Brave trait – the character can be brave and courageous most of the time but crumble in the face of their biggest fear! Phobias can sometimes be gained during the course of an adventure if the character encounters something particularly scary that'll leave a lasting impression like giant rats or clowns.

Effect: The character will receive a -2 penalty to any attempt to approach the subject of their phobia or stay calm in its vicinity (see 'Getting Scared' on pg. 94). The Brave trait does not help with this roll.

SELFISH (Minor Bad Trait)

"But what's in it for me?" It's all about me. Me, me, me, me, me. The character may go along with the rest of the group, helping civilisations out of trouble or rescuing people in danger, but at the back of their mind is always the thought that they may be able to get something out of it: a reward, riches, hidden treasure, technological knowledge, or just information about the future that they can exploit.

Effect: Selfish doesn't interfere too much with the way the character acts – they'll help and join in as usual – but there may be times when they sneak off to see what they can plunder or gain. The Gamemaster may reward this action with Story Points for playing

in character if it moves the adventure in an exciting or unexpected direction at the character's expense.

SLOW REFLEXES (Minor/Major Bad Trait)

A character with this trait is constantly surprised by events, unable to get a word into a conversation, last to react in a confrontation and often hit in the face when a ball is thrown to them.

Effect: As a Minor Bad Trait, the character always goes last when multiple people are acting at the same time in a round. Others will always go first. However, as a Major Bad Trait, the character always goes last in a round (see pg. 80), going after everyone else, as they try to take in all the information and work out what is the best course of action.

Note: Cannot be taken with the Quick Reflexes Good trait.

TECHNICALLY INEPT (Minor Bad Trait)

Technology seems to hate the character. Things break when touched, using advanced technology is frustrating and annoying, trying to fix technology presents the character with a mass of wires and welding that is so completely confusing that they hardly know where to start.

Effect: Technically Inept means that any attempt to fix technology or devices, or use particularly complex technology, suffers a -2 penalty to the roll. If the Gamemaster thinks it is suitable to the story, an electronic device being used by the character can fuse or fail at a dramatic moment.

Note: Cannot be taken with the Boffin or Technically Adept traits.

UNADVENTUROUS (Minor/Major Bad Trait)

The idea of exploring or seeing the world and the universe just doesn't seem to appeal. Why spend money travelling across the world when you don't have anything to show for your expense afterwards except some trinkets and fading photographs? Sometimes, it's just laziness, fatigue or bad experience, but either way the excitement and thrill of travelling or experiencing the new just isn't there, or has faded.

Effect: It is rare that characters have this trait at creation but it can be gained during play due to repetitive injuries, being captured too many times, or just growing tired of the constant peril and relentless danger. If the Gamemaster thinks the character is getting captured or injured too often, they may gain Unadventurous as a Minor Bad Trait. They can try to buy this off with good roleplaying (see pg. 109), but in the meantime they are disinterested in some of the wonders of the universe, and can even dread the experiences a life of adventure can bring.

This can increase to a Major Bad Trait if they continue to have bad experiences. Again, the player can try to fuel the character's interest and buy off the trait, but it'll become obvious that the character is really unhappy to be involved in the travels. The Gamemaster may apply a -2 penalty to rolls during the game – not every roll, but certainly those where a level of enthusiasm is needed.

If the bad experiences continue still, the character can get so fed up with the constant peril, danger and repeated injuries that they decide to leave. They demand that they are returned home (or to a time and place where they can be happy) and leave the TARDIS crew, usually for good. They may return for a guest appearance, but other than that, the player should create a new character (see 'Dying or Leaving the TARDIS' on pg. 97).

Note: Cannot be taken with the Insatiable Curiosity Bad Trait.

UNATTRACTIVE (Minor Bad Trait)

For every stunningly gorgeous individual there are those whose faces do not launch a thousand Jathaa Sungliders or stop traffic on the New New York motorways (unless that face is the Face of Boe). They're not necessarily ugly or hideous, but their looks may hinder when it comes to some social situations.

Effects: The trait comes into play whenever doing something that their looks can influence, suffering a -2 penalty to rolls. On rare occasions, their appearance (especially if it is somewhat menacing, such as scarred) can provide a +2 bonus if they are trying to intimidate someone.

Note: Cannot be taken with the Attractive Good Trait.

UNLUCKY (Minor Good Trait)

Call it a curse, call it chance, but fortune hasn't smiled for a while. The traffic lights turn red whenever approached, the character pressed the wrong button

on the control panel and shorted the autopilot or their attempt at being diplomatic has resulted in insulting the city's patron and her entire family.

Effect: The character is unlucky! Simple as that. If you roll two '6's on your dice, you'd normally cheer as this would be a huge success. At least, normally. Characters with the Unlucky trait **have** to re-roll when double '6's are rolled, increasing the random chance of rolling something worse. If you get double '6's again, well, your unlucky streak isn't so bad – you can keep that result.

WANTED (Minor/Major Bad Trait)

You are actively hunted by a group. They may believe you have committed a crime, but they might just as easily want to worship you as the chosen one. Either way, you don't want them to catch up with you.

Effects: As a Minor Bad Trait the group will sometimes come across you, but they have limited resources and are unable to send a large force to bring you in.

As a Major Trait the group are very powerful, and if they catch up with you, you are as good as captured.

WEAKNESS* (Minor/Major Bad Trait)

The Weakness trait reflects a single area where the character is susceptible to harm or temptation. This could be anything from an allergy like hay fever or wasp stings (not so good when fighting giant wasps!), to being weak willed and susceptible to mind control, or suffering from occasional - but paralysing - drive glitches.

Effect: The player should discuss the chosen weakness with the Gamemaster and come to an agreement over the exact nature of this Bad Trait. In most cases, when the character encounters the thing that affects them, any rolls suffer a -2 penalty. In the case of a substance like pollen or stings, the character should suffer a -2 penalty to all actions while they're within range or exposed to its effects.

For example, being stung by a wasp (not a giant Vespiform but a normal-sized one), when allergic to wasp and bee stings will result in suffering a -2 penalty to all actions for at least eight hours (or until an anti-toxin is administered), while he's feeling weak and groggy from the poisons.

Weakness as a Major Trait is best suited for villains and aliens who need a definite exploitable weakness to give the characters a chance against them, such as weakness to acetic acid, or an extreme reaction to water or gold. Major Weaknesses actually cause injury rather than a penalty and exposure to the effective element will actually inflict 4 levels of damage, reducing their attributes (see Injuries, on pg. 85).

⚙ SPECIAL TRAITS

ALIEN (Special Good Trait)

Aliens come in all shapes and sizes, but in the majority of cases these aliens are basically humanoid in shape, with certain abilities and features that set them apart. By purchasing the Alien trait, the character is of an alien race, alien to humanity, and one of the infinite varieties of lifeforms.

Effect: Alien is a 'gateway' trait, opening a selection of additional traits that are normally unavailable to humans, and costs 2 Character Points to purchase. The Gamemaster should approve the selection of this trait. The Alien trait means that the character is from another planet. Initially, they are of human appearance and look similar to everyone else on Earth. This trait does open up the opportunity to purchase other specifically Alien traits, and enables attributes to be above level 6. As a downside, if discovered as being an Alien, they may suffer severe consequences (such as being captured by the government and experimented upon). Additionally, some of the Alien-only traits that are now open may mean that the character will have an alien appearance. For more information on creating aliens and alien characters, and additional Alien traits, see **Chapter Five: All the Strange, Strange Creatures** (pg. 143).

> The humanoid form is a hard design to beat, and many of the alien races the Doctor has encountered are indistinguishable from humans. These races have no need to purchase the Alien trait.

ALIEN APPEARANCE (Special Bad Trait)

While many aliens can pass for human under some circumstances (or low lighting), the character with this trait will have an obviously alien appearance. It could be that they're basically human but green, or have a large head to accommodate their massive brain power, or pointy ears, or obviously reptilian features. Players should feel free to be creative. This trait could also be taken by a human whose physical form has been altered by mutation or experimentation.

Effect: Alien Appearance is a Bad Trait that can provide either 2 Points or 4 Points. The more severe the Alien Appearance trait, the more 'alien' the character looks.

As a 2-point Bad Trait, Alien Appearance means the character is basically humanoid but with a distinctive alien feature. In most cases, when they encounter people who are OK with aliens there will be nothing out of the ordinary, however when meeting the inhabitants of more-primitive planets (see Technology Levels, pg. 65) who may not have met aliens before, social rolls will all suffer a -2 penalty (that is if they don't just run away!).

As a 4-point Bad Trait, the 'alien-ness' of the character is more extreme. The may have tentacles instead of limbs, or a face like a squid – they could look like anything! Again, on advanced planets that are used to aliens, this isn't a problem, but if they meet less experienced peoples they will suffer a -4 penalty on social rolls (possibly even become the target of scared locals who assume the alien is a monster to be destroyed!).

CLAIRVOYANCE (Special Good Trait)
Prerequisite: Psychic
A true clairvoyant has the ability to see distant locations through intense concentration as if they were actually there. In the past, this talent was found in tribal 'seers' and visionaries. During the Cold War this was called 'Remote Viewing' as teams of intelligence psychics tried to spy on distant countries to uncover secret bases and weapons.

CLAIRVOYANCE TABLE

RESOLVE	RANGE	DURATION
1	up to 5m	Brief flash
2	up to 10m	A few seconds
3	up to 200m	30 seconds
4	up to 1km	A minute
5	10km	3 minutes
6	100km	5 minutes
7	500km	10 minutes
8	1000km	20 minutes
9	Anywhere on the planet	30 minutes

Effect: Clairvoyance is a Special Trait, requiring the character to already have the Psychic trait. Clairvoyance costs 2 points. The character can see into other locations without actually being there or having to rely on technology. It will cost a Story Point to activate this ability and the range is limited to the

character's Resolve – the higher their Resolve, the further away they can see. Often these 'visions' will be flashes or mere glimpses into another place, but with practice, concentration and a high Resolve, the experience can be prolonged and immersive.

Clairvoyance uses the character's innate abilities, rather than a skill, so Awareness and Resolve are used to view distant locations. People at the spied location with the Psychic Training trait can sense they are being watched or observed and may try to resist.

CYBORG (Special Good Trait)
On some high tech worlds machinery can be used to replace body parts lost due to an injury, improvement or simply old age. The character is such a merging of flesh and machine. The cybernetic part is able to act like a Gadget, but it does also mean the character could be subject to discrimination in certain parts of the galaxy, where cyborgs are regarded as second class citizens.

Effect: Cyborg is a Special Good Trait that costs either 1 or 3 Character Points. At the lowest level, the cybernetic parts of the character are obvious. They can be hidden, but they will have to be careful. Bannakaffalatta is like this, his cybernetic chest section is something that can be hidden, but it is bulky and is obvious if he removes his shirt.

At the 3-point level, the cybernetic elements are completely disguised under fairly realistic looking, plastic skin.

The Cyborg trait allows the character to have a permanent Gadget (which must be purchased separately) that will not run out of power or get lost (see Gadgets, on pg. 112). Major cybernetic overhauls, such as Max Capricorn's or full Cyberman conversion are not suitable for a character in the game, except at the Gamemaster's discretion.

Note: Cannot be taken with the Robot trait.

EXPERIENCED* (Special Good Trait)
The character creation rules are suited to companions and normal heroes. Players may find it tricky to create a character as experienced or as powerful as River Song or Captain Jack Harkness. This trait provides the character with additional Character Points and Skill Points, at the cost of Story Points. This reduction in Story Points not only applies at character creation, it also reduces the number of

Story Points the character can carry over between adventures.

Effect: Experienced reduces the maximum Story Point pool for the character by 3 and provides the character with an additional 2 Character Points and 2 Skill Points. This trait can be purchased additional times, though no character can be reduced to zero Story Points because of this. That's far too dangerous! Not every character should be as experienced as this, and their lower Story Points help to balance the character with their less experienced companions.

FAST HEALING (Special Good Trait)
See the Fast Healing Good Trait (pg. 32)

FEAR FACTOR* (Special Good Trait)
The Fear Factor trait is designed for monsters, and those truly scary individuals who can send people running in terror. They don't have to be ugly or monstrous – people cowered at the Master's feet in fear of their lives – but sometimes just looking at the alien with the mouth full of sharp fangs that fills them with fear.

Effect: Fear Factor is a Special Trait that is only suitable for Villains. It costs 1 point, but can be purchased multiple times. Each purchase of the Fear Factor trait adds +2 to any roll when **actively** trying to strike fear into people's hearts. See 'Getting Scared' on pg. 94.

FEEL THE TURN OF THE UNIVERSE
(Special Good Trait)
Not many people experience the clarity and the wonder that is feeling the whole universe. Knowing you're just a small part in the vast, almost endless universe of planets and possibilities. It can drive some people mad, and others can sense when something is wrong.

This trait is not available to companions, and is normally only for Time Lord characters (see pg. 56). However, a rare few aliens and even a few humans may possess this trait as the result of being exposed to the Vortex, or possibly being on the verge of madness like Vincent Van Gogh.

Effect: Feel the Turn of the Universe costs 1 point and gives the character an innate ability to sense when something is amiss or unnatural and what needs to be done to set the universe right. This can be anything from sensing that a person has unnatural indestructibility, to knowing that something is disturbing nature or sense if something is tampering with time. They may not know exactly what it is, but they'll know something isn't right. The character will sense something is wrong with an Awareness + Ingenuity roll with a +2 bonus – the more successful they are, the clearer the problem will appear, as well as the potential solution.

HYPNOSIS
(see the Hypnosis Good Trait pg. 33)

IMMORTAL (Major Good/Special Good Trait)
Prerequisite: Alien Trait

There are two types of Immortal being in existence. The first never gets old, never ages and will never die of old age. They simply continue on. While it's rare for them to die from a disease, they still can, and can certainly be killed through violence or accident. Immortal at this level is a Major Good Trait and while it doesn't affect the actual game (as they can still be killed through violence) they could have already lived a long time. The Gamemaster may allow them to recall something from their past if it suits the story, or something from their history could resurface, provoking a whole new adventure. If they have lived 'ages', then they should purchase the Time Traveller trait for the past eras that they were alive and active, at the Gamemaster's discretion.

The second type of Immortal cannot be killed through violence, accident or disease. This version is a Special Good Trait. They may get a little older in appearance, but their longevity is so epic that their ageing is hardly noticeable. They can be shot, electrocuted, drowned and fried, but they just don't seem to die. They may fall down and look dead, but it isn't long before they're up and active again. Again, if they've been alive for a long time, they should also purchase the Time Traveller trait for the eras they were alive – they have time travelled, they've just done it the slow way.

Effect: Immortal is either a Major Good Trait that costs 2 points, meaning the character never ages and will not die of natural causes, or a Special Trait, which means the character cannot be killed. Both may be unbalancing to the game and if a player intends to take either version of the Immortal trait, they should discuss it with the Gamemaster.

Immortal as a Special Trait costs 5 Character Points, as well as reducing the character's maximum Story Points by 4. If killed during the course of an adventure, the character looks dead and is unable to be revived. Without the Fast Healing trait, the character will heal at a normal rate (this is usually 1 level of attribute per day of rest). When they have healed all of the damage they have taken, and returned to their full health, they will wake and be fine. If the damage is really severe, the Gamemaster may keep track of how far into the 'negative' your character's attributes go, and they will have to heal all of these before they can recover. Any extreme damage, such as loss of limb, may lead to further Bad Traits unless they also have the Fast Healing trait, though these may heal over a long period of time at the Gamemaster's discretion.

Note: The Alien trait must have been purchased before selecting Immortal, though in rare circumstances (such as Captain Jack Harkness) Immortality may be granted to humans at the Gamemaster's discretion.

INEXPERIENCED* (Special Bad Trait)

The character creation rules here are suited to companions and normal heroes. Players may find, however, that this doesn't reflect very inexperienced or young characters. Courtney would be a perfect example of this. She's still in school, hasn't finished growing, and is very inexperienced when it comes to adventuring through time and space. But, she is brave and keen to help the Doctor in the most dangerous situations.

Effect: This trait costs 2 Character Points **and** 2 Skill Points. In return, the character's maximum Story Point pool is increased by 3. These additional Story Points will help them to keep up with the more experienced character while reflecting their lack of skills.

This trait can be purchased additional times for even less experienced characters, though this will have to be approved by the Gamemaster. If, however, during the game the character's skills and total Character Points increases through experience to the levels of a normal character, the character's maximum Story Points are reduced to their normal level.

LAST OF MY KIND (Minor Bad Trait)
Prerequisite: Alien Trait

Being the last of your kind can be a burden as well as lonely. To know that there is no one else like you out there, and that an entire race dies when you do.

Effect: Last of My Kind is a Minor Bad Trait, and has the prerequisite of the 'Alien' Special Trait (unless, during the course of the game, every other human in the universe is wiped out... but that's what the Doctor's around for, to prevent things like that happening!). As the last of their kind, the character can often get moody and depressed, and needs the companionship of others to stop the weight of the responsibility and loneliness from getting too much.

When travelling alone, the depression can affect everything the character does, imposing a -2 penalty on every action unless engaged in combat. At particularly bad times, the Gamemaster may impose this penalty even when travelling with others – for example when reminded of their situation, anniversaries of the destruction of their homeworld, or similar.

PRECOGNITION (Special Good Trait)
Prerequisite: Psychic Trait
Some people, such as the Sybilline Sisterhood, are gifted with the ability to see the future. In many civilisations, they become the town 'seer', or are outcast from society due to their strange abilities. Most of the time, these abilities manifest as visions – incomplete fragments of a potential future seen as a strange and abstract dream. The future is usually in flux, ever changing, except for certain fixed points in history, so the visions of the future are fairly vague to reflect the potential for the events to change.

Effect: This trait costs 1 point to purchase and can only by taken by characters with the Psychic trait. When appropriate to the story, the Gamemaster may give the character flashes of information to help or encourage them to pursue a particular course of action to aid the adventure. If the player wants the character to actively try to sense what is to come, they should spend a Story Point, and the Gamemaster will supply as much useful information is they think necessary (without ruining the story!).

PSYCHIC (Special Good Trait)
Psychic is a Special Good Trait, costing 2 points to purchase (or 1 point if the character already has the Psychic Training trait) that allows them to reach into another person's mind and try to access hidden information, though the target can resist. Companions or humans are rarely Psychic, but it occurs in a scarce few. The Gamemaster should approve selection of this trait.

Effect: To see into a target's mind, the player must succeed at a Resolve + Awareness test. The target must be within visual range (with the naked eye) and the trait provides the character with a +4 bonus on the roll. However, if the target is unwilling, they can resist such a mental intrusion with a Resolve and Ingenuity roll. Both sides can spend Story Points if they're concentrating intently. Psychic also gives a +4 bonus when the character attempts to resist having their mind read, and to resist possession.

ROBOT (Special Good Trait)

Instead of flesh and bone they are made of steel, wires and plastics. Instead of an organic brain their mind is made of circuitry and a powerful computer. Robot is a Special Good Trait that costs 2 points as a robot of normal appearance – that is, they look like a robot, such as K-9, a Host, a Roboform or even Kamelion (one of the Doctor's earlier companions). However, the trait can be purchased at a higher level, costing 4 points, which means externally you look convincingly human – most of the time people will assume you are human unless you're injured or display inhuman abilities.

Effect: Robot means the character is a robot. They have attributes, skills and traits, just like a living character. However, their attributes can be raised above level 6, and they can purchase Gadget Traits (see pg. 112). These are traits normally used only in Gadgets, but this means that traits such as Forcefield or Scan, can be built directly into the robot character!

Robot also means that the character does not die from old age (though their power supply may need replacing). When a robot takes a physical injury, it loses attributes just like a person, though it will not heal itself over time – either itself or another suitably skilled technician will need to conduct repairs (using

Ingenuity + Technology), with a level of injury repaired equal to the level of success. A robot character can be 'killed' and repaired, returning to fully operational level, though if the damage is severe enough (such as being disintegrated or dropped into a furnace or vat of molten metal) the robot is unlikely to be salvageable.

Robots normally learn over time, and can increase their mental skills just as a human, however physical skills and attributes will require some form of 'upgrading' to take into account the increased ability. Of course, in most cases a robot does have the disadvantage of standing out in a crowd and scaring primitive civilisations!

Note: Cannot be taken with the Alien or Cyborg trait.

TELEKINESIS (Special Good Trait)
Prerequisite: Psychic Trait

Telekinesis, sometimes called psychokinesis, is the power to move something with thought alone. Just concentrating on something can make it move, bend, float or break. This power is usually limited to line-of-sight. That is, if the character cannot see it (because it is too far away or in another room) they cannot concentrate enough on the object to lift or manipulate it (though characters with Clairvoyance may be able to see the object psychically, though

they will be limited to adjacent rooms). Telekinesis is a Special Trait that costs 2 points to purchase, and should only be picked with the approval of the Gamemaster. It can only be purchased if the character already has the Psychic trait (see pg. 53).

Effect: The Telekinesis trait uses the character's Resolve rather than Strength to determine how much they can lift by thought alone. For example, if the character has Resolve 1, they can lift something with their Telekinesis as if they were physically lifting it with a Strength of 1. The only difference is, they're not using their hands – they're using their mind. To just lift an item, the character is using their innate abilities, so the player should make a roll using their Ingenuity + Resolve.

To throw an item at a target using Telekinesis, Resolve replaces Strength and the character would need to succeed at a Resolve + Marksman roll. Picking a lock, for example, would use Resolve + Subterfuge, but the character would need to be able to see the mechanism in some way (either an x-ray scanner or clairvoyance) to telekinetically manipulate it.

TELEPATHY (Special Good Trait)
Prerequisite: Psychic Trait
Telepathy is the ability to communicate with others through the power of the mind. Telepaths can project their thoughts directly into someone else's head and they'll hear it as if they're speaking to them. Usually, the person isn't too far away, but if the character's Resolve is high, they could communicate to someone up to a kilometre away or even further. Very handy if you need to call for help!

Once a link has been established, they can hold a short conversation as long as they are not distracted or under stress. The moment they are distracted (for example being surprised by a loud noise or a sudden attack) the link is lost and the character will have to try again at a calmer moment when they can concentrate.

Effect: Telepathy is a Special Trait that costs 1 point to purchase. Approval from the Gamemaster will be required before selecting this trait. The character must also have the Psychic trait before they can purchase Telepathy. Telepathy uses the character's innate abilities, rather than a skill, so Ingenuity and Resolve are used for the roll to establish communication. If the target doesn't want to be contacted, they can resist with a similar roll. The distance over which the character can communicate with the Telepathy trait depends upon their Resolve.

TELEPATHIC RANGE	
RESOLVE	RANGE
1	Touch Only
2	Line of Sight
3	Adjacent Room
4	Adjacent Building
5	Within the same city
6	Within the same country
7	Anywhere on the same planet
8	Within the planet's system
9+	Across the universe!

TIME AGENT (Special Good Trait)
Time Agents are special operatives of the Time Agency, a shadowy group performing undercover espionage work involving time travel. Little is known of them, only that their operations spanned the galaxies and all of time. When Jack Harkness returned to Cardiff after the Harold Saxon encounter, he was told that there were only seven surviving operatives (including the renegade agents Captain Jack Harkness and Captain John Hart). They are usually equipped with Vortex Manipulators, and 'bounce' through time to their assignments.

Effect: Time Agent is a Special Trait that means the character has worked (or still works) for the Time Agency. They will have familiarity with 51st Century technology (Tech Level 8 is their 'home' era), and usually have a Vortex Manipulator that allows them to communicate, time travel and interact with computer technology (although whether or not this still works to its full capabilities is up to the Gamemaster). They may suffer from partial amnesia, having their memory wiped after particularly secretive missions, reflected by purchasing the Amnesia trait.

The Time Agent trait means they automatically gain the Vortex trait, and will (usually) have a Vortex Manipulator in their equipment. Time Agent costs 2 Character Points and 2 Story Points to purchase, and players should discuss with the Gamemaster if having a Time Agent (or former Time Agent) in the group is going to upset the game.

TIME LORD (Special Good Trait)

The Time Lords of Gallifrey were one of the first and most powerful civilisations in the universe. Pioneers of time travel technology, they became self appointed custodians of time before their fall during the Time War with the Daleks.

Effect: The rarest and the most special of all Special Traits is 'Time Lord'. This Special Trait costs 2 Character Points and 4 Story Points. Only two Time Lords are known to have escaped Gallifrey at the end of the Time War, so you'll probably only use this trait when playing the Doctor. Close discussions between player and Gamemaster is essential before creating a Time Lord character.

This trait gives the character all of the abilities of a Time Lord – they can regenerate, automatically gain

the Code of Conduct, Feel the Turn of the Universe and Vortex traits and gain 2 levels of the Ingenuity attribute (even if this takes the attribute above 6). They also get a Gadget at no extra cost. The Gamemaster will decide if they have access to a TARDIS or not – there is no additional cost for this as it may be essential to the Gamemaster's plans for the story.

Time Lords **must** have a couple of Bad Traits – they can be eccentric, aloof and have superiority complexes, or be just plain crazy. Staring into the Untempered Schism can do that to you! Time Lords are usually mildly Telepathic, so players wishing to have a Time Lord character may wish to purchase Psychic and Telepathy traits.

Further rules for playing a Time Lord character, their abilities, regeneration and TARDISes, see **Chapter Four: Time and Time Again**, and the **Time Traveller's Companion** supplement.

Note: Although Time Lords are alien to humanity, they look so outwardly alike that there is no need to purchase the Alien trait.

TIME LORD (EXPERIENCED)* (Special Good Trait)
Prerequisite: Time Lord
The experienced Time Lord has been around for centuries, gaining a vast repertoire of skills and knowledge. Although, in gaining all of this experience, they may have exhausted a regeneration or two in the process.

CHAPTER TWO: OLD-FASHIONED HEROES FROM OLD-FASHIONED STORY BOOKS

Effect: This trait means that the character is older (and hopefully wiser) than a novice Time Lord. The player can choose any additional number of years to add to their age, between 100 and 200 years. If you'd prefer to choose this randomly, roll two dice and multiply the result by 10, and add 80 (2D6x10 +80). This will produce a figure between 100 and 200. This is the number of years added to the Time Lord's age.

By taking this trait, the Time Lord uses up one of their regenerations. The player should decide how and when this was, creating a suitably interesting and exciting background for the events that led up to his regeneration. Each regeneration can change the character's attributes and will change their appearance. If the Gamemaster prefers, each regeneration could be handled using the regeneration rules in **Chapter Four: Time and Time Again** (see pg. 121).

The character gains 4 additional Skill Points, and an additional Time Traveller trait for a different time period.

Experienced Time Lord is a Special Trait that costs 1 Character Point to purchase and requires the character to already have the Time Lord trait. Benefits of Experienced Time Lord are cumulative with Time Lord, and Experienced Time Lord can be purchased more than once – though remember, every time it is purchased, it reduces the character's regenerations by one...

VORTEX (Minor Good / Special Trait)

The Space-time Vortex is a swirling maelstrom that requires great knowledge and skill to navigate. The character may not have access to a TARDIS, Vortex Manipulator or another time travel device, but they have experience in travelling through the Vortex and are familiar with its dangers.

Effect: Vortex is a Special Trait, costing 1 point, and is not for beginning characters (unless they have a background of using a TARDIS or other Vortex Manipulators). Selecting Vortex as a trait at character creation has to be approved by the Gamemaster.

The Vortex trait adds +2 to any roll that involves piloting a time travel or Vortex-manipulating device. Controlling the TARDIS (or other such time vessels) is so tricky to the unskilled, that it is almost impossible to actually be able to succeed at the task without having the Vortex trait.

An additional 'level' of Vortex is available to characters with the Alien trait (see pg. 49), and costs 8 points. This high level of Vortex means the character can time travel without the need of a ship or device, literally stepping through time. This is an Alien trait and is best reserved for Villains or NPCs.

To step through time requires an Ingenuity and Resolve Roll to use, and the expenditure of two Story Points. The more successful the roll, the more accurate the 'jump'.

CHARACTER CREATION EXAMPLE - TRAITS

Continuing our character creation example, Edward has 6 Character Points left to spend on traits after purchasing his attributes. He wants to enhance his smarts even further and decides to purchase the Boffin Major trait (2 points) and the Technically Adept trait (1 point).

He also thinks that having the Photographic Memory trait (2 points) and the Resourceful Pockets trait (1 point) would be very handy. He'd also like to have the Voice of Authority Minor Trait (1 point), to compensate a little for his low Presence, but he's already spent his 6 points. He can gain another point by opting to take a Minor Bad Trait, so he opts to take the Obligation Minor Bad Trait which gives him the point necessary to buy Voice of Authority as well.

So, that gives him:

Boffin (Major, 2 points), Photographic Memory (Major, 2 points), Resourceful Pockets (Minor, 1 point), Technically Adept (Minor, 1 point), Voice of Authority (Minor, 1 point) and Obligation (Minor Bad, -1 point)...

... for a total of (2+1+2+1+1-1) = 6 character points

If Edwards wants, he can still opt to take another Bad Trait or two to give him extra points to increase his attributes, purchase more Good Traits, or to spend on skills.

⚙ SKILLS

You've defined what your character is like with their attributes and traits, now we need to define what they know. Skills represent accumulated knowledge, the abilities they can use in their journeys and adventures to protect them and to defeat the villains that would threaten humanity.

To keep things simple there are just twelve skills. Want a super cool computer hacker? No problem, they have a good Technology skill. Adventuring archaeologist? They'd probably have a high Knowledge to cover that history, maybe with some Athletics to take their active nature into account. If you're just itching to have a skill that is not on the list, first of all think whether one of the skills listed below covers it already. It could be that focusing the skill with an Area of Expertise (see sidebar) will give your character the skillset you'd like.

Skills, just like attributes, are rated numerically. A skill of 1 indicates a basic knowledge in the area, someone who has just started to learn the subject or has a little experience in the field. A skill of 2 or 3 means they've become quite confident. If it's an academic skill, they may have a good qualification in it (maybe some A-levels or a certificate or two), or they've gained a reputation at being reliable in that area. A skill level of 4 or 5 is really showing some expertise, they may have a degree, some commendations, and are the go-to people for their skill. Above that, 6 or more, you're talking real experts in the field. They may be doctors or masters, but not **the** Doctor or **the** Master – they have skills even higher than that!

ASSIGNING SKILL POINTS

Characters have 18 Skill Points to allocate to their skills. They don't have to allocate points to every Skill; after all, most people aren't good at everything. Players should pick one or two skills that reflect their occupation or pastimes and put 3 or 4 points into those, then pick a skill or two that they think will be handy for the coming adventures and put 2 points in them. The remaining points can be distributed as they see fit, bearing the concept of the character in mind.

AREAS OF EXPERTISE

The Doctor and his companions have a wide range of abilities and skills, seemingly able to deal with anything the story throws at them. The **Doctor Who Roleplaying Game** is designed to reflect this by keeping the number of different skills to a minimum. However, adding a bit of specialisation to a character can make them more individual and vital to the team. "Areas of Expertise" are a great way to add this level of detail.

Each skill covers a wide area, but just because you have a good Science skill, it doesn't mean you're an expert in biology, chemistry and astrophysics. As you learn a skill, you get to a level where you can focus your studies and interest, getting better at one particular facet of it. This is an Area of Expertise.

When you have a skill at level 3 or above, you can opt to select an Area of Expertise where you excel in this skill. At character creation this just costs you a single Skill Point.

For each skill there are many Areas of Expertise. Each skill description gives you some suggested Areas of Expertise, though this list isn't exhaustive.

You can have more than one Area of Expertise for each skill, but each one must be purchased separately. At character creation this still costs just one Skill Point per Area, but the skill must be at level 3 or above.

If you are called upon to use a skill during the game, and the Gamemaster agrees that your character's Area of Expertise applies to the task at hand, you gain a +2 bonus to the roll. If your Area of Expertise doesn't cover the task, the skill roll is made without this bonus as normal.

For example, Edward's character is particularly good at working with computers, with Technology 3 and an Area of Expertise in Electronics. Whenever he rolls to mess about with an electronic gadget, he adds his Technology skill of 3 to the roll as well as a +2 bonus for his Area of Expertise, giving him an effective skill of 5.

If, however, he is using his Technology skill for any other purpose besides working with an electronic device, such as fixing a broken car, he only adds his basic skill of 3 to the roll.

SPARE CHARACTER POINTS

If at the end of character creation, players have Character Points to spare, deciding that higher attributes or additional traits do not fit their character, the remaining Character Points can be spent on skills, as if they were Skill Points.

Note that the opposite is not true, so make sure you spend all your Skill Points or you will lose them! If you have too many Skill Points for the sort of character you have in mind, it may be worth considering the Inexperienced Bad Trait (see pg. 52), which will reduce the number of Skill Points (and Character Points) you have to spend, but will give you more of those vital Story Points to play with.

While the character can advance and have skills above 5, it is rare for a starting character to have a skill above that. During character creation, no skill can be above level 5 unless this has been discussed in detail with the Gamemaster and authorised. If you want to play, for example, a university professor or a medical diagnostician you may be allowed to put more than five points into a skill, but then it should only be in the skill that reflects the character's profession. Besides, you don't want to pile all those points into one place and become too much of a specialist to be of any use, do you?

❀ LIST OF SKILLS

Below is a list of the twelve skills along with descriptions of the areas they cover and when they are used. For details on how skill rolls work, see pg. 70 of **Chapter Three: I Can Fight Monsters, I Can't Fight Physics**. Within each skill there is guidance for how the skill is used, and a list of possible Areas of Expertise (see sidebar on pg. 58). Remember, this is not exhaustive and the Gamemaster and players should feel free to add Areas of Expertise (or even whole skills) if it best suits their game.

ATHLETICS

The character is used to being physically active. Depending upon the level of this skill, they could work out, go to the gym every week or just eat healthily. Or, at higher levels, they could be a professional athlete or a highly trained soldier.

Athletics is used if the character has to run for a prolonged time away from charging Futurekind, hold their breath underwater to swim into the secret alien base or to jump over a chasm of lava. The Athletics skill is also used when riding horses (as it is a more physical activity than using the Transport skill). Almost any physical act the character has to perform can be covered by Athletics. However, blocking a punch should be accomplished with the Fighting skill (paired with Coordination), which is more appropriate to the situation. As a basic rule of thumb, if it's physical, it's Athletics. If it's combat, use the Fighting skill.

Areas of Expertise: Running, Jumping, Riding, Climbing, Parachuting, Scuba, Swimming.

CONVINCE

Convince is all about getting people to do what you want. You can use this to sway people to your way of thinking, to prove to strangers that you're not a threat or to delay the villain from commencing the attack on Earth long enough to let your companions foil their plan. It can mean you're a convincing liar, or just the most commanding military leader. Most of the time, Convince rolls are contested (see pg. 77).

After all, you're trying to change someone's mind. Convince is usually paired with, and resisted by, Presence or Resolve.

Areas of Expertise: Fast Talk, Bluff, Leadership, Seduction, Interrogation, Charm, Lie, Talk Down.

ROLE-PLAY VS ROLL-PLAY

Convince is used for many types of social interaction, from convincing someone that the lies you are telling is the truth, to convincing them you are a sincere and trustworthy person. Many social interactions will rely on the Convince skill but it shouldn't be as simple as rolling dice and getting what you want.

Players should try to act out the dialogue, the amusing lines and the attempts at bluffing. If the player's attempts at the table are good enough, the Gamemaster may even apply bonuses to the roll or reward the player with Story Points for good roleplaying.

CRAFT

Craft is an all-encompassing skill that covers all manners of creative activities. Whether the character is good with their hands and can carve an ornate chess set from wood, or maybe just great at playing the guitar or singing, the Craft skill covers it. Boat building, metalworking, knitting a good scarf or rapping can all be covered by this skill. This skill is very broad and benefits from using Areas of Expertise (see pg. 58) as it reflects which Craft the character is particularly talented in. A blacksmith, for example, may have Craft 5 due to his mastery of metalworking, but that doesn't necessarily make him a virtuoso musician, brilliant painter or a witty knitter as well.

Areas of Expertise: Building, Painting, Farming, Singing, Guitar, Woodwork, Metalwork, Dancing.

FIGHTING

It may not be the Doctor's chosen form of resistance, but sometimes there is no way out of a situation other than to fight. Fighting as a skill covers all forms of close combat, whether this is with fists, feet, swords, axes or cat claws. This skill is purely for when it gets up close and personal. The Fighting skill is typically used with Strength to not only land a punch, but also to block that nasty jab. Any combat that involves attacking from a distance (like guns,

LEARNED SKILLS AND INSTINCT

When it comes to parrying and blocking, as used in close combat, let's look at the difference between a learned skill and a reaction or instinctual act. There are a few areas where the difference between a skill roll and an sttribute roll can be a little confusing.

BLOCKING AND DODGING

Blocking and parrying is a learned skill. Anyone who has done martial arts or fencing will know that learning when to block or parry an attack takes knowledge and skill. When blocking or parrying in the game, the character uses Strength + Fighting.

Dodging is different. A lot of the time, dodging relies on natural reactions and instinct. When it comes to dodging gunfire or moving out of the way of a rockfall, the character uses innate abilities only, relying on attributes alone – usually Awareness + Coordination. If you're a skilled fighter or martial artist you'll be able to bend out of the way of a punch or kick, so you could use Coordination + Fighting to dodge in close combat, but they will still use attributes alone when dodging gunfire or that rockfall.

Of course, the character has to be aware of the attack to begin with in order to block or dodge. If the character is taken by surprise, or if the attacker is hidden (for example, a sniper shooting from a distance), they will be unable to react to it first time. The attack will just be rolled as an unresisted task against a fixed Difficulty as defined by the Gamemaster.

As a guide:
Punching or Kicking (or any physical attack):
Strength + Fighting

Blocking or Parrying a physical attack:
Strength + Fighting

Dodging a physical attack:
Coordination + Fighting

Dodging gunfire or environmental hazards:
Awareness + Coordination (if they see it coming).

Dodging gunfire or environmental hazards (if they are surprised): No chance to dodge

NOTICING OR SPOTTING SOMETHING

Spotting an important clue is another tricky one that can be handled in a couple of ways. If the character is not actively looking for something and the Gamemaster wants to give them a chance to see the giant bug before it attacks, they will have to make an attribute-only roll, usually Awareness + Ingenuity.

However, if they are searching books for a clue, looking into medical records for information, or something similar, the character is actively looking and their skills come into play - in this case it's Awareness paired with a skill that reflects the subject.

As a rough guide:
Passively noticing something (not actively looking, but there's a chance of seeing it):
Awareness+ Ingenuity.

Actively searching for something:
Awareness + Skill (related to the subject, such as Knowledge, Medicine, Technology, and so on).

disintegrators or even the trusty bow and arrow) uses the Marksman skill.

Areas of Expertise: Unarmed Combat, Parry, Block, Sword, Club.

KNOWLEDGE

The Doctor has proven that his knowledge of the universe can defeat the most powerful of villainous dictators. Of course, not every character has that brain power, but the Knowledge skill is a guide to how much they know.

This is a broad and almost all-encompassing skill that covers most areas of knowledge. The exceptions are those covered specifically by other skills such as Medicine, Technology or Science. Knowledge typically covers academic and humanities fields, such as law, sociology, psychology, archaeology, history, literature, or languages. The skill is most often paired with the Ingenuity attribute. The Knowledge skill can also include alien areas of knowledge, such as alien cultures, the history of alien worlds and times. Alien Areas of Expertise are not for beginning characters, especially contemporary companions. However, the

Gamemaster may allow alien Areas of Expertise if it suits the character's background.

Areas of Expertise: History (choose an area), Law, Psychology, Language (select a specific language), Literature, Sociology, Alien Cultures, Earthonomics, Gallifrey History, The Dark Times.

MARKSMAN

It's a dangerous universe out there, and the time might come when the characters are forced to take arms against the alien invaders. The Doctor rarely uses guns, preferring to outwit or out-think his opponents, but his companions have resorted to firearms from time to time.

COMMON KNOWLEDGE

Having just twelve skills means that some of them, especially Craft, Knowledge and Science, require a little bit of adjudication on behalf of the Gamemaster.

For example, if the character is a lawyer, their Knowledge skill should have an Area of Expertise that refers to all things legal. An archaeologist's Areas of Expertise will reflect years of education in history, geology and archaeology. Even if you are not using Areas of Expertise in your game, the reason the character has the skill should be taken into account if they are trying to do something they are unfamiliar with.

If a character is trying to use their skill for something obviously not in their field - a quantum physicist trying to give a lecture on Ancient Roman history for example, the roll should incur some penalty to reflect this.

Think of how far removed from the actual knowledge the character has from what they'd like to do. If

it is fairly similar to something they'd know (but not of the actual Area of Expertise), a low penalty should be applied of -1 or -2. If it's something very different (like the talented guitarist trying to forge horseshoes) then the penalty could be as high as -4, the usual penalty for being completely unskilled (see pg. 72). If it's something incredibly technical or difficult, such as a veterinarian trying to perform brain surgery, the Gamemaster may simply decide that it is impossible for them to do.

Another element to take into account is the character's home era. The average person from present-day London is unlikely to have the skills to survive in the palaeolithic era and will be confused by 51st century technology.

The character sheet has a space to note the planet, time period and technology level of the character's origin, and trying to use your skills outside of that frame of reference can sometimes be difficult. More information on Technology Levels can be found on pg. 66.

The Marksman skill is used for any weapon that fires a projectile or shoots at a target that is outside of close combat range. Everything from bows, thrown rocks or knives to guns, machine guns, Dalek weapons, or even starship missile systems use the Marksman skill.

For weapons that require physical aiming, such as a pistol, use Coordination + the Marksman skill. Other more technical weaponry, such as computer controlled systems or artillery, use Ingenuity + Marksman, to reflect the less physical approach to operating the weapon. More information about ranged combat is detailed on pg. 87 of **Chapter Three: I Can Fight Monsters, I Can't Fight Physics.**

Areas of Expertise: Bow, Pistol, Rifle, Automatic Weapons, Thrown Weapons, Ship Weapon Systems, Cannon, Plasma Weapons, Disintegrators.

MEDICINE

Injuries are bound to happen when trying to save the universe, so it is always useful to have someone aboard the TARDIS who has a little medical knowledge. The Medicine skill, at low levels, reflects the character's ability to perform basic first aid, CPR or to stabilise wounds. At higher levels, they may be medical students, fully fledged doctors or nurses, or at Skill 5 they could be surgeons. Medicine also reflects other Areas of Expertise, depending upon the background of the character, such as forensic, veterinary medicine or alternative therapies.

Medicine is usually paired with Ingenuity, though if the medical procedure is particularly tricky or requires delicate work, then Coordination should be used. Usually, the success of the roll dictates how many levels of injury are healed: Success heals 1, Good heals 2 and Fantastic heals 3 levels of injury. More information on healing, injury and damage can be found on pg. 96 of **Chapter Three: I Can Fight Monsters, I Can't Fight Physics**.

Areas of Expertise: Disease, Wounds, Poisons, Psychological Trauma, Surgery, Forensics, Veterinary Medicine, Alternative Remedies.

SCIENCE

The Doctor frequently blinds his companions with his scientific knowledge, and the Science skill measures just how knowledgeable the character is when it comes to and all the stuff that makes the universe go around. There's a little crossover with the Medicine and Technology skills, but if the task requires less repairing people or gadgets, and more contemplating the wild pseudoscience or in-depth theory, then Science is going to be the skill of choice. Most of the time, Science will be paired with Ingenuity, only apt when you think of the ingenious scientific theories and inventions that they'll be coming up with! On rare occasions it can be paired with Presence or Resolve if debating scientific theory.

Areas of Expertise: Mathematics, Physics, Chemistry, Biology, Astrophysics.

SUBTERFUGE

In the course of saving the world, you can be forgiven for breaking and entering secret bases, employing a bit of stealth to avoid being spotted by patrolling guards, for opening a safe to read the classified files or pickpocketing the guard's access keys. In these cases, the Subterfuge skill is used, usually paired with Coordination or, if the task is of a more intellectual nature, Ingenuity can be used, especially for tasks like safecracking or creating a disguise.

Areas of Expertise: Sneaking, Lockpicking, Sleight of Hand, Pickpocketing, Disguise, Safecracking, Camouflage.

SURVIVAL

The universe is a harsh place, and many a companion has been stranded in a hostile environment, waiting for the Doctor to come and rescue them before they freeze, roast or suffocate to death. The Survival skill is used to help them to stay alive in these harsh or exposed environments, from knowing what native plants can be eaten to building shelter and a fire. Some Areas of Expertise will help in other environments such as knowing how to protect yourself from exposure to space, from an oncoming sandstorm or the safe way to decompress from deep sea pressures.

Areas of Expertise: Space, Desert, Swamp, Mountain, Icescape, Underwater, Wilderness.

TECHNOLOGY

Some people are a whiz with computers, gadgets and electronics. Technology as a skill represents the character's know-how when it comes to all of these things. Whether it is hacking into the Torchwood computers, mixing odd parts of existing tech together to make a 'timey-wimey detector', programming a virus to thwart the alien fleet or just fixing the microwave, Technology, paired with Ingenuity, is the skill to use.

Fixing things on the TARDIS can only be done by someone with the Vortex trait (see pg. 57); trying without it may make things worse. Creating Gadgets can only be done with the Boffin trait (see pg. 30) unless you want a technological disaster on your hands!

Areas of Expertise: Computers, Electronics, Gadgetry, Hacking, Repair, TARDIS.

TRANSPORT

Sometimes, you need to get from A to B, and you won't have access to the TARDIS. Transport covers the ability to drive cars, ride motorcycles, fly hover vans in New New York or pilot an aircraft or starship. Like other broad skills, knowing how to drive a car doesn't mean you can pilot a 747, but when it comes to vehicles many are similar enough to give you a good place to start. Steering wheel, accelerator, what more do you need? If the technology is similar enough, you can probably allow the players to use the skill without penalty.

The only method of transport that isn't covered by the Transport skill is riding an animal, such as a horse. Riding is a very physical action, so the Athletics skill is used. If you are steering the horses pulling a carriage, then Transport is used as you're not engaging in the physical exertions used during riding.

Areas of Expertise: Cars, Trucks, Helicopters, Aircraft, Spaceships, Temporal Ships, Motorcycles.

CHARACTER CREATION EXAMPLE - SKILLS

Edward has 18 points to put into skills. He's already decided that his character is going to be smart and observant, rather than strong. He decides that Knowledge 3, Science 4 and Technology 3 will make him something of a brainbox. He also thinks that Convince 2 will come in handy.

That's 13 points spent so far, leaving 5 to spread throughout his other skills. Edward decides to spend two of these points on a couple of Areas of Expertise and rounds out his list with some useful non-combat options. His final skills are:

Athletics 1, Convince 2, Craft 1, Knowledge 3, Science 4 (Physics +2), Subterfuge 1, Technology 3 (Electronics +2), Transport 1.

That equals 16 Skill Points, +2 for the two Areas of Expertise, which is 18 in total. He's certainly the brains of the outfit, but he's no fighter.

⚙ STORY POINTS

Story Points are very important. We'll cover how Story Points are actually used in **Chapter Three: I Can Fight Monsters, I Can't Fight Physics** (see pg. 69) but for now all you need to know is how many points the characters have. We've already mentioned the Story Points and the allocation at the beginning of character creation (see pg. 102) so you know that most characters should start with 12.

However, some of the Special Traits are so major that they effect the very story of the game, and adjust the maximum Story Points a character can keep between adventures!

Whatever the characters have left to start the game with, the players should mark it into the box on their character sheets (though use a pencil, just like all of the other numbers, as Story Points may change from adventure to adventure). Before you start to play each session, each player takes a number of tokens equal to this figure so they can keep track of the rapid increases and decreases you'll come to expect during the course of the game, without having to keep rubbing the number out and writing a new one in every five minutes.

Some Villains have Story Points as well that can be used in just the same way as the player's characters. This will mean that major villains are harder to defeat, and can spend Story Points to make their escapes if the characters look to be victorious too early in the game.

⚙ FINISHING TOUCHES

There are lots of little touches that finish the character off and make them more than just a string of numbers. There are some places on the character sheet to keep track of some of these, or you may wish to go into greater detail and write up something more in depth.

NAME

Each character needs a name! Most of the Doctor's companions have normal and everyday names. If you can't think of something immediately, try flicking randomly through a phonebook, or one of those baby-name books you can find. Maybe use a friend's name, and switch the surname to something new, or pick a couple of actors from TV or movies and change their names around. Above all, you have to like it, and it shouldn't be immediately funny.

Even alien characters shouldn't be called something silly that'll disrupt the game. No one should be called 'Squid-roon' or 'Duckbar' (all names suggested by real players in the past). The character is going to have to live with that name, and so will the player during the game. The more sensible and the more normal the better. Though that doesn't mean the Doctor hasn't travelled with strangely named characters in the past – after all, how many people do you know called Perpugilliam or Vislor? As long as it doesn't upset the tone of the game.

ALIEN CHARACTER NAMES

Of course, it could be that the character is alien. If the player needs to create a new alien name, it needs to be relatively easy to pronounce, even if it's not so easy to spell. If it's complicated, like the Mighty Jagrafess of the Holy Hadrojassic Maxarodenfoe, think of a cool nickname for them (Max) so it's easy for the other players to talk to them. Not every player is going to remember Blon Fel Fotch Pasameer-Day, but they'll remember Margaret Slitheen.

APPEARANCE

What do they look like? The player could have a very distinctive idea of what their character looks like, or imagine a particular actor playing their part. If they're feeling artistic, they could even draw a sketch so everyone knows how the character looks. Think about how tall they are, what their build is, hair colour, or any distinguishing features they have (sideburns, big ears, ginger hair, something like that).

BACKGROUND

Just who are they? You won't have to write a huge essay or draught up a family tree, but it's often good to have a basic idea of who they are, what they do and where they're from. You can get a pretty good idea of who a character is just by writing a simple paragraph about them.

For example – he's a Maths teacher at Coal Hill School and runs the cadet squad. He used to be a sergeant in the British Army but left after a particularly 'bad day'. He's put all that behind him now and has started dating Clara Oswald...

That pretty much sums up Danny Pink after his first encounter with the Doctor in **The Caretaker**, and this information gives the Gamemaster a little to work on. It may give them ideas to spice up the average adventure and make it more personal.

Of course, players could go into even more detail than this if they'd like. Though sometimes the details and personal background develop as the game progresses, so just a basic concept is a great starting place.

HOME TIME PERIOD AND TECHNOLOGY LEVELS

This can be a very important element when travelling through time. There is a space on the character sheet to define the character's home time period. This is so the Gamemaster can work out if a character using technology in an adventure that they'd be unfamiliar with. Have a look at the Tech Level table and see where the character is from.

Most characters are from level 5 – modern day Earth. Robin Hood is from the Middle Ages, so he'd have a home time period listed as 'Middle Ages, Tech Level 2.' The Doctor is a Time Lord, so he has 'Gallifrey, Tech Level 10'. Clara and Danny are from modern Earth, so they'd have '21st century Earth, Tech Level 5'.

More information on Technology Levels and how they affect your character can be found in **Chapter Three: I Can Fight Monsters, I Can't Fight Physics** (see pg. 110).

TECHNOLOGY LEVELS

12	Beyond comprehension – Abilities available only to the Eternals
11	Ancient Time Lord – The Dark Times, Rassilon and Omega
10	Time Lord
9	Advanced Time Faring – Daleks
8	Time Faring – 51st century Earth
7	Advanced Interstellar Empire – 31st-49th century Earth, no time travel
6	Star Faring – 22nd-30th century Earth, Faster-than-light travel, transmats
5	Space Faring – late 20th and 21st century Earth, Colonisation of the Solar System, system-wide travel
4	Industrial – 18th-20th century Earth, Industrial Revolution, steam, manufacturing
3	Renaissance – 15th-17th century Earth, gunpowder, sailing ships and art
2	Metalworking – Bronze Age to Middle Ages, swords and steel
1	Primitive – Stone Age

PERSONAL GOALS

Each character has a goal, and we're not talking football here. Players should give some thought to what the character is like and come up with something that they'd like to achieve. Most of the

Doctor's companions are not about money or fame, but if that's something the character would have at the forefront of his mind during the adventure, then the player should pencil it in. It could be anything – to explore, to find the love of their life, to further humanity, to advance the course of science, to boldly go where no one has gone before... you get the idea.

If a player cannot think of something straight away, they can leave it blank and add something as they get to know the character. It is important though – when the character is actively pursuing their Goal, the Gamemaster will reward the player when they achieve it with either Story Points or something even cooler. It's down to the Gamemaster though.

For example, Clara's a teacher, and is responsible for the kids in her care. She takes this responsibility seriously, and not just at school, looking out for the innocent and defenceless. If Clara puts herself at risk to protect someone, not only will she get Story Points for his selfless act, but she may receive additional Story Points or even an increase in a skill, trait or attribute at the end of the adventure to reflect her accomplishing her Goal. Further advice on this can be found on pg. 108.

EQUIPMENT AND PERSONAL ITEMS

The Doctor and his companions rarely adventure to gain things. They travel to experience the adventure, the excitement and to make the universe a better place. It is rare that someone is accepted into the TARDIS if they're only in it to make money and collect some valuable treasures on the way. Of course, the Doctor can make mistakes in judgement.

All characters should have the basics. Have a think about what you carry about with you when you go out – phone, purse or wallet, a little cash, make-up, mirror, notebook, bottle of pop, MP3 player and that's about it. It's unlikely you'll be starting the game with climbing gear, mapping tools, nightvision goggles, torch or guns. If you're really prepared you may have a car-boot full of clothes, but that's about it. Any weird and bizarre equipment you need to suit the environment might already be somewhere in the TARDIS in the wardrobe or another of its myriad rooms.

If you're planning on starting the game with any unusual item of equipment you should talk it over with the Gamemaster and see if it is acceptable. If it's going to be too useful or unbalancing, the Gamemaster may consider it a Gadget (like the Sonic Screwdriver) and there are special rules for purchasing or creating those (see pg. 112).

ANY QUESTIONS?

At the end of this process, each player should have a character fit for the TARDIS. Now, all you need to know is the rules of the game. Luckily, we're coming to that bit in the next chapter. Get yourself a cup of tea and settle down... it's time to learn how to play the game.

EXAMPLE (CONTINUED)

Continuing the story of Edward's character, he has all the numbers filled in that he needs, but his character isn't really a 'person.' He knows he's good with technology and science, but a bit shy and not terribly strong. First of all, he needs a name.

Edward gives it a bit of thought and comes up with 'Adrian Davies'. He's going to be a fellow teacher at Coal Hill, alongside Clara, Danny and the Doctor (in his guise as the Caretaker). It's only a matter of time before he gets swept up on one of their adventures.

Edward decides that Adrian is 31, somewhat shy and with a unique sense of style – he wears a bow tie – but he's friendly and loyal, and the kids love his science lessons. He's from England, 2015, so his Tech Level is 5 (contemporary Earth).

His Personal Goal is to find a steady girlfriend, and to have some more fun! Edward then lists some handy equipment he may have, like a pen, a set of screwdrivers, a torch, a mobile phone and a laptop.

With that, he's ready to play!

I CAN FIGHT MONSTERS, I CAN'T FIGHT PHYSICS

This chapter covers the rules of the game. Everything players need to know, from how a character can run, jump, swing from ropes, or dive for cover, to talk down an alien with a gun, outsmart an evil mastermind or drive a car, is in here.

While this may look complicated at first, there is just one simple rule to remember that works in every situation in the game. Bearing that in mind, it is not going to be as hard as it might seem.

⚙ RUNNING THE GAME

As we've already discussed, every player has a character to control with their details written down on their Character Sheets. The Gamemaster introduces the adventure, and the rest is done through conversation. The players describe what their characters are doing, the Gamemaster allows the plot to develop and describes how events progress and the actions of any additional people, including the Villains.

Check out the example of play in **Chapter One: The Trip of a Lifetime** (pg.13) to get a feel for the game in action.

Most of the time if the player wants his character to do something, they can do it with very little worry. If

they want to talk, walk, eat or read something, they don't require any rules to do so. If the player wants their Character to do something that may or may not be successful, that's when numbers and dice come into play. For example, if they want to hit a switch by throwing a cricket ball across the room, run down a staircase without tripping, mend a broken computer or something else that requires a level of skill or chance – or that might have a chance of failure – it's time to roll those dice!

THE BASIC RULE

The **Doctor Who Roleplaying Game** uses the same basic rule for every action. Whether it is fighting, convincing someone, researching, creating a gadget or piloting the TARDIS, it all comes down to the same basic rule:

> **ATTRIBUTE + SKILL (+TRAIT) + TWO SIX SIDED DICE = RESULT**
> (try to match or beat the Difficulty of the task)

Attribute: Select the most appropriate attribute for what the character is trying to do. Trying to lift something? Then Strength is the one you need. Trying to remember something important or invent a device that is crucial to saving the group? As this uses brainpower, you need to use Ingenuity. Trying to solder an intricate component, walk along a narrow beam or aim a sonic disruptor, they all require some sort of dexterity so Coordination is the attribute for that task. Once you've picked a suitable attribute, it needs to be paired up with something.

Skill: Next find the skill best suited for the task. Are they running for their lives? Having some Athletics would mean they could run faster and for longer. What about if they're trying to cobble together household electrical items to make an alien detector? It would

be hard to do such a task without the Technology skill, so that would be the skill to use. Sometimes there's no suitable skill to use, so they'll have to use a second attribute instead.

Trait: Do any traits come into play? If so, have a look at the trait description and see if it applies any modifiers to the roll. For example, jumping a gap between two buildings will use Strength + Athletics, but the Gamemaster may decide that the Brave trait will add a bonus to the jump – you'd have to be pretty brave to attempt such a feat, after all. If you think one of your character's traits would come into action, then take it into account – even if would apply a penalty. Playing to your character's weaknesses means you're acting in character, which makes the game more interesting, aids the storytelling and is rewarded with Story Points.

Dice: There's always an element of chance in these things – it keeps us on our toes. Roll two six-sided dice, add them together and remember the number.

The Result: Add the value of the attribute you've selected, the skill you have and any adjustments from traits, to the total dice roll. If the total is equal to or higher than the Difficulty of the task (as determined by the Gamemaster), then you've succeeded! If it is lower, then they've failed. It's as simple as that.

EXAMPLE

Clara is running through tunnels in Bristol, with the 3D paintings animated by the Boneless giving a slow and juddering chase. However, the tunnel itself is rippling with the Boneless themselves, and Clara must jump over an open shaft to escape.

The Gamemaster, Peter, asks Clara's player, Samuel, to make a roll. It's going to be a physical jump, and Peter and Samuel agree that it's going to use Clara's Coordination (as she's going to have to control where her feet go) combined with her Athletics (as it's a physical jump that will be aided with a little athletic practice). Coordination of 3, Athletics of 3, for a total of 6.

Peter says that it's a fairly tricky jump and assigns a Difficulty of 15. Samuel needs to equal or beat that with whatever he rolls, plus the 6 from Coordination + Athletics.

Samuel rolls two dice, and gets a 5 and a 5 = 10. The 10 from the dice roll, plus the 6 from the Attribute + Skill, equals 16, which is more than the Difficulty of 15. It was hard, but Clara leapt over the shaft and escapes the tunnels.

WHICH ATTRIBUTE OR SKILL TO USE

In most cases, which skill and attribute to use are fairly obvious. However, in some cases, there may be two attributes or skills that could be used equally well.

For example, Danny Pink, played by Ingrid, has found a strange alien device in the boiler room at Coal Hill School. It's flashing ominously so he tries to investigate it further. He could use Ingenuity + Technology (as it takes brains to know what to do), or Awareness + Technology (as he needs to be able to spot which bit goes where) or Coordination + Technology (as it is intricate work to try to investigate the device without setting it off).

In this case Ingrid would choose whatever her character is better at, or the Gamemaster, Peter, would choose whichever is more apt to the way they are attempting the task. Peter, in this instance, decides that Coordination is the most relevant to the task as it is incredibly fine work, and an unsteady hand could have unforeseen consequences!

If two skills or attributes are relevant, the Gamemaster should keep the **unused** skill or attribute in mind when deciding the outcome of the roll. You'll see on the Success Tables (see pg.74) that the results can be interpreted in different ways depending upon the roll. If the Gamemaster chooses, he can bring the unused attribute or skill into the result.

Continuing the example, Danny uses his Coordination + Technology and makes a great roll to disable the alien device, getting a Fantastic result. Peter remembers that Awareness could have been used just as well, and says that while Danny did a great job of disabling the device, he also spotted that the device has a symbol on it – perhaps a clue to where it came from.

Or, if the roll had failed, the same could be said. If Ingrid had rolled and got a Failure result, Danny might have failed to work out what the device was, but spotted in time the trap wired into it.

The Gamemaster doesn't need to bear this in mind all of the time, but it can be a great way to inspire cool additions to the action and plot.

UNSKILLED ATTEMPTS

Usually, attempting to do something without the relevant skill results in failure. You wouldn't normally try to fix the wiring inside a computer if you didn't know what you were doing, and you wouldn't try to perform surgery without medical training. However, in desperate times, characters may have to try despite being untrained.

Even without a skill you use the same formula as before. Of course, without a skill to add in there, the result is going to be lower, which reflects their lack of training, and in most cases, trying to do something without any skill could actually make things worse.

Any time a character tries to do something that they have absolutely no skill in, the roll suffers a -4 penalty. They might have a skill that could help a little, but isn't completely related – if the Gamemaster agrees they can try with a smaller penalty of -2.

⚙ HOW A ROLL WORKS

Rolling dice and adding numbers is fine, but what are you rolling for, and how do you interpret the outcome? First of all, decide what the character intends to do.

INTENT

The player needs to decide exactly what they want their character to do and describe it as best as they can. This helps the Gamemaster to decide how difficult the task is so they can assign a Difficulty. This will also help in deciding how well the character did and whether they achieved what you wanted to do!

For example, the player could say "Clara tries to hide from the approaching Cybermen, ducking for cover behind the smouldering remains of a car." This tells the Gamemaster what they want to do, how they're intending to do it, and how difficult it is. Both the player and the Gamemaster can start thinking of what would happen if they succeed or fail.

DIFFICULTY

Some tasks are going to be more difficult than others. After all, reprogramming an alien computer is going to be much harder than replacing the batteries in a TV remote control!

Whenever the characters have to do something that requires a roll, the Gamemaster will determine the Difficulty. This is the number the player will have to beat to succeed with the task. The average human Attribute is 3, the average Skill is 2-3, and the average die roll is 7, so an average person should be able to accomplish something with a Difficulty of 12 more often than not. The table below provides you with suggested Difficulty levels, though the Gamemaster can adjust these to suit a particular situation.

HOW WELL HAVE YOU DONE?

Looking at how far above or below the Difficulty the Result was, you can imagine how well or how badly the task went. After the first couple of task resolutions, this will come quickly to players in the game and the flow of the story shouldn't be slowed down by looking at numbers and making calculations. Rolling dice furthers the story and resolves any conflicts and tests of skill or chance.

If the roll was successful, have a look at how far above the Difficulty the Result was. The wider the difference between the Difficulty and your Result, the better you've done. Remember what the Intent was and consider the question "did you succeed?" Looking at the Success Table on the following page you can see that as the result gets better and higher, you progress through 'Yes, But' to 'Yes' and finally 'Yes – and'.

The same also applies to failures. Sometimes, if you're attempting something you're really not skilled for, you could make matters worse just by trying. Look to see how far under the Difficulty you failed by. The lower your result, the worse things could get. Again, think of what your initial Intent was, as this will give you ideas of what actually goes wrong (see the Failure Table on the following page).

TASK	DIFFICULTY	EXAMPLE
Really, Really Easy	3	Really simple, should be an automatic success. Opening a can of drink, using a phone, eating chips.
Really Easy	6	Looking something up in a dictionary, operating a microwave oven, hitting an unaware alien with a cricket bat.
Easy	9	Setting the DVR to record a program, jumping a low fence, operating a smartphone, finding information on the internet.
Normal	12	Driving a car in traffic, shooting at a stationary target, swimming in the sea, uncovering a useful but not secret fact.
Tricky	15	Driving at speed, shooting a moving target, climbing a cliff.
Hard	18	Picking a lock, lift twice your weight, treat a gunshot wound
Difficult	21	Climb a Venetian bell-tower in the rain, charm your way into a government facility, escape from rope bonds.
Very Difficult	24	Recite a Shakespearian soliloquy without mistakes, charm your way into the White House.
Improbable	27	Hit a very small target with a slingshot, hack into a government computer system, create a DNA scanner out of radio parts.
Nearly Impossible	30	Close a rift in time and space with a chocolate bar, climb the outside of a skyscraper in the rain, shoot a small target in an adjacent room without looking.

SUCCESS TABLE

AMOUNT ABOVE DIFFICULTY: 9+
RESULT: Fantastic!
"DID YOU SUCCEED?": **Yes, And**... something unexpected happened as a result of the outstanding success. The character not only gets what they wanted, but something extra happens that the player decides, with the Gamemaster's approval. The greater the difference, the more dramatic the effects.

For example: Clara has dressed as a lady-in-waiting to infiltrate Nottingham Castle, where she suspects something odd is going on – she's very successful in her attempt to blend in and can walk around the castle uncontested AND she's told in passing by one of the maids where the strange mechanical knights are being repaired.

Damage: If attacking someone or something, the damage is multiplied by one and a half (x1.5) times (round down).

AMOUNT ABOVE DIFFICULTY: 4-8
RESULT: Good
"DID YOU SUCCEED?": **Yes**... the character has managed to do what they wanted. If the result is 4-8 above the Difficulty assigned the character has certainly accomplished what they wanted, and pretty well.

Continuing the example, Clara tries to convince a (human) guard that she is to deliver a tray of food to the knight – at the request of the Sheriff. She's successful, and the guard lets her past.

Damage: If attacking, the weapon damage inflicted on the target is normal and unmodified.

AMOUNT ABOVE DIFFICULTY: 0-3
RESULT: Success
"DID YOU SUCCEED?": **Yes, But...** it may not have gone as well as the character had hoped, or something unexpected has occurred. The roll was still successful, but only just. It was a close call, but they managed to scrape through. The player (at the Gamemaster's discretion) should add some sort of complication or secondary problem.

While investigating the (dormant but definitely robotic) knight, the Sheriff of Nottingham himself comes into the chamber to give it new orders. There's a scuffle and Clara tries to club the Sheriff round the head with her tray. She's successful at stopping the Sheriff from crying out to alert the guard, BUT the Robot Knight begins to activate...

Damage: If attacking, the weapon only inflicts half of the damage (round down). The target was still hit, but only just.

FAILURE TABLE

AMOUNT BELOW DIFFICULTY: 1-3
RESULT: Failure
"DID YOU SUCCEED?": **No, But...** it could have been much worse. The character failed, and didn't manage to achieve what they'd hoped, but it wasn't a horrible failure. The Gamemaster may allow the player to gain something out of the attempt, but it may not be what they'd expected.

Continuing the example, the Robot Knight awakens from its slumber. Clara shouts "Stop! I can explain everything!" The Robot Knight looks at the dazed Sheriff and prepares to disintegrate Clara BUT the Sheriff comes round at that very moment and shouts "Halt!"

Damage: If receiving damage from an injury or attack, the character is harmed but only sustains half of the damage (round down).

AMOUNT BELOW DIFFICULTY: 4-8
RESULT: Bad
"DID YOU SUCCEED?": **No...** the character has certainly failed at the task, but it wasn't a total disaster.

Hoping to avoid a fight, Clara tries to convince the Sheriff "My lord, I just wanted to hear about your dastardly plan," however the Sheriff is having none of it. "I know a ploy to make me launch into a villainous monologue when I see it", he says, grabbing Clara's arm "Come with me."

Damage: If taking damage, the character sustains the normal, unmodified amount.

AMOUNT BELOW DIFFICULTY: 9+
RESULT: Disastrous
"DID YOU SUCCEED?": **No, And...** something else has gone wrong. Not only was the failure bad enough, but there may be worse consequences.

The Sheriff of Nottingham marches Clara along the battlements towards his tower. Clara tries to escape by leaping off the wall and into a passing haycart but the Sheriff is wise to her and grabs her. She is still the Sheriff's prisoner AND she's dangling over the edge of the wall, the haycart gone! Things are just getting worse!

Damage: When taking damage, the character sustains one and a half times the amount of damage (x1.5) (round down).

OPTIONAL RULE: THE DRAMA DIE

If calculating the levels of success slows your game down, the Gamemaster may decide to discard them and stick with a simple Success or Failure. Alternatively, if you'd still like the detailed and varied result without having to work out the difference between the Difficulty and the Result, you could roll an additional die to generate the degree of success randomly. A "drama die" could be a single, different-coloured die that is rolled with the other dice that can determine the degree of success.

Die		
1	Success (Yes, But...)	Failure (No, But...)
2-5	Good (Yes)	Bad (No)
6	Fantastic (Yes, And...)	Disastrous (No, And...)

It can be a little random, but it does speed things up and may allow a more extreme level of success that may normally be out of reach to the character.

CHAPTER THREE:
I CAN FIGHT MONSTERS, I CAN'T FIGHT PHYSICS

DAMAGE

You'll have noticed that the Success Tables also mention damage and how it is affected depending upon how well or how badly you've rolled. All weapons or forms of injury have a fixed damage. This number is modified depending on the roll (either how well you shot at someone, or how badly you dodged the harm). Halving, or multiplying the damage by 1.5 (one and a half times), may result in half or quarter numbers – always round down to the nearest whole number, unless the number is zero (0). Damage has been done in some form, so the lowest it can be is one (1). We'll discuss damage and conflict later (see pg.85).

USING STORY POINTS

Didn't do as well as hoped? Don't worry, all is not lost. If you imagine all the levels of success and failure as a ladder, you can spend a Story Point to move up one 'rung', so to speak, turning a Success into a Good, or a Good into a Fantastic Result.

Failed miserably at a task that was vital? You can spend Story Points to recover from a particularly bad result, moving up a rung per Story Point. However, spending Story Points in this way does limit you to a highest level of just 'Success'. More on spending Story Points to effect the outcome of a roll can be found on p.102.

If a player is low on Story Points and it suits the story, they can do the reverse and turn a Success into a Failure to regain Story Points. The Gamemaster has the final say, and doing this too often should not be encouraged, but it can stir things up a little and can be a good way to build up Story Points in times of need. More on awarding and spending Story Points can be found on pg.106.

THE SUCCESS TABLE LADDER

9+ above	Fantastic
4-8 above	Good
0-3 above	Success
1-3 below	Failure
4-8 below	Bad
9+ below	Disastrous!

COOPERATION

Sometimes a task is so tricky or complicated, the characters are going to have to call in help. Many hands make light work! One person with the required skill will take the lead in the task. The helpers, if they have a suitable skill that could help, each add +2 to the leader's attempt. The Gamemaster may put a limit on how many people can help in any given circumstance, and which skills are suitable to assist.

Example: Madame Vastra is having a bad day. She is in pursuit of a gentleman thief who's stolen a potentially lethal piece of alien technology from her; she doesn't have the time or patience to argue with a steward as to why she should be allowed into the glamorous ball that the thief has ducked into. Fortunately, Jenny keeps a cool head and, in the role of servant, offers 'suggestions' to Vastra and the steward as to how her invitation has been misplaced. Madame Vastra rolls Presence + Convince skill , but because because Jenny is helping she adds an extra +2 to her roll.

THIS MAY TAKE SOME TIME...

Another way to deal with incredibly hard tasks is to take your time and work at it over a longer period. The Gamemaster determines how long it is going to take for the character to complete the task. At the end of that time, make the roll as normal to see if you succeed. If the character spends longer than necessary on a task, taking their time and being extra careful, they are more likely to succeed. Taking twice as long adds a +2 bonus to the roll, three times as long adds +4, and so on up to a maximum bonus of +10.

Example: *The Doctor is experimenting with a mix of chemicals that will hopefully eat through Dalekanium in a very short time. The Gamemaster, Peter, knows the Doctor is brilliant, but it's going to take a while to get this right. Peter says "It's going to take at least an hour of mixing and trying formulas before you come close to a solution." The Doctor's player, Jenna, isn't in a rush, and this is vital to the success of the players. She decides to spend two hours on the experiment and gains a +2 bonus on his Ingenuity + Science roll at the end of this time.*

The opposite can be said if the character is rushing something. Trying to do things quickly can result in fumbling hands! Halving the time it would normally take to do something means the roll receives a -2 penalty, and so on, just like taking extra time.

⚙ CONFLICT: CONTESTED ROLLS

Rolling dice and adding some numbers together to beat a set Difficulty is all well and good, but what if you're actively opposing someone or something else? Luckily, this is just as easy as a normal task, only the Difficulty is determined by the opponent as they try to stop whatever you're doing.

Most of the time, Conflicts are between the players' characters and antagonists controlled by the Gamemaster, so the Gamemaster will state what the bad guys are trying to do and make a roll on behalf of them first – this will be what the characters will have to try to beat, just like the Difficulty of a normal

task. In effect, they are setting the Difficulty of the player's roll by making things difficult to succeed against them.

Don't worry if this sounds confusing, we'll take you through how it works stage by stage.

INTENT

This works just as before. The player says what they want to do, and the Gamemaster determines what the Non-Player Character is doing to prevent it – looming to attack, opening fire, dodging, and so on.

WHAT ARE YOU USING?

Next, see which Attribute + Skill you're using to do what you're intending, and if any traits are relevant. Both sides work out what they need to roll, relating to their planned action. This is done in just the same way as any other task.

ROLL THE DICE

Just as before, the Gamemaster adds the Attribute + Skill (as well as taking any traits into account) to the dice roll, determining how well the antagonists do. The player does the same and informs the Gamemaster what the result is. The Gamemaster uses the antagonist's result as the Difficulty for the player's rolls, and works out if the player is successful or not. If the player fails, then evil prevails and the antagonists take their action. If the player succeeds, their intended actions go ahead – and they agree with the Gamemaster what exactly happened.

This is how it is done for any Conflict, from fighting to arguing, everything works in exactly the same way.

Example: *Clara and the Doctor are exploring a strange mansion, rumoured to be haunted; in true horror-movie style, they split up. Investigating the strange banging in the basement, Clara finds the cause of the haunting – there are coffins full of Whisper Men, controlled by the Great Intelligence! She tries to back quietly out but is spotted by a Whisper Man who has just appeared out of thin air behind her! The Gamemaster, Peter, asks Clara's player, Samuel, what Clara is going to do.*

Samuel knows that the Doctor is upstairs and will be able to rescue her if she can delay the Whisper Man long enough. Samuel decides to attempt to persuade the Whisper Man to stop it from attacking, to tell it that its master might prefer her alive. Peter thinks this sounds good, and says the Whisper Man is intending to seize Clara and stop her heart.

Samuel checks his character sheet, and Peter looks up the Whisper Man's attributes and skills. They add the necessary attributes and skills together – in Clara's case it will be her Presence + Convince to tell the Whisper Man to let her live.

Peter looks up the Whisper Man's Coordination + Fighting skills to see what he needs to roll. Even though it may be talked down, the Whisper Man still uses the Attribute + Skill it would use if it had no resistance.

The Whisper Man looms, and Clara tries to stop it from killing her. Both Samuel and Peter roll their dice, and add their respective attribute and skills, taking into account any traits. Samuel has a higher result, but only just. Samuel decides the outcome of the conflict and determines that the Whisper Man doesn't attack. However, the result was only a "Yes, But" so Samuel decides that the Whisper Man takes Clara prisoner to take to the Great Intelligence. She's alive, but held captive! She needs to keep an eye out for another opportunity to escape.

COMPLICATIONS

If you wish to add more realism or detail into a Conflict, certain environmental factors can be taken into account. If the task at hand is tricky or complicated,

or there are conditions such as rain, darkness or the character is hurried, the Gamemaster can have a look at the examples provided below and apply a modifier that seems suitable. These are just a guideline, and Gamemasters should feel free to modify the rolls as they see fit, though it makes for a speedier and smoother game if these modifiers are used sparingly.

Of course, modifiers should be taken into account in a Conflict only if one side alone is affected by it. If both are affected equally (for example, the room is in complete darkness and neither side has a light or nightvision goggles), you don't need to worry about this sort of thing.

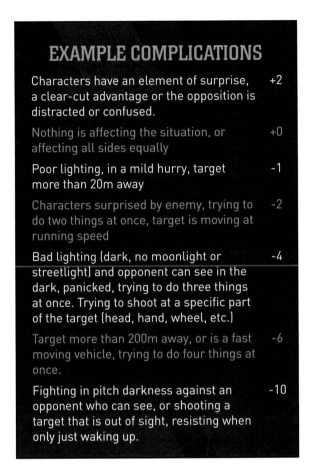

EXAMPLE COMPLICATIONS

Characters have an element of surprise, a clear-cut advantage or the opposition is distracted or confused.	+2
Nothing is affecting the situation, or affecting all sides equally	+0
Poor lighting, in a mild hurry, target more than 20m away	-1
Characters surprised by enemy, trying to do two things at once, target is moving at running speed	-2
Bad lighting (dark, no moonlight or streetlight) and opponent can see in the dark, panicked, trying to do three things at once. Trying to shoot at a specific part of the target (head, hand, wheel, etc.)	-4
Target more than 200m away, or is a fast moving vehicle, trying to do four things at once.	-6
Fighting in pitch darkness against an opponent who can see, or shooting a target that is out of sight, resisting when only just waking up.	-10

MULTIPLE OPPONENTS

Often in Conflicts, there will be more than one adversary actively opposing the characters. Instead of rolling for each individual opponent, the Gamemaster may use the Cooperation rules (see pg.76) for the adversaries to keep things running quickly.

The Gamemaster should choose one of the adversaries to function as the leader for the group, such as the Cyberleader or Sontaran General. The leader makes the main roll against the characters, gaining a +2 bonus to the roll for each of their 'troops' with the appropriate skill. In 'ranged' combat, where people are shooting at each other, there are fewer limitations to how many can shoot at a single target, so the four maximum may be disregarded in some conflicts. With very large groups of opponents, these modifiers make things very difficult for the characters. No character should try to face off against multiple Daleks or Sontarans without something serious up their sleeves.

For large conflicts, the Gamemaster can split the enemy forces into equal, manageable 'chunks'. In such a case, the opponents should be split into an equal number of groups to the characters. For example, a whole squad of Sontarans faces off against the Doctor, Clara and Danny. The squad is 10 Sontarans, so the Gamemaster splits the enemy into three groups, 3 against Clara, 3 against Danny and 4 Sontarans against the Doctor.

Each group would be given a 'leader' temporarily (if there isn't already a leader in the group as a whole). Larger scale conflicts like this are covered in more detail in **Defending The Earth: The UNIT Sourcebook**.

Example: *The Doctor and Clara are onboard the spaceship Aristotle, talking to Colonel Morgan Blue in advance of an attack by the Combined Army Resistance on a Dalek outpost. The Doctor has to convince the Colonel to call off the attack – it has to be a trap! Colonel Blue's right-hand man, Lieutenant North, who is secretly a Dalek puppet, argues that the outpost must be seized!*

The Doctor tries to use his Presence + Convince on Colonel Blue, and the Colonel uses his Resolve +Convince to argue back, determined that the Combined Army Resistance must prevail. The Doctor is a very talkative and persuasive person, but Colonel Blue also has Lieutenant North talking into his ear at the same time, warning him that the last time the Doctor appeared they nearly lost the ship – and the war! North's Convince is called into play as well, adding to Colonel Blue's roll.

Dice are rolled, using Colonel Blue's result to determine the Difficulty for the Doctor's roll. The Doctor gets a Failure – Colonel Blue isn't going to be convinced not to launch the attack, BUT he heeds the Doctor's warning that it might be a trap and instructs his troops to be on their guard.

The Doctor may have failed but it wasn't a complete disaster. Now, he just needs to get into the Dalek outpost himself to try to foil whatever it is the Daleks have planned!

⚙ EXTENDED CONFLICT

Resolving smaller tasks with just one dice roll is all well and good, but if the situation is more intense or involved, such as a chase or fight scene, you may wish to break the action down into a series of rolls. Not only does this add tension, but it also allows everyone to create more involved and exciting action scenes as the tables can turn quickly with a good or bad roll.

SETTING THE SCENE

First, the Gamemaster 'sets the scene' for the players, describing the location as best they can so everyone knows where their characters physically are. If they have maps prepared, the Gamemaster can reveal these to the players, or draw a rough diagram so everyone can get a feel for the place. It's not essential, just as long as everyone knows where they are, what it looks like and any important environmental conditions (is it raining, misty, dark, slippery or freezing cold?).

Example: Jenny has been taken prisoner by the Cybermen. They've dragged her unconscious body back towards the processing centre, and the Doctor and Madame Vastra are giving chase. They follow the Cybermen from a distance, watching them enter the building. They sneak in through the doors and look around. It's here that the Gamemaster sets the scene.

The Gamemaster says, "You enter the processing centre. Sprawled around you is a mass of dark and steaming machinery, whirring away, and you can hear the distant cries of people being converted into yet more of the metal men. It's relatively dark, low-level spotlights are dotted around the corridors that squeeze between the machines. As doors open and close, amber and red warning lights flash, and sirens alert you to another batch of unsuitable candidates being incinerated.

The steam of the machinery makes the place hot and sticky, but nothing can disguise the horror of what this place is for. About 100 metres ahead of you, you can see Jenny being dragged along by two Cybermen. As you notice her, you see her regain consciousness and start to struggle."

The Gamemaster has set the scene, given a feel for the location and what is going on, and the tone of the encounter to come. The players can now decide what they're planning to do.

ACTION ROUNDS

Once the Gamemaster has set the scene, the events in an Extended Conflict are broken down into action rounds. Basically this means that everyone gets a turn, and by the end of an action round you'll have gone 'round the table and everyone will have had their go. You can try to do more than one action in a round, but that's harder than it sounds. We'll cover that a little later. First thing to do is to decide what everyone's planning on doing for that round.

INTENT

Just as in the normal Conflict, players decide what they will try to do. They may discuss their plan amongst themselves in detail, or it could be as simple as running while shouting, "You go that way, I'll cut them off!" The Gamemaster decides what the adversaries will do in this round, and in what order things occur.

WHO GOES FIRST?

Now you know what everyone wants to do on both sides, the big question is who gets to go first and who does what? Each character can only take one action at a time, and they'll get to act in the order below, which depends on the type of action they take.

Talkers: "No, no, no... wait!" Talking, or shouting, has proved to be very important in the Doctor's adventures, words being far more powerful (and usually quicker to use) than weapons. The place can be exploding or you could be held at gunpoint, but before anyone starts shooting or tying you up, you get to say your piece.

Movers: "When I say run, run! RUN!" Running is a frequent option, and often when facing an alien threat people start a round running. They could be running away from something or just running into the location, but they're on the move so they get to go next. Even if you're sneaking into the secret base as quietly as possible, trying to avoid security cameras, you're moving from one place to the next, so you're next in the pecking order.

Doers: "I've just got to reverse the polarity of this circuit, and we'll be fine!" It can be as intricate as rewiring a circuit, or it could be as simple as opening a door. If you're not running or talking to the enemy, you're probably planning on doing something that'll help the situation.

Fighters: "Open Fire! All Weapons!" Finally, the people who choose to fight or shoot take their turn.

The Gamemaster goes through this list in order, and the players and villains take their turn when it's their part of the action round. For example, the Gamemaster roughly knows what the players have planned, so starts from the top. "OK, any characters want to do any Talking this round?" Any players intending on shouting at the villains to try to stop them hold up their hands. After those players have gone, the Gamemaster calls for the next lot: "Now that's done, anyone planning on just running around?" And so on.

CHARACTERS ROLL AND PERFORM THEIR ACTIONS

When it's their turn to go in the action round, it's time for the characters to do their thing. In many cases, their opponent will resist the intended action in some way, whether this is arguing, bluffing, punching, shooting or trying to mentally control someone. Other times it will be a simple roll against the Difficulty of their action, if they are doing something with no resistance, such as running, fixing a computer, defusing a bomb or if the target is completely unaware of the first attack. If someone resists the character's actions, there will be a 'Reaction' to determine how hard it is for the player to act.

REACTIONS – RESISTING THE ROLL

During a Conflict, the character will want to defend themselves from an adversary's action. Whether this is parrying a sword, dodging Dalek weapon fire or countering an argument to stop a war committee from making a terrible mistake, these defending actions are Reactions.

This works in the same way as any other Contested Roll (see pg.77). The character declares their intended action, and the character they are "attacking" has a chance to make a Reaction. The defending character makes their Reaction first, setting the Difficulty for the attacker, just like a normal roll. Reactions should only be allowed, however, if the character is aware of the opponent's impending action.

The sidebar suggests some sample actions and reactions. These represent only a small sample of possible combinations, and depending upon the circumstances entirely different skills and attributes may come into play.

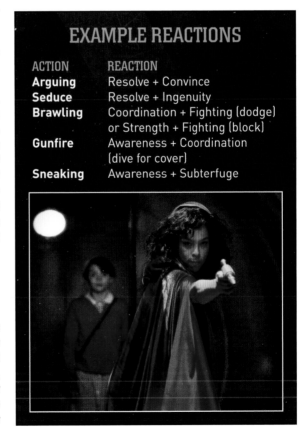

EXAMPLE REACTIONS

ACTION	REACTION
Arguing	Resolve + Convince
Seduce	Resolve + Ingenuity
Brawling	Coordination + Fighting (dodge) or Strength + Fighting (block)
Gunfire	Awareness + Coordination (dive for cover)
Sneaking	Awareness + Subterfuge

MAKING MORE THAN ONE ACTION IN A ROUND

You only get one action in a round, whether it's running, talking, doing or fighting, but that doesn't mean that you won't be targeted by more than one

Conflict. Resisting is technically a Reaction, but you can't do more than one thing at a time without things getting difficult. You get your action as normal, but every other different action you take in the sequence, such as shooting or shouting, receives a -2 penalty. This penalty is cumulative as well, so each additional action after that gets another -2 on top!

Example: *On a heist with the Doctor, Psi is running away from a Dalek apparently unimpressed by his theft of the saucer's data-vault. He's hoping to hack into the saucer's computer with his mind to close a bulkhead behind him. His first action is going be hacking into the computer as that's a 'Doing'. He rolls as normal. However, he's getting shot at by the Dalek. It fires, and Psi dives out of the way, but as he's already acted this round, this Reaction receives a -2 penalty. If Psi wants to do anything else it'll be at a -4 penalty.*

You can voluntarily do more than one thing in a Round, but again, every action after the first is at a cumulative -2 to the roll.

Reacting works a little differently.

MAKING MORE THAN ONE REACTION IN A ROUND

You can make more than one Reaction roll in a round, but in many cases you don't actually need to. Once you're leaping around and dodging, you're harder to hit for everyone who's shooting at you – you don't need to try to dodge every single shot. If you have to react in a round, roll as normal (with any necessary penalties for when you make the roll). That Reaction roll counts for every similar attempt against you in that round.

Let's say the Doctor is being shot at by three Silurians while he's trying to adjust the settings on his Sonic Screwdriver to knock out their guns. The 'Doing' comes first, so setting the Sonic Screwdriver is rolled as normal. Then comes the fighting. The Doctor's Sonic Screwdriver isn't going to be ready to use until next round so the three Silurians open fire. He's going to dodge, jumping for cover. The Doctor's already acted this time (adjusting the Sonic Screwdriver) so his dodging is at -2. He only needs to roll once, and that result sets the target for all three of the Silurians trying to hit him.

If the Silurian's leader was trying to command him to surrender earlier in the round, 'Talkers' come first, so he would resist that before trying to adjust the Sonic Screwdriver. His resistance against being

talked into surrendering would be rolled as normal (and would count against any other attempts to talk him out of what he's doing). Setting the Sonic Screwdriver would be next in the round, with a -2 penalty. Then the dodge against all three shots would be rolled at -4.

Using the same roll for multiple resistances only works with Reactions, not with actions.

MITIGATING CIRCUMSTANCES

As with any of these rules, there can be times when the Gamemaster may have to decide the actual events. For example, if you start an action round while you're already running, the Gamemaster may swap the order of the Talkers and the Movers. They're already running, so the Talkers aren't going to get much of a chance to shout at you as you breeze past them. The Gamemaster will decide if special circumstances mean that characters go in a different order.

CHANGING YOUR MIND?

If a player decides that they want to perform an action belonging to an earlier phase, and have not acted yet, they can jump in straight away. This is usually because they may have had something planned for the round, but it was resolved before they had an opportunity to act.

Example: *Kate Stewart is planning to shoot at a Vitrus the Cruel, an alien bounty hunter, but Virtus acted earlier, activating his forcefield. Kate knows that shooting at the forcefield is going to be pointless as her gun will have little effect. She changes her mind, and decides to run for help – however the Movers phase has already passed!*

Kate's player, Tom, jumps in and declares what he wants to do, and the Gamemaster, Peter, lets Kate run for assistance before any further Doing or Fighting actions take place. The Gamemaster may apply a -2 penalty to any actions like this if they require a roll to reflect the character changing their mind at the last minute and being unprepared.

ACTING SIMULTANEOUSLY

What if two people are trying to do the same thing at the same time? If two or more people are intending to Fight or to Run then the characters go in order of the highest attribute used. For example, if two people plan on shooting at each other, the one with the highest Coordination goes first. If they both have the same level attribute, then the highest skill goes first. If they are alike in every way, their actions are simultaneous!

EXTENDED CONFLICT SUMMARY

Sound too complicated? Don't worry, just take it one stage at a time:

1) **Establish the Scene**
    Where is everyone and what is the environment like?
2) **Establish Intent**
    What is everyone planning to do? What are the NPCs planning to do?
3) **Take Actions**
    Everyone gets their action (including the NPCs) in order of what they're planning to do:
    Talkers – any people who are just going to speak, they go first.
    Movers – people who are moving or running, they go next.
    Doers – non-combat actions, such as fixing something, or doing something.
    Fighters – finally, the combat actions go last.
    Actions directed at another character or NPC can be resisted with a Reaction as they occur.
4) **Do it all again**
    If the Conflict hasn't been resolved, go back to Step 2 and decide what everyone intends to do next.

DO IT ALL AGAIN...

When everyone has had their action, and you've worked your way through the talkers, movers, doers and fighters, you can start the process again. Return to the Establish Intent phase when you're discussing what your characters are all going to do – then run through another action round. This continues until the Conflict is resolved and you progress on to the rest of the adventure.

A problem with breaking Conflicts into shorter rounds, especially combat, is that players can sometimes get stuck in a rut, repeating the same action over and over again. Besides being a colossal bore storywise, any intelligent enemy will eventually figure a way to counter such predictable tactics.

If the players have used the same tactic or action against the enemy for three rounds in a single scene, the Gamemaster should start giving the enemy a cumulative +1 bonus to resist for that and every additional round that the characters uses the same tactic or action again (to a maximum equal to the enemy's Ingenuity).

Example: *The Doctor is holding the Daleks at bay with a biscuit by Convincing them that it is a TARDIS self-destruct. The third time he does this, they get a +1 to resist his Convince attempts, and an additional +1 for every round after that (up to +4, which is equal to their Ingenuity) until the Strategist Dalek sees past the ruse.*

"Alright, it's a Jammy Dodger! But I was promised tea!"

LOSING A CONFLICT

Losing can mean many things depending upon what sort of Conflict our heroes were engaged in. Physical conflicts, such as fighting or combat, will result in physical injury or even death. Mental Conflicts, such as a battle of wills or attempts at mind control, may result in losing control of their actions, unconsciousness or on rare occasions, death. Social Conflicts can result in losing prestige, respect or even the trust of others.

In many cases, losing a Conflict will result in the temporary reduction of one or more of the character's attributes. The Gamemaster will discuss this with the players to determine exactly what happens and what the outcome of the Conflict is, allowing you to make a failure interesting to heighten the action of the adventure.

How severe this reduction is, or even the very survival of your character, will depend upon the strategic expenditure of Story Points, and how badly your character lost in the Conflict. In most cases, you'll need to see how badly you were defeated, whether this is a Failure, a Bad or, even worse, a Disastrous result.

We'll go through the various types of Conflict below and discuss how to handle losing.

MAKING LOSING EXCITING

Of course, failing isn't always bad. It can, with some imagination, actually make things more exciting and the game more interesting. Failures will still mean that you lose a Conflict, but it doesn't mean that you can't make this a cool part of the story. Making it more dramatic and exciting makes the adventure more interesting for everyone, and the Gamemaster will reward players who go with their downturn in fortune by awarding the character Story Points for keeping things running smoothly.

Losing can be really cool for the story as well. After all, how many great stories come from something going wrong at the beginning of an adventure, then spending the rest of the story trying to right the mistake? Whether this is getting captured by villains, or setting in motion a chain of disastrous events that need fixing, it all makes for a great story.

If a player is running low on Story Points, and if the Gamemaster agrees, the player can opt to adjust a successful roll to a Failure (or worse) to advance the plot (just the reverse of spending Story Points to improve a roll), making things more interesting, and giving the player some Story Points that they can save for the adventure's climactic finale. Of course, the Gamemaster has the final say on all of this, and gaining Story Points in this way should be done sparingly and when the adventure allows.

Example: *Danny Pink has managed to escape the Skovox Blitzer, losing it in a derelict factory. He was hoping to lead it into the Doctor's trap, but his escape route is blocked and he's out of Story Points. There's no signal here, so he has no way of communicating with the Doctor or Clara and is unsure where they are. His player, Ingrid, rolls to sneak past the Blitzer and succeeds, but instead of wandering around aimlessly, decides to reduce the result to a Failure. This moves the plot along by alerting the Skovox Blitzer to Danny's presence, but it still gives him time to get out of the way of its weapons fire. The Gamemaster, Peter, rewards Ingrid with a Story Point for reducing her success to a Failure, and then works a new event into the story. As he's leaning by a wall, catching his breath, Danny knocks over a pile of rusty pipes, alerting the Skovox Blitzer. He has time to make a run for it, but the sound also attracts the Doctor's attention, who's still preparing his trap – time to put it into action!*

CHAPTER THREE: I CAN FIGHT MONSTERS, I CAN'T FIGHT PHYSICS

✸ LOSING A PHYSICAL CONFLICT

It's bound to happen sometime. The universe is a dangerous place and people get hurt. Whether this is just tripping over when being chased by robotic Yeti, to getting shot by a Cyberman's particle gun, getting hurt isn't fun and doesn't do your character any good. Most of the time, such injuries can be prevented with the careful expenditure of Story Points. See, we told you they'd be useful! (See pg.102 for more on Story Points).

Sometimes the injury is so small that there's no heavy paperwork involved. The Gamemaster may just remember the injury and say that the character may be walking slower due to that twisted ankle, or that they can't reach that item on the top shelf because of the pain in their arm.

If injuries are severe enough, you may find that one or more of the character's attributes are reduced. Which attribute is down to the actual source of injury. It should be logical to the story and to the event – for example, falling a distance and failing to land safely may result in a loss of Coordination from a leg injury or possibly Strength. Getting shot could mean you'd lose Strength, Coordination (if it's in a limb), or Resolve. In most cases, the Gamemaster will dictate which attributes are affected.

Most sources of injury will have a number or a letter next to it to indicate the damage the character will take from it. These are explained in the handy sidebar below.

LEVELS OF INJURY

All sources of injury, whether they are weapons, falls, poisons or worse, have a value attached to them. This is usually a number, or in some cases the letter "S" or "L".

Numerical Values

Most sources of injury will have a number next to them. This indicates how many levels of damage the character will suffer, and how many levels attributes will be reduced due to the injury. The Gamemaster will discuss with the player which attribute is most suitable for the injury and works best with the story.

Getting hit by an arrow will deplete physical attributes, whereas being hypnotised or drugged will lower mental attributes. We'll cover the various sources of injury later and give you guidelines for how this works.

Most numerical damages are presented in the following format: N/**N**/N. This represents the normal value for the damage, as well as the halved (rounded down) value, and the 1.5 times value (rounded down). For example, a weapon with a value of 3/**6**/9 would normally do 6 levels of damage for a Good Result (to hit, or a Bad Result when trying to avoid getting hit), but would only do 3 levels of damage for a Success Result, or a dangerous 9 levels of damage for a Fantastic Result.

The bold number in the middle is the Good/Bad result and is considered the average amount of damage taken, while the Fantastic/Disastrous result represents an extremely damaging outcome. The lower Success/Failure level represents a graze or a lucky break that reduces the damage.

S (Stun)

"S" stands for Stun and means that the target has been knocked unconscious. If the Gamemaster allows, they may be able to perform one last heroic act before falling unconscious, such as shouting a warning on the radio, pressing the button that opens the doors or something else that is quick and simple. How long they are unconscious will depend upon how badly they've failed. A normal Stun lasts for around 30 minutes (15 minutes for a Failure, 45 minutes for a Disastrous Result). The Gamemaster may change these times to suit the source of the stun, or whatever best fits the story. Besides being stunned, the poor victim is unharmed and will eventually wake up with a headache or feeling a little nauseous.

L (Lethal)

Dalek death-rays, Cybermen particle cannons or Judoon blasters, they all have one thing in common: just one zap and it's disintegration in a red flash or glowing blue skeleton time. Weapons flagged as Lethal are just that. You shouldn't go face to face with a Dalek.

On a Success/Failure, the Lethal weapon didn't hit fully and the target will sustain some damage (usually 4 levels). On a Good/Bad or higher result, the damage is Lethal and only the expenditure of Story Points will allow their survival. If the character is out of Story Points, it could mean their demise – the Gamemaster will discuss this with the player to ensure a suitably dramatic and epic end to the character, but players should look at Dying or Leaving the TARDIS on pg.97. Lethal weapons, if used against massive targets such as dinosaurs, vehicles or buildings, have the equivalent of inflicting 4/**8**/12 levels of damage.

⚙ SOURCES OF PHYSICAL INJURY

Besides the usual perils of the environment (fire, cold, vacuum and falling, see pg.92), the most common form of injury in the universe is, unfortunately, violence. But how much does something hurt when you've been hit?

FIGHTING DAMAGE

When it comes to close, physical combat, it's all about how strong you are. Getting hit by Amy is certainly going to hurt, but not as much as being punched by a Judoon Trooper. Basically, the damage for a punch or kick is the character's Strength attribute. If the character has a Strength of 3, they will do 3 points of damage on a Good Roll (and 1 on a Success and 4 on a Fantastic). If they have a Strength of 5, they do 5 points of damage on a Good result (2 on a Success and 7 on a Fantastic). If they are using a weapon, the damage is increased depending upon what sort of weapon it is that they're swinging around. Follow this simple checklist, and for every 'yes' add +2 to your character's Strength.

Is it sharp? Does it have a cutting edge, sharp points or something equally nasty designed to puncture or slash the target?

Is it heavy? Does the average person need two hands to lift it?

Is it dangerous? Does it do damage with just a touch, like a Sycorax whip, a laser sword or a chainsaw?

For every one of these, add +2 to the Strength of the character when working out damage. So if it's something like a sword, the damage is your character's Strength +2. If it's a big sword, like the Sycorax's, and you really need to use it two-handed then it's both heavy and sharp so it's Strength +4.

CHAPTER THREE:
I CAN FIGHT MONSTERS, I CAN'T FIGHT PHYSICS

WHERE DOES IT HURT?

The Gamemaster usually determines which attribute is affected, according to the source of the injury. If it's a severe injury, the Gamemaster may apply all of the damage to a single attribute, effectively stopping the character from using that attribute until they can get medical attention. A less severe injury may take a little off multiple attributes.

For example, if the character is shot in the leg with an arrow, taking 3 levels of damage, the Gamemaster may decide that a point should be removed from the character's Strength, due to their newly weakened state. They should also lose a point from Coordination as they're less able to move around, and finally a point should be removed from Resolve as the injury will reduce their drive and determination.

With a little imagination, an injury can lead to great story effects and plot developments.

Imagine where the character has been injured and then think of how this injury would affect them. If you need to determine the location randomly, roll two dice and use the table below.

Roll	Location	Attribute Reduced
2-4	Leg	Coordination, Resolve, Strength
5-8	Body	Resolve, Strength
9-10	Arm	Coordination, Resolve, Strength
11-12	Head	Awareness, Coordination, Ingenuity, Presence, Resolve

If the location doesn't suit, or if the area hit is behind cover, you can either roll again, or decide that the cover absorbs the damage.

If it's something really nasty like a chainsaw, it's sharp, dangerous, and heavy, so it gets the full +6 to the Strength.

If you're throwing a weapon (such as a knife or rock) at someone this also applies. The stronger you are, the more force you can put behind the throw doing more damage. So a thrown rock would do damage equal to the character's Strength, a thrown knife would add +2 to that for being sharp.

If the propelled object is being thrown by something else, such as a catapult, or gunpowder, then it's a whole different matter, and you'll be looking at Marksman Damage for shooting things.

MARKSMAN DAMAGE

Shooting something is a different case. It's not about how strong you are – it's about how accurately you can shoot, and the type of ammunition used. In most cases, a bullet or a laser will do the same amount of damage if it hits, no matter who fires it. The table presents some of the most common weapons and their normal (Good/Bad) damages.

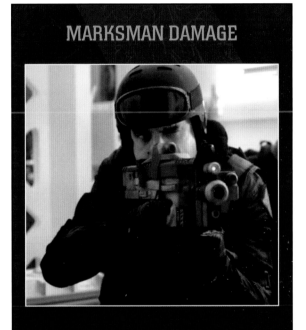

MARKSMAN DAMAGE

Weapon	Basic	S/G/F
Arrow:	3	(1/**3**/4)
Crossbow Bolt:	4	(2/**4**/6)
Flintlock Pistol:	4	(2/**4**/6)
Pistol (9mm):	5	(2/**5**/7)
WWII Rifle:	6	(3/**6**/9)
Shotgun:	7	(3/**7**/10)
Assault Rifle:	6	(3/**6**/9) *
Machine Gun:	7	(3/**7**/10) *
Sniper Rifle:	8	(4/**8**/12)
Laser Pistol:	L	(4/**L**/L)
Laser Rifle:	L	(4/**L**/L)
Cyberman Particle Gun:	L	(4/**L**/L)
Dalek Ray:	L	(4/**L**/L)
Judoon Blaster:	L	(4/**L**/L)

* Damages assume a short burst of 1-3 bullets at a time. In most cases, firing a fully automatic weapon on full auto rarely hits anything – it'll probably hit with those 1-3 bullets, the rest will spray the surroundings and shoot up the scenery.

KNOCKOUT!

Often, brawling damage isn't designed to do serious damage in a fight. Most of the time the character just wants to knock an enemy out for a little while so they can get away or get past them.

When hitting someone with fists or other non-sharp or dangerous weapons, the damage will reduce the target's Resolve only. When it reaches zero, the target is Stunned. Damage taken during the course of being knocked out is removed when the character wakes, though they may have a headache and a few bad bruises to remind them of the encounter.

If the Gamemaster decides that the damage taken like this is too severe (5 points or more), not all of the damage will be recovered. For every 5 points of damage taken, only 4 points should be recovered when they wake from being Stunned.

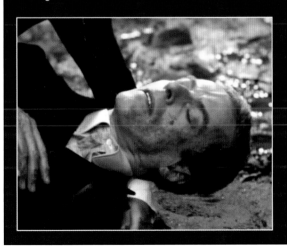

COMBAT

In the Doctor's adventures things are rarely resolved with gunfire. While the villains may resort to firepower, the Doctor and his companions almost never take up arms. It doesn't stop more militaristic agencies such as UNIT or Torchwood though. It's unlikely that you'll have many fights per adventure, but sometimes you have to fight fire with fire.

Luckily, combat runs the same as any other conflict, and isn't just about shooting at each other. Just because the aliens are pointing guns at you doesn't mean you have to point a gun back. The Doctor uses his greatest weapons – his brains and his mouth because he's smart and he can certainly talk!

GUNS ARE BAD

We're not going to preach to you about how bad guns are, it's a simple fact that guns are dangerous, guns kill and guns shouldn't be pointed at someone lightly. Guns will come into play and 'combat' will crop up frequently, but the Doctor hardly ever (we won't say never, as he has once or twice in his 2000 years) aims a gun at his foes.

Guns and other weapons should be treated just as they are in real life – as something to be feared and regarded with care. Actual gunfire is incredibly loud and terrifying. Getting hit is not like they portray in those action movies – it is likely to result in a lot of

blood, passing out, going into shock or worse. You're not going to be able to take a bullet hit like a Cyberman. The bad guys will frequently resort to guns and violence, but there are many ways to stop them from pulling the trigger, and plenty of things your character can do if you're not used to handling guns.

Plan Ahead: The best way to avoid a getting into a gunfight is to make sure the situation doesn't come to shooting. Simply avoid the fight. There are many ways of doing this, especially if your character isn't a gun loving soldier. If you're a scientist or good with technology, you could come up with a great way to make the enemy's weaponry ineffective. Remember when the Doctor boarded the Dalek Emperor's ship to rescue Rose? Walking around a Dalek ship is going to get you killed. Knowing what they were up against, Captain Jack modified the Slitheen tribophysical waveform macro-kinetic extrapolator to create a forcefield that surrounded the TARDIS allowing the Doctor to talk to the Daleks without worrying about being exterminated before he could speak. You could create a gadget to jam frequencies, to temporarily blind the opponent or something similar.

Hide and Sneak: Another way to avoid conflict is to not be seen. There's nothing quite as exciting as sneaking around an alien installation trying not to be discovered. It's tense, and provides great dramatic opportunities as you sneak from room to room, avoiding the patrols, sensor arrays and guards. Knowing that you have to go into a heavily fortified location doesn't mean you have to 'tool up' and go in all guns blazing with a team of UNIT commandos at your side. That's not what the Doctor would do. It doesn't mean you can't do this, however it may be safer to find a way to sneak in, get what you need, and try to sneak out before you are discovered rather than risk casualties on both sides from a frontal attack.

Talking Down: "Hold it. Before you shoot, before you do something you may regret, listen to me..." The Doctor has done this on many occasions, talking a hostile foe down from the brink of opening fire. Whether it is purely to distract the enemy, or to convince them of the errors of their ways, it is handled in just the same way as any other Conflict resolution.

If you've been discovered sneaking in and your gadgets are ineffective, there's one thing you can always rely upon – you can always try to talk your way out of the situation. As you'll have seen in the Extended Conflict section (see pg.80), 'Talkers' go before 'Fighters', so before the guns start firing you can always try to convince them of a better solution rather than pulling the trigger.

If successful, the character's speech is convincing enough to halt the enemy before they fire, even if it is just for a moment. How successful they are in the

roll dictates how well they do talking down, whether it is a brief respite giving them chance to think of something else, or getting the enemy to lower their weapons. It may be that this is the lesser of two evils, allowing the character to be captured rather than be killed; after all, you can always try to escape later, not something you can do if you've been exterminated.

Distraction: It may be that instead of getting them to stop shooting at you, you could try to distract the enemy long enough for you to make your escape. This could be as simple as pointing at someone else and telling them they have the wrong guy (though this just gets someone else into trouble, not something the Doctor would do) to blinding the opponents momentarily – or something else that allows you to get away.

Take the Guns out of the Equation: Of course, if there are no guns, there's nothing to worry about. Weapons are pretty dangerous so if you can make them ineffective then the enemy is going to have to think of something else to do rather than shoot at you. Unfortunately, the Doctor has discovered that it is often the other way around – bullets are rarely effective against the creatures that are encountered. Create forcefields, use perception filters (if they can't see you they won't need their guns) or draw the enemy somewhere where gunfire attracts the wrong sort of attention... like the police.

Call the Police: As Banto asked in his DVD store, why doesn't anyone just go to the police? Sure, it's not much of an option on an alien world, but on present day Earth the sound of gunfire is bound to alert the authorities. This can be handy if you're unarmed and about to be attacked by gun-wielding aliens. Not so good if you're the ones doing the shooting. If the situation is bad enough, you may end up having to answer to UNIT.

Surrender: He who turns and runs away may get shot in the back! It may just be easier in some circumstances to give in and let yourself be captured. You can always work out a plan to escape later, or even plan in advance for such an eventuality.

Diving for Cover: Sometimes the best thing to do is just hit the dirt, throw yourself behind something suitably solid and hoping for the best. Often this can provide you with those valuable seconds that can give you time to think of Plan B.

If the enemy opens fire before you can distract them or talk them out of it, all you can do is dive for cover or run away. The Doctor may have powers beyond our imagination, but even he is not bulletproof (though he has been known to use his Sonic Screwdriver to create a wall of sound to stop bullets). When the bullets (or lasers) start flying, the characters can use their Coordination and Athletics (and any suitable trait). If they beat the enemy's attempt at hitting with their weapons, the characters successfully make it to cover.

Running for your life!: When faced with unstoppable numbers, and an unbeatable force, sometimes the best thing you can do is just run away. At least it gives you a second chance at defeating the villains. Running away is probably the easiest of options, though if the enemy is persistent it can lead to a dramatic chase (see Chases on pg.98) or having to dodge weapon-fire while running (see 'Diving for Cover' on the opposite page).

Shooting back: Desperate times call for desperate measures, and while the Doctor hardly ever takes up arms against any living thing, his companions have frequently needed to return fire on encroaching aliens. This is certainly the case when it comes to UNIT or those trigger-happy Torchwood employees.

If a character is going to resort to violence, they have a couple of choices when it comes to firearms. They can lay down a covering (or 'suppressive') fire at the enemy. This means they're not really aiming at them, just in their general direction. It is unlikely that they'll hit the enemy, but the gunfire will have them diving for cover. This is almost 'intimidating' the opponents into hiding by shooting at them. The targets will have to resist with a Strength + Resolve roll to have the guts to poke their heads above cover to act back.

On the other hand, the characters may decide that the only option left to them is to try to hit the enemy. If this is the case, it is best resolved with an Extended Conflict (see pg.80).

Of course, just because some of your group are shooting at the enemy, it doesn't mean that the less combative characters can't be doing something else. While Captain Jack was barricading the floors from the Daleks and shooting at the metal menace with the survivors of Satellite 5, the Doctor was busy building the Delta Wave Projector. While the fighters are holding off the enemy, the others can be doing plenty of things, like tending to the wounded, working on a way out, cobbling together technological devices, breaking into computer systems or other helpful actions.

DUCK AND COVER

Hiding behind things is probably the safest bet when the bullets are flying and the death rays are turning folks into an electric shade of blue. Cover provides two advantages - one is that it is harder to hit the small area that is exposed, and the second is that the cover provides protection against injury.

Imagine how much of the character is visible, and how much is behind cover. The more of the character that is hidden, the harder it is for the attacker to hit them. If they are aiming specifically for the exposed areas, they suffer a modifier to hit the smaller target.

HOW MUCH IS BEHIND COVER?	MODIFIER TO HIT THE EXPOSED TARGET
1/3 - Low boxes, or kneeling	-2 modifier to hit
2/3 - Head and shoulders visible, target laying on floor	-4 modifier to hit
Completely behind cover	-10 modifier to hit

If the attacker isn't aiming specifically for the exposed area, and just shooting at the target, there's a chance they will hit but the cover will get in the way.

How much protection does it offer?
Shooting someone who is behind some form of protection reduces the amount of damage they take. It all depends upon how tough the cover is – some objects can only take so much damage before it is destroyed or before damage starts going through.

As before, determine how much of the target is behind cover, and use the Random Location Table (see "Where Does It Hurt?" on pg.86). If that part of them is exposed, they are hit as normal. If the location is behind cover, then that location could be hit if the damage is enough to go through the protection of the cover (see table below).

Example: If Robin Hood is shot by a Robot Knight's disintegrator for 4 points of damage while ducking behind a wooden palisade, the fence 'absorbs' 1 point of damage, and Robin takes the remaining 3 points. The fence he is using as cover can only take another 4 points of damage before it is considered destroyed.

If he was hiding behind a castle wall, he would take no damage as its armour protection is greater than the damage done, however, the disintegrator would take 4 points off of the wall.

If the cover is very large, and the chances of hitting any part of the target behind the cover is minimal, the Gamemaster may suggest the use of Story Points to even get a hit in!

Armour
Just like cover, armour works in the same way, reducing the amount of damage taken. This armour normally only protects against bullets or other physical weapons. Laser or other high energy weapons (anything with a Lethal (L) damage) will cut right through it, although protective forcefields will defend against everything.

Alien armour, such as Dalekanium and the forcefields that Daleks employ are covered in **Chapter Five: All the Strange, Strange Creatures.**

ARMOUR TYPE	ARMOUR PROTECTION
Leather Jacket	1
Bulletproof vest	4
SWAT Body Armour	8
Full Metal Plate (Medieval armour)	8

COVER TYPE	ARMOUR PROTECTION	DAMAGE IT CAN TAKE BEFORE IT IS DESTROYED
Wood	1	5
Brick Wall	10	50
Concrete Wall	15	70
Steel Wall	30	250

OTHER SOURCES OF INJURY

Swords, firearms and physical conflict are not the only way to get hurt in this dangerous universe. What happens if a character accidentally falls or if they're cornered by fire in a trap set by the evil villain?

Falls: Falling can result from failing at climbing something, failing to jump over a gap or around obstacles. The distance fallen determines how much damage taken from hitting the ground. If they've just fallen from tripping over something, they're not really going to take any damage – at least not physical damage. The Gamemaster may stun the character if they fail particularly badly, if they hit their head or something.

Damage from falling any distance is easy to calculate as well. For every metre your character falls, the value of the damage is 1. So if you fall five metres, the damage value is 5. This is the value for failing a Climb, Jump or Running roll with a Bad result, it will be halved if the result was a Failure or multiplied by 1.5 if you get a Disastrous. This reflects something breaking your fall, managing to land on a ledge (albeit a little painfully), catching yourself on the way down or, in the case of a Disastrous Result, landing particularly badly or on something sharp.

Crashes: Most vehicles are designed to protect the passengers (with the exception of bikes, and other forms of transport where the driver is exposed). If the character hits something at speed, or is hit by something travelling at speed, the damage is equal to the number of Areas it travelled in the last action. For example, getting hit by a car that was travelling 8

Areas in its action does 8 points of damage (on a Bad result when trying to avoid it; halved for a Failure, or x1.5 for a Disastrous). Passengers in a vehicle that hits something suffer the same damage, but reduced by the armour protection of the car. If the car that was travelling at 8 Areas then hits a brick wall, if the car provided 4 levels of armour protection (see vehicles, on pg.111), each passenger takes 4 levels of damage.

Drowning: Drowning, like falling, is the result of failing a roll. This time it comes from failing at swimming or holding your breath in a flooded area. Not being able to breathe, unless you're indestructible like Jack, is pretty bad and will usually be a fatal experience.

A Bad result will mean the character sustains 8 levels of damage (usually to Strength and Resolve). A Failure reduces this to 4 which would mean that you've swallowed a lungful of water, choked a little and have hurt yourself but you're OK to try again. Disastrous result is Lethal, so let's hope you have some Story Points left...

If you're trapped in a flooded room or location, you're going to take this damage every ten seconds or so, so you're going to have to find a way out quick. The Gamemaster may be lenient and have the character black out to be recovered by the villains, waking up as their prisoner.

Fire: Fire's a tricky one, as it can depend upon how big the fire is. The way we'll handle it is actually avoiding catching on fire yourself. This way, you can run through a burning building, fight back a blaze, try to put out a burning document that has been thrown into an open fireplace – it's all handled the same way.

The Gamemaster will change the difficulty if the fire is particularly intense, but a failure means that you've caught fire in some way – an item of clothing has caught alight, or worse. A Disastrous result is Lethal, as it doesn't take long for the flames to totally engulf a person. A Bad or Failure result means that you've managed to put out the fire after suffering some burns, reducing the damage to 8 or 4 respectively. Again, Story Points are going to be the lifesaver in this situation.

Extreme Cold/Heat: Cold is all about exposure with the Gamemaster assigning a damage level depending upon how extreme the temperature is. Characters will have to make rolls using their Strength and any suitable skill (usually Survival, modified by traits) to avoid exposure. This may have to be repeated every hour (or more often if the temperature is suitably frosty, such as the surface of Volag-Noc), the character gradually losing attributes until they freeze to death.

The same effect can be used for exposure to extreme heat, like being caught in the open under the hot desert sun or exposed to the heat and magma of Pyrovilia. Again, the Gamemaster will assign a damage level depending upon how hot it is, and Strength + Survival rolls are required to avoid taking damage from the heat.

EXTREME COLD / HEAT

TEMPERATURE	DAMAGE
Above 55°C	5 every 5 minutes
Above 45°C	3 per hour
Above 30°C	1 per day
Below -5°C	1 per day
Below -20°C	3 per hour
Below -40°C	5 every 5 minutes

These figures are approximations based on exposure without the correct clothing or protective gear. The Gamemaster should feel free to adjust these figures or make up their own to suit the situation.

Radiation: Radiation is nasty stuff, invisible and deadly. It's rare that characters will encounter sources of high radiation, but here are some guidelines just in case the characters stumble into a nuclear power plant that has been set to meltdown by the vengeful younger brother of a Time Agent.

Radiation is measured in rems (or Roentgen Equivalent in Man, who said games weren't educational?). The higher the rems received, the more severe the damage. For example, an unshielded power plant core gives out around 500 rems per hour, a nuclear fallout cloud around 1000 rems per hour, and being at a nuclear plant when there's an accident you're looking around 2000 per hour. Exposure to any of these levels for an hour is usually fatal without a radiation suit (which halves the dosage). Even then, under 500 rems and you're taking 12 points of damage an hour (on a Bad result, half of that on a Failure to 6, or 1.5 on a Disastrous to 18) and looking forward to weeks of hospital treatment to recover.

Vacuum: Without a spacesuit, going out into the vacuum of space is a one way trip to doomsville. Science fiction writers constantly argue over whether being exposed to vacuum results in suffocation, explosive decompression, instantly freezing due to the cold of space or cooking from unprotected exposure to the sun. However, we've seen that it's not as violent a death as some would have us believe, and exposure to vacuum is treated like drowning (see above). A Disastrous result at holding your breath (remembering to exhale first) while you're exposed to vacuum is Lethal, Bad or Failure results in 8 or 4 levels of damage respectively as the lungs struggle against the pressure. This will have to be repeated every thirty seconds with a Difficulty that gets harder every time (you can't hold your breath forever!).

⚙ LOSING A MENTAL CONFLICT

It's not just physical threats that can harm our heroes. There are many terrors out there that can sap the will or invade the mind. In most of these cases, this will be conducted just as any other Conflict. It can be as simple as failure resulting in being mentally controlled, scared, possessed or worse. In more detailed mental Conflicts, characters take 'damage' from the encounter, just like a physical Conflict. The only difference is the damage inflicted is temporary.

Mental damage is inflicted just like physical damage, but using Ingenuity or Resolve instead of the Strength attribute. The Gamemaster may apply bonuses if weapons are used such as a MITRE headset or other mind-bending equipment. Damage is usually taken from the character's Resolve, until it reaches 0 and the character has lost his will to resist or falls unconscious. This 'damage' is restored quickly afterwards, though the effects of losing may be longer-lasting if they've been subjected to possession or mind control, sometimes gaining Bad Traits if the effects are severe enough.

GETTING SCARED

It is not hard to get scared when facing the unspeakable horrors of the universe and it's not just the innocent villager who gets terrified out of their wits. Many of the aliens the characters will encounter are just plain terrifying, and it'll be a brave individual who doesn't stand there quaking in fear.

Facing something scary is simply another Conflict. If the alien is particularly scary, it will have the Fear Factor trait that'll modify the monster's Resolve and Presence. The character facing it will have to beat these with their own Resolve and Ingenuity, modified by any suitable trait like 'Brave'. Remember, the Fear Factor trait doesn't come into effect unless the creature is **actively** scaring the character.

If the character wins, they may be scared but they're able to continue as normal. However, if they fail against the creature, it the character can do very little other than stand there and scream. Failing by a lot, a Bad or Disastrous result, and the character may faint, run away or suffer from horrible nightmares for months.

Example: *Clara is walking through the vaults of the Bank of Karabraxos, wondering where the Doctor has got to. As she turns a corner, she spies the Teller, sniffing out the guilty. She's scared, having seen what it can do, and makes a Resolve + Ingenuity roll against the Teller's Resolve + Presence. The Teller hasn't seen her, so its Fear Factor trait doesn't come into play. She succeeds and prepares herself to sneak across the corridor and away. The Teller senses her, and turns. It roars at her, and Clara stands in abject terror. She needs to make the roll again, as it has seen her and is actively scaring her, getting the bonus from its Fear Factor! Clara gets a Failure on her roll and can do nothing but stand there, terrified!*

FREEZE!

In many of the Doctor's adventures there are moments when things happen that are so mindboggling that people just stand there and stare. For example, the characters encounter a group of people intent on taking over the world. The stand face to face with the villains when they reach to their foreheads and unzip their skin-suits! The shake off their disguises to reveal a group of Slitheen!

In the game, the players would usually take those 5-10 seconds of dramatic reveal as an opportunity to run, attack or do something while the aliens were helpless and busy wriggling out of their skinsuits. It is during these shocking and dramatic moments that the Gamemaster can demand that the player characters freeze. They're stunned into inactivity while the reveal happens.

Character who wish to act can spend a Story Point to do so, as long as it doesn't upset the Gamemaster's plans for the adventure. As long as the characters are in no danger while this reveal occurs, it makes things more dramatic.

BEING POSSESSED

There are many alien beings in the universe that can take over a character, controlling their every action and thought. The living sun in the Torajii system could turn people into homicidal agents of its vengeful thoughts, and the Beast took over Toby Zed on Sanctuary Base 6 to become the living vessel of the its consciousness.

Defending yourself against an alien presence that is trying to control your mind is a normal Conflict,

with the alien's Resolve + Convince resisted by the character's Resolve + Ingenuity (if a battle of wits) or Strength (if a battle of pure mental power). Any applicable traits can modify the attributes of each side. If the character wins, they retain their control and sanity. If the character fails they can opt to spend Story Points to retain control. If they're out of Story Points, the alien will take control, and the Gamemaster will dictate what they wish to do.

There may be moments when the character can retain control for a couple of seconds – stopping themselves from pulling that trigger, trying to tell the others what the alien's evil plans are or how to defeat it. It's not easy, but the Gamemaster may allow you to do this if it fits the story.

How to shake the thrall of the alien? It's going to cost Story Points, but if you're already possessed it probably means you've already run out of Story Points, so you're going to have to get them from your friends. They can donate Story Points: a rousing speech of support, a meaningful dialogue to remind you of who you are, anything that might bring you back to your senses may help.

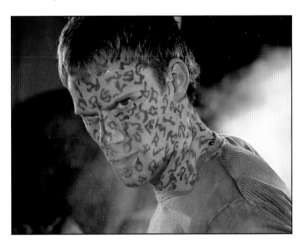

⊗ LOSING A SOCIAL CONFLICT

Sometimes you simply lose an argument. Losing doesn't mean that you suffer physical damage, but you may lose face or respect in the eyes of others, or just fail to persuade the opponents to your way of thinking. A Disastrous result in an argument might mean that you'd pause for a while and possibly even contemplate their side of the argument.

Imagine the Conflict is a fistfight, only using brains and words instead of brute strength and fists. The Conflict runs as a combat, only the players use suitable oratory or mental skills instead of Fighting and Marksman. They can dodge, just like a fight, using their skills. They will also take 'damage' just as if they've been punched!

This is temporary damage, and it reduces the character's attributes (usually Resolve) for the duration of the combat, just like actually getting hurt. When the character's attributes get low, they react in just the same way as being injured but their injuries are to their pride, thoughts and social standing. They can turn and run away, or they can fight until their attributes reach 0 – at which point they have lost and will be completely convinced, persuaded or humiliated by their opponent. The damage to their attributes is then restored, but a severe humiliation or loss will result in a change in the way people act around you. Major damage like this can result in gaining Bad Traits. The actual amount of damage done is based on the character's Ingenuity (if a battle of wits) or Presence (if charm or charisma is involved). Just like a physical fight, every level of the attribute is a level of damage they can inflict in a social Conflict.

Example: *Kate Stewart and Osgood are attempting to renew humanity's peace accord with the Zygons, with the Doctor keeping a careful eye on proceedings. This is a Social Conflict, with each side using their Presence + Convince, against their opponent's Resolve + Convince. The terms are argued back and forth, with each side reducing the other's Presence or Resolve until one is reduced to 0. At this point, the debate calms down and everyone's attributes are restored as they reach a decision – the loser agreeing to the terms.*

⚙ HEALING

Most of the time, injuries or reduced attributes will be restored to normal between adventures. Time passes, you get better and recover from your wounds.

Some wounds are severe, and if the character has lost a lot of Attribute Points, the Gamemaster may give

them a Bad Trait. For example, losing a lot of Resolve due to being scared at a particular moment, trapped in the enemy ship in the dark with aliens crawling around, the Gamemaster may let them recover their Resolve between adventures, but the experience was so traumatic that they have developed the Phobia (Darkness) trait. This will almost certainly happen if an attribute has been reduced to 0.

If medical aid is at hand and you need to get back into the action as quickly as possible, someone with the Medicine skill can try to patch the character up. A successful Medicine roll will 'heal' an injury, restoring levels of attributes that have been lost. For a Success, 1 level is restored, 2 for a Good and 3 points for a Fantastic. The Gamemaster may apply modifiers if the injuries are severe or when treating someone with an unfamiliar biological make up.

This sort of medical assistance can only be done once for each injury. That is, if you are injured from a fall, reducing your Coordination by 1, someone can try to patch you up and restore that missing level. If they fail, it cannot be attempted again until the character sustains another injury. However, if you receive a further 2 points of injury and your resident medic gets a Fantastic result, you will have all 3 points of injury restored.

Without medical aid, or after aid is given, natural healing is at a rate of 1 level of attribute per day of full rest – that is, nothing more strenuous than making a cup of tea.

Normally, when one adventure ends, any injuries are healed and attributes are restored to normal. However, there are exceptions – if the Gamemaster is planning a two or three part story, where very little time passes between, injuries will be kept, or only partially healed at the Gamemaster's discretion.

MULTIPLE INJURIES AND REDUCED ATTRIBUTES

There could be a time when the character has lost a lot of points. When an attribute reaches 0, the character is unable to do anything related to that attribute.

Zero Awareness

One or more of the character's senses have been temporarily impaired, leaving them unable to move around on their own. They're so dazed they cannot interact properly with their environment. They may be unaware of what is going on around them and may be unable to communicate.

Zero Coordination

The character will be flailing around as if they'd had one too many at the local pub. They'll keep falling over or tripping over the slightest thing, over reaching for items, knocking everything over. Probably best just to sit down and hope to recover.

Zero Ingenuity

This is not one that'll drop very often, but when it does it will mean the character is so tired or confused they're unable to think sensibly or come up with any ideas. They may do foolish things, like blindly following foolhardy orders or believe what people say unquestioningly.

Zero Presence

The character will probably be unconscious, unable to talk or communicate until revived by medical means or given time to recover. If remaining conscious, they will refuse or be unable to communicate with anyone, shunning contact with others, as everyone seems threatening.

Zero Resolve

The character has given up completely, admitted defeat and will sit around not really wanting to do anything. They become open to suggestion and likely to do anything they're told. If inundated with suggestions or orders they may react badly to the overwhelming instructions, striking out at everyone nearby.

Zero Strength

The character will collapse to the floor, unable to even stand. The character will have to be carried and will probably not have enough strength to defend or help themselves.

Hitting 0 in an attribute is pretty bad, and it may be that your character may develop a Bad Trait to reflect the lasting effects. Reach 0 in more than one attribute and things get serious. If three or more attributes reach 0, not only will the character be almost unable to do anything, they're so badly injured that there is a good chance that they'll die.

DYING OR LEAVING THE TARDIS

Without Story Points to save you, taking too much damage can be fatal and an unlucky hit from a 'Lethal' class weapon will put an end to the character's

adventures. If that seems harsh, the Gamemaster can just have the character be knocked unconscious and captured, or allow another character to spend Story Points on their behalf, pushing them out of harm's way.

However, if the character suffers multiple injuries and three or more of their attributes have been reduced to 0, there's a good chance they may be killed. If this is the case, the Gamemaster can offer the player a deal – the character gains the Unadventurous Bad Trait, in return for a Story Point that'll heal some of the character's health (see It Was Just a Scratch! on pg.104). The character will still be unconscious and likely captured, but alive.

The Unadventurous trait reflects the character's dislike of constantly being injured in their travels. They will continue, but the dissatisfaction will soon become evident. If this happens again, the Unadventurous trait can be increased from a Minor to a Major Bad Trait as the constant threat to their life takes a further toll on their adventuring spirit. If the Unadventurous trait grows higher than a Major Trait, the character will leave. They will ask to be returned home, or will settle somewhere that they will be happy, and leave the game. The player should then create a new character.

Although companions can die, more often they leave the TARDIS through their own choice or circumstances that the Gamemaster develops with the player to 'write them out'. It doesn't mean they won't return briefly in the future, but their return will be limited. If the original character died in a suitably heroic way, the player's new character may receive additional Story Points at character creation, or other bonuses, to reward such a great sacrifice in the name of a good story.

⚙ CHASES

The Doctor once remarked that being scared was a superpower, allowing you to fight harder, to run harder. And there's an awful lot of running to be done in the Doctor's adventures. So how do you keep track of everyone running around, and how do you know if the characters have escaped their pursuers?

MOVEMENT

Most of the time, you can move from one place to the next without any problem. No need to use those dice, though there are certain instances when moving about is difficult, or when you're being pursued.

When movement is important, we start to discuss things in Areas. Most of the time the actual size of an Area isn't important. They can mean different sizes depending upon the situation, from around 3m x 3m if you're on foot, to 30m x 30m if driving cars, or even larger when in space. You can move as many Areas as your effective Speed.

On foot, your Speed is equal to your Coordination. So if your Coordination is 3, you can move 3 Areas on foot. Simple! Some traits modify this, such as Run for your Life! or Slow (common in 'stomping' villains like the Cybermen).

If you're in a Vehicle, your Speed is equal to the speed of the vehicle plus your Coordination. More details of vehicles and their speeds can be found with the equipment (see pg.111).

If the path is without barriers, obstacles or other problems, then moving is pretty easy and you don't need to roll. Simple obstacles, such as low pipes, slippery floor or the sudden appearance of a cat jumping out in front of you will need a roll, Coordination + a suitable skill – Athletics if you're running, Transport if you're in a vehicle.

You can go faster than your Speed as well, but it'll require a roll (again, Coordination + either Athletics or Transport). If you succeed, you increase the number of Areas you move depending upon the Result (+1 for a Success, +2 for a Good or +3 for Fantastic!). If you fail, you've tripped or scraped the vehicle and it's slowed you down – that's the risk you take for pushing yourself a little too far. You reduce the number of Areas you travel an equal amount for the failure (-1 for a Failure, -2 for a Bad, or -3 for Disastrous). On top of that, a Disastrous Result could mean that your vehicle, or yourself, takes some damage from crashing or tripping over.

TERRAIN MODIFIERS

The way forward isn't always open roads and clear skies. Indeed, most Chases take place on busy streets, in forests at the heart of a starship or through miles of twisting and complex corridors. Terrain can make the Chase more complicated, but it can give the players additional ideas and opportunities to shake their pursuers, or to catch up to their target.

Using different terrain shouldn't slow the game down, though. Terrain is a simple Difficulty that the movers will have to beat to try to go faster than their normal Speed. Trying to go faster on an average street is Difficulty 12, for example, but trying to go faster on ice is far more treacherous and is Difficulty 21.

Failure means that the terrain has slowed them down in some way, whether this is due to traffic, or a difficult surface. A Disastrous result could mean that they have crashed, bashed their head on a low pipe, slipped on the ice or something similar.

TERRAIN	DIFFICULTY
Open Road	6
Open ground, field	9
Average street, normal traffic, pedestrians	12
Busy street, stairs, undergrowth, rock quarry	15
Rush hour traffic, forest, ladders, loose rubble	18
Swamp, mountains, ice	21

PURSUIT!

Chases are a simple case of comparing how fast the two (or more) people are moving. If you make a line of Areas, you can place miniatures, jelly babies or counters on them to represent the characters. In the back of this book you'll find photocopiable Area squares that you can cut out, draw on obstacles or plot out maps, or you could use Post-Its or beer mats. Most Chases will start with the various people 2 or 3 Areas away from each other, but it'll depend on the situation and how the Chase starts.

A Chase is an Extended Conflict. The winner gets away or catches up, depending on where they are in the Chase. If the way is tricky, there can be modifiers, however, Chases are meant to be played fast, quick and exciting, so the rules are designed to be as simple as possible. If at any time, the Gamemaster decides this is slowing things down, ignore the rules and run with it. However, if it is important to resolve an outcome of a Chase in detail, the following rules should break it down into a simple, yet exciting series of action rounds.

Each action round, simply compare the Speeds of both characters involved. Look at the Speed of the person running away, and take away the Speed of the person pursuing them.

Let's look at an example to explain it all. Courtney Woods is running away, being chased down the corridors of Coal Hill School by the Skovox Blitzer. Her Coordination is 3, the Skovox Blitzer has 2. There's a difference of 1, so every round, Courtney will increase the gap between them by one Area.

However, both sides can make rolls to push themselves a bit faster. Continuing the example, the Skovox Blitzer lurches forwards and tries to increase its Speed, and Courtney will have to do the same. The terrain is normal, so the Difficulty starts at 12. The Skovox Blitzer rolls Coordination + Athletics, getting a Success, so it gets +1 to its Speed this time, increasing it to 3. Courtney rolls her Coordination + Athletics as well, getting a Good Result, so she gets +2 on her Speed, increasing it to 5. Despite the Skovox Blitzer pushing itself, Courtney has managed to increase the gap between them by 2 Areas this round.

If the number of Areas between the characters is reduced to 0, then the pursuer has caught up with the pursued. If the number of Areas between them increases over 6, then the pursuant usually escapes.

In some circumstances, where visibility is particularly poor, this may be reduced (such as a busy city centre). The same goes for the reverse, in open space or the countryside, where you can see the target a long way off, the number of Areas required to escape may be increased at the Gamemaster's discretion.

RUNNING ORDER

If you'll pardon the pun, sometimes you need to know who goes when in a Chase. Most of the time, it is just a matter of comparing Speeds and seeing if there is any ground gained or lost between the parties involved. This happens simultaneously.

However, if one of the people involved decides to pull a Stunt (see below), or open fire during the Chase, then the person with the highest Awareness goes first. Yes, Awareness, not Coordination. You may be faster, but most of the time things are happening quickly and you'll need your wits about you, so being able to notice what's going on in the heat of a Chase will give you the advantage. Whoever has the highest Awareness can act first (or choose to go second if they think it'll be an advantage).

COMBAT IN CHASES

You've seen the cool action movies where they shoot at each other while careening down multi-laned streets with traffic weaving between them. They make it look easy, but it's not. However, characters can shoot at each other while engaged in a Chase. Shooting at a target ahead while running or driving

is easier than shooting behind. Remember, they will have used their action running or driving, so will have a -2 penalty before taking into account that the target will be moving (another -2 penalty, or more if they are in vehicles travelling at very different speeds, and another -2 if shooting behind them). It's not going to be easy to hit them, so the best bet is to try to catch up or force them to stop.

STUNTS: DOING SOMETHING CRAZY

There's nothing like doing something crazy to make a Chase more exciting. If you're feeling daring, you can opt to perform a 'Stunt'. It can be anything that has a bit of danger involved, from vaulting over a fence when running on foot, driving your motorcycle on the pavement or driving a car through a shopping mall or the wrong way down a motorway. The crazier the Stunt, the more difficult it is going to be, however if you're successful it could mean a quick escape. The player can determine what it is, as well as the Difficulty of the Stunt. The player will have to beat this Difficulty to perform the Stunt – failing this and the Stunt goes wrong and they risk crashing or tripping over. If they succeed, the NPC will have to repeat the Stunt to keep up, at the same Difficulty. Any difference in success levels (Fantastic, Good or Success) between those performing the Stunts can widen or shorten the distance between them by as many Areas as the difference.

Example: *Two Spider Germs are chasing Clara through the moonbase. The corridors are filled with junk but the Spider Germs are keeping up.*

Clara decides she'll have to do something drastic to shake them, doubling back and leaping over a stack of crates. She's quick and dextrous, and decides that she'll be easily able to make a jump over the obstacle, knocking things over to block her pursuers way. Clara's player, Samuel, suggests to the Gamemaster, Peter, that the Difficulty of the task should be 17. Peter agrees, and Clara has to succeed to perform the Stunt. She rolls, adds her Coordination + Athletics (and spends a Story Point just to be sure), and easily leaps over with a Good result. The first Spider Germ reaches the tumbling crates and has to beat the same Difficulty. It succeeds, but only just with a Success. The second doesn't make it, getting a Bad result. The crates pin it to the ground. That's one of the two Spider Germs out of the picture (she'll have gained 4 Areas on this Spider Germ, and then it will spend next action extricating itself from beneath the crates). Clara's roll was a level higher than the Spider Germ that made it through, which means that she's widened the gap between them by one additional Area.

You can try many Stunts to get away. You could try evading, jumping or turning down a side alley, hoping the pursuers fail to see where you went. Or stopping completely to hide somewhere (turning the Chase into a Conflict to hide – though you need to be far enough away that the pursuers don't see you trying to hide), or performing the wildest Stunts imaginable like jumping over rooftops, darting in front of a train, or other dangerous moves. The risks may mean that the Difficulty is high enough to deter your pursuers, but it may be so hard that you fail and put your own life at risk!

COOPERATING IN A CHASE

Of course, if there are multiple people involved in the Chase each should roll separately. This way, if someone is particularly slow, there's a good chance that they'll be caught. It'll be up to the rest of the group to see if they hold back and wait for them. If someone is slow and holding the group up, they can act as a whole, with the faster characters helping the slower ones to escape. In this case, the characters all roll separately as before, but the slow character can be helped along with the other characters, providing a bonus using the Cooperation rules (see pg.76).

Example: *Madame Vastra, Jenny and Strax are running from a group of Clockwork Robots, however Madame Vastra has twisted her ankle and her Coordination (and therefore her Speed) has been reduced to 1. Strax and Jenny aren't pushing themselves, so they don't have to roll; instead they*

help Vastra along so their Speed is reduced to match hers. Vastra is pushing herself to move faster, rolling her Coordination + Athletics, gaining a +4 bonus from Strax and Jenny helping her to run. She gets a Good result from her roll, adding +2 to her Speed, making it 3. They've gained some ground on the Clockwork Robots, but not as much as they could otherwise have.

CHASE SUMMARY

Determine Initial Distance
Determine how far away each person is, usually 2-3 Areas away

Calculate Speed for Each Person
Coordination if on foot, Coordination + Vehicle Speed if using a vehicle

Determine the Difference
Subtract the Speed of the person being chased from the Speed of the pursuer. This is the number of Areas the pursuer will gain (or lose) each action round.

Chase Actions
See if any of the participants wish to push themselves to increase their Speed, pull a Stunt or attempt Combat, and make the necessary rolls.

Determine New Distance
Reduce or increase the distance between the characters depending upon the outcome of any rolls, and see how far apart they now are. If this is less than one, they have caught up. If it is greater than six, they have escaped and the Chase is over. Otherwise, return to Stage 2 (bearing in mind the characters' Speeds may have changed due to injury or damage to the vehicle).

✸ STORY POINTS

Story Points are used to change events in a player's favour. There may be times when you hardly have to use them, or in the heat of a climatic battle with superior enemy forces, you may find that Story Points are changing hands faster than the vinegar in a chip shop. It's not just the players that have Story Points – some Villains have a number of Story Points too, which the Gamemaster can use to keep them alive longer, or so they can escape to plot another master plan that the players will have to thwart. They didn't get to their position of power only to be foiled by a player with a few strategic Story Points. They have Story Points of their own to allow them to provide a bit of a challenge at least!

You've heard the term Story Points used many times so far, and each player will have some marked down on their character sheet. Before everyone starts playing, the Gamemaster will hand out a number of tokens to each player equal to their Story Points. That way, when they spend a Story Point, they simply hand the token back to the Gamemaster rather than having to constantly rub out numbers on the character sheet. If the Gamemaster rewards the players for good play or aiding the story, he'll hand some back to you. Simple as that. But what do they do and how are they used?

SPENDING STORY POINTS

Story Points can be spent to bend the laws of reality so that characters succeed where they normally would fail, or survive where they normally would

have been killed. See, we told you they'd be useful, didn't we? Of course, it's not all spend spend spend!

Players can gain Story Points through good play, by acting in character and keeping the game running smoothly, ensuring everyone has fun. And, it's not just characters who have these Story Points. Vital items of equipment or scientific devices have points that aid in the adventure too.

Story Points can be used in many different ways. The Gamemaster will advise if it's a good or bad time to use them and, as always, the Gamemaster will have final say. The Gamemaster may also limit the number of Story Points used in any particular adventure or session. Below we suggest some uses for Story Points, explaining how they work in the game.

"I dunno... I'm stumped..."

The characters should be able to follow clues from one place to the next during the story, gradually leading them to the villains and the culmination of the plot. However, there can be times when the characters miss a clue, get stumped and simply do not know what to do next. If the players are really stuck and don't know where to go or what to do next, they can opt to spend a Story Point and the Gamemaster can give them a subtle nudge in the right direction. The character that spends the point suddenly realises the way to go and makes a suggestion to the rest of the party.

"We only get one shot at this."

If the character knows beforehand that the outcome of a particular roll is vital to their success, that the fate of the universe may revolve around that one roll, then the player might want to spend a Story Point to add a little to the roll. The character steels themselves for the task, and takes a deep breath. The character spends a Story Point and adds an additional two six-sided dice to the roll. This isn't a guaranteed success, after all you could roll two '1's – but there is a chance you could succeed phenomenally well. The player will have to judge if the task is worth spending a valuable Story Point.

If the Gamemaster agrees, for a particularly vital action that may affect everything in the game, the player may spend more than one Story Point to add an extra six-sided die for each additional Story Point spent. So if you spend 3 Story Points, you get the two extra dice from the first Story Point, and another two from the second two Story Points, meaning you'd roll four extra dice on top of the two you'd normally roll! It must be a desperate action that requires so many dice!

"That was close, nearly didn't make it!"

Failing at something can be disastrous. Worse, it can be fatal if the task is life threatening. Luckily, if you fail at a roll, you have the option to 'tweak' the result a little and succeed. This must be done straight after the roll in question – there's no jumping back in time to fix something an hour or a week later.

As soon as you know you've failed at something you have the option to spend Story Points to improve the result. A single Story Point will bump the result up one level in the character's favour. For example, a Disastrous result – which can often be fatal in a Conflict – can be bumped up one to a Bad result. A Bad becomes a Failure, a Failure becomes a Success result, and so on (see pg. 75).

If it's a truly essential roll and you simply **have** to make it, you can spend more than one Story Point at a time to succeed from a horrific fail. One point per bump in levels means that you can move from a Disastrous to a Success result with three Story Points.

The only limit in doing this is that you cannot bump a roll in your favour higher than a Success result. After all, you would have normally failed, so there's **no** spending five Story Points to get a Fantastic result. Reality can bend a little, but you can't bend it **that** far. It'd break!

Of course, you can end up spending more points than planned. Villains have Story Points as well, and it may be that a pivotal Conflict becomes a match between who is willing to spend the most Story Points to win.

Example: *Journey Blue is being chased through the corridor of a spaceship by a couple of Daleks. As she runs, one of the Daleks opens fire with a mighty shout of "Exterminate!" Journey's player, Nick, hopes to have her dive behind a bulkhead for protection, and rolls the dice, adding her Coordination + Athletics. Nick rolls and gets a meagre 8. The Dalek shoots and the Gamemaster, Peter, rolls a couple of very lucky 6s, making the Dalek's result 18. A Fantastic result for the Dalek (and a Disastrous result for Journey Blue, meaning instant extermination as the Dalek's weapon is Lethal). Rather than see Journey die in a flash of light and a glowing skeleton, Nick opts to spend Story Points to save her bacon. Nick spends 3 Story Points, bumping the Disastrous result up to a Success. The Dalek has a Story Point as well, and Peter decides that Journey shouldn't get away quite so easily – he spends the Story Point and knocks Journey back to a Failure.*

Nick doesn't want to spend another precious Story Point, and accepts the 4 levels of Damage suffered from slamming into the bulkhead awkwardly. A small price to pay for not getting exterminated!

"It Was Just a Scratch"

The rules usually mean that a character will only really receive an injury when they have run out of Story Points and cannot avoid taking damage (by spending points to bump the results as above).

However, characters may opt to accept the injury, possibly to gain Story Points for making things dramatically exciting (see 'Gaining Story Points' on pg.106).

Injuries are usually ignored from one adventure to the next, unless the Gamemaster decides that the injury is particularly severe or long term (which can sometimes involve gaining a Bad Trait). The Gamemaster may allow players to 'buy off' injuries for Story Points at suitably quiet moments or if the character needs that extra boost just before the climax, when they get their second wind. This can be particularly handy in two- or three-part adventures where the characters have little time to recover.

Every Story Point spent in this way restores half (round up this time, we'll be generous) of the attribute levels that have been lost due to injury or losing a Conflict.

Example: Danny has taken a couple of hits and last lost 5 levels of attributes from these injuries, so could spend a Story Point and recover 3 of them (2.5 rounded up). His player can decide which attributes are restored, but it should be rationalised with a suitable explanation (second wind, grim determination, five minutes sat down, nice cup of tea, or something similar).

"Doing something remarkable!"

Sometimes the Doctor does something absolutely remarkable, and his companions have been known to do the impossible when the chips are down. In this game, everything is possible, but it comes with a high price. For example, the Doctor traps the Family of Blood in various places for eternity, Rose absorbed the heart of the TARDIS to banish the Dalek fleet to dust, and the Doctor managed to escape the Pandorica by popping back in time to give Rory the Sonic Screwdriver so he could free the Doctor to allow him to go back in time to give him the Sonic Screwdriver. How could this be possible and how can you do this in the game?

In preparation for the coming game, the Gamemaster chats with the Doctor's player and they decide that the most fitting and dramatic way to deal with the Family of Blood is to give them a suitably dramatic demise. The Gamemaster and the Doctor's player do not know what that'll be yet, but they think it's going to be big, and may require a lot of Story Points for the Doctor to pull it off. The Gamemaster says he'll give the Doctor's player a whole load of Story Points to accomplish this but he'll have to do something really dramatic to earn these points. The Gamemaster has an idea for a cool adventure, turning the Doctor human for a while. It'd make a great story, add some dramatic tension and challenge the player to be someone else for a while. In return, the Gamemaster says that when the time comes, the Doctor will have a whole heap of extra Story Points that should be used to dispatch the Family at the climax.

In the other example, the Gamemaster discusses with the Doctor's player about dealing with the end of the last game session, which saw Rory turned into an Auton, Amy dead by his hand, and the Doctor trapped in the Pandorica. The Gamemaster gives the Doctor a load of extra Story Points to save the universe, with the understanding that the Doctor will have to make a massive sacrifice in the end to complete the task.

Hopefully, these examples give you an idea of how all this works, without going into too much detail with numbers and points and such. Basically, if you do something suitably dramatic, brave or selfless, that makes a great story, the Gamemaster will award you extra Story Points that can be used to do dramatic and cool things that make a great story fantastic.

"Hang on, I have an idea!"

This is where things get a little radical. Story Points allow you to bend the plot and manipulate the story to save yourself in times of need. The 'unlikeliness' of what you want to happen determines how many Story Points this costs. It could be anything: The major villain decides he won't kill the entire group because he's taken one look at Clara and fallen madly in love, or the TARDIS just happens to know where to go to rescue the rest of the group who are trapped, despite you not knowing how to pilot it. The possibilities are endless. However, the Gamemaster will have to approve, and will determine how expensive it is going

to be. They may decide that there is no way that your idea will work, but instead of the villain falling for Clara, his chief guard will as it is more likely and less upsetting to the plot. In fact, it may lead to a whole new plot twist!

"What's that you're building?"

Some objects and devices are so intrinsic to the story that they are known as Gadgets (note the capital there, it's important!). Gadgets such as the TARDIS or the Doctor's Sonic Screwdriver have Story Points that can be used by anyone who has the item.

Gadgets with Story Points can sometimes do things that they're not designed for. The Sonic Screwdriver, for example, can open doors but it can be used for so many other tasks outside of "sonic-ing and

STORY POINT GUIDELINES

Just how many Story Points should you gain or spend from a dramatic turn of events? Below are a few guidelines on how many to spend to "bend reality" or how many a character should gain for doing something that will move the story along or aid the Gamemaster's plot. In extreme and dramatic circumstances – and with the Gamemaster's approval, of course – players may spend their Story Points together to achieve suitably grandiose effects.

POINTS	EFFECT
1-2	**Tiny:** It's a small expenditure to make a change, but it's only small stuff. You remember your hat at that particular moment when not wearing a hat would have been a tremendous faux pas, or you remember where you dropped a vital piece of equipment.
3-4	**Minor:** This is still fairly expensive for your average character, but it doesn't bend reality too drastically. At that vital moment, they work out how to generate the power needed to restart the ship, or make the villain's henchman fall in love with the character, allowing them to escape later.
5-6	**Medium:** This is a pretty hefty amount for a character, but this could be a lifesaving plot twist - a squad of UNIT soldiers turn up to investigate the strange happenings, just as the characters are finding themselves outgunned, or they learn that the only way to save another character is through an extreme sacrifice of their own.
7-8	**Serious:** We're getting into real plot-changing details here. The TARDIS materialises around the characters after they have been thrown out of the ship's airlock into space, or the player agrees that their character should be captured and work for the villains as a double agent for the entire adventure.
9-10	**Massive:** It is rare that something quite as plot defining as this will boil down to spending or receiving Story Points, but this is reaching the levels of Rose absorbing the heart of the TARDIS, and the sacrifice she (and later the Doctor) makes to remove the Daleks from the universe.
11+	**Climactic:** There are few events so massively important that they would need this many Story Points, and it's rare that a character will have so many points to spare. This is up there with trapping villains for eternity in the heart of a star or rebooting the universe, and a character would have to do something serious to earn that many points, such as being trapped by an alliance of enemies in an eternal prison, or turning human and changing the character's memories to blend in (see "Doing Something Remarkable!").

entering", such as plugging the Sonic Screwdriver into a microwave oven to send a communication signal into space. Story Points spent like this come from the Gadget's Story Points, not the character's. These can be topped up by the character, or by the Gamemaster if they think it serves the plot. The Gamemaster may reward the device a bit like 'Doing something remarkable' above, if the device is removed, put in danger or temporarily destroyed as part of the story.

Wild superscience devices can be created as well with a little 'jiggery-pokery'. Devices can do fantastic things or just aid the story such as the 'Timey-Wimey Detector' or the genetic analyser that the Doctor cobbles together in Manhattan. These items have Story Points that are from the person who creates them, as if the item's creator is investing points into the device. It can also be a handy way of transferring Story Points from one character to another in times of need, by passing the Gadget on.

Further information on creating superscience devices and 'jiggery-pokery' is on pg.113.

"Like this, Doctor?"

With a little instruction, even if the character is totally unskilled at doing something they may be able to help. In this case, as long as someone has told the character what to do and how to do it, by spending a Story Point, they can do something technical that they've no skill in. This is limited to very basic things, like pressing the right sequence of buttons, cutting the right series of wires at the right time or using the Sonic Screwdriver to open doors. If you've been shown exactly what to do, you spend a Story Point and effectively have the same skill as the person who showed you how to do it, ignore the unskilled penalties, and roll using your character's attribute + the tutor's skill, as if you know what you're doing. This will only last for one specific scene, and cannot get a result higher than a Success.

Example: The Doctor needs to rush off and work on the TARDIS' engines while it spins out of control into a black hole. He tells Courtney that she needs to keep pressing a sequence of buttons (and hitting the console at the right moment) that'll control the tribophysical waveform macro-kinetic extrapolator and offset the black hole's inexorable pull. She hasn't a clue what she's doing, but after a quick lesson it looks a bit like a game she has on her smartphone. Her skill, after spending a Story Point, is equal to the Doctor's when rolling to activate the extrapolator. Courtney cannot get higher than a Success on the rolls, but it should be enough to protect the ship

while the Doctor sorts it out. If, in a later scene, she's asked to do the same again – she can spend another Story Point and be shown again what to do, or just admit that she didn't know what she was doing and was just pressing buttons randomly (which seemed to work!).

"You can do it, I know you can."

It's getting near the end of the adventure, things are getting desperate and you're out of Story Points. You know you've got a frantic dash across an open courtyard while Sontarans are shooting at you, and it's going to be almost suicidal without some Story Points. Luckily, the Doctor has loads – he's done some really daring and astounding things so far, and put himself in terrible danger to help the hopeless. If only you had some of his Story Points...

That's no problem. Characters can donate Story Points to each other to help through a particularly major moment. This can be done in many ways, a dramatic and rousing speech, a word of encouragement or even a kiss. If it's dramatic, moving, rousing and encouraging, and the other player is willing to share their Story Points to keep you going, then this should be encouraged.

GAINING STORY POINTS

The Gamemaster awards Story Points for many reasons. Often, just completing a set task will be enough to net the player a couple, though more will be awarded for making the adventure dramatic, exciting and playing 'in character'. Good roleplaying is essential, and the Gamemaster will reward this. Good roleplaying and achieving your goals (both the ones in the story and your Personal Goal (see pg.66) will not only result in gaining Story Points, but may lead to improving skills, traits or even attributes!

Making the story dramatic doesn't mean that you should be acting foolishly or recklessly, unless that is part of your character's personality and nature. Showing ingenuity, bravery and above all making the adventure (and the game as a whole) fun will be rewarded.

Have a look at a few of these examples to see how players can gain Story Points for doing something dramatic.

"I won't leave them behind!"

Heroes do heroic things, like risking their lives for their friends or putting themselves in danger to save an entire planet of innocent victims. Most of the time, the characters will be heroic in every adventure, but every now and then they will be placed in a situation where they can choose to save themselves and escape or put their own lives at risk for the sake of others. Putting the safety of innocents and their friends before themselves is what makes the characters special. Choosing to act heroically at the appropriate moment deserves reward. If the Gamemaster decides it is fitting and the character isn't acting foolishly or out of character, they will award 1-3 Story Points for their bravery.

"Captured... yet again."

Sometimes it suits the plot better to just give in and get captured, rather than force another fight. The Doctor will usually allow himself to be captured rather than resist violently. After all, you can always plot your escape later if it means that you prevent a fight where innocent people could be hurt or killed.

Giving up and getting captured, if it suits the storyline and doesn't cause major problems for the Gamemaster (it shouldn't do), will mean the character will gain one or two Story Points to use later – usually to help execute their escape!

"I can't do that, I just can't..."

Bad Traits are there for many reasons – they make the character more interesting, give them some foibles that spice them up a bit and provide restrictions to their abilities and behaviour.

A character with the Distinctive trait, for example, will act and/or dress in ways that make them stand out ("I wear a Fez now, Fezzes are cool!"), and having the Phobia (Spiders) trait, it is assumed that you will remember this fact when you come face to face with the Empress of the Racnoss. If you play to your weaknesses and remain in character, throwing in some moments every now and then that show your limitations, you will receive a Story Point (sometimes two if it is a Major Bad Trait and excellent timing for the plot). Examples include accidentally dropping something vital down a lift shaft due to your Clumsy Bad Trait, or wading into a situation without checking first due to your Impulsiveness, or refusing to allow the alien to die because of your Code of Conduct.

LOSING STORY POINTS

"As if I would ask her to kill."

Killing is wrong. Simple as that. The Doctor will not allow it and knows that killing is always the worst possible solution to any problem. Even when you have to kill from mercy or necessity, it leaves things with a bitter aftertaste and people are noticeably changed from the experience. Even during his time with UNIT, the Doctor preferred risking his own life trying to negotiate with hostile species like the Silurians, rather than greeting them with hostile force.

There will be times when the characters have to defend themselves, or times when they have to leave people behind, but the Gamemaster will know when you're doing the right thing.

However, killing in cold blood – deliberately – against unarmed opponents, is **very** wrong. If the Gamemaster feels that the character has killed someone or something that was unnecessary, they will lose ALL of their Story Points. If it is done in a particularly cold-hearted way, the Gamemaster may even deduct half of all of the other players' Story Points too, as they should have stopped you.

MAXIMUM STORY POINTS

When the characters were created they ended up with a Story Point total – this is their maximum number of Story Points between adventures. In most cases this is 12, though if the character has purchased some Special Traits this might be lower (or higher!). As the adventure progresses, the character can hold more Story Points than this, though usually this is building up to a big expenditure at the story's climax. When the adventure is over, the characters usually heal all their wounds, and if their Story Points are above their maximum, they are reduced back to 12 (or whatever their maximum is). If they have less than that, the Gamemaster will just replenish what they think is fitting depending upon how well they have played.

⚙ GROWING FROM EXPERIENCE

Sounds like one of those new-age evening classes, doesn't it? Here's where we go into detail to look at improving the characters over time.

The Gamemaster will reward good roleplaying and teamwork in many ways. It won't happen every session, but usually at the end of an adventure full of exciting gaming when the players are really getting involved and doing lots of cool stuff, the Gamemaster may reward them with the chance of improving the characters.

If they've played in character, made the game fun and exciting, and helped to tell a great story, the Gamemaster may reward them by allowing the player to increase a suitable skill, gain (or remove) a trait, or in rare cases even increasing an attribute. Such rewards are especially forthcoming if the character has, in some way, achieved their personal Goal. Here's how:

ATTRIBUTES

With exercise, practice and dedication, a character's attributes can increase. It's not easy, and isn't likely to happen very often, but with work, attributes can grow to reflect the character's development and experience in time travelling adventures and saving the universe. Increasing an attribute is very rare, but it can happen – usually no more often than once in a dozen adventures.

Has the character done enough to warrant an increase in an attribute? Have they done something that reflects the attribute in question? Have they been particularly ingenious over the last few of adventures, or have they shown great determination and drive? The attribute in question should be something that has come into play significantly over the last couple of adventures or sessions.

Increases in attributes are rare, but these increases are particularly rare in above average attributes. Travelling with the Doctor (or simply striving to make the universe a better place) usually brings out the best in people, and makes them above average. Amy was just a kissogram who went on to save the universe with her boyfriend, Rory. Attributes that are less than average (2 or worse) are more likely to be improved than those that are already above average (4 or better). However, if the Gamemaster and the player agree that an attribute has come into play a lot in recent adventures and warrants an increase, then it can be done.

People don't suddenly get stronger or smarter overnight, and this is why you need to rationalise it with the player. Maybe the increase will be the result of a story suggested by the Gamemaster or increased over time through a sub-plot that'll cover many adventures. It may take a little while, but attributes can be raised if the story permits it. Of course, if you're a normal human, your attributes can never go above 6. For alien or extraordinary characters, attributes can grow above level 6, but this is incredibly rare.

SKILLS

Skills are more likely to improve over time, but again they require some practice. Using a particular skill a lot means you're bound to get better and better at it (even if you keep failing all the time, as we do learn from our mistakes). Whereas attributes only increase maybe once in a dozen adventures, skills can improve more often, but only when it is fitting to the development of a character.

Increasing a skill cannot be done at the same time as raising an attribute, and again there should be some rationale behind it: have they shown some great skill at driving during a car chase, for example? Then their Transport skill should be increased. If you want to increase something different, you can, but players should discuss things first with the Gamemaster to try to come up with a good reason for their sudden improvement. And it's not just skills that can improve: you could gain a new Area of Expertise if you've really developed an affinity for something.

REMOVING BAD TRAITS/
BUYING GOOD TRAITS

Bad Traits are a nuisance. They can be detrimental to the character and hinder their progress. Sometimes they have been gained through injury or psychological trauma, though often they have been picked during character creation to make the character more interesting and to gain extra points. As these traits can be such a pain, it's only sensible that you may wish to remove them.

This isn't easy. It's not like you can suddenly regain the use of a missing hand (unless you've recently regenerated). The Gamemaster will listen to the request to remove the trait and together with the Gamemaster players can formulate a way to work removing the trait into the storyline of one or more adventures, whether it is gaining the technology that will remove a physical impairment, or working at their fears to overcome that particular phobia.

In a similar way, the character could develop a new Good Trait if it suits both the character and the story. In most cases, these are just Minor or sometimes Major Traits, but in rare occasions (especially if it suits the plots the Gamemaster has planned) a Special Trait can be developed. A prime example of this is Captain Jack and his indestructibility. Jack goes from being a debonair con man to Earth-defending hero and if this was part of the game, the Gamemaster could bestow Jack with the regenerative powers that Rose gives him accidentally, making him a more important character. Such major changes can unbalance the

game, and character's maximum Story Point totals may alter to reflect this.

Again, removing Bad Traits or gaining new Good Traits does not happen overnight, and only really occurs after great gaming that deserves an equally great reward.

CHANGING YOUR PERSONAL GOAL

Personal Goals are quite deep-seated in the character's personality, but it doesn't mean that they cannot change. It doesn't happen often, and will need some rationalisation with the Gamemaster. It may occur after a Goal has been satisfactorily reached, or if there's something new the character wants more. It should only happen in between adventures, and then not very often, only to reflect an important change in the character's motivation or personal storyline.

INCREASING STORY POINTS

Story Points are replenished a little in between adventures, but sometimes characters deserve a helping hand. They could be particularly brave ordinary people, but their actions deserve a reward. The Gamemaster may offer the character a boost to their Story Point limit, raising it above their usual maximum. Again, this isn't common, but sometimes great and dramatic storytelling means that their Story Point max should be raised to encourage even more dramatic storytelling.

GROWING AS A PERSON

Ignoring points, it could be that the character simply grows. Not physically (unless they're were a child when you started playing the character), but as a person. Don't forget that character development can be more than just numbers. The Gamemaster can reward the players with Gadgets, equipment, an interesting sub-plot like a romantic encounter or a spotlight adventure where their character can really shine. There are many ways a character, and the player, can be rewarded for a great bit of game playing without just increasing numbers on the character sheet.

⚙ BOYS AND THEIR TOYS

There are two kinds of item in the **Doctor Who Roleplaying Game:** Equipment and Gadgets. Equipment refers to normal items that you use, such as tools, torches and so on. Gadgets are something special, they do cool things and can be the focus of whole adventures.

EQUIPMENT

Equipment is the everyday sort of item you see around you. Nothing too important – a can opener, a map, a torch or a gun. They may be useful and help you during adventures but, aside from doing their job as a tool, they have no extra abilities and do not give the user any additional skill.

Example: If Danny's trying to open the side of a computer terminal on a spaceship, he takes out his trusty screwdriver (a normal one, not one of these fancy sonic or laser things) and has a go at opening it.

Normally, his player, Ingrid, wouldn't need to make a roll, but if there's something that makes it tricky (it's dark, or the bad guys are beating down the doors and time is of the essence), the Gamemaster, Peter, may ask for a Coordination + Technology roll. The screwdriver itself doesn't affect the roll – but it would make the task much harder, almost impossible, if he didn't have it!

The only things to look out for are vehicles (not a tremendously common thing in the Doctor's adventures) and equipment from outside of your time and technological experience. This is why each character has their place of origin and the Technology Level they are accustomed to marked on their sheet.

TECHNOLOGY LEVELS

There are times during the game that characters may encounter technology from outside of their home time period. This could be flintlock pistols, crystal computers, space ships or Bakelite radios. To help space- (and time-) faring species avoid any technological or cultural mistakes, such as arriving in the Palaeolithic Era and accidentally leaving a TV remote control behind, planets and places are labelled with a Technology Level.

As noted many times in the Doctor's adventures, Earth in the late 20th and 21st century is a Level 5 planet (see the table on pg.66).

If a character uses technology from outside their home Tech Level, they incur a penalty to the roll. Every level the technology is more advanced than the character imposes a cumulative -2 penalty. Every level the technology is below the character results in a -1 penalty (it is easier to use items from your past than it is your future).

Example: *Clara is trying to get the TARDIS to work while the Doctor isn't present. The Gamemaster normally wouldn't allow such an action as she doesn't have the Vortex trait, but she just wants to move it to another part of the building to rescue the Doctor, not to time travel. Clara is from 21st century Earth (Tech Level 5), whereas the TARDIS is Tech Level 10. That's 5 levels above her experience, so that'll be 5 x -2 penalties = -10. It's unlikely that she's going to be able to get it to work, at least not how she wants it to.*

VEHICLES

The Doctor doesn't use many vehicles. He has his TARDIS, so he's doesn't usually need any other form of transport. There was a time when he was exiled to Earth and had a couple of nice cars (Bessie, and the Whomobile), but the Doctor is a little too mobile (both in time and space) to rely on vehicles.

We'll look in greater depth at spaceships, space stations and time craft in a future expansion, but for now all we need to worry about is how fast vehicles can travel in a Chase, and how much damage or protection they can offer in a Conflict.

Vehicles have an Armour Rating and a Hit Capacity, just like forms of cover (see pg.91). These numbers tell you how much damage they can protect the occupant from, and how much damage they can take before they are destroyed. If they take more than half of their hit capacity, their effective Speed is halved as well. If its hit capacity is reduced to zero, the vehicle stops working and either crashes or comes to a stop.

When it comes to how fast a vehicle can travel, the number of Areas it travels is determined by the vehicle's Speed added to the driver's Coordination (reflecting their reaction speed). The total determines how many Areas they can travel in an action round. For example, a car has a Speed of 8, being driven by someone with a Coordination of 2, giving them a total Speed of 10.

You can go faster than the vehicle's normal Speed, but it's more difficult and you'll have to make a roll, using their Coordination + Transport (see Chases, pg.98). Some faster vehicles offer more than the usual bonus Areas. The Speed given for a vehicle like this is its best controllable Speed – vehicles can travel slower than this.

Example: *The Doctor and Strax are chasing after the Half-face Man. The Half-face Man is galloping off on a pony and trap, Strax is giving chase in his stagecoach and the Doctor is left to follow on foot.*

First action round, the Half-face Man, Strax and the Doctor all check to see how well they do in the Chase. The Half-face Man is on a pony and trap, which has a Speed of 6 to add to his Coordination. The stagecoach adds 5 to Strax' Coordination. The Doctor is still on foot so he only has a Speed of 5. The Half-face Man starts 3 Areas ahead of Strax and the Doctor. He adds his Coordination of 2 to the Speed of 6 to get a total of 8. Strax added his Coordination of 4 to the stagecoach's 5 to get 9. Every new round, Strax will catch up by 1 Area. The Doctor has a Speed of 5 from being on foot so the horses will gain 3+ Areas every round on him, so they will quickly vanish into the distance after a couple of rounds. He stops and leaves Strax to continue the chase.

With the Half-face Man 3 Areas ahead, Strax will catch up in 3 rounds. The Half-face Man can see Strax is gaining and tries to pull a Stunt to get away. He hopes to swerve around a cart of straw that is blocking the street ahead, hoping to shake Strax. He's going to leave it to the last minute, and sets the Difficulty at a tricky 15, which is going to be a long-shot. He has a Coordination of 3, Transport skill of 1, and rolls a 10 for a total of 14. He fails, the pony pulls up short and the trap smashes into a wall. At a Speed of 8 hitting the wall does half of that in damage (so, 4 levels of damage). However, Strax has to make that roll too, adding his Coordination of 4, Transport skill of 3 and a roll of 10 for a result of 17. He just makes it and swerves the stagecoach around the cart in time. The Stunt didn't work out as the Half-face Man planned – he is injured and the trap has been damaged. It has lost half of its Hit Capacity, so the trap's Speed is halved to 3.

With its vehicle damaged, Strax is going to catch up very soon.

SAMPLE VEHICLES			
VEHICLE	ARMOUR	HIT CAPACITY	SPEED
Motorcycle	0	6	8
Car	4	12	8
Truck	6	18	5

⚙ GADGETS

Gadgets are a whole different matter. They're something really special, and can do amazing things. The Doctor's Sonic Screwdriver and Psychic Paper are Gadgets, and they have a number of traits that can help your rolls. For example, if the Doctor decides to help Danny with that computer terminal, he takes out the Sonic Screwdriver and makes the same Coordination and Technology roll, adding the bonus from the Screwdriver's Open trait into the roll. Things are certainly easier with a Gadget!

OWNING A GADGET

These remarkable little items are rare to have at character creation and should be approved by the Gamemaster. Having a Gadget isn't free, Gadgets purchased in this way reduce your maximum Story Point totals, but it does mean that the Gadget is rarely lost. The good thing about getting a Gadget this way is that if it goes missing or is broken, the Gadget is assumed to be fixed or replaced at the beginning of the next adventure. After all, the Doctor's Sonic Screwdriver may overload and get fried or run out of power for an adventure, but it's working good as new in time for the next one.

This doesn't mean that the Gadget can't be removed permanently. If the Gamemaster thinks that the Gadget is being over used, or misused, it can be lost as part of the storyline, the Gadget being removed (with the character's Story Point maximum restored by the Gadget's cost). Who knows, the recovery of the item could be a whole story in itself, and maybe the players will learn not to rely on such gadgets all the time.

Gadgets come in various sizes, just like traits: Minor, Major and Special.

Minor Gadgets cost 1 Story Point and can hold a single Minor Trait. They may hold a Major Trait (or two Minor), but must take a Bad Trait to 'pay' for the extra cost, such as Restriction or One Shot. They hold 1 Story Point, and this can be used so the Gadget can do something novel or different, though the effect of this will be fairly small. Creating an item like this during the game with Jiggery-Pokery has a Difficulty of 12-18, and takes around an hour to complete.

Major Gadgets cost 2 Story Points and can hold one Major or two Minor Traits. They may hold an additional Major (or additional two Minor Traits – up to 4 points' worth in total) but will need to take a Bad Trait or two to 'pay' for the additional ability,

such as Restriction or One Shot. They hold 2 Story Points, and these can be used so that the Gadget can do something that it is not normally designed for, the effect of which can be fairly significant. Creating an item like this during the game with Jiggery-Pokery has a Difficulty of 17-21, and takes around a day to complete with the correct components.

Special Gadgets cost 4 Story Points and can hold up to 4 points worth of traits (two Major, four Minor, or any other combination). They may hold double this, but will need to take Bad Traits to pay for the additional abilities. They can hold 4 Story Points to do odd or remarkable things, with some major effect on the story. Creating an item like this during the game with Jiggery-Pokery has a Difficulty of 21+, will require the correct rare components and will take days (if not longer) to complete.

For example, the Sonic Screwdriver is a Major Gadget and has four Good Traits: Open/Close, Scan, Transmit and Weld; and two Bad Traits: Restriction (Dead Lock) and Restriction (Complex Controls). It can hold 4 Story Points, which can be used to do things that the Sonic Screwdriver hasn't done before. It costs 2 Story Points from the characters' Story Point pool if purchased at character creation (though some traits, such as Time Lord, give the character a 'free' Gadget of this worth).

JIGGERY-POKERY

The Doctor frequently cobbles together a wild gadget with a little jiggery-pokery. Whether this is creating an alien DNA scanner from a radio or a 'Timey-Wimey' detector from various household appliances, these gadgets work just the same as one gained at character creation. Characters with the Boffin trait can create these gadgets – without that Trait they'll just cobble together a non-functioning mess of wires.

When creating a Gadget in the middle of an adventure, the character needs to make an Ingenuity + Technology skill roll to ensure they have tweaked the right bits and soldered the correct connections. Then they spend enough Story Points to temporarily purchase the Gadget.

For example, the Doctor creating the 'Timey-Wimey' Detector (a Minor Gadget) is an Ingenuity + Technology skill roll with a Difficulty of 15. If the Doctor succeeds he spends a Story Point and decides what traits the Gadget has, with guidance from the Gamemaster. It's designed to scan for people being transported back in time after an encounter with the Weeping Angels, so it needs the Scan trait. The Doctor could also spend a second Story Point and give it another trait, like Transmit, if he wanted, but it's not necessary for this item. It takes around an hour to complete, and requires the use of a few household items (a tape recorder, a lunch box, and a telephone handset amongst other things).

Gadgets created this way are temporary items, and the Story Points used to create them are not deducted from the character's maximum total, just from their current points. They'll get them back in time.

More complicated items (Major, or Special Gadgets) can take a lot longer to create and can require rare and difficult to find items that will be the focus of a whole adventure. The big question to ask before going ahead with creating any of these gadgets is "Why do they need them?" If they're just making something 'cause it's cool, then that's not really good enough to warrant the time spent creating it. There needs to be a dramatic need for the item – such as the Gravity Bubble Generator that will lift a wing of Spitfires into orbit or the Perception Filter Keys used to avoid the Master.

⚙ GADGETS TRAITS

The Gadget, as mentioned above, has Good Traits that affect the character's rolls when they are used. These can be traits listed already for creating characters (see pg.29) or aliens (see pg.165), or something new. For example, a cool jetpack might award the user the Flight trait (one usually restricted to aliens with wings or hover abilities). Or, the Gadget can use one or more of the Gadget-specific traits listed below. These Gadget-specific traits can be taken by Cyborg or Robot characters as normal traits, as the trait reflects part of the machinery that makes them.

Gadgets can have Bad Traits. Usually these are restrictions on their use. For example, the Sonic Screwdriver is very handy at opening and closing things, scanning and all sorts of cool stuff, but it can't open a deadlock and it has the Restriction (Deadlocks) trait.

Traits that can be purchased multiple times are marked with an asterisk (*)

GOOD GADGET TRAITS

Bigger on the Inside
(Minor/Major/Special Good Gadget Trait)
This trait can be applied to any object with an interior space or holding area, like a bag, backpack or vehicle interior. In effect, the interior of the item is a pocket dimension of greater size than is possible for the actual volume of the object, allowing one to store vastly larger items inside, assuming they can fit through the opening.

As a Minor Good Trait the item has an interior roughly 10 times its apparent volume. As a Major Good Trait, the object holds roughly 30 times its apparent volume. Weight is still a factor in both cases, so even if you can fit a hundred gold bars into your 'magic bag' you still have to be able to lift it. As a Special Good Trait, the item has 30 times capacity and its weight is negligible. This counts as two Major Traits.

All TARDISes are assumed to have the Special version of this trait by design (even if not specified in their profile), but their interior space is infinite and the exterior is as weightless as the operator chooses.

Compress
(Minor/Major Good Gadget Trait)
A compression field squeezes molecules closer together, making things smaller. It's not dimensionally transcendent – it's a lot smellier than that! Compression fields show up in all sorts of places, from Miniscopes to the Master's Tissue Compression Eliminator to the Teselecta justice vessel to the Molecular Nanoscaler that allowed the Doctor to go inside a Dalek. The Minor Good version of this trait is a one-way shrinking – it can make big things small, but cannot unshrink them. The Major Good version can instantly shrink or unshrink a target.

Delete
(Major Good Gadget Trait)

This means that the Gadget can remove something from existence, almost like a one-way teleporter. It transforms the item into its component molecules, and records it. Usually, the item stored in its memory is deleted later, literally thrown into the object's memory trash. However, it can be stored for up to an hour and reconstructed ('digital rewind' if you like). While the Gadget is holding the item in its memory, it cannot be used to delete something else, without 'trashing' the first item zapped – it can only hold one thing at a time. The size of the object that can be deleted like this is usually up to a metre in diameter, though this can be doubled if a Story Point is spent. Items with the Delete trait usually have a safety function to prevent its use on living tissue, which can be taken as the Restriction (Living Tissue) trait.

Dimension Modification
(Major Good Gadget Trait)

The Dimension Modification trait allows a Gadget to modify the length, width, height and volume of an object to any size, large or small with little or no harm to it. The target can be made as large or small as the user likes. The effect will only last 2D6 hours unless the item is constantly trained on it and functioning.

Disable
(Minor/Major Good Trait)

The Disable trait stops another Gadget from working. As a Minor Good Trait the effect only works on one particular target – it might Disable a Dalek forcefield, or stop one sort of weapon from working within its area of effect. The Major Good Trait is more likely to drain the power from every Gadget nearby. Disable effects are usually temporary, but a One-Shot Disable may destroy its targets at the Gamemaster's whim.

Entrap
(Minor/Major Good Gadget Trait)

The Entrap trait means the Gadget is able to entangle, restrain, capture or otherwise hold a target. Entrapment is equivalent to a Stun result except it doesn't go away after 15 minutes. Instead, it remains in place until the target is released, or until they find a way to escape. As a Minor Good Trait, escape will usually be a Difficult task. As a Major Good Trait, escape is usually an Improbable task.

Forcefield
(Minor / Major Good Gadget Trait)

The Gadget can project a protective forcefield that automatically knocks any damage sustained down by a level. Damage the character or item would receive due to a Disastrous Result from the character (or

a Fantastic from the attacker) is knocked down to a Bad (or Good), and a Bad to a Failure. The Major equivalent of this trait knocks the damage down by two levels. Many repeated hits might deplete the item's Story Points until the forcefield is useless.

Innocuous
(Minor/Major Good Trait)

A Gadget with the Minor Good Trait looks like something perfectly ordinary. That Engineer's Mate looks just like a wrench until you switch it on, the Scanner's built into your bog-standard laptop, and your jeep looks completely normal until you switch it to flight mode. In fact, your Gadget won't even show up as alien technology until you're actually using it. A Gadget with the Major Good Trait has a perception filter built into it. People ignore it except when it's in active use, and sort of forget about it afterwards.

Open/Close
(Minor Good Gadget Trait)

This trait gives the Gadget the power to open locks, and to seal things shut again if necessary. If used with the Subterfuge skill to pick a lock, it gives the character a +4 bonus to the roll. Locking a door is far easier than opening it, as most locks (mechanical or electronic) tend to lock when they are tampered with, giving the character a +6 bonus if the Gamemaster decides a roll to lock the door is necessary.

Scan*
(Minor Good Gadget Trait)

The Scan trait means that the Gadget can investigate something from a range of a metre and see what's going on inside it. Whether this is a medical function, checking inside someone to see what's wrong or what species they are, or a technical function looking at the wiring and circuitry of a device, it all works on the same basic principle. In most cases, the user has to make an Awareness roll coupled with a suitable skill (Medicine for a medical or biological scan, Technology to scan the workings of a device or computer). The Scan trait provides a +2 bonus to this roll if the device is designed for general scanning.

If the Gadget is used only for a specific purpose, for example a Medical Scanner, then the trait provides a +3 bonus when used for medical purposes, and +1 when used for anything else – Medical Scanners aren't the best thing to look inside a computer, but it may help a little. If the Gadget is designed for a specific purpose, this should be discussed with the Gamemaster, and recorded on the Gadget's sheet. It could be that using the Gadget outside of its specific purpose is useless, in which case it can be considered a Restriction.

Skill*
(Minor Good Gadget Trait)
The Gadget is programmed or designed in such a way that it can perform a specific skilled task when the user has no ability. It could be an electronic lock pick (Skill: Subterfuge) or an auto-aiming feature on a pistol that aids the user (Skill: Marksman).

The Gadget has a Skill of 2 in a single skill, which can be used in place of the character's skill if higher. This is particularly handy for characters who completely lack the skill as it allows them to ignore the -4 penalty for unskilled rolls.

The Gadget is only Skill 2, and provides no bonus to the user if their own skill is higher – the operator either leaves the device to work on its own, or they can use their own skill, not both. The trait can be taken multiple times, increasing the Gadget's skill by 1 each time, up to a maximum of 5.

Track
(Minor/Major Good Gadget Trait)
The Track trait means the Gadget can find things for you. As a Minor Good Trait it can locate the target as long as it is on the same planet, by showing the operator how close they are and guiding them towards it. As a Major Good Trait the device can find the quarry anywhere in the universe, able to offer coordinates to its general whereabouts where it can be tracked on the ground as with the Minor Good Trait.

Transmit
(Minor Good Gadget Trait)
Transmit is a general Gadget Trait that means the device can pick up and/or send out signals, from picking up radio or phone transmissions, to intercepting calls, blocking the transmissions of a teleporter, or something similar. It can be used anywhere that signals are transmitted or received to block, listen in or alter the message. To use the Gadget like this will require an Ingenuity + Technology roll,

the Gamemaster deciding the Difficulty depending upon the signal being intercepted or received, and how powerful or distant the signal is, and whether it is encrypted.

Teleport
(Major Good Gadget Trait)
Teleport means the user can disappear from one location, and instantly appear in another. This is usually very draining on the Gadget and it will require recharging frequently. Teleporters, or 'Transmats' are usually dedicated devices as it takes a lot of processing power to not only transport the user, but also to check the exit location is clear and avoid any nasty materialisation mishaps. The distance travelled is usually limited to around 400km (enough to get from a planet's surface to orbit, or to an awaiting ship), although this range can be increased with the further use of Story Points.

Weld
(Minor Good Gadget Trait)
The Weld trait covers all sorts of incendiary uses;– the Gadget can be used to burn something, cut through thin substances or even solder and weld small items together. While the trait doesn't give the task any bonuses, it works as a great multi-purpose tool for all your sealing and cutting requirements!

Zap
(Minor or Major Good Trait)
The Zap Trait turns the Gadget into a ranged weapon. As a Minor Good Trait it has two versions: either the Zap does 4/L/L damage on people, or it does 4/8/12 damage but can also make things explode and burn. As a Major Good Trait it also has two versions: either the Zap can hit multiple targets standing close together with a single shot, or it is strong enough that it can blast vehicles or even spaceships. If you are creating a Gadget with the Zap trait, remember the Doctor's stance on weapons (see pg. 88).

BAD GADGET TRAITS

Bulky
(Minor or Major Bad Gadget Trait)
This Gadget is bigger and heavier than it should be. As a Minor Bad Trait, the Gadget can be carried by a single person, but it's the size of a heavy rucksack. As a Major Bad Trait, the Gadget fits on the back of a truck.

This Bad Trait only applies to Gadgets that you'd expect to be small. Trying to argue that your flying car is Bulky will just make the Gamemaster laugh at you, but a Sonic Screwdriver the size of a tuba is a perfect example of Bulky.

One Shot
(Minor Bad Gadget Trait)

The Gadget has one use, and one use only, so you better make it count. One shot, and it's history. Some items just burn out or explode – others are designed to break after doing what they're supposed to. If the Gamemaster feels the use of the Gadget is dramatic enough, they may refund the Story Points used to build the item.

Restriction*
(Minor Bad Gadget Trait)

Most Gadgets have their limitations. The Sonic Screwdriver cannot open deadlock seals and psychic paper doesn't work against people with psychic training. A Restriction is a specific limitation of the Gadget's current function, not a list of things the item doesn't do. For example, though the Sonic Screwdriver can do many things, it can't make a good cup of tea. This isn't a restriction, as the Screwdriver doesn't have a Brew Tea function!

The Restriction should be discussed with the Gamemaster: it should be something reasonably common, but not so common it makes the device useless. Does it not work through lead? Need a special type of fuel to operate? Tricky controls so that only one person can use it? These are all great Restrictions that can make the device more interesting and cheaper for the character to purchase or create (though a Gadget will never cost less than 1 Story Point).

Slow
(Minor/Major Bad Trait)

This Gadget does what it's designed to do, but it takes its time about it. As a Minor Bad Trait the delay between activating the Gadget and something actually happening is at least two minutes. As a Major Bad Trait the Gadget can take hours or days to get going.

GADGET STORY POINTS

Gadgets are also really handy as they can hold Story Points. The Gadget can spend these if their use is particularly vital to the story. In most cases, these work a little like a character's Story Points. They can be spent to add an extra two dice to an essential roll or to do something extraordinary.

The Story Points the Gadget spends can only be used when the Gadget itself is actively being used; you can't spend the Psychic Paper's Story Points to help lift a heavy cave-in to rescue a trapped child!

The Gadget's Story Points can be used, as long as the Gamemaster approves, to allow the Gadget to do something it's not normally known for.

For example, the Doctor finds himself in quite a predicament where the only way to proceed is to freeze the particles in a chamber. The Sonic Screwdriver has done many things, but freezing isn't something in its trait list. The Doctor really needs these particles frozen! He opts to use one of the Screwdriver's Story Points, allowing it to do what is necessary.

When the Gadget runs out of Story Points, it is essentially out of power, broken or otherwise out of action. Characters can donate Story Points to 'fuel' the Gadget, or the dramatic use of the item can mean it is awarded Story Points.

This is also a great way of helping a character when they're low on Story Points, by entrusting them with a Gadget.

EXAMPLE GADGETS

2-Dis (Minor Gadget)
The 2-Dis was a device created by the Doctor to return objects and people flattened by the Boneless to their normal states. It resembled a pocket calculator with a webcam and aerial stuck to the top. The Doctor was inordinately proud of its name, a play on TARDIS, but Clara was unimpressed.
Traits: Dimension Modification, Restriction (Restores flattened objects to their original size only).
Story Points: 1

51st Century 'Squareness Gun' (Minor Gadget)
Handy gun that deletes and restores walls and other items digitally, as used by River Song and Capt. Jack Harkness.
Traits: Delete, Restriction (doesn't work on living tissue).
Story Points: 1

Datapad (Minor Gadget)
All purpose scanner, ideal for taking readings from ancient monoliths or detecting approaching battle fleets.
Traits: Scan.
Story Points: 1

Lockpick (Minor Gadget)
Traits: Open/Close, Restriction (doesn't work on deadlock seals).
Story Points: 1

Electronic AI Lockpick (Major Gadget)
Traits: Open/Close, Skill: Subterfuge 3, Restriction (Electronic locks only, not on deadlock seals).
Story Points: 2

Engineer's Mate (Minor Gadget)
An electronic and futuristic Swiss Army knife of the tech world. Able to diagnose tech problems and helps the user to try and fix it.
Traits: Scan, Technically Adept (gives the user the same bonus as if the character had the Technically Adept Trait), Restriction (scan technological items only).
Story Points: 1

Engram Eraser (Major Gadget)
As used by some governments to erase memories of witnesses to extraterrestrial incidents.
Traits: Delete, Psychic, Restriction (Delete function only works on memories).
Story Points: 2

Hallucinogenic Lipstick (Minor Gadget)
River Song's escape method of choice, making people see whatever she wants them to see.
Traits: Hypnosis (Major), Restriction (Effect limited to 30 minutes).
Story Points: 1

Molecular Nanoscaler (Major Gadget)
A Molecular Nanoscaler was a large device used in the future to miniaturise surgeons so they could operate on a patient from within. The device the Doctor encountered onboard the spaceship *Aristotle* was put to a different use, however: to allow the Doctor and his companions to physically enter a malfunctioning Dalek.
Traits: Compress (Major), Teleport, Bulky (Major).
Story Points: 2

Psychic Paper (Minor Gadget)

Psychic Paper shows the viewer whatever the user wants them to see, or what the viewer thinks they ought to see.

Traits: Psychic, Restriction (doesn't work on psychically trained).

Story Points: 1

Rear View Scanner (Major Gadget)

Strange mounted devices that allows you to see invisible creatures and identifies them, but only when viewed in the mirror.

Traits: Restriction (only works in reflection), Scan, Special (reveals invisible entities).

Story Points: 2

Sonic Screwdriver (Major Gadget)

The most recognisable of Gadgets, variations of this device exist across time and space, from Sonic Pens to Sonic Lipsticks. However, none are as special as the Doctor's, the subject of over 1200 years worth of customisation and tinkering.

Traits: Open/Close, Restriction (Cannot open Deadlock Seals, Tricky Controls), Scan, Transmit, Weld.

Story Points: 2

Vortex Manipulator (Special Gadget)

As used by 51st Century Time Agents. This version is not usually for player characters and costs 10 Story Points, more than double that of a normal Special Gadget, as its time jumping abilities are fully functional. The Gamemaster may design a game around a group of characters whose only transport is with one of these, at which point the Gadget is 'free', like a TARDIS. See **Chapter Four: Time and Time Again**. Jack's Vortex Manipulator is a Major Gadget version, without the Vortex trait (though it can be activated for short periods if the story warrants it, with the expenditure of Story Points).

Traits: Scan, Transmit, Teleport, Vortex (Special Trait), Restriction (Short Temporal Jumps only).

Story Points: 10

TIME AND TIME AGAIN

⚙ TIME TRAVEL

So how does time travel work? Can you mess around in the past without changing the future? If you can't change the future what's the point in messing around? What is the past and future anyway if you can be anywhen you like? As the Doctor says, it's complicated, very complicated.

For most of us, time happens in a straight line. Actions are followed by reactions and consequences and the world makes sense. We know that things in the past affect things in the future. This makes life a lot easier to manage, as you only have to worry about the consequences of your actions after you are committed to them.

When you have the ability to travel in time, things get more complicated. Events still occur to you in the same order, however as far as the universe is concerned, actions you take in the future can influence the past. Your personal timeline and the linear chronology of the universe go out of sync. What you get up to in 1867 still happens in 1867, even if you did it after you'd visited 2036.

To make things more complicated, you might choose to interact with your own timeline. You shouldn't, but we'll come back to that later. This allows you to receive messages from the future or realise the strange hermit whose journal has been so useful is your future self who went to the past to ensure you had what you needed at the right time.

What this all means is that time is still occurring to you in a linear fashion, but not as a straight line. When you map your actions (which bounce from one time frame to another in no apparent order) onto the set chronology of the universe, your timeline appears to be very bendy and curvy, even though for you it seems to be a straight line of cause and effect.

Any single traveller has a warped timeline and can twist the timelines of those they come into contact with to a greater or lesser degree. Even a single time traveller can cross paths with many, many people in the course of their lives. Their timelines curve about and bend those they cross. When multiple time travellers move around the temporal space of the universe everything gets even more complicated. Timelines cross and twist around each other and link in the most surprising ways. As these curved paths of linear time wrap around each other and interact, they create the temporal shape of the universe, a big ball of timey-wimey stuff.

GRANDFATHER PARADOX

Even though the past may yet become your future when you time travel, confusion is not the only problem a time traveller has to face. The main problem with time travel is that your actions might create paradoxes. This is best explained by the classic 'grandfather paradox', which goes like this:

You hitch a lift in a TARDIS and travel back in time to meet your grandfather, in the days before your father was born. He's pleased to meet you and invites you in for tea where you have a lovely chat. You get on so well he shows you his gun collection and while admiring his shotgun you accidentally pull the trigger and tragically kill your grandfather.

The paradox is this: if your grandfather died before you were born, how can your father (and therefore you) be born. If you weren't born you couldn't shoot your grandfather. If he's alive, you must be also, so you must have gone back in time. Neither option can possibly be correct as you are alive and you have killed your grandfather. A paradox occurs and that can often be very, very bad for the universe.

When the Time Lords watched over the universe they watched for these paradoxes and took measures to deal with them. They may have visited you and told you not to go back in time to see your grandfather before you leave. If that doesn't work they may even use their incredible technology to warp time to heal the breach, which might ensure that neither you or your grandfather ever actually existed. While these measures might seem drastic and dangerous, the effects of a paradox on the fabric of space and time can be catastrophic. Such breaches can allow creatures such as the Reapers to manifest, tear holes in reality or can even destroy the universe in the blink of an eye.

Even the Master was careful to avoid some paradoxes. When he returned to Earth from the end of the universe he could have easily removed Martha Jones before she even met the Doctor. It would also have been rather simple to sneak up on the Doctor and destroy him before he knew what to look for. However, if he did a paradox would have occurred. If the Doctor or Martha died or were unable to travel to the end of the universe they would never have found the Master and restored him. Even at his worst, the Master had no desire to mess around with his own timeline. However, as soon as the Doctor returned from the end of the universe the Master was ready for them and his plans could begin in earnest. After all, the pre-planning and manipulation of Martha's family caused no paradox. So he prepared and patiently waited for the Doctor to return from the end of the universe and a final confrontation could ensue.

TIMEY-WIMEY TO THE RESCUE

So how are such paradoxes avoided? The key is that when a paradox occurs, time doesn't stop. If other agents can time travel they can interfere with a developing paradox and stop it happening. All those curved linear timelines wrapped around each other can influence things for the good, even things that haven't even happened yet. If the paradox is solved, time resets and things carry on as usual. It would alarm most people if they realised how often this was actually going on in the universe.

Many paradoxes are stopped before they even start. It may change history and save lives if you assassinated Hitler. However, before you even considered the idea, some other time agent went back and stopped you doing so to preserve the timeline. Someone may even have stopped him stopping you, but had then been stopped by another agent, and so it goes on. You don't know this before you set out on your attempt to stop the Second World War, but you have already failed before you started.

The universe is sometimes the way it is because the actions of the time travellers have made it so. In fact, in some cases time travellers may have even been responsible for starting essential historical events, through accident or design. You might not have meant to knock over a candle in Pudding Lane, but it still started the Great Fire of London. You haven't changed history; instead you've just done what you're supposed to.

Luckily, not every manipulation of the past can create a paradox. Only a direct contradiction creates one, such as you needing to be both dead and alive at the same time. If you happen to change the results of an election you may find many changes to your future, but if none of them stopped you going back in time there is no paradox. A true paradox only occurs when two facts of history cannot both be true, but absolutely are. When the universe is bent out of shape that badly it gets very weak and fragile and that's when bad things happen.

REAPERS

Reapers are best described as the antibodies of space-time. They are huge creatures that exist outside of time and space, drawn to paradoxes and tears in the fabric of space-time. Rather than cleaning the wound by fixing the problem, they repair the paradox by destroying and feeding on everything in the spur. When the Time Lords oversaw time travel, there was a barrier to prevent the Reapers from feeding on intelligent creatures.

Reapers have great mouths in their chests, and their favourite feeding tactic is to sweep a victim up in the cloak of their wings and swallow them whole. Reapers have a voracious appetite and feed not only on the meat and bone, but also on the potential timeline of their victim. They are immune to gunfire and conventional weapons, and are fast and strong.

They can teleport themselves easily, so the physicality of any barrier proves no object. The only protection against them is something old. To pass a barrier Reapers have to break down its temporal structure and find a gap in its history. So, if the Reapers come for you, find somewhere old to hide, but don't hide for long, for if the Reapers have arrived reality itself is falling apart.

Reapers are naturally occurring creatures that effectively prevent paradoxes and changes caused by time travel from going out of control and changing history. They are not necessarily 'evil', though their methods are violent and predatory, feeding upon the youngest affected with great delight. Their cleansing actions may kill hundreds, but they do stop paradoxes from wiping out or changing the lives

REAPERS

AWARENESS	4	PRESENCE	2
COORDINATION	3	RESOLVE	3
INGENUITY	2	STRENGTH	5

SKILLS
Athletics 3, Fighting 3,
Knowledge (Space/Time) 2

TRAITS
Alien
Alien Appearance
Alien Senses (Temporal Disturbances)
Flight (9)
Immunity (all weapons)
Natural Weapons (see below)
Teleportation
Weakness (Ancient Structures)

WEAPONS: Bite 3/**7**/10, Tail/Sting 5/**11**/16

STORY POINTS: 3-5

TIME SPURS

Sometimes, no matter how much care a time traveller takes, paradoxes occur, often as a result of taking inexperienced passengers on temporal joy-rides.

If a paradox occurs and is relatively localised, reality often protects itself by creating what time travellers refer to as a 'spur'. Essentially it cuts the area out of the space/time continuum and lets it work itself out, freezing the rest of the universe out until a conclusion is reached. No matter what occurs in the spur, time as a whole is safe and secure. When things have been resolved, usually by the elimination of all concerned – though more peaceful solutions are possible – the universe reintegrates the area into the time stream and life goes on.

Those trapped inside a spur are in real trouble. Communications break down instantly, and any time vessels are cut off from the Vortex. Other dimensions will be cut off as well, and a TARDIS doorway will be cut off from the 'inside', which it can no longer reach; your time travelling blue box becomes just a blue box.

The only way out of a time spur (alive, that is) is to resolve the paradox. The universe doesn't mind how you do it, as long as it's done. The Gamemaster should feel free to throw careless characters into time spurs when they fail to avoid a paradox – once is usually enough to make sure they watch their step in the future.

THE BLINOVITCH LIMITATION EFFECT

If you make a mistake while time travelling or things don't work out as planned, why not go back and change them again? It's a tempting idea when so much could go wrong. Surely the point of having a time machine is giving yourself a second chance?

Unfortunately, returning again and again to redo what you've been trying to do weakens the space-time continuum. In a sense the very fabric of reality gets worn away by repeated trips to the same place. To protect itself, the universe creates what is known as the Blinovitch Limitation Effect (named after a Russian who reversed his own time stream and reverted to infancy). The Blinovitch Limitation Effect simply states that repeated attempts to change a set event have less and less effect the more you try to do it. Preset events will conspire more and more to protect the timeline as it stands the more you try to fight them. Where the fabric of reality is worn it protects itself by losing its elasticity and becoming more rigid and set.

Essentially, if you didn't get it right first time, going back again is less likely to succeed than before, and

even less likely on your third or fourth trip. This effectively makes returning to sort your mistakes, not only dangerous (due to the potential paradox) but ultimately pointless. It is the great irony of time travel that you only really get one chance to get it right.

CHANGING TIME

Thankfully, the universe can easily avoid minor paradoxes. Time is very much like a river, able to roll round most stones dropped into it without changing course too badly. In this way the careful traveller can go to the past and future without doing much damage, as long as they stay out of trouble. If you tread on a butterfly you won't destroy the world as the universe does its best to ensure time develops along the right path. It basically ensures a different butterfly does what the one you stepped on was meant to do. Without a solid (albeit confusing) structure to space-time the universe would fall apart, so the fabric of reality does its best to tidy up after you.

Of course, no river survives long if you throw enough big stones into it, or dig up the banks. If you know the trail of events and influences of your actions in any time frame, you can do an awful lot of damage. A concerted attempt to change the proper order of events can succeed, if you know what you are doing. Temporal manipulation isn't easy though. For instance, you might think killing Hitler would be enough to stop The Second World War.

However, the war began due to a complicated series of events enacted by many various individuals. So killing Hitler isn't enough alone, in fact, you might not need to kill anyone at all. Perhaps getting England into a treaty with Germany before the invasion of Poland might do the trick. But then a vast Anglo-German alliance might crush most of Europe. As you

can see, blundering about in time often does no good at all. Without an intrinsic instinct for the flow of time it is very hard to see the right 'nudge points' to get the best effects.

It is also important when manipulating time to stick to the small stuff and play the long game. Major adjustments to history (such as the death of renowned historical figures) get noticed very quickly. Not only does the universe react badly to such blatant attempts, but so do the various races that govern time travel. The Time Lords came down hard on rogue agents who didn't tread carefully. That is if the universe itself doesn't edit the marauder from existence in self defence.

RIPPLES AND NEXUS POINTS

Having established that interference in temporal events is possible, you need to know the best place to do so. Any temporal manipulator must master the use of ripples and nexus points to stand a chance of success.

Ripples are the side effects of interfering with time. No action happens without influencing the actions of others. Change one action and you change any further events that action influenced. Those actions in turn influence other actions, and so on. As you move further and further from the centre of such a disturbance, its influence might fade, but it could just as easily build into a cascade. This chain of actions that spread out from the spatial and temporal centre of the disturbance is like ripples on a pond after you throw a stone in it. Travellers must take care of the ripples their actions create on the pond of universal time. Their effects are hard to predict and often more far reaching than you expect. As with a stone, when the initial interference has sunk and been forgotten, the ripples might still continue. Many amateur interventionists are surprised at the damage they do when they focus only on the initial change to causality and fail to deal with the further consequences of their actions.

Luckily, not all places in time and space send out ripples in the same way. Some places are more important to the fundamental fabric of space-time. These places are referred to as nexus points. Both Earth and Gallifrey are good examples of powerful and important nexus points. Gallifrey's history had such an impact on the universe that the Time Lords banned all interference in its timeline. Earth is important given the way humans have spread out to every corner of the galaxy. To change the history of the cradle of humanity would influence every world they ever touched.

While most time travellers have the sense to leave nexus points alone (it's safer that way) they often become primary targets for temporal marauders. There will always be those who think they can interfere with time for personal gain and either control its effects or don't care about the damage they do. Such beings are sadly in no shortage. Earth has become a battleground for alien invasion on countless occasions as changes to the timeline here can create galaxy-wide changes to causality. This is also due to Earth's development being quite primitive compared to most time-aware cultures. It appears simple to manipulate such primitives to create far reaching temporal interference effects. However, their position as 'knots' in the weave of the fabric of space-time grants nexus points a kind of destiny. Such places seem to find heroes to defend them, and keep them safe. These heroes and those who inhabit such nexus points are bound to play a major part in the universe.

PREDESTINATION OR 'WHAT'S THE POINT?'

This all leads to the question of predestination. If you were actually responsible for a historical event, all you are doing is following a set course. Your life has been predetermined for you the moment you step into the time machine. So why bother going back in time at all?

Firstly, you still don't know what's going to happen to you. Whether you are already fated to perform certain actions or not is unimportant. You are free to do as you please, knowing that everything you do has been sorted out by the universe without messing with history. If you are not actively trying to mess with time, you are probably OK. Secondly, it might be vital that you do, as you may be fated to stop some other temporal manipulation from happening.

It is possible to change the future if you work at it. Other time travellers might be working to pervert the universal timeline. Your successful plan to stop them could already be a matter of history, or it might not be. If time is altered, the universe might follow a different path. Alter history enough and no one might be able to fix the damage. That might have been the fate of the universe all along. You just never know what you're meant to do, but does that mean you don't try? If you told a soldier from either side of the Second World War what the outcome would be, do you think he'd fight any less? He knows what's at stake, he can't just trust fate to sort things out without him. Everyone has a part to play in the drama of the universe. In the case of time travellers, the universe simply has a lot more work for them to do.

When Sally Sparrow finally talks to the Doctor through a DVD extra, she was already predestined to say what she said. However, she was still able to ask the Doctor what she wanted to know as she didn't know what she was predestined to do! It just so happened that whatever she wanted to know or would have thought to ask was ready to be answered by the Doctor. But it isn't all fun; you can argue that occasionally predestination can still take control of your actions. Sally's conversation with the Doctor ends with his telling her there is no more transcript, which he assumes means the Angels are coming. It is this that makes Sally check where the Angels are. Could Sally have talked longer with the Doctor if he hadn't said that? Could the Angels have attacked earlier? They could have chosen to, but predestination implies they didn't, and if you don't know what you're meant to do, how can you change it?

With time travellers going from the future to the past with alarming regularity, it is possible for them to even engineer predestination sequences on purpose. If the Doctor had wanted to use Sally Sparrow to deal with the Angels for no better reason than he didn't want to get too close to them, he could have done so. However, working out the variables to create the right chain of events can often take a lot more time and energy than just doing the job yourself, though simple predestination sequences are easily possible and can be fun, if only to mess around with temporal physicists. For instance, you know your friend will spill his cup of tea. So you tell him not to worry that he'll spill it, which causes him to fumble with the cup and to spill his tea anyway. Would he have still spilt it if you'd not told him it didn't bother you? Is that a form of predestination or are you just messing with his head?

Temporal philosophers have wrestled with the problem of predestination for millennia. How do you know if your actions have been pre-planned and you are following a path you are unable to deviate from? If you are, then that just makes us all unthinking puppets of an uncaring universe. Mind you, that is a very 'glass half empty' way of looking at it. If you don't know the intentions of the universe, it doesn't matter if it is a plan or not. You still never know what is around the next corner, and what adventures might need you.

NEAR AND FAR

It is also important for a time traveller to be careful how far they travel in time. It is very tempting to go to the end of the universe, and maybe eat their picnic while watching suns fade away. You might also fancy a trip to gaze at the Big Bang and see the universe created.

Even the Time Lords never travelled to the end of existence. It isn't a very good idea, for two reasons: firstly, these are momentous events, and interference in either might have dire consequences for the universe as a whole. The tiniest particle added to the Big Bang could cause the universe to form in a totally different way. The end of time is just as delicate, with

whole species evolving into new forms or on the cusp of their universal destiny.

The second reason is simply for your own safety. These times are very, very dangerous indeed. Beings at the end of the universe might be more advanced than you, and decide to use you or your technology as some way to escape the final days. In the early days of the universe, strange and god-like entities, some that eat time itself, swim in the forming matter. These beings might drive you mad with a touch or destroy your timeship. Even with these beings gone the universe is still dangerous. The laws of physics themselves are still forming. You might arrive to find time travel is impossible due to the state of the universe, and these are not very pleasant or forgiving environments to be stuck in. In some cases your very existence might not function in reality, and it is a pain to be erased from existence the moment you step out of the door.

SIDEWAYS IN TIME

If you can travel forwards and backwards in time, what happens if you go sideways? The answer is that you visit a timeline where different decisions have led to a different outcome for the world, an alternate universe. The theory of alternate universes suggests that every time you make a decision, a whole new world is created where the path you didn't take is also followed through. If that decision was whether to have a bacon sandwich or a boiled egg for lunch, the world that is created wouldn't be very different from the other reality. However, if the decision was whether or not America should have entered the Second World War, or whether Bill Gates should get involved in the computer market, the world may be very different indeed. Especially as each of these decisions creates ripples that flow out into the alternate world and offer new opportunities and tragedies to plenty of other people. For example, if America hadn't entered the war, not only might Germany have conquered Europe, but all the American soldiers who died fighting would have lived. Who knows what these soldiers might have done with the lives the battlefield stole from them? The potential for them to change the world is vast.

Alternate worlds are a playground of 'what ifs' filled with copies of everyone you know that are often slightly different. Visiting such places is a fascinating way to find out what you might have become if things had been just a little bit different. As such they are an incredible source of adventure and exploration. Especially as you won't know what your alternative version has been up to until you investigate. Will you be mistaken for someone wanted for murder or treated like a president?

Before the Time War, the barriers between these dimensions were thin and a TARDIS could easily pass between them. However, the damage wrought by the Time War caused the universe to shut down such access in an attempt to limit the damage to reality. The walls between the worlds went from paper to stone as the universe tried to heal itself.

That is not to say getting to an alternative universe is impossible, it's just that it isn't a very good idea. There are still holes and tunnels to such places that failed to close and certain powerful machines might exist to force open a gateway. However, once you are there, getting back can often be an issue. The power systems of most devices will be slightly different, making it difficult to repair any damaged systems and get them working again. Given how hard it is to punch through the universe, and traverse the Void between, it is unlikely you'll arrive without any damage to your timeship at all. While some places are paradises of peace and tranquillity (on some worlds even humans get things right) others are hostile and barren. You never know what you'll find until you get there. Just imagine what the Earth might be like if the Doctor hadn't been around to save it and you get the idea. Boiled and sold off to the Slitheen, a slave farm for the Sycorax or even the centre of a new Human/Dalek empire. Donna discovered just how harsh a reality without the Doctor could be when she 'Turned Right'. Sometimes the world is mostly the same – it just has more Zeppelins in it, and someone you once knew is now sporting an attractive eye-patch.

This travel to other worlds doesn't only go one way. There may be alternate worlds that are actively developing such devices so they might invade other worlds, including ours, for their resources. After all, if you have run out of oil in your world, you know there are plenty of other Earths you could visit to get more.

PRESENT IS PAST

Most people mark the 'present' as the point they step into a timeship. Sure, they may lose a couple of days, and have adventures that last a week or two while returning a few hours later. However, the year is still usually the same and an experienced guide can use the Blinovitch Limitation Effect to steer their companions along a more linear timeline with everyone else.

Although you can't revisit your own timeline very easily you can 'bookmark' your last visit to a place and return there after you left. Time travel isn't an exact science, however, and the Doctor himself once promised to return in five minutes and ended up twelve years in the future of a very annoyed Ms. Pond.

TIME IS NOT THE BOSS OF ME!

If this time travel thing is so complicated, how on earth do you make sense of it in adventures? Few gaming groups are lucky enough to have an actual Time Lord running the adventure. So how can a poor human Gamemaster stay in control of potential paradox and predestination?

Luckily, it isn't as hard as it looks, as long as you are prepared to cheat.

The fluidity of time is a big help here. The only actions that will change time are the things the Gamemaster wants changed. If the player characters knock over a candle in Pudding Lane, it need not start the Great Fire of London. As the Gamemaster

you can decide that luckily the city watch managed to get the fire under control. Conversely, if you want the thug they just defeated be a key figure in the destiny of nations you can do just that. The players will need to tread carefully, as they don't have that sort of control. However, if you keep the adventure fluid you can make sure time is messed with only in the way you want it to be. If you need them to save someone to create a temporal disturbance, don't spend hours trying to convince them to save 'Bob', just make the important person the next one they save, whoever it may be.

When it comes to paradox, things can be trickier, but here is where the players can help. In general, they will be playing characters that want to safeguard the universe and take care of it. When a paradox occurs, it isn't your problem but theirs. If their solution sounds plausible to you, let them get on with it. If they can't figure it out they'd best try harder. Putting them in a time spur means you can let them mess up as much as you like without damaging the universe (giving them the option to create new characters if things go really badly!). If things go really wrong, you can always have the Doctor (or one of his other incarnations if someone is playing the Doctor) turn up and sort everything out.

Predestination is also quite simple if you are happy to reverse engineer it. You can't plan for it very easily, but when something happens in the game it is quite easy to tell the players they were destined to do that all along. Sure, it's cheating, but that is half the fun. Be careful not to overuse it though, as no one likes to think their characters are just puppets of the

universe. Small things are easy though, and can help you out of trouble too. If the players are stumped, a note or device can turn up, sent by themselves from the future.

Predestined events are also quite easy if you are vague with the details until they actually happen. The Gamemaster need not know where the Doctor will be during any specific part of an adventure in order to deliver a message from a Ms. R. Song trapped in the past. It arrives wherever he is, whenever he needs to get that clue or the Gamemaster sees fit to give it to him. River may later reveal to the characters that she addressed it to that specific building or had it delivered by Western Union messenger at that specific time because she was told by a future incarnation of the Doctor that he would be there. The players, for their part, will assume some sort of complicated temporal planning was involved, but it's all just a bit of fast improvisation on the part of the Gamemaster.

So in general, time travel is a tool for the Gamemaster to create adventures, not a rope to tie yourself up in. You can make it work for you rather than against you as the game and all of time is yours to control. If you do it right the players will be amazed how you are able to plan for their every action and be suitably impressed. Of course, this is just the mouth of the Vortex, and you'll find more advice about time, time travel and the history of the universe in **The Time Traveller's Companion** supplement.

⚙ THE TIME LORD

While they may look the same, a Time Lord is very different to a human. Not only are there a few quirks of biology, but there are plenty of traits that separate the two races as well. A Time Lord has an innate connection with the ebb and flow of the universe: the term 'Time Lord' is not merely ceremonial. They can feel the turn of the universe and sometimes see the timelines of those they meet stretching out in front of them. The Doctor often seems distracted by things humans cannot perceive; his mind functions on a higher level, comprehending variables no one else can possibly fathom.

GALLIFREYAN PHYSIOLOGY

While they look the same on the outside, Gallifreyans are very different to humans on the inside. Their evolutionary process has been almost entirely internal, granting them incredible resistance to environments and radiation that might kill any other species. Time Lords may not look that impressive, but they are incredibly tough.

While their skeletal structure is essentially human, and they have most of the same organs, just about everything in their body works much better than a human's does. The most obvious difference on initial examination is that a Gallifreyan has two hearts. This 'bivascular' system allows their whole body to effectively run at double pace when necessary. A Gallifreyan can often exert themselves and survive brutal stress to their system far in excess of any human. It doesn't mean they don't feel it though. Kicking two hearts into overdrive is often painful and dizzying, but if that gives you the stamina to reach a vital switch on a ship crashing into the sun, then it's all worth it.

Having two hearts also ensures you have a spare. Gallifreyan children practice shutting down their heartbeats to minimal levels, which induces a death-like trance state. The heartbeats are so low that it is easy to fool even a qualified doctor. While it is a game for Gallifreyan children, for a renegade traveller it is often a life saving ability. Plenty of Time Lords have escaped prisons and battles by pretending to be dead and being passed over by their enemies.

The advanced nature of the Gallifreyan system allows them to handle the vacuum of space and powerful radiation far better than any human. They are not immune to such hostile environments, but they can survive them roughly twice as well as an average human can. No Time Lord looks forward to getting thrown into space, but if it happens they have a better chance of surviving long enough to get back inside than anyone else.

By the same token they are better in hot, cold and occasionally poisonous environments and are immune to certain types of radiation. The advanced nature of Time Lord biology also makes them better equipped to resist disease. They contract illnesses very rarely and usually less severely. However there are a few diseases that will incapacitate a Time Lord that don't even affect humans due to the differences in their biochemistry.

The most amazing ability of the Time Lords is their ability to regenerate. Should they suffer enough trauma to kill them, a Time Lord's entire body automatically rejuvenates. In a burst of energy, every cell in his body rebuilds itself, healing all wounds, viruses or poisons that might have hurt them. Despite changing their entire cellular structure, the Time Lord's memories remain, although their personality can undergo quite a dramatic change. As different as they are and however different their personality, their basic essential self remains. It is almost as if they are reborn and their memories are based on a different experience of events – in the same way two twins have different life experience and so become different individuals based on the same template. In this way, a Time Lord with a strong moral (or amoral) streak will keep it, although they might become a practical joker where they were quite serious, or even take to wearing a bow tie.

While it might appear to take place in a few moments, regeneration takes quite a while to fully complete. After the initial change the Time Lord's body takes at least fifteen hours to settle and 'fix' itself. This grants the Time Lord an incredible healing ability while their system is in flux. They seem to have boundless energy (when not asleep) and can even re-grow limbs in moments. However, during this time they are physically and mentally at their least predictable. While their body is working on overdrive their mind is confused and disoriented. Companions are forced to do without them until their faculties return.

The problem with regeneration is that you never know what you are going to get. How pleased or disappointed with a new body a Time Lord might be will also depend on their new personality. It is a sad fact that it is a Time Lord's companions that usually suffer the brunt of these changes. Few Time Lords are really aware of how different they are, assuming any mood changes are quite reasonable or an improvement at worst. Not surprisingly, few wish to believe they have become difficult, unreasonable or just plain crazy since regenerating.

RADIATION AND TIME LORDS

Time Lords have been known to play and experiment with incredibly dangerous forms of radiation, and learn how to manage their effects on their bodies. A Time Lord can spend a Story Point to negate a single exposure to radiation or electricity, ignoring any damage effects from that source. Of course, extended exposure can still be dangerous, and a high enough dose can be too much for even a Time Lord. If the Gamemaster decides the exposure is too high, it may be that even Story Points cannot help and the Time Lord will need to regenerate to survive. In the right situations, this ability can be used to reverse the effects of poisoning, as long as a Story Point is spent and they have access to the right elements to stimulate the inhibited enzymes into reversal and expel it from the body.

RESPIRATORY BYPASS SYSTEM

Besides the "two hearts" thing, Gallifreyans also have another biological trick up their sleeves. They have a respiratory bypass system that allows them to survive strangulation and to exist in the vacuum of space with no ill effects. This does not work over extended periods, and even a Time Lord will eventually need a supply of air. The Time Lord can go for an entire Scene without air as long as they are not shocked or hurt. For example, the Doctor has to walk across the surface of the Moon to the TARDIS, but there are no spacesuits. It'll take about ten minutes of walking to get there, and the Gamemaster allows this with the expenditure of a Story Point (it's a long time to go without air). If he's shot at on the way he'll have to start making Strength and Resolve rolls to avoid exhaling and suffocating.

REGENERATION

If the Doctor is killed in the course of the adventure, hopefully he will have one or more of his regenerations remaining (and some Story Points from sacrificing himself in a suitably heroic manner). So what exactly happens in game terms?

If the Time Lord is reduced to 0 in three or more attributes, or is hit by a Lethal weapon, the player can keep the character active for ten minutes for every level of Resolve they would normally have if they weren't injured. At the end of that time, regeneration kicks in, and in a flash of energy the Time Lord is renewed.

How do you know what you're going to be like after regeneration? As the Doctor has proved, he's still able to use all of the skills he's gained from his previous incarnations, so skills do not change. However, attributes and traits can.

ATTRIBUTE CHANGES

It is common for a Time Lord's physical appearance to change dramatically from one incarnation to another, from old to young, tall to short, brown haired to grey. The player should take all three physical attributes (Awareness, Coordination and Strength) and redistribute the points. Remember, no attribute should be lower than 1. If you'd prefer a more random way of redistributing the points, roll a die on the table below:

ROLL	AWARENESS	COORDINATION	STRENGTH
1	Up	Same	Down
2	Up	Down	Same
3	Same	Up	Down
4	Same	Down	Up
5	Down	Same	Up
6	Up	Down	Same

TRAIT CHANGES

In most cases, Traits will remain the same, though this is a great opportunity to tweak the points. Just as you did with character creation, you can reduce an attribute to purchase another Trait, or vice-versa.

APPEARANCE

Possibly the most dramatic change of all is appearance, but what will they look like after regeneration? If you're unsure, you could roll randomly on the table below. Roll a separate die for height, build, appearance, hair and age. If it doesn't make sense, especially considering the attributes, roll again. It's just a guide.

ROLL	HEIGHT	BUILD	LOOKS	HAIR	AGE
1	Very Short	Thin	Different	Auburn	Teenage
2	Short	Slim	Plain	Brown	20s
3	Average	Average	Average	Blonde	30s
4	Average	Average	Interesting	Black	40s
5	Tall	Stocky	Attractive	Ginger	50s
6	Very Tall	Chunky	Stunning	Grey	Old

In addition to these physical changes (and new teeth, and a new voice) the character's personality is likely to change. There are a couple of ways of doing this: firstly, it could be up to the player. The Time Lord's existing player can try something new, though it is easy for them to slip back into their old ways. A better way is to have the character shift to another player! This way their actions and dialogue will be very different, and more like the regenerations we've come to know.

If this is the case, the players can simply swap characters. The player who used to play the Time Lord can take over playing one of the companions, or that companion can choose to leave and the player can create a new character. Either way, the players keep their Story Points, not the characters – and all players must agree to the swap.

Once regeneration is complete, the Time Lord is usually incapacitated for a while. Use six hours as a guide, though you can roll a die and reduce the time by that many hours. The Gamemaster may modify the time spent recovering depending upon how much damage the Time Lord took. For that time period, they are almost continually unconscious, waking for moments to utter a sentence or do something vital before passing out again. For example, the Doctor spent hours in bed after absorbing the power of the Vortex from Rose, but after absorbing lethal amounts of radiation and regenerating again, he was active moments after.

OTHER EXTRAORDINARY ABILITIES

The Doctor has many other abilities that continue to surprise and amaze. Some abilities or weaknesses may be exclusive to the Doctor, others are traits of the Time Lords as a whole.

We know that the Doctor has a problem with Aspirin (a single pill could be fatal). He also has learned to overcome the voice changing effects of helium, and has displayed a level of psychic ability, linking with others to read or implant thoughts. Of course, the Doctor can do a great many other things as well, his abilities seem to grow with every day that he travels.

Similarly, a Time Lord character may 'reveal' some new ability which may be a facet of Time Lord biology or a trick he's picked up somewhere on his travels by spending a Story Point. New abilities should only be allowed on rare occasions, maybe once every other adventure at most, and the Gamemaster must agree.

The amount of change in appearance and personality often depends on the stress and trauma that forces the regeneration. The system is designed to save a Time Lord from the ravages of old age, not absorbing the power of the Vortex or being blasted by gunfire. When forced in this way, regeneration can be a very difficult procedure. It leaves the Time Lord disoriented and a little crazy for a while.

The release of energy that rejuvenates them also gives them an energy and vigour that can make them very excitable. All of this makes them very difficult to get along with for the first few days! Even Time Lords who regenerate in peace and tranquillity rarely know how things will turn out, even if the process is a little easier.

In the days of Gallifrey, each Time Lord was limited to twelve regenerations. Even the Time Lords understood that everything must end one day, including them.

However, with Gallifrey gone the rules may have changed. **The Time Traveller's Companion** supplement provides additional information on Gallifrey, Gallifreyans and Time Lords, as well as more advanced rules for playing Time Lord characters.

✪ THE TARDIS

One of the most incredible devices in the universe is the TARDIS, its initials standing for Time And Relative Dimension In Space. However, to its creators, the Time Lords of Gallifrey, it was considered an item of little importance, being referred to merely as a 'Time Capsule'. To them it is a utilitarian device that simply gets you from point A to point B, like a car or a bicycle. While such nonchalance to such incredible technology might seem strange, the TARDIS is just one of an array of amazing Time Lord technologies.

Even though several other cultures eventually built timeships of their own, none were ever as advanced as even the Doctor's rather clapped out blue box. A TARDIS can travel to any place and time in the universe, and survive in the harshest areas of the Vortex. Not only that, but it can carry a vast amount of people and protect all of them from the ravages of the Vortex, as well as feed and clothe them. If you want to travel anywhere and anywhen you like in comfort and safety, no better device has ever been crafted. Though you may need to stop off on Earth from time to time for milk...

BIGGER ON THE INSIDE

The most astounding thing about a TARDIS is that its interior is far larger than its exterior dimensions allow for. In other words, it's bigger on the inside. All TARDIS units (and a good selection of Gallifreyan technology in general) share this particular trait, which is referred to as being 'Dimensionally Transcendental'. This means that the inside of the device is not actually inside what appears to be the outside, instead, it exists in a separate dimension.

The shape you see materialised being little more than a three dimensional doorway referred to as the 'real world interface' that the device extends into reality. The inside of the TARDIS exists outside time and space, effectively nowhere at all, extending its door into reality or the Vortex as it lands or travels.

While this might seem an overcomplicated way of building a device, it has several advantages. Firstly, infinite (or near infinite) interior space means you can pack a TARDIS with everything you need. No one has to share a room and you can stock up on any equipment you need, and there's room for a pool - even in the library.

With the 'door' dematerialised the TARDIS exists purely in the Vortex and outside time and space. The less a device is part of reality, the easier it is to do the

impossible - such as travel in time. When you aren't part of the universe, it is easier to slip through the cracks.

Finally, the most useful effect of being separated from reality is that you are a lot safer. TARDIS units are remarkably resistant to damage. Not even the assembled hordes of Genghis Khan can break into a TARDIS (and they've tried). This is because they need to not just break down a door but cross over into another dimension. You can surround a materialised TARDIS with explosives, but unless that explosion is powerful enough to pass into the inside dimension there will be no actual damage.

That is not to say it is impossible. Both the Daleks and Cybermen developed powerful explosive devices capable of damaging a TARDIS. There are also certain devices that can reach across the dimensional divide and get into a TARDIS, such as powerful transmat beams and Huon particles.

TRAVELLING THE VORTEX

Whatever other abilities it has, a TARDIS is designed and built for travelling in the Space-Time Vortex. The Vortex is a great swirling tunnel that any time vessel must travel through to move from one place in time to another, a turbulent place of madness and time-storms. Generally it appears red when you travel forward in time and blue when you travel backwards. Otherwise it is a mesmeric pattern of colour, and a little frightening to anyone not used to

it. There is something about its seemingly innocuous appearance that has an aura of vast power. It is like staring into the heart of the universe and the raw power and chaos that created it. Needless to say, travelling the Vortex without any form of protection is fatal to most species. Most low-end forms of time travel have barely adequate protection, leaving their passengers feeling ill and exhausted after their journey. It is really, really not recommended to try and hang onto the outside of a TARDIS as it takes off.

What makes the Vortex so dangerous is that it doesn't truly exist. There was no Vortex before anyone travelled in time, but as soon as they did it had been there forever. The problem is to travel in time you need to be outside the normal flow of space-time, which means you need to be outside reality. Unfortunately there is nothing outside reality, but if you create a device that can travel there, there must be something. Even if you go nowhere you must still end up somewhere. So the Vortex came into being, created by a loophole in physics and tamed by the Time Lords.

Piloting a time vessel through the Vortex is very hard indeed. Most timeships use powerful computers to plot a direct course and barge through. This puts enormous stress of the vessel and reduces the time it can spend in the Vortex or the distance it can travel. Vessels like a TARDIS work with the Vortex flow, riding the eddies and currents and guiding itself along its tides. While this means a TARDIS can go as far as it likes and stay in the Vortex as long as it likes, it also means it requires a skilled operator and a computer with more than a little sentience.

Travelling the Vortex is a strange and occasionally confusing experience. This oddity comes mainly from being outside time and natural existence. However good the protection in your timeship, your whole being feels the disconnection inherent in being in a place that doesn't exist. You suffer a yearning at a cellular level to be somewhere real. Also, while you feel as if you are moving, actually it is the Vortex that flows around you. In the constantly churning tunnels of flux and chaos your time vessel remains almost exactly where it is. However, every possible point of reference sweeps past you. It is like being on an escalator, knowing you have to jump off when you see your stop. However the escalator is actually still and the entire world is flashing past you. If you stare into the Vortex for long enough you will see all reality pass by you. It can be a terrifying and humbling experience; many people just close their eyes.

Extensive travel through the Vortex results in exposure to artron energy, a type of time radiation. It isn't necessarily harmful and can even be used by some alien races such as the Daleks and the Bane. However, this radiation can reveal – to technologically advanced species who can detect such things – that the person has travelled through the Space-Time Vortex.

TARDIS HISTORY AND MODEL TYPES

Before the destruction of Gallifrey the Time Lords built several models of TARDIS and continued to refine and advance the basic design. In many cases the newer models simply worked a lot better, but many had new or experimental features that separated them from the others. In all there were around 100 different models of TARDIS. The Doctor's is a Type 40TT Capsule, and not an especially good example of that model either. Most Time Lords would see it more as a rusty Ford Cortina than as a vintage car.

TARDIS SYSTEMS AND ABILITIES

While a TARDIS is a useful space and time vehicle, it can do so much more. Here is a brief guide to the systems that make up this amazing device and the sort of things of which it is also capable.

Architectural Configuration Circuitry: The TARDIS's interior layout and design is very simple to manipulate. The general look of the inside can be modified much like a desktop theme on a computer. It takes a little longer as the TARDIS must grow into its shape, but it's a lot quicker than physically redecorating.

The ability to manipulate the inside of the TARDIS is not limited to just the décor though. Using the architectural systems the operator can create new rooms, add corridors and then move them around. New occupants don't need to find a room, the operator can just create one and put it near the control room. There are some rooms and systems that come 'as standard' such as a Wardrobe Room, Zero Room and obviously a Console Room. However, any and all of them can be moved around. So while it is more convenient to have the Console Room near the outside doors, if you want an atrium or a foyer in your TARDIS you can have one.

Chameleon Arch: A common feature installed on most TARDISes is designed to allow a Time Lord to change their genetic structure so they may disguise themselves. The Arch makes use of the Gallifreyan's ability to regenerate to manipulate their body and mind at a cellular level. Most Chameleon Arches are set to change a Gallifreyan into a human, mainly as they are one of the most populace races throughout time and space. However, it is possible the device might be set to mimic other life forms and species. The process of changing is extremely painful, so it is not used lightly.

When the transformation is complete the Time Lord's true essence and memory is stored in a convenient device, often a pocket watch. Given it carries the mind of a Time Lord, this device has a powerful aura that might be detectable to beings of even undeveloped psychic potential. The Time Lord's new personality can be set to ignore the device, sometimes until a certain date. At that time, all they need to do is open the device to restore their natural form, a remarkably painless process that takes moments.

The device was originally intended to allow a Time Lord to fully immerse themselves in a culture without interfering. To this end the Arch gives them a new personality and manipulates causality to give them a place to live and work in the new culture. The new personality is not necessarily based on the Time Lord's original personality and can in some cases be almost diametrically opposed. In this way they can learn and record events, even take part in them, and not interfere with the timeline. When they reverse the process they can record their findings.

In the final days of the Time War the device found another use: one of disguise. A Time Lord so disguised is as good as vanished from the universal stage. Who knows how many may still be out there, unaware of who they truly are.

Chameleon Circuit: TARDISes are incredibly alien devices. Any vessel that can travel in time must be able to exist slightly outside reality, even when outside the Vortex. So an undisguised timeship may look normal on first glance, but upon further inspection it is clearly not. Its skin might seem to ripple and change, as if it isn't quite there. Something about it just seems wrong or unreal, almost like a dream of an object. Plenty of crashed timeships have been the seed of myths and legends about gods, dreams and monsters. Soon after they began travelling in time, the Time Lords realised they would have to disguise their vessels. This led to the creation of the Chameleon Circuit, perhaps the most useful system on a TARDIS.

Every time the TARDIS materialises in a new location, within the first nanosecond of landing it analyses its surroundings, calculates a twelve-dimensional data map of everything within a thousand mile radius, and adapts the 'real world interface' (or three-dimensional doorway) to any appearance that will fit in with the TARDIS's surroundings (a tree in a forest or a computer bank in a research station). In most models the operator can override this function and decide what form the TARDIS will adopt upon landing, although the circuit often becomes faulty in

older models, locking the TARDIS into a single form or even oscillating between wildly inappropriate shapes.

There are a few limits to what form the TARDIS can take. It needs to be big enough to put a human size door in it. After all, the occupants need to have space to get in and out of the machine. It is also prone to inaccuracies when copying certain objects. Finally, the biggest problem is that it won't be connected to anything, so certain parts won't work. If it becomes an organ, it could be played, as the keys are still there. However, if it were a phone box, the phone wouldn't work.

Part of the Chameleon Circuit is a Distraction Field. This energy aura works as a perception filter for anyone passing by the TARDIS. Essentially the field gets into the senses of those who pass by it to make them ignore the TARDIS. It isn't powerful enough to confound those actively looking for the machine, but most casual passers by will never notice it, even if the chameleon circuit is a bit dodgy. If you craft a bit of gadgetry onto a TARDIS key you can access this field to use it as a personal cloaking device. However, strong willed people, those with psychic training or those looking for you specifically may see through such deception easily.

PERCEPTION FILTERS

A Perception Filter can be built by giving a Gadget the Face in the Crowd Trait. This Trait may be purchased multiple times for the Gadget, giving it a cumulative +2 bonus for the user's Subterfuge rolls. At the first level, the Filter simply encourages people to ignore the target, but at higher levels the Filter can disguise their appearance or make them effectively invisible.

Cloister Bell: Every ship needs an alarm system, and for the TARDIS this is the cloister bell. This deep and resonant alarm bell tolls through every area of the TARDIS when activated. It usually sounds when terrible danger is imminent for the TARDIS and its occupants. Given that it takes something very bad to harm a TARDIS, whatever is coming must be dreadful indeed. The bell often sounds when there is danger to the universe as well as the TARDIS, the overly cautious Time Lords feeling that their operatives should be aware of such dire occurrences so they can do something about them.

The cloister bell is especially useful as it is linked to the flow of the universe itself. It doesn't merely sound when danger is imminent in the physical sense; it often sounds if it senses there is something badly wrong with time, or if events might lead to a danger that is not yet present. In general it is not a good idea to ignore the call of the cloister bell, it never sounds for unimportant or trivial events.

Control Console: When most people step into a TARDIS, the first thing they are faced with is the Console Room. While the design is often very different depending on the TARDIS and its operator, the controls themselves are usually much the same. All TARDIS systems are controlled from a single hexagonal control console that surrounds a time rotor. To properly pilot a time capsule requires six operators, one for each section of the console. This is why a single operator often needs to run around quite a bit to get the machine travelling to the right place. Luckily a companion can often help by holding down the right switch now and again.

The time rotor in the centre of the console moves up and down when the TARDIS is in flight. It often glows with power and energy, providing the light for the room as well. Beneath the time rotor and the console is said to reside the Heart of the TARDIS. This heart is the seat of the machine's sentience and its connection to the Vortex itself. To stare into the heart of the TARDIS is to be one with the universe and all time and space. Not even a Time Lord can control such energy for long, or predict what sights and powers might come from such a union.

The Eye of Harmony: All TARDIS units drew their energy from the raw power of a tamed black hole called the Eye of Harmony. Technically, this name is applied to the first of these hungry monsters the Time Lords controlled, and originally all TARDIS units and Gallifreyan systems drew energy from it as it was an infinite source of power. However, with the destruction of Gallifrey the TARDIS has to resort to 'refuelling' from places of temporal activity, such as temporal rifts (like the one in Cardiff) or drawing power from cosmic events.

Energy Manipulation: As a side effect of being able to control a black hole, TARDIS units are very good at manipulating energy. The shields and force fields that keep the Eye of Harmony in check can be extended around the TARDIS or used to absorb explosive energy. This allows the TARDIS operator to create tractor beams and zones of null-gravity. They can use the TARDIS as a lightning rod for all kinds of energy explosions. You can even use a TARDIS to plug a hole in space time, using its abilities to keep the forces of chaos at bay until you can find a better fix.

Hostile Action Displacement System (HADS): In addition to being able to disguise itself, and having its materialised form almost impenetrable to most weapons, the TARDIS has an emergency system known as the Hostile Action Displacement System (or HADS for short) that detects when the TARDIS is under attack, and automatically dematerialises the TARDIS, relocating it a short distance away (ensuring the attacker has gone) in a safer location. The HADS has to be enabled every time the Time Lord leaves the TARDIS. Needless to say, the Doctor usually forgets to do so.

Internal Weapon Deactivation System (IWDS): It is said that due to its position outside time and space, a TARDIS exists in a state of 'temporal grace'. The IWDS feature makes use of this tranquillity inherent in the violence of the Vortex as a safety feature. The IWDS ensures that no hostile actions can be taken aboard a TARDIS. While this applies to only physical violence in older models, more advanced IWDS may even put a stop to harsh language. The IWDS is not especially powerful though, allowing particularly violent or immoral individuals the ability to fight against its effects. The system on the Doctor's TARDIS has proved extremely unreliable, and some operators find ways to bypass the feature entirely. A few TARDIS mechanics have been known to attune the system so it doesn't affect them but works on others.

Nesting: Given that a TARDIS is bigger on the inside, it can land on large items and engulf them into its interior, appearing to just replace them if it assumes their form. This tendency to absorb rather than crush is good news to anyone being landed on. In general, such engulfed people and things appear in the console room as the TARDIS lands, but it is a simple matter to have them appear anywhere in the TARDIS. For instance, if you want to capture a particular person and they are stationary, you may materialise on top of them so they end up in a prison in the TARDIS. The reverse can also be set up, allowing the TARDIS to take off without some of its passengers if need be. However, unless the TARDIS is programmed to land on someone or something it automatically materialises in an empty space, however exact the coordinates.

One of the best uses of this ability it to materialise over an existing example of whatever your TARDIS is disguised as. Effectively this allows you to take the place of some innocuous-looking item rather than add your disguised TARDIS to a place. If you are worried about the abilities of your chameleon circuit you can then measure the dimensions of a real version of your disguise in the comfort of your control room.

This is all fine as long as the object you are materialising over is not another TARDIS or other dimensionally transcendental artefact. Then things get very messy, as the multi dimensional nature of both devices curves around each other infinitely. Effectively both TARDISes end up inside each other. If you leave one you end up in the control room of the other, leaving that TARDIS puts you back in your own control room again. If both TARDIS pilots work together the ships can be separated with minimal danger. However, if one pilot has chosen to try and trap his opponent's TARDIS in this way you are both in trouble. It is very hard for a TARDIS caught in such a way to break the loop without help.

Sentience: Every TARDIS is sentient and aware as each is grown rather than made. The level of sentience is quite minimal, a simple self-awareness rather than full artificial intelligence. However, like any living thing a TARDIS develops as it ages, becoming more and more aware and intelligent.

The reason for this sentience being part of the design of a TARDIS is twofold. Firstly a sentient machine can assist the pilot in navigating the complexities of the Vortex. It can predict the patterns and shifts and keep the capsule on course without the pilot needing to make every correction. It also allows it to anticipate the occupants' needs and try to keep them safe. All sentient life has a self-preservation instinct, meaning a TARDIS does not blindly land in hostile places or lead its occupants into danger.

The second need for sentience is that it allows the device to make a psychic link with the operator and occupants. This link's prime use is to draw on the intellect of the occupants and pilot to operate more efficiently. The living minds of the occupants create an essential part of some of the systems such as the translator (see below).

Shields: As part of an extensive array of safety features, all TARDISes are equipped with shielding against a variety of sources.

The shields protect the occupants from damage by radiation and energy attacks, as well as space and the Vortex. They also protect against temporal incursions from other time craft, and the damage that ensues from hitting a flying cruise liner. Unless actively turned off the TARDIS manipulates these shields to protect the crew whenever necessary. So if you open the doors in the vacuum of space it places a shield across the door to prevent everyone from being sucked out. The same applies for most planetary hostile environments too.

The Doctor's TARDIS shields have been modified and improved through the use of technology gained from the Slitheen. Blon Fel Fotch Pasameer-Day Slitheen's Tribophysical Waveform Macrokinetic Extrapolator was wired into the TARDIS systems by Jack Harkness to create an extended forcefield to defend them against the Daleks, and the Doctor used this to shunt the TARDIS away from the Racnoss. This type of shielding is not standard on non-combat orientated TARDIS units.

TARDIS Key: Every time capsule is protected by an advanced lock, requiring a key to enter. Spare keys can easily be created by the operator, but only when inside the TARDIS. Without a key, your chances of getting inside are pretty negligible. While many look like simple Yale type locks they are not, and no amount of lock picking will get you inside. They are a transdimensional key to a mathematical equation, whether they look like one or not. So the key can take any form, anything from a normal Yale key to a strange alien design to a coloured crystal. More advanced models might use a palm/retina scan or psychic scan on known passengers to open the door as losing the key can make life really difficult.

Sometimes, however, the psychic link between the Time Lord and the TARDIS can strengthen to such an extent that the TARDIS can recognise its 'pilot' and allow entry without a key. After hundreds of years travelling in the TARDIS, the Doctor can gain entry with a snap of the fingers.

Telepathic Circuits: Besides linking the mind of the Time Lord operator to the TARDIS and providing the empathic link between them, this circuit is also a psychic transmitter that uses Artron Energy to send telepathic signals through the Vortex to any place or time. Its other important function is to create the telepathic field which provides instant translation of speech and even writing to the Time Lord operator (see below). This field extends to others in the Time Lord's immediate presence and the operator may even choose to 'gift' specific individuals with the ability to use the field on their own. The operator's brain is an important part of this circuit, however, and should they become incapacitated, get mind wiped or enter into a self-induced coma, the link is broken. The TARDIS console also possesses a Telepathic Interface, a gel-like substance allowing its pilot to directly connect their mind to that of the TARDIS, effectively piloting it by focusing on a particular memory or location.

Translation Systems: The universe is home to infinite diversity, and therefore infinite languages. For a civilisation as advanced as the Gallifreyans, creating a portable translator was not beyond their abilities. However, such devices are cumbersome and might be mistaken for a weapon. Worse yet, if they are lost the traveller is stuck without any ability to communicate. Machine translation is also famously unsubtle often missing the nuances and details that make true communication possible and trouble free.

Each TARDIS is equipped with its own translation device. Using the psychic link it has to the occupants it simultaneously translates any spoken and written language for the occupants. Such travellers are often unaware of the way the TARDIS is manipulating their brain patterns, as anything they see or hear simply appears to be in their native language. By using a living mind the translators pick up all the nuances of the conversation, overcoming most cultural and intellectual barriers to communication as well as the purely linguistic ones.

The only problem with the translator systems is that it is tuned to Gallifreyan mental patterns. So if the only Gallifreyan occupant is incapacitated, the link may fail given that human minds are not strong enough to do the work.

⚙ THE TARDIS IN THE GAME

The TARDIS is a complex machine. It is first and foremost a vehicle and has the characteristics of one. It is also an extremely complex and useful Gadget with Story Points of its own. But even beyond that, the TARDIS is alive and has many of the characteristics of a character. It can think, feel, sense danger and can pilot itself when it desires. As the TARDIS can do all of these things, it is almost a character of its own, even through it isn't a player character.

It is, almost, the ultimate NPC. It should do whatever the Gamemaster requires of it to suit the plot, and is almost entirely under Gamemaster control (except when it is letting its pilot choose a destination). The skills and traits are provided to give you an idea of the many things it can do.

For example, if the Doctor wanted to scan a planet for life, he could use the Scan trait of the TARDIS, adding to his own Awareness + Ingenuity. If the Doctor was in trouble and there was no one aboard the TARDIS to pilot it, the TARDIS could make its own Awareness + Ingenuity roll, with a bonus from the Scan trait, to detect the Doctor's distress. Or the Gamemaster may simply decide that the TARDIS gets involved and materialises to his aid (whichever is the best option for the story).

Although the TARDIS has an Armour Rating and can take damage to its system, it is practically impossible to destroy. Damage reduces its functionality, reducing some of its attributes, but this can be repaired by the Doctor or by the TARDIS itself. The threat of destruction should only come as a plot device or the focus of an entire adventure.

More information on TARDISes can be found in **The Time Traveller's Companion** supplement.

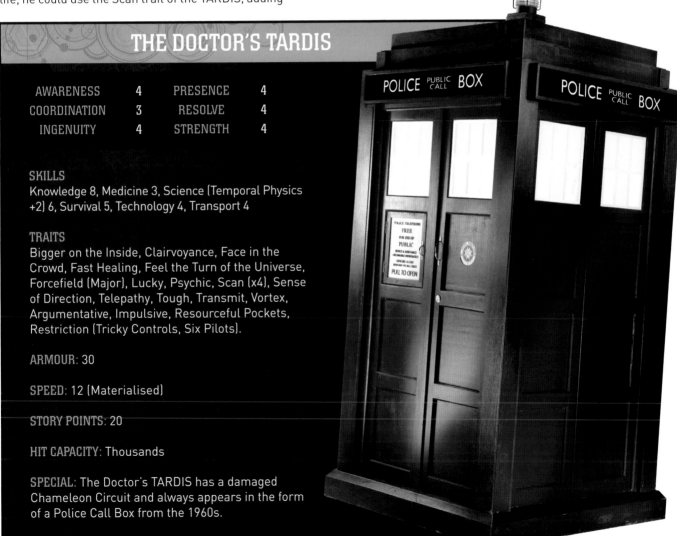

THE DOCTOR'S TARDIS

AWARENESS	4	PRESENCE	4
COORDINATION	3	RESOLVE	4
INGENUITY	4	STRENGTH	4

SKILLS
Knowledge 8, Medicine 3, Science (Temporal Physics +2) 6, Survival 5, Technology 4, Transport 4

TRAITS
Bigger on the Inside, Clairvoyance, Face in the Crowd, Fast Healing, Feel the Turn of the Universe, Forcefield (Major), Lucky, Psychic, Scan (x4), Sense of Direction, Telepathy, Tough, Transmit, Vortex, Argumentative, Impulsive, Resourceful Pockets, Restriction (Tricky Controls, Six Pilots).

ARMOUR: 30

SPEED: 12 (Materialised)

STORY POINTS: 20

HIT CAPACITY: Thousands

SPECIAL: The Doctor's TARDIS has a damaged Chameleon Circuit and always appears in the form of a Police Call Box from the 1960s.

⚙ GAMEMASTERING THE TARDIS

The TARDIS can be used in a number of ways in the game, and we've included some guidelines below. Remember, the Gamemaster has the final say on what is and what isn't feasible, and sometimes the TARDIS' functionality will have to be limited for the sake of the story.

TRAVELLING THE VORTEX

The main function of the TARDIS is to go from one time and place to another. The TARDIS has the equivalent of the Vortex Special Trait (see pg.57) though it is much more efficient in its travel and only uses a single Story Point for each trip (though the Gamemaster may increase this cost for extremely long journeys).

When the characters are setting the coordinates, they use their Ingenuity + Technology, with the bonus for their Vortex trait (without it, they will have great difficulty getting the TARDIS to go anywhere).

A Success means that the TARDIS has a minor misjump in space or time, missing the target location by 1-6 kilometres or days (roll a die to determine how far out). A Good Success lands the TARDIS very close to the target, within a few yards or minutes of its planned arrival.

A Fantastic Success is an incredibly accurate landing and is necessary for programming coordinates that require extreme precision (such as landing in a space only just big enough to fit the TARDIS).

A Failure lands the TARDIS in a bad position that requires a "micro-jump" to correct (such as arriving with its doors against a cliff face) or possibly distant from the target. A Bad result indicates landing in a place of potential danger that may put the TARDIS out of reach of the characters, such as activating the HADS and dematerialising shortly after the characters exit. A Disastrous result could place the TARDIS in a dangerous location, such as the engine room of a starship falling into a sun, or the middle of the control room of a Dalek saucer – whatever is appropriate for the story.

The Gamemaster should make piloting the TARDIS more difficult if they feel that the players are using its abilities to cheat or to gain easy access to buildings or locations. This can be justified by saying that the constant TARDIS use is causing ripples and disturbances in the space-time continuum, making piloting difficult. Otherwise, the TARDIS could be grounded for a time due to a system malfunction caused by the constant wear and tear.

THE TARDIS AS SUPER-GADGET

With the wide variety of systems and functions, the TARDIS is essentially the most multifunctional Gadget in the history of the universe. In essence, it has its own set of Other Extraordinary Abilities just like a Time Lord (see pg.134), but this extends to almost anything you can imagine a piece of hyper-advanced technology like the TARDIS may be able to do.

Characters should spend some time inside the guts of the TARDIS setting it up to perform complicated functions by rewiring controls, modifying circuits and making an Ingenuity + Technology roll, though anyone attempting to do this to the TARDIS should not only have the Vortex trait, but also Boffin. All but the simplest of these special modifications should be "One Shot" and for a single use only. Sometimes these modifications may be so major that the TARDIS may be grounded until the jiggery-pokery is repaired.

PLOT DEVICE

The TARDIS is a great means of getting the characters involved in the adventure, and also a way to keep the characters there. There are many instances where the TARDIS has landed only to be stolen, captured in a forcefield or otherwise grounded, forcing the Doctor and his companions to find the source of the trouble in order to recover his beloved blue box.

There have been times when the TARDIS has become the centre of an adventure, with whole stories taking place inside it, or even as the focus of an entire story arc.

Finally, with the TARDIS being semi-sentient, it can act on its own and lead to an adventure as well. What if the TARDIS tires of all the trouble the Doctor keeps putting it through and decides to take a holiday, leaving them stranded in time? What if a villain infects it with a virus that turns it against the characters? The possibilities in that small blue box are as expansive as its interior...

ALL THE STRANGE, STRANGE CREATURES

The universe is a vast place, and with the whole of space and time as your playground you're bound to encounter some less-than-hospitable forms of alien life. This chapter details some of the most common creatures, both hostile and friendly.

Of course, there isn't enough space here to cover every alien or adversary from the Doctor's recent adventures, never mind the hundreds of other races in the universe. This chapter is just going to cover the more important or more familiar races. Rules for other races and enemies, as well as for creating your own adversaries, is covered in greater detail in the **Aliens and Creatures** supplement, as well as the sourcebooks for each of the Doctor's incarnations.

WHERE IS RUSTY THE DALEK?

If you're looking for a specific alien, you may not find them in here. We had to make some tough decisions to narrow down the races and villains covered in this book. There are only so many pages we could squeeze in here, so we decided to look at races as a whole, and ignore specific characters (with one exception).

For example, we'll cover the Daleks here, but not Rusty the Dalek or the Dalek Prime Minister. If you need a specific character for your game, simply use the generic stats provided for their race, though for major Villains their attributes and skills may be

higher, and they should have access to more Story Points.

VILLAINS HAVE STORY POINTS TOO...

In the write-ups for the various races we've provided some suggested Story Points in their stats. This number is for minor characters, whereas more specific characters and major Villains will have more Story Points depending upon how powerful they are. For example, you could easily create the Supreme Dalek by taking the basic Dalek provided, increasing the Ingenuity a little, and also increasing the Story Points to around 8-12, to give it a better chance to foil the characters and to successfully escape when it would otherwise have been defeated.

⚙ CLOCKWORK ROBOTS

Humans have always found a need for robots, and in the 51st century they perfected a very stylish design using clockwork. While programmed for maintenance, the Clockwork Robots were also distinctive works of art in their own right.

The standard Clockwork Robot is encased in tough plastic shaped like a sculpted human form. Its gold and brass gears can easily be seen ticking away as they go about their tasks. The constant ticking sound they make is audible, but not much louder than a clock.

Specific robots can vary from this baseline depending on their circumstances. Some models may lack the power to teleport, or might be equipped with flamethrowers. Some have replaced their casing so they appear like a normal person. Artificial skin is not hard to come by in the far future, but some robots might decide to use the real thing.

In the 51st century, two sister ships went into space with clockwork crews: *SS Madame de Pompadour* and *SS Marie Antoinette*. Both ships were lost.

The *SS Madame de Pompadour* was badly damaged. The clockwork robots repaired it using organic parts from the crew, and sought the brain of the real Madame de Pompadour to complete their work. They managed to open time windows into the past, but the Doctor, Rose and Mickey closed the windows and the Clockwork Robots shut down.

The *SS Marie Antoinette* fell through time into Earth's distant past. The robots maintained the ship for millions of years, and they too killed humans and animals for repair materials. They were discovered by the Doctor, Clara and the Paternoster Gang in London in the late 19th Century, and when the control node (a particularly self-aware Clockwork Robot known as the Half-face Man) died, they all shut down.

Clockwork Robots are highly logical and even pedantic, but they display great ingenuity when it comes to repairing and maintaining their systems. They are also capable of imaginative development, for example, the control node for the *SS Marie Antoinette* developed an awareness of beauty and a belief in paradise (although this change did take millions of years).

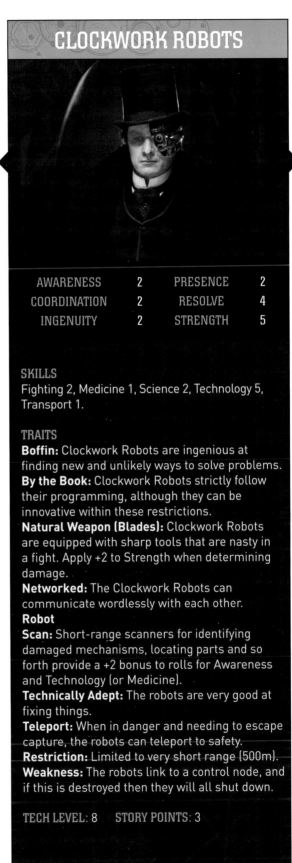

CLOCKWORK ROBOTS

AWARENESS	2	PRESENCE	2
COORDINATION	2	RESOLVE	4
INGENUITY	2	STRENGTH	5

SKILLS
Fighting 2, Medicine 1, Science 2, Technology 5, Transport 1.

TRAITS
Boffin: Clockwork Robots are ingenious at finding new and unlikely ways to solve problems.
By the Book: Clockwork Robots strictly follow their programming, although they can be innovative within these restrictions.
Natural Weapon (Blades): Clockwork Robots are equipped with sharp tools that are nasty in a fight. Apply +2 to Strength when determining damage.
Networked: The Clockwork Robots can communicate wordlessly with each other.
Robot
Scan: Short-range scanners for identifying damaged mechanisms, locating parts and so forth provide a +2 bonus to rolls for Awareness and Technology (or Medicine).
Technically Adept: The robots are very good at fixing things.
Teleport: When in danger and needing to escape capture, the robots can teleport to safety.
Restriction: Limited to very short range (500m).
Weakness: The robots link to a control node, and if this is destroyed then they will all shut down.

TECH LEVEL: 8   **STORY POINTS:** 3

⚙ CYBERMEN

Cybermen are humans who gave up their humanity to become cold steel soldiers. They are determined to upgrade the rest of humanity to join their silver legions.

A Cyberman is essentially a human brain and nervous system wired into a powerful robotic body, although many conversion methods simply encase the whole body in a metal shell and rewire the person's brain. Emotional suppression is essential to keep Cybermen functioning. If they experience real understanding of what they have become, they will go mad, or worse.

Unusually, the Cybermen have two parallel histories. In the Doctor's universe, the Cybermen originated on the solar system's lost tenth planet, Mondas. Millennia ago, Mondas drifted away through space, and its people gradually became metal cyborgs to survive the extreme environment. Their souls were also transformed and they became the conquering Cybermen. When Mondas returned to the solar system, the Cybermen attempted to drain Earth of its power but Mondas exploded, leaving the Cybermen as homeless nomads. The following centuries saw several further attacks on Earth by the Cybermen, until the decisive Cyber Wars knocked them out of history.

The second origin of the Cybermen was on Earth in a parallel universe. Wealthy lunatic John Lumic of Cybus Industries designed the Cybermen as a way to improve the world. Converts would be released from the limitations of the flesh, but also from prejudice and disease, and perhaps even death. He had no understanding that immortality in a world with no art, love, culture or variety would be no life at all. The Cybermen eventually escaped Lumic's control and crossed realities to invade the Doctor's Earth. The invasion was halted by the Doctor in what became known as 'the Battle of Canary Wharf'. Most Cybermen were thrown into the Void, but some fell through time and escaped.

Surviving Cybermen from both origins eventually met. The two branches merged their technology and resources to create a new breed of the metal monsters. Most of the Doctor's recent encounters with Cybermen have been with these hybrids. One

dramatic encounter with the hybrids threatened the transformation of the whole of Earth's population, living and deceased. This was the masterplan of the Doctor's old enemy Missy, who had taken control of a force of Cybermen. She adjusted Cybermen technology to allow the conversion of dead bodies as well as living victims, and arranged for dead people's minds to be preserved so they could be restored at the moment of cyber-resurrection. Missy's Cybermen were destroyed by one convert, Danny Pink, who retained his identity. He won control of the Cyber army and ordered them all to self-destruct.

CYBERMEN

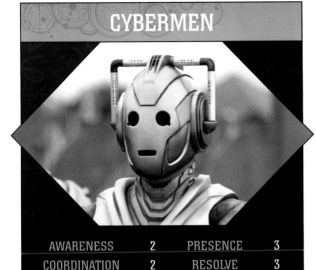

AWARENESS	2	PRESENCE	3
COORDINATION	2	RESOLVE	3
INGENUITY	2	STRENGTH	7

SKILLS
Convince 2, Fighting 3, Marksman 2, Medicine 1, Science 1, Technology 4.

TRAITS
Armour (Major): Heavy metal armour reduces damage by 10, but reduces Coordination to 2.
Cyborg
Flight: Cybermen have rockets in their boots that allow them to fly at the same speed as a commercial airliner.
Fear Factor (3): Cybermen are scary and gain +6 on rolls to actively scare someone.
Natural Weapon – Electric Grip: The Cyberman's grip delivers a powerful blast of electricity, increasing the damage in close combat to (4/9/13).
Natural Weapon (Particle Beam): Cybermen have arm-mounted particle beams (4/L/L).
Networked: Cybermen are connected by wireless technology to a collective hive mind.
Slow
Special – Quicksilver: A Cyberman can move in short bursts of lightning speed, quicker than the human eye can follow. Each burst of speed costs 1 Story Point and gives the Cyberman a speed of 20 for one round.
Weakness (Minor) – Magnetism: A Cyberman must make a Resolve + Strength Roll (Difficulty 18) when exposed to strong magnetic force. A Bad Result means the emotion inhibitor shuts down, driving the Cyberman crazy. A Disastrous Result destroys the Cyberman.
Weakness (Minor) – Gold: Gold particles are lethal to Mondas Cybermen only.

TECH LEVEL: 6   STORY POINTS: 3

⊛ DALEKS

In the entire universe, no race has caused more death and destruction or incited more fear and terror than the Daleks. Those who see a Dalek for the first time often underestimate them. They look like little more than an armed pepper pot, some sort of silly robot that will have a problem getting up stairs. Nothing could be further from the truth.

The Daleks were created by Davros, a crippled scientist from the planet Skaro. He developed tank-like 'travel machines' to help his people, the Kaleds, survive the war-torn environment of Skaro. Wartime weapons mutated the Kaleds and Davros accelerated this mutation to ensure their survival, creating the brain-like creatures named Daleks.

The Daleks were born in war, and they continued along that path. This reached an apex in the Time War, perhaps the greatest war ever fought, where the Daleks and the Time Lords strove to wipe each other out of history. It was the Doctor who put an end to this war, apparently wiping out both sides.

This was just one of many times the Doctor engineered defeat for the Daleks. He fought them on Skaro at their genesis and several times after, and he has stood against their invasions of other worlds numerous times, not least their conquest of Earth in the 22nd century. The Time War should have been the end of the Dalek threat, but the Daleks found a way to survive. Small groups scattered through history launched various schemes to rebuild the Dalek population, such as the secret conversion of humans into Daleks, the evolution of a new form of Dalek, and the rescue of lost creator Davros from the Time War. Eventually one of their schemes succeeded, and the Dalek population exploded once again.

The Daleks built a fearsome empire, complete with subject worlds pockmarked with prison camps and secretive sleeper agents inserted into rival forces. Although different varieties of Dalek do not normally mix, they now come together in a great Parliament when appropriate; after the Time War, the Daleks have found a way past the brutal purity disputes that once set different strains against each other in deadly civil wars. This unified Dalek force anchored the siege of Trenzalore, maintaining it for many centuries before the regenerating Doctor destroyed their fleet. Unperturbed, the Daleks continue to plot in the darkness, always planning to re-take their position as the highest form of life in the universe...

DALEK TRAVEL MACHINE

A Dalek is not a robot, but a crippled mutant encased in an armoured battlesuit. This battlesuit is armed with a weapon that can fire in a 360-degree arc and spells instant death for any life form it strikes. It is encased in both armour plating and a forcefield, making it immune to almost every form of weaponry. Built-in survival systems allow a Dalek to survive easily under water or in hard vacuum. Even the heat of falling through a planet's atmosphere from space cannot destroy the suit or kill the mutant inside. Energy thrusters in the casing allow the Dalek to fly in space or in atmosphere at low altitudes. Finally, advanced computers allow the Dalek to hack into most computer networks, downloading huge amounts of data in moments. Everything about a Dalek is designed to kill and destroy – even their plunger-like manipulator arm can suffocate a man to death, crush their skulls or extract their brainwaves.

DALEK

AWARENESS	3	PRESENCE	4
COORDINATION	2	RESOLVE	4
INGENUITY	4	STRENGTH	7

SKILLS
Convince 4, Fighting 4, Marksman 3, Medicine 3, Science 8, Survival 4, Technology 8.

TRAITS
Armour (Major): The Dalekanium casing reduces damage by 10. This does reduce the Dalek's Coordination to 2 (already included in their Attributes).
Cyborg
Environmental: Daleks are able to survive in the vacuum of space, or underwater.
Fear Factor (4): No one who has faced a Dalek can consider them anything less than terrifying, getting a +8 to rolls when actively scaring someone.
Flight (Major): Daleks are able to fly. When hovering their Speed is effectively 1, when in open skies or space they have a Speed of 6.
Forcefield (Major): Bullets appear to stop in the air before the Dalek, appearing to dissolve on contact with the Dalek's powerful forcefield. Damage is reduced by two levels (from Disastrous to Bad, from Bad to Failure, and so on).
Natural Weapon – Exterminator: The legendary Dalek weapon usually kills with a single shot (4/L/L).
Scan: The Dalek can interface with computers and with living beings and absorb data in great quantities.
Special – Self Destruct: If under threat of being captured, the Dalek will self destruct, causing (3/6/9) levels of damage to those within 10m of the explosion.
Technically Adept: Daleks are brilliant at using and adapting technology.
Vortex: As a last, desperate measure, some of the higher-ranking Daleks, such as the Cult of Skaro, can activate an 'Emergency Temporal Shift', literally throwing themselves into the Vortex to escape. There is no control over where they will emerge, and this usually exhausts most of their energy supplies, leaving them on emergency reserves.

TECH LEVEL: 9   STORY POINTS: 5-8

SECONDARY THREATS

Daleks fight their own battles from the front, flying their saucer ships into battle or charging forward into the lines of enemy ground forces. The travel machine is the most common threat faced by those targeted by the Daleks. However, Dalek technology and culture does allow for other kinds of threats under their control. Daleks sometimes keep and use slaves (modified humans or bestial Ogrons, for example) or trained beasts (like the deadly Slyther). They use tiny security robots to maintain the bodily security of their travel machines, and similar robots could be encountered at normal size protecting Dalek facilities. The most upsetting additional Dalek threat is their use of sleeper agents - the agents often don't realise they are controlled by the Daleks until orders to exterminate finally come roaring through their minds, when a Dalek eyestalk grows abruptly from their forehead.

DALEK PSYCHOLOGY

All Daleks believe they are superior to all other forms of life. They alone have the right to command and dominate. They believe in no greater force than themselves and insist that no form of morality applies to them. It is their mission not only to control the universe, but also to cleanse it of all non-Dalek life. Even with advanced technology, as the Time Lords learnt to their cost, it is hard to face such a determined and aggressive enemy. Daleks feel no fear, will kill in an instant and feel no remorse, and consider the universe only in terms of war and murder. Daleks have no art or culture, they exist only to fight and conquer. Anything that cannot be used as a weapon or a defence is no use to them.

As one of the most technologically advanced races in the universe, mere weapons and armour are rarely enough to destroy the Dalek threat. One of their only weaknesses is their predictability, due to their reliance on logic. The Doctor's cunning, ingenuity and abstract thinking has led to their defeat each time. The Daleks are also extremely pragmatic, which has often given their enemies respite from their attacks. Free from emotion the Daleks never get angry or upset over the results of battle. If resistance proves too strong they will not push forward out of pride or martial spirit, they will retreat and reconsider. However, if they believe they can overcome an obstacle they will sacrifice slaves and other resources, even themselves, to achieve their objective. Daleks are subservient to their own race, seeing the individual as unimportant compared to the glory of the Dalek race as a whole.

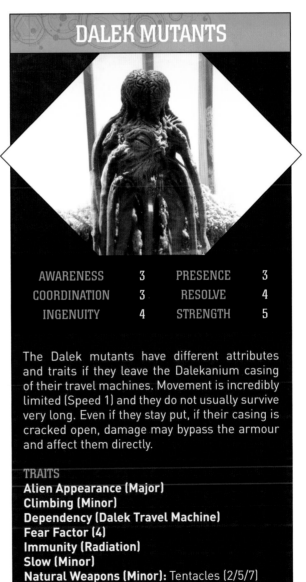

DALEK MUTANTS

AWARENESS	3	PRESENCE	3
COORDINATION	3	RESOLVE	4
INGENUITY	4	STRENGTH	5

The Dalek mutants have different attributes and traits if they leave the Dalekanium casing of their travel machines. Movement is incredibly limited (Speed 1) and they do not usually survive very long. Even if they stay put, if their casing is cracked open, damage may bypass the armour and affect them directly.

TRAITS
Alien Appearance (Major)
Climbing (Minor)
Dependency (Dalek Travel Machine)
Fear Factor (4)
Immunity (Radiation)
Slow (Minor)
Natural Weapons (Minor): Tentacles (2/5/7)
Technically Adept

DALEK ANTIBODIES

AWARENESS	3	PRESENCE	2
COORDINATION	3	RESOLVE	2
INGENUITY	2	STRENGTH	3

These tiny antibodies keep the Dalek safe from microscopic infections and other threats. They are programmed to disintegrate any intruding organic material and dump the remnants into a disposal system.

TRAITS
Alien Senses (detect life signs)
Flight (Major)
Immunity (Radiation)
Natural Weapons (Major): Disintegration beam (4/L/L)
Networked
Robot
Tiny (Major)

DALEK SLEEPER AGENT

Anyone converted into a Dalek sleeper agent appears to be normal, with their usual range of attributes, skills and traits. However, when their Dalek programming is triggered, an eyestalk will emerge from their head and a gunstick from their hand, and they will serve the Daleks.

ABILITIES AND SKILLS:
As the converted character.

TRAITS
As the converted character, but also:
Alien Appearance (Major): Eyestalk emerging from forehead
Alien Senses (Dalek Eyestalk)
Enslaved
Natural Weapons (Major): Gunstick hand (4/L/L)
Networked
Shapeshift (Minor)

⚙ MISSY (THE MASTER)

Missy is the latest incarnation of the Doctor's oldest friend and most determined enemy, the Master. Since reappearing in the Doctor's life during his exile on Earth, she has been a recurring thorn in his side. She is responsible for many horrors and may well be irredeemable. She has apparently died time and time again but always found a way back.

Missy is a middle-aged woman wearing exaggerated Victorian clothing – complete with flying umbrella. She has abandoned the smooth charm that has marked some of her previous incarnations, and doubled down on the eccentricity. She gleefully says she is "bananas" as she murders people for the slightest infractions. Above all else she enjoys discomfiting the Doctor.

HISTORY
At the age of eight, children of Gallifrey are taken out into the mountains of Solace and Solitude and made to stare into the Vortex. Their reaction determines their course in life. Some, like the Doctor, run. Others, like the boy who would become the Master, are driven insane. That boy would go on to commit countless atrocities – perhaps more than anyone else in history.

The Master grew interested in Earth during the Doctor's exile there. The Doctor thwarted several attempts by the Master to conquer or destroy the planet. When the Doctor's exile ended, the two went on to battle further across several other planets. Later, in his final incarnation, the Master returned to Gallifrey and corrupted members of the High Council. The Doctor thwarted his revenge, but could not stop the Master soon after taking over the body of Tremas of Traken. In this body, the Master set about his most audacious plan ever; holding the universe to ransom as a wave of entropy swept across the stars. Again, the Doctor stopped him.

Some time later, the Master was put on trial on Skaro and exterminated by the Daleks. The Doctor retrieved his ashes, but this was another of the Master's schemes, and he forced the TARDIS to land in San Francisco at the turn of the millennium. He took over another new body, and tried to steal the Doctor's remaining lives. Instead he was sucked into the Vortex and lost.

Later still, as the Last Great Time War began to reach its peak, the Time Lords resurrected the Master to be their perfect warrior. The Master fled, however, using a Chameleon Arch to hide as a human at the end of the universe, the kindly "Professor Yana". He worked for years to build a rocket capable of taking the last surviving humans to a fabled 'Utopia', where they could survive the collapse of everything. When the Doctor arrived, the Master's memories awoke and he regenerated into a new younger body. He stole the Doctor's TARDIS and infiltrated the British government in the early 21st century. As "Harold Saxon" he took the office of Prime Minister. Once again the Doctor and his companion were able to stop his schemes, but his wife shot and killed him before the Doctor could take him into his care.

Soon after, a death cult managed to resurrect the Master, and he used the so-called Immortality Gate to turn every human on the planet into his double. This was all part of a grander scheme to bring back Gallifrey from its place in the Time War, but when Rassilon and the High Council appeared, the Master assisted the Doctor in defeating them. He was dragged back into the Time War where he was trapped on Gallifrey. This was not the end. Gallifrey survived the Time War, and the Master escaped, regenerating into a new, female body and taking as a new alias "Missy", short for "the Mistress". She found the Doctor and embarked upon a lengthy plan that involved capturing the minds of everyone who died on Earth, and also many others who died close to the Doctor's adventures in other times and places. She stored these minds in a stolen slice of the Gallifreyan matrix called the Nethersphere, gently convincing them to divest themselves of their emotions.

Meanwhile, she established the 3W Institute on Earth, which convinced wealthy people that the dead still suffered unless their bodies were suitably cared for. The super-rich around the world entrusted their bodies to 3W's care as they died.

MISSY

AWARENESS	4	PRESENCE	6
COORDINATION	4	RESOLVE	6
INGENUITY	10	STRENGTH	3

SKILLS
Athletics 2, Convince 5, Craft 2, Fighting 2, Knowledge 6, Marksman 3, Medicine 4, Science 5, Subterfuge 5, Survival 4, Technology 5, Transport 4.

TRAITS
Adversary (The Doctor): The Doctor always turns up to thwart Missy's plans.
Boffin: Allows Missy to create Gadgets.
Distinctive: Missy dresses as a mad Victorian governess, so stands out in a crowd.
Eccentric: Megalomaniac, control freak, twisted game player, psychopath: take your pick!
Hypnosis (Special): +2 bonus to control another's actions and feelings and may attempt to possess another subject.
Impulsive: While she does have long, complicated plans, she often acts on a murderous impulse.
Indomitable: +4 bonus to any rolls to resist psychic control.
Obsession (Major): Missy is obsessed with trying to win the Doctor over.
Photographic Memory: Missy can remember everything she has seen or done.

Quick Reflexes: She is light on her feet and quick to act.
Selfish (Minor): Missy only ever thinks of herself (and the Doctor).
Technically Adept: +2 to any Technology roll to fix a broken or faulty device.
Time Lord
Time Lord – Experienced (Special Good)
Time Traveller (Special): Familiar with all Tech Levels.
Voice of Authority: +2 bonus to Presence + Convince rolls.
Vortex Born: May re-roll a failed test involving time or time travel.

EQUIPMENT: Laser Screwdriver (Special Gadget; Traits: Open/Close, Scan, Transmit, Zap, Weld; Story Points: 1); **Umbrella** (Minor Gadget; Traits: Flight; Story Points: 1)

TECH LEVEL: 10

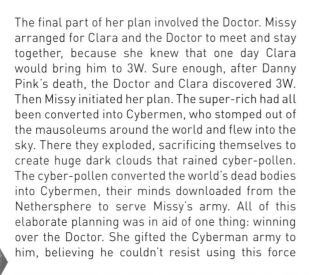

The final part of her plan involved the Doctor. Missy arranged for Clara and the Doctor to meet and stay together, because she knew that one day Clara would bring him to 3W. Sure enough, after Danny Pink's death, the Doctor and Clara discovered 3W. Then Missy initiated her plan. The super-rich had all been converted into Cybermen, who stomped out of the mausoleums around the world and flew into the sky. There they exploded, sacrificing themselves to create huge dark clouds that rained cyber-pollen. The cyber-pollen converted the world's dead bodies into Cybermen, their minds downloaded from the Nethersphere to serve Missy's army. All of this elaborate planning was in aid of one thing: winning over the Doctor. She gifted the Cyberman army to him, believing he couldn't resist using this force for good, and expecting him to be corrupted by the power it gave him. The Doctor refused the gift, and Missy was apparently disintegrated by a renegade Cyberman. However, on past performance, Missy will find a way to return…

✸ THE BONELESS

The Boneless are from a universe that has only two dimensions. They crept into three-dimensional space on a Bristol estate, and killed several dozen humans by 'flattening' them to examine and dissect them. After they encountered Clara and the Doctor, they manifested directly as three-dimensional beings, but their behaviour was destructive and malign.

BONELESS

AWARENESS	3	PRESENCE	3
COORDINATION	1	RESOLVE	4
INGENUITY	3	STRENGTH	3

SKILLS
Fighting 2, Marksman 2, Science 4, Subterfuge 3, Survival 3.

TRAITS
Alien
Alien Appearance (Major): The Boneless are two-dimensional beings, and even when manifesting in three dimensions they still look 'wrong'.
Climbing (Major): There is no such thing as "up" to a Boneless. They can travel smoothly over any surface.
Environmental (Minor): The Boneless are native to a two-dimensional environment and exist comfortably in such conditions.
Immunity: The Boneless cannot be harmed by any physical object; the object would be flattened as soon as it touched them. However, a 3D Boneless does take damage. It is reduced to 2D if it is overcome, and must expend a Story Point to regrow into 3D shape.
Natural Weapon (Major): At a touch, the Boneless can 'flatten' a target, instantly killing them (L/L/L).
Special – Use Dimensional Energy: The Boneless can absorb dimensional energy and expend it as tendrils of orange lightning.

The Boneless can drain dimensional energy from three-dimensional targets, "flattening" them.
- The Boneless must be touching the target to use this power.
- When an object is flattened, it can become a confusing mess like an abstract painting or a clean image like a photograph.
- When used on a living target, the victim dies immediately. The victim can then be experimented upon, dissected or turned into a clean image like a drawing of the person.

The Boneless can also expend dimensional energy, which appears as red lightning.
They can restore a flattened object to normal.
- They can give themselves three-dimensional bodies. (This costs 1 Story Point.)
- They can create short-term 3D forms, like a giant hand to grab a victim. (This costs 3 Story Points.)

TECH LEVEL: Unknown   **STORY POINTS:** 6

The Doctor threw them back to their home dimension and warned them not to return, but that might not stop them.

The Boneless appear as a distortion on a flat surface, like running water but moving with direction and purpose. They cannot jump from one surface to another. They can also make themselves appear as a moving image of a person they had flattened. The three-dimensional forms they tried out in Bristol were flickering, warped versions of the same people, shambling awkwardly through the unfamiliar 3D world.

⊛ THE TELLER

The Teller was one of two surviving members of a telepathic humanoid species. Both survivors were enslaved by Madame Karabraxos; one was locked away in a special vault to provide leverage over the other, forcing it to work for the Bank of Karabraxos. The Teller's ability to detect guilt and sift through minds to confirm criminal intent made it a supremely useful asset to bank security.

The Bank's manager kept the Teller in a misty hibernation chamber, waking it for periodic sweeps to detect guilt and also whenever she suspected trouble. If the Teller locked on to someone's mind and found criminal intent, it was permitted to devour the mind, which it did with little fanfare: its eyestalks came together to create a beam of light that struck the target's head, and in moments their mind was turned into soup and their skull had collapsed in on itself.

There is no known way to escape this fate, although keeping your mind blank makes it harder for the Teller to locate you. Of course, keeping your mind blank is easier said than done!

Once the Teller has locked on to a target's thoughts, it cannot be shaken loose, and it can begin to feast at any time. It is possible to lure a Teller into releasing a target, but only by offering it an even more appealing guilty mind as an alternative meal.

THE TELLER

AWARENESS	4	PRESENCE	4
COORDINATION	4	RESOLVE	4
INGENUITY	2	STRENGTH	3

SKILLS
Survival 2.

TRAITS
Alien
Alien Appearance (Major): The Teller is humanoid but has eyes on stalks. long claws, and a stubby tail.
Alien Senses: The Teller can use its psychic abilities to detect guilt in the minds of those around it. It can also follow the thought trails of those it has previously examined telepathically.
Enslaved: The Teller is fully owned and controlled by the Bank of Karabraxos.
Fear Factor (1): The Teller is used as a threat by the Bank. +2 on rolls to actively scare or intimidate.
Psychic

Slow: The Teller is ponderous and sure in its movements. Its Speed is 2.
Special (Mind Wipe): After it has locked on to someone's thoughts, the Teller can devour their mind. No additional roll is needed – the victim's Awareness, Ingenuity, Presence and Resolve attributes simply start losing 1 point each turn until they are all at 0.
Telepathy: The Teller can directly contact and sift through someone else's mind, looking for evidence of criminal intent (or anything else it wishes). It needs to win an opposed Ingenuity + Resolve roll to lock on to someone's thoughts.

TECH LEVEL: Unknown

STORY POINTS: 5

The Doctor was asked by a dying Madame Karabraxos to go back in time and remedy the injustice she had done to the Teller and its mate. The Doctor and his friends launched a daring heist, but they had to hide their true intentions to pass through Bank security.

Nevertheless, once they reached the secret vault, the Doctor opened his mind to the Teller. He allowed it to scan through his memories because he knew it would be able to break through the mental block. The Teller saw that the Doctor's mission was actually to rescue its companion. It released the Doctor, and the Doctor and his friends in turn freed the Teller's mate and took them home to be free.

⚙ ROBOT KNIGHTS

The Doctor's encounter with Robin Hood was enlivened by robots disguised as armoured knights. They were the size and shape of muscular human adults, and only if their helmets were opened would an observer see their unemotional metal faces.

The robots were the crew of a spaceship from the 29th century that had fallen through time and crashed in Nottingham. After the crash they were discovered by the Sheriff of Nottingham, who took control of the robots and disguised them as knights. In return, the Sheriff endeavoured to repair the ship's circuits, a task requiring a great deal of gold.

The robots took to their new duties with mechanical zeal. They worked as the Sheriff's enforcers throughout his lands, and they also ruthlessly managed the slave workforce beneath the castle who worked the gold into parts for the ship. Workers who had exceeded their potential work capacity were no longer useful, and were simply disintegrated.

The robots also offered to use their technology to physically enhance their ally, the Sheriff. They performed simple surgeries on his body that transformed him into a cyborg.

The Robot Knights were seeking to reach "the Promised Land", the Nethersphere trap that was laid by Missy. They appeared to believe they could pilot their ship to this destination. It is unclear how they acquired this belief in a Promised Land, just as

it is unclear how their ship became damaged and fell through time to the 12th Century.

Although all the robots in Nottingham were destroyed along with their ship, it is possible that before it was destroyed, their ship communicated to other vessels with robot crews, sharing data about the knightly disguise and the Promised Land. Thus, ships full of crusading armoured robot knights could be encountered almost anywhere in time and space.

ROBOT KNIGHTS

AWARENESS	2	PRESENCE	2
COORDINATION	3	RESOLVE	3
INGENUITY	2	STRENGTH	5

SKILLS
Fighting 3, Knowledge 3, Marksman 3, Medicine 2, Technology 3, Transport 2.

TRAITS
Armour (Minor): The knightly armour of the robots reduces damage by 4.
By the Book: The robots diligently follow commands from their controllers.
Natural Weapon (Disintegrator): These robots fire a purple disintegration ray from a slit in their face (4/L/L).
Restriction: The disintegration ray does not affect a reflective metal surface, in fact it is reflected back at the robot and may destroy it.
Robot

EQUIPMENT: Sword (3/7/10)

TECH LEVEL: 6   STORY POINTS: 3

⚙ SILURIANS

Human beings were not the first race to dominate the Earth. Long before them, long before even the dinosaurs roamed the great plains of the prehistoric planet, another race of creatures were kings of the planet's lush, jungle environments. The Silurians (also known by many other names, most commonly Homo Reptilia) were a race of humanoid lizards who ruled a vast empire stretching the continent - and even beyond, delving deep under the oceans.

A peaceful race, the Silurians were the true masters of the Earth in its early prehistoric existence. Their mighty empire spanned millions of years, and they were known of throughout the galaxy. When the earliest humans began to evolve, Silurians treated them much like animals, a far lesser species to their own. When humans became an annoyance, they would be simply disposed of using a virus fatal to humans created by Silurian biologists.

Like many races, the Silurians were split into several sub-species. While all shared rough scaly skin, and crown-like crests atop their heads, various species of the race evolved differently. Some Silurians developed a third eye in their forehead, while others grew to have more human features, which they hid behind masks.

Those Silurians that evolved beneath the waves of the oceans (known as Sea Devils) grew webbed feet and hands, better suited to their undersea environment.

At some point during their history, the Silurians detected a planetoid headed in the direction of Earth; they became concerned that it was on a collision course with the planet, and that it would spell the end of their vast civilisation. Preparing themselves against the fear of destruction, the race hid underground, building huge hibernation chambers deep beneath the surface.

With the planet's surface clear of Silurians, none saw that the planetoid was eventually pulled into the Earth's gravity to form the Moon.

Though the Silurians had planned to re-awaken and take back their world once they believed the threat had passed, the technology was created in a hurry, and didn't function as expected. The creatures remained buried under the Earth's surface for millennia, sleeping unaware that on the surface, humanity had risen up and claimed the world for their own.

At various points throughout history, some sub-sets of the Silurian species have re-awoken when their technology was disturbed. These small groups believe that the Earth is still rightfully theirs, and that the Human beings need to return to their rightful place. During the 20th century, a small group of Silurians re-awoke in England and infected the country with a dose of their poison. The Doctor was able to establish a cure and convince the Silurians to return to their hibernation.

Disturbed by their claim over the planet, however, the peace was to be short lived, and the group was attacked by UNIT, under orders from Brigadier Lethbridge-Stewart. He ordered that the group be destroyed and their hibernation chambers were blown up.

This kind of rocky reception was often the type that met with the re-awakening of any Silurian group. In the early 21st century, the Doctor again encountered the Silurians, and thought he could broker a deal between them and humanity.

Fear and tension rose between the two species again, however, and the talks nearly descended into warfare when the Silurians turned upon even their own kind in the pursuit of their planet.

It is possible that one day, the Silurians can return to living on the surface of the world they once owned. The Doctor is a keen champion of this idea and following the conflicts during his last meeting, re-wired their hibernation technology to give them just a thousand years more sleep; hoping that they can try again at that time.

SILURIANS

AWARENESS	4	PRESENCE	4
COORDINATION	3	RESOLVE	4
INGENUITY	3	STRENGTH	5

SKILLS
Athletics 3, Convince 1, Fighting 3, Knowledge 3, Marksman 2, Medicine 2, Science 2, Subterfuge 1, Survival 3, Technology 1.

TRAITS
Alien Appearance (Major)
Armour (Minor): Silurians have incredibly tough, lizard-like skin. From head to toe, their rough scales provide a natural armour. Silurians reduce all damage made against them by 5.
Climbing
Environmental (Minor) – Extreme Heat
Natural Weapon (Major) – Tongue: A Silurian's long lizard tongue can be fired out from its mouth at incredible speed and to a distance of one metre. If it comes in contact with a human, it injects poison into them. The infected person must make a Strength + Resolve check once every hour to avoid mutation or death.
Weakness (Minor): Cold.

SILURIAN GUN: Lethal (4/**L**/L); also has a Stun setting, firing a cloud of incapacitating gas.

TECH LEVEL: 6   STORY POINTS: 3-5

SEA DEVILS

AWARENESS	3	PRESENCE	4
COORDINATION	2 (Land) 5 (Water)	RESOLVE	4
INGENUITY	4	STRENGTH	4

When the Silurians walked the Earth, millions of years ago, they employed foot soldiers of a distantly related breed which came to be known as Sea Devils. Like huge, bipedal, humanoid turtles, these warriors hibernated when the Silurians feared for the continuation of their species. With a thousand underwater colonies across the globe, their hibernation technology was not as advanced and left them in a weakened state when they started to wake.

SKILLS
Fighting 4, Marksman 4, Science 2, Survival 3, Technology 2.

TRAITS
Fear Factor 2: They are lizards, crawling out the sea towards you, and that's frightening.
Environmental (Major): They can live underwater.
Armour (Minor): Scales reduce injury by five levels.
Weakness (Major) – High frequency sound: High frequencies make Sea Devils unable to take any other actions than walking slowly.

SEA DEVIL GUN: Lethal (4/**L**/L). It can also be used to burn through walls and doors, even those made of thick metal.

TECH LEVEL: 6   STORY POINTS: 4

 SKOVOX BLITZER

Skovox war machines are created to fight in devastating wars that reduce whole planets to smoking ruins. They are designed and built by Skovox Artificers, who also command them in the field. One of their machines is the Blitzer, which is essentially a mobile artillery platform. It has a humanoid robot torso that is mounted on a sturdy platform with four insectoid legs. Both the Blitzer's arms terminate in weapons - it has no hands, and manipulates its environment using other means.

The Doctor, Clara and Danny encountered a Skovox Blitzer that had found itself on Earth. It homed in on Coal Hill School in London due to the area's high level of artron energy. The Doctor attempted to trap it in a time tunnel, but after this failed he imitated an Artificer and convinced it to accept a shutdown code. He then deposited the deactivated Blitzer in space.

Skovox war machines have some understanding of time technology. The Blitzer that came to Coal Hill School was able to detect artron energy and was attracted to it; it likewise was able to detect and correctly interpret the temporal disruption that was the Doctor's trap for it. Skovox machines are sensitive to time energy emissions of all varieties and time travel does not confuse them.

The Skovox Blitzer is certainly not the only variety of Skovox war machine. Skovox Artificers have designed and created an enormous variety of deadly machines to serve all aspects of their war effort.

There are machines specialised for underwater and arboreal engagements, machines dedicated to forward observation, machines dedicated solely to digging tunnels to undermine enemy fortifications and countless more.

SKOVOX BLITZER

AWARENESS	3	PRESENCE	1
COORDINATION	2	RESOLVE	2
INGENUITY	2	STRENGTH	3

SKILLS
Athletics 2, Fighting 2, Knowledge 3, Marksman 4, Subterfuge 2, Survival 2.

TRAITS
Alien Senses: The Blitzer can detect heat traces.
Armour (10): The Blitzer is covered with military-grade protection.
By the Book: The Blitzer is calibrated for military action and rigidly follows orders from its commanders.
Restriction: The Blitzer relies on visual identification to confirm targets and objectives, and it can be foiled by invisibility.
Robot
Scan: The Blitzer can scan to detect energy sources and life forms in an area.
Special (Payload): The Blitzer carries enough explosives to destroy an entire planet. If its standard weapons aren't doing the job, it will quickly escalate to the use of massive weapons. Furthermore, if it is attacked and harmed by conventional weaponry, these armaments may detonate, with devastating consequences.

Special (Self-destruct): The Blitzer is programmed with a self-destruct protocol that engages whenever it receives end-of-service orders. (A special input code can cause shutdown without self-destruction however.) Its eyes turn red and it counts down from ten. If it gets to zero, it explodes with devastating consequences for the planet it is on.

WEAPONS: Blaster (4/L/L), Machine Gun (4/8/12), Explosives (4/L/L).

TECH LEVEL: 6   **STORY POINTS:** 3

⚙ SONTARANS

The Sontaran race was known millennia ago as one of the most talented and cultured species in the universe. The race was devoted to the arts of music and painting, and many came to their planet of Sontar to view the works of the great Sontaran Renaissance. Sontar itself was a world of majestic beauty, featuring vast plains of grass, blowing in a cinnamon breeze, stretching out to the horizon, where deep canyons fell thousands of feet to the rich-blue oceans below. Around 50,000 years ago all of this changed for the planet and its inhabitants. The Sontarans found themselves caught in a war with the shape changing Rutan Host. Putting aside their arts for what they expected to be a short war, the Sontaran race went on to a military footing – a state of affairs they've been on ever since.

SONTARAN PHYSIOLOGY

In an attempt to build their numbers quickly, the race defied nature in the early centuries of the war, and developed cloning technologies. The art galleries of Sontar were torn down and replaced with cloning facilities, all in the aid of the great Sontaran military. At one time, it was said that a million Sontarans were born at every hatching.

The gravity on Sontar is very strong, which causes the Sontarans to be short and stocky, most standing around 1.5 metres. Some Sontarans, notably those in the Scientific Corps, stand taller. They have immense physical strength, and can lift weights two or three times their own. They have dome-shaped heads, with tough, wrinkly brown skin. They wear battle scars with pride, as proof of their duty to Sontar.

Sontarans do not eat or rest in the way many races of the universe do, but rather they 'recharge' through the use of a probic vent in the back of their neck. The vent has to be left uncovered, making it a weak point on the Sontaran body. A sharp point, such as an arrow, or a pen, jabbed into the vent will cause the Sontaran great pain. Similarly, a hard blow to the outside of the vent will stun them enough to make a quick getaway. Sontarans, however, do not see the vent as a weakness, as it forces them to always enter battle face-to-face with the enemy. They are also susceptible to coronic acid, which eats away at their skin, effectively causing them to melt.

SONTARAN TECHNOLOGY

The technology of the Sontaran race has varied wildly over the course of the war. As they face victories or defeats, so their technology becomes more or less advanced. They have at times been known to field great battle fleets consisting of ten million ships, all lining up for war. Most Sontaran fleets contain a central battle ship, from where the generals can amass their armies, survey plans and prepare for the attack. These ships hold millions of Sontaran warriors and thousands of individual scout ships. Large enough to hold just a single Sontaran at the controls, these spherical ships spin as they are piloted through space. These ships contain everything a single Sontaran officer needs to collect information about a planet or a species. They're used to scout out planets, searching for resources to build weapons or use as cannon fodder.

The weapons used by the Sontaran military vary greatly, ranging from small pistols to laser guns and big, bulky weapons. Generals carry batons that can shoot a deadly beam of energy to either stun or kill an opponent. Sontarans often use a Cordeline signal to assist them in war, which causes the copper in ballistic projectiles to expand in the barrel of the gun, blocking it, and rendering the weapon useless.

ETERNAL WAR

As the years have gone by, the war with the Rutans has passed into legend. Still raging across time and space, none can recall what started the fighting, just that both sides are truly devoted to the fight, and to victory. The Sontaran military is split into many different sectors, each devoted to a different element of the war. Battle Fleets, Research Scouts, and Scientific Divisions all work independently, but for the greater good of the war. Some Sontarans lack the need to fight that characterises the species, and these are sent to work on other projects, such as mining for resources or building ships and weapons; it is the duty of every Sontaran to benefit the war, whether they agree or not.

At first the war was contained in the small space between the worlds of its two occupants, but soon it spread and stories of it reached all civilised words. The planet Earth has been of importance in the war on several occasions.

The first Sontaran acknowledgement of the planet was in the Middle Ages of Earth's history, during which time they didn't consider it to be of strategic importance. All this was to change, however in the following millennia.

The planet first became of note in the Early 21st century, when the Tenth Sontaran Battle Fleet attempted to covert it into a clone world on which to breed more soldiers, giving quicker reinforcements to the troops fighting. Following their defeat, some of their teleportation technology remained behind on the planet, and was converted for use by UNIT personnel in New York. Whilst it is still in its early stages, 'Project Indigo' continues to undergo refinement.

The Sontaran War Council was furious at being denied entry to the Time War, which had started between the Time Lords and the Daleks. Locked out of the war, it became invisible to the Sontaran Race, who were considered no more than brutes. The War Council set about devising their own plan; if they could not join the Time War, then they would start one of their own.

The first attempt by the Sontarans to steal time-travel technology came in the form of the Kartz-Reimer module, which was being developed by two human beings aboard a research station in the late 49th century. Allying themselves with people aboard the facility, they launched their attack, unaware that the Time Lords were one step ahead, and had sent the Doctor to stop the experiments, before the Sontarans could get to them. It took two incarnations of the Doctor, but between them, they defeated the Sontarans in Seville, Spain, in the 1980s.

It was after this that the Sontaran race fell quiet. The war with the Rutans waged across the many galaxies, and the Sontarans even seemed to be losing. In reality, they were simply planning their biggest and most daring feat ever: the invasion of Gallifrey.

Using a 'lesser' race – the Vardans – and the Doctor himself, they forced their way into Gallifrey, planning to steal the secrets of the Eye of Harmony, the heart of the Time Lord civilisation and the core of their power. Planning to destroy the Eye, the Sontarans intended to bring chaos by unleashing the raw power of the Vortex upon it. The Doctor ultimately defeated them, using a de-mat gun to wipe the Sontarans on Gallifrey out of time itself, marking the Sontarans' greatest defeat.

SONTARAN TROOPER

AWARENESS	3	PRESENCE	4
COORDINATION	4	RESOLVE	6
INGENUITY	3	STRENGTH	6

SKILLS
Athletics 2, Convince 2, Fighting 5, Marksman 5, Medicine 1, Science 4, Subterfuge 3, Survival 4, Technology 2, Transport 3.

TRAITS
Adversary: The Sontarans have been at war with the Rutans for thousands of years.
Alien
Alien Appearance (Major)
Brave: a Sontaran fears nothing! They receive a +2 bonus to any Resolve rolls against fear.
By the Book: A Sontaran never disobeys an order from their superior officer.
Tough: being bred for war means that they are incredibly tough, reducing any damage to attributes by 2.
Weakness (Minor) – Probic Vent: the Sontaran's only weak spot is the probic vent on the back of their necks. A single hit will disable a Sontaran (effects like a normal Stun). Hitting the vent is tricky though, and the Sontaran needs to be facing away. There is a -4 penalty for aiming at the vent.

WEAPONS: Sontaran Rifle (4/**L**/L), Shock Staff (S/**S**/S)

ARMOUR: Sontaran body armour is incredibly strong, reducing any damage taken by 5.

TECH LEVEL: 6   **STORY POINTS:** 3-5

⊛ SPIDER GERMS

There's a dragon in the moon. It may be unique or there may be millions more like it, other huge creatures gestating inside planetoids like chicks in eggs, waiting to hatch.

The huge scale of these creatures, combined with a physiology and life cycle that flies in the face of all logic and scientific understanding, means their immune systems operate on a different level to other forms of life. Their parasites are equally unusual.

There is a whole ecosystem of creatures accompanying the moon dragon, like bacteria on a human body. Prominent among them are countless huge spider-creatures. Although they prefer to lurk deep below the eggshell surface, where the moon dragon itself lies dormant and warm, they can and do roam freely from time to time, and if they find other potential food sources they will eagerly hunt them down.

It should be noted that visitors to the moon make excellent food sources, as the 2049 moon expedition discovered, along with the Doctor, Clara and young Courtney Woods.

The spider creatures are essentially giant germs. The Doctor described them as "prokaryotic unicellular life forms, with non-chromosomal DNA". They have the body plan of a hunting spider, with a mouth full of needle-sharp teeth. Their behaviour is much like a hunting spider as well, stalking prey and then lunging quickly to seize and overpower it.

SPIDER GERMS

AWARENESS	3	PRESENCE	1
COORDINATION	4	RESOLVE	2
INGENUITY	-	STRENGTH	4

SKILLS
Fighting 2, Subterfuge 2.

TRAITS
Alien
Alien Appearance: Spider Germs are badger-sized spiders with bright red leg joints.
Alien Senses: Spider Germs are highly sensitive to fast movement (+4 to relevant Awareness rolls).
Climb (Major): Spider Germs can climb on nearly any surface, including ceilings.
Impaired Senses: Spider Germs do not have good vision (-2 to relevant Awareness rolls), relying on their motion detection.
Natural Weapon (Fangs): Spider Germs have sharp, deadly fangs (2/4/7).
Weakness (Minor) - Sunlight: Spider Germs are sensitive to sunlight. They take a -2 penalty on any actions taken in sunlight and avoid it if at all possible.
Weakness (Major) – Anti-Bacterial Chemicals: Spider Germs are highly vulnerable to any chemicals that wipe out bacteria, taking 4 levels of damage for each contact.

STORY POINTS: 1

⚙ WEEPING ANGELS

On first appearance, the Weeping Angels seem to be harmless static statues; classic marble sculptures that have adorned churches, graveyards and tombs for centuries. In reality, they are an ancient alien race that can destroy lives with just a touch. Their origins are unknown, and are thought to be as old as the known universe itself. Dubbed the 'Lonely Assassins', they are possibly one of the most dangerous and terrifying foes the Doctor has ever faced.

The Doctor encountered the Angels with Martha at Wester Drumlins and was sent back to 1969 after the Angels targeted the TARDIS as a source of unlimited power. Luckily, with the help of Sally Sparrow and Larry Nightingale, the Angels were tricked into staring at each other, permanently turning them to stone.

These Angels were weak, however, stranded on Earth for centuries. The Doctor would face stronger Angels at the crash of the Byzantium, a category 4 starliner that crashed in the 51st century. While seeking to stop an Angel from feeding on the radiation from the crash, the Doctor, River, Amy and a squad of Combat Clerics stumbled upon hundreds of desiccated Angels, waiting to be restored by the radiation from the exploding wreckage. Once they absorbed the radiation from the explosion they would be restored and spread out across time and space to devour everything in their path.

The Doctor, Amy, Rory and River encountered the Weeping Angels once more in Manhattan, where they had created a battery farm by trapping their victims in the Winter Quay apartments and feeding off of their energies. The Doctor stopped them, but not before Amy and Rory fell victim to a Weeping Angel.

ANGEL PHYSIOLOGY

Weeping Angels are often found in a weakened state: a statue, decaying after years of neglect and unable to unleash its full potential. They can regenerate from nearby radiation sources, but it is chronon energy that will truly revive and sustain an Angel. They attack by sending their victims back in time, feeding on the potential temporal energy of the days that their victims will never have lived. The potential energy powers the Angel's regeneration, while their victims are left to live the rest of their natural existence abandoned in a different time.

When they are stronger, or facing larger numbers, their attacks can be simpler and more brutal, ripping their victims apart with their talons and fanged teeth. However, neither of these are their most dangerous weapon or ability: the Weeping Angel can move unnaturally fast. At their strongest, they can cover many metres in the blink of an eye, which is when they have to attack.

When observed the Angel cannot move; they are 'quantum locked', and become like stone. And, as the Doctor pointed out, you can't kill stone. They gained the name Weeping Angels from the fact that as a statue they hide their eyes behind their hands as if they are crying, often to hide their own gaze from each other for fear of quantum locking themselves into eternal paralysis.

Weeping Angels are timeless and eternal. They can regenerate any physical damage, though this is a slow process that can take decades if they cannot access a radiation source to feed upon.

WEEPING ANGELS

AWARENESS	3	PRESENCE	3
COORDINATION	4	RESOLVE	3
INGENUITY	2	STRENGTH	3

SKILLS
Fighting 3 Knowledge 4 Subterfuge 4.

TRAITS
Alien

Alien Appearance (Minor)

Alien Senses (Blind Sense)

Armour (Special): When quantum-locked, the Weeping Angel is made of the toughest stone. Bullets may chip it a little, but they are incredibly tough and resilient to damage, reducing any damage sustained by 15.

Immortal (Special): Weeping Angels are timeless and eternal. They can also regenerate any physical damage they may have sustained, though this can be a slow process taking decades and a source of radiation.

Natural Weapons (Minor) – Teeth and Claws: A Weeping Angel gets +2 to Strength on attacks. Damage (2/5/7).

Weakness (Being Seen): If the Angel is seen by anyone, quantifying its existence, it cannot move.

Special – Don't Blink: Angels move at incredible speeds so long as they are unobserved and may act once in every phase, talking (if they have some method of communicating), moving, doing and attacking all in the same round. Alternately, they may forgo the first three phases in order to rend a victim to shreds, attacking four times in one round. An Angel at full strength moves like the wind but as it weakens from hunger or damage, it will slow down. As such, an Angel's Speed is equal to their current Story Point Total.

Special – Infection: The Weeping Angel, at their strongest, can infect anything that can record its image, becoming another Angel. If a living being stares into the eyes of an Angel for long enough, the Angel makes a Presence + Resolve roll (opposed by the target's Resolve + Strength). If the victim gets a Bad or Disastrous Result the Angel has infected them and they will gradually become an Angel themselves. The victim will have to succeed at Resolve + Strength rolls every hour (with a Difficulty of 12, +3 for every hour that passes after the first). Failure results in losing Resolve (1/**2**/3) and when the victim's Resolve

reaches 0 the transformation is complete. Curing the infection is difficult, and involves removing the mental image or memory of the Angel from the victim. The Doctor lured the Angels into the crack in the universe to erase the one in Amy, though memory alteration may also prove to be successful.

Special – Lights Out: Angels can interfere with the normal flow of electricity by spending their own energy, typically to short out light sources that are keeping them visible to their victims. The amount of Story Points varies from 1 to short out all the flashlights in the immediate vicinity for a round or permanently suppress one light source, to 6 or more for countering a magnetic lock. Groups of Angels can and will pool Story Points for large tasks, especially if there's a meal at the other end.

Special – Temporal Exile: The Angels consume potential temporal energy by ripping living beings out of their time line and throwing them backwards in time. If the Angel is striking to feed and lands a successful physical attack, the victim is thrown back in time a number of years equal to the roll of two dice multiplied by ten, per level of Success. The Angel gains 1 Story Point for every Level of Success it scores on this attack, up to a maximum of 9 Story Points.

TECH LEVEL: Unknown   **STORY POINTS:** 6-8

⚙ ALIENS AS PLAYER CHARACTERS

Players have the option to create all manner of strange and bizarre aliens, but as with anything in character creation, they need to make sure they have built a character that is going to function properly in the group and in the adventures the Gamemaster has planned.

Before they even consider playing an alien they should consider how cosmopolitan the adventures are likely to be. In adventures on other worlds where even humans are different and unusual, having blue skin, a tail or horns shouldn't be a problem. However, this may not be true for worlds where alien contact is not a regular occurrence, such as Earth. Luckily, there are plenty of alien creatures that can at least look human. Some aliens might be shape shifters, or able to adopt a human form like Multiforms. Others can disguise themselves.

After looking at their ability to fit into their surroundings, you need to think how suitable the alien species is as a player's character. Some unassuming races are inappropriate due to their strange cultures and attitudes. An Ood is not a powerful character, but may be a little slow and docile for many of the Doctor's adventures. A Tree from the Forest of Cheem might sound fun, but they are a little obvious and are easily set on fire.

In general it comes down to why does the player want to play an alien? What can they do with this character that they can't with a human? If they want their character to look different, there are already plenty of humans who can look different, and humans from different periods in history can have strange ways and odd habits. If what attracts the player to the alien race is that it is simply more powerful, they are probably interested in it for the wrong reasons.

If the Gamesmaster allows you to create an alien character, you will need to take certain traits and ensure you have the right levels of certain attributes. If you want to play a Silurian, you have to purchase the traits that make up a Silurian. You don't get all their abilities for free, as that would be unfair on the other characters. So you may find (especially in the case of 'good' Daleks) that they just don't have the points to create that sort of character.

'GOOD' VILLAINS

At some point, someone is going to want to play a 'good' Dalek or Cyberman, and to be fair this is not unprecedented. The Doctor once infected a group of Daleks with the 'Human Factor', Rory once became an Auton Duplicate, and Madame Vastra and Strax have become some of the Doctor's most trusted allies. However, in many of these cases, these good characters were short lived. The humanised Daleks were wiped out in a civil war, Rory was returned to flesh after the universe was reset. They make difficult player characters so the Gamemaster shouldn't feel bad about not allowing them in their game. Such races often have a reputation that will precede them and cause trouble for the rest of the group. Even the legendary Madame Vastra and Strax have to be careful how they're seen in 19th century London.

⚙ ALIEN TRAITS

Below is a list of Alien Traits that the character can have to set them apart from mere humans. The list includes traits that are usually best reserved for villains (and they will be indicated in the text). Just as other traits that can be purchased, they come in Minor, Major and Special Good and Bad Traits. To get started creating your alien, you simply need to purchase the Alien Trait (see sidebar), and then you can pick any of the Alien Traits presented here, as well as those available to human characters.

Of course, the list of Alien Traits presented below is just a sample of what can be done, though most of the aliens the Doctor has encountered to date can be built using these traits. If you wish to design your own trait, you should feel free. If the Gamemaster is creating an alien as a villain or enemy for the characters in an adventure, they don't really need to worry about costs and how many traits they have, whatever it takes to make a cool alien character. However, you can total up the traits you've used to see just how many points you would have spent, so you can see how powerful the alien is compared to the average character (who usually has between 6-10 points' worth of traits).

As usual, Minor Traits cost 1 Character Point to purchase (or provide the character with 1 point if they're Bad). Major Traits cost 2 Character Points to purchase (or provide 2 points if they're bad for the character).

Traits that can be purchased multiple times are marked with an asterisk (*).

ALIEN (SPECIAL GOOD TRAIT)

By purchasing the Alien Trait, the character is of an alien race, alien to humanity, and one of the infinite varieties of lifeforms.

Effect: Alien as a trait is a 'Gateway', opening a selection of additional traits that are normally unavailable to humans, and costs 2 Character Points to purchase. The Alien trait means that the character is from another planet. Initially, they are of human appearance and look similar to everyone else on Earth. This trait does open up the opportunity to purchase other specifically Alien Traits, and enables attributes above level 6. As a downside, if discovered as being an Alien, they may suffer severe consequences (such as being captured by the government and experimented upon). Additionally, some of the Alien-only traits that are now open may mean that the character will have an alien appearance.

⚙ GOOD ALIEN TRAITS

ADDITIONAL LIMBS* (Minor Good Alien Trait)
Many hands make light work, or so they say (though try saying that to Alexander Monro). Taking this trait means that the alien has an additional pair of limbs. This can mean arms or legs or an odd alien limb or tentacle that functions as both. Of course, taking an additional pair of limbs means that the character is usually very obviously an alien in appearance, and will automatically get the Alien Appearance Bad Trait (Minor). The Additional Limbs trait can be taken a second time, giving the alien a cumulative bonus, but their Alien Appearance trait becomes Major.

Effect: Additional Limbs is a Minor Good Alien Trait, and costs just 1 point for every additional pair of limbs. If the alien has additional legs, their effective Speed (when calculating chases and alike) is increased by +2. If the limbs are arms, the first additional action in any action round receives no penalty (as they can effectively do two things at once). This trait can be taken twice to create an eight limbed alien, though they will be obviously more alien. Additional limbs can be had on top of this, but they receive no bonus and cost no extra – there comes a point when you have so many legs or arms that it just becomes confusing and you can end up tripping over your own feet.

ALIEN SENSES* (Minor Good Alien Trait)

Most of the time, simply having a really high Awareness means that your senses are particularly acute. However, some aliens have senses that go above and beyond what is considered normal. It could be that they can see infra-red or ultraviolet ends of the spectrum, they could see the eddies and flows of time, see paradoxes or simply smell their prey from a dozen rooms away. The cost of this trait could easily be offset by the Alien Appearance trait, saying that the character can see phenomenally well, but has big alien eyes.

Effect: Alien Senses is a Minor Good Alien Trait. At character creation, the sense that is particularly good (whether this is sight, hearing, smell or something more exotic) should be specified and the particulars of the extraordinary perception (what is so special about it and what is sensed). When the alien uses the sense, it gains a +4 bonus to Awareness rolls but only when using that sense.

If the environment effects the sense, this bonus may be reduced. For example, an alien that can see into the infra-red range of the spectrum can see the heat given off by people. He gains a +4 bonus to his rolls when he spots the approaching Sontaran in the dark, but once the shooting starts, and things start exploding, everything will be hot and the bonus from his alien sense will be lost. This trait can be taken multiple times - specify a different sense each time.

Note: Cannot be used with the Keen Senses trait.

ARMOUR* (Alien Minor/Major/Special Good Trait)

Armour as an Alien Trait means that the alien has 'natural' armour that protects it. Armour counts as 'natural' if it cannot be removed. For example, a Sontaran wears very heavy battle armour, but can remove it. Cybermen and Daleks are literally built into their armoured casings and the armour cannot be removed. If it's a permanent feature (whether this is a cybernetic suit, or just very tough, leathery skin) it is an Alien Trait.

Effect: Armour as an Alien Trait can be purchased at various levels. As a Minor Trait the alien has a tough hide that is able to reduce injury by 5 levels. If the alien is hit by a weapon and receives 6 levels worth of damage to reduce its attributes, this 6 is reduced by the 5 of the Armour to a single point. This makes the alien quite a tough cookie! Even Lethal damage is resisted: treat it as 8 levels of damage and reduce it accordingly.

As a Major Trait, the damage reduction is increased to 10. In most cases, this armour will be thick plating, such as metal or scales. However, their Coordination is reduced by 1 (to a minimum of 1).

As a Special Trait every additional Character Point spent increases the armour by a further +5 (and reduces their Coordination by an additional -1 to a minimum of 1) – so if you spend 3 points on the trait, the creature will have Armour 15 and -2 Coordination. This means you can create huge and heavily armoured creatures, but they don't move particularly fast.

CLIMBING (Minor/Major Good Alien Trait)

The alien is exceptionally good at climbing. As a Minor Trait, they can climb walls particularly well, and as a Major Trait they are equally adept at clinging to the ceiling!

Effect: As a Minor Good Trait, Climbing means that the alien can climb up sheer and difficult surfaces. While they cannot climb surfaces without any grip, such as glass, they certainly find it easy to climb walls. They receive a +4 bonus to Coordination and Athletics rolls when climbing.

As a Major Trait they have suckers, fine hairs or secrete some sort of substance that provides them the same +4 bonus, making them able to climb smooth surfaces such as glass or metal, as well as clinging to the ceiling like a spider.

ENVIRONMENTAL (Minor/Major Good Alien Trait)

Environmental is a catch-all trait that means the alien can exist in strange or harsh environments. It could be that they are aquatic, and can exist just as well underwater as on land. They may be able to survive in the vacuum of space, endure the harsh heat of a volcanic world, the extreme cold of Volag-Noc or exist in the Vortex itself.

Effect: As a Minor Good Trait, the alien suffers no ill effects from one particular harsh condition. If it's something like being able to survive underwater, their ability should be explained. Do they have gills, or can they store oxygen in some way?

As a Major Good Trait, the alien suffers no effects from any environment – for example, a Dalek can fly through space or drive along the bottom of the Thames. Again, there should be some rationalisation of this, such as the Dalek's battle armour.

FEAR FACTOR* (Minor Good Alien Trait)

The Fear Factor trait is designed for monsters, and those truly scary individuals that can send people running in terror. They don't have to be ugly or monstrous – people cowered at the Master's feet in fear of their lives – but something about the alien fills them with fear.

Effect: Fear Factor is a Special Alien Trait and is only suitable for Villains. Each purchase of the Fear Factor trait adds +2 to any roll when actively trying to strike fear into people's hearts. See Getting Scared on pg.94.

FLIGHT (Minor/Major Good Alien Trait)

Flight is quite a common feature of aliens, whether it is the hovering of Daleks over the city, the flapping of leathery wings heard when the Krillitane are about to feed or the silent gliding of sharks in a crystalline cloud belt. This trait means that the alien has wings, gas bladders, jetpacks, anti-gravity devices or rotors, but one way or another they can leave the ground for extended periods.

Effect: Flight as a Minor Good Trait means that the alien can take off, hover, and travel slowly at a limited height. In most cases, this is just hovering, like a Dalek climbing the stairs. Their Speed is half of their Coordination (round down, minimum of 1), and they can usually only ascend to a height of around 100 metres.

As a Major Good Trait, they can really take to the skies. Above 100 metres, their effective Speed is 3x Coordination. They can fly as high as they like (though the Gamemaster may want to take other factors into account such as air, cold and other environmental effects). If they're travelling below 100 metres, they will probably travel slower to avoid obstacles and the Gamemaster may impose a limit (or make the alien's player roll additional Awareness + Coordination checks to see if they can react in time to any dangers).

GADGET (Minor/Major/Special Good Trait)

Aliens sometimes have in-built cybernetic or mechanical enhancement, giving them Gadget traits. Bannakaffalatta had an EMP device, Daleks have forcefields as well as the ability to "Emergency Temporal Shift!" Gadgets are purchased as normal, but how and where the gadget is 'plugged in' (and if it can be removed) should be defined.

Effect: See Gadgets and Jiggery-Pokery on pg.113 of **Chapter Three: I Can Fight Monsters, I Can't Fight Physics**

IMMUNITY* (Major Good Alien Trait)

Many aliens are immune to one form of harm or another. A former head of UNIT once commented how nice it would be to face an alien enemy that **wasn't** immune to bullets! However, being immune to the effects of certain weapons is not as common as he'd liked to believe, and often the cost of this trait is countered by taking the Weakness trait (see pg.48). For example, Autons are immune to bullets – they can be shot many times – but are vulnerable to having their control signal cut off.

Effect: Immunity is a Major Good Alien Trait. When taking this trait, the specific thing that the alien is immune to must be clearly defined, whether this is something as simple as bullets, acid, mind control or poison. If the immunity is particularly powerful, such as bullets, the Gamemaster may balance this immunity with a weakness, especially in major Villains or player characters. The trait can be taken multiple times – specify a different immunity each time.

IMPERVIOUS (Major Alien Good Trait)

The Impervious trait means the alien is extremely resistant to damage from any form of weapon. This might be due to an almost insubstantial form or a body of stone or metal.

Effects: When hit by a weapon, shift the damage result down by one step (for example, Fantastic becomes Good) before applying any other abilities. Successful attacks will always do a minimum of 1 point of damage though.

INFECTION (Major Good Alien Trait)

Some aliens have the nasty ability to transmit their 'alien-ness' into other beings. Sometimes it can start as a strange green rash that comes from a bite or scratch that takes over the victim until they become alien themselves, or it could mean that the unsuspecting target becomes host to the alien's consciousness.

Effects: Infection can work in a couple of ways, both are Major Good Alien Traits. As a transmittable disease, the target needs to be scratched, bitten or take some form of physical damage. If the damage penetrates any armour worn, or if the victim failed with a Bad or Disastrous result, they become infected. At regular intervals (usually every hour or day) they will have to make a Resolve and Strength roll, against the Resolve and Strength of the alien.

Failing this will mean the infection has spread. The Gamemaster should decide how many failures mean the target has become alien (one fail spreads to a whole arm, two fails to the chest, etc.). It should give the characters time to find an antidote! The other way it can work is by making the target susceptible to possession, making them host to the alien, and the infection is actually the alien moving from one host to another. Again, this is usually from sustaining an injury. Once infected (as above), the target will have to make similar rolls, though instead of resisting the infection spreading, this is to resist becoming possessed (see Being Possessed on pg.95).

NATURAL WEAPONS*
(Minor/Major Alien Good Trait)

The alien has some form of weaponry that is part of their form. This could be something as simple as toxic breath, a poisonous bite or sharp claws, to built in guns or being able to fire sharp spines. As long is it is not something that is usually dropped or carried (like a gun or sword), and is part of the alien (like a Dalek's gun or a Weeping Angels' claws) then it is technically a 'natural' weapon.

Effect: This is a Minor or Major Alien Good Trait that can be purchased multiple times if the creature is particularly dangerous.

As a Minor Trait, the weapon is only for close combat. These are usually teeth, claws, spines or electrical shock or something similar. A weapon like this increases the damage of the usual physical attack by +2, so the alien's damage is equal to their Strength +2. This increase is just like normal close combat weapons, as the trait adds blades or 'dangerous' damage to their physical attack.

As a Major Trait, the weapon shoots something (like a poisonous spine, fingernail, flaming breath or built-in gun). A ranged Natural Weapon will have the same damage (2/**5**/7) but can reach a greater distance than a simple swipe of a claw.

This trait can be purchased multiple times to reflect various forms of defence that the creature has, or it can work on a single weapon and increase the damage cumulatively. For example, a Dalek has only one weapon (the Exterminator 'death ray'). It's a long range weapon that usually kills with one shot, so the Exterminator is worth two Major Natural Weapons Traits, if not more.

NETWORKED (Minor/Major Good Alien Trait)

The Networked trait means that the alien is connected in some way to others of their kind. Whether this is an inbuilt gadget this connects them to others, a telepathic field or a 'hive mind', it means that if one is in trouble or injured, it can call for aid. Whether others are in close proximity to help is another matter...

Effect: Networked is a Minor or Major Good Trait. As a Minor Trait, the aliens simply sense each other,

and know when one is in trouble. They don't really 'talk' to each other, but they can congregate in one place or know where to go in a similar manner to the Autons.

As a Major trait, they have the equivalent of the Telepathy Trait connecting them to each other, or even to a hive mind. Cybermen are more like this; they have the ability to send communications to other units. Most of the time, the range of this communication is limited. You can use the Telepathy Psychic Trait as a guide (see pg.55).

POSSESS (Special Good Alien Trait)

This is technically the highest possible level of the Hypnosis trait (see pg.34). Possess allows the alien to take over another person and control their actions. While in the host body, the alien can make it do or say almost anything (though they cannot make the host kill themselves; their survival instinct is too strong for even that). Possessing someone is an exhausting affair, and if the alien has a normal body that it has left behind somewhere, it will need protecting (and may die of starvation if they're out of their body too long).

Effect: Just as with the Hypnosis Trait, the target will have the opportunity to resist becoming possessed (with an Ingenuity + Resolve test) The possessing alien receives a +4 bonus on their first roll to possess someone, though if they fail this every attempt that follows loses this bonus.

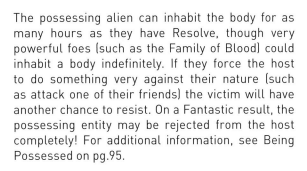

The possessing alien can inhabit the body for as many hours as they have Resolve, though very powerful foes (such as the Family of Blood) could inhabit a body indefinitely. If they force the host to do something very against their nature (such as attack one of their friends) the victim will have another chance to resist. On a Fantastic result, the possessing entity may be rejected from the host completely! For additional information, see Being Possessed on pg.95.

REPLICATION (Major Good Alien Trait)

Unlike the Infection trait, Replication means that the alien can multiply itself by various means without the need of transmitting its alien-ness to another life form. It could be that they 'bud' and create a youthful clone of themselves without natural reproduction, or it could be that any limbs lost or removed will grow into a duplicate version of themselves.

Effects: As a Major Good Trait, the alien can replicate itself outside the normal expected means of reproduction. This can mean spawning a childlike

offspring or creating a duplicate of the original. The alien will have to make a Resolve and Strength roll, Difficulty 15. A result of Success or higher means that the replication is successful and another version of the alien has been 'born'. It will be confused and disorientated for a few minutes. A childlike offspring will grow at a normal rate unless artificially accelerated and will learn as it goes. A duplicate will be 'born' with the same Attributes and Skills of the original.

If a player character takes this Trait, the duplicate will not be 'playable' by the same player, unless the original is incapacitated or killed. Gamemasters should be aware of the way this Trait can produce an army of clones or duplicates that could threaten to take over the world or otherwise quickly unbalance a game.

RESISTANCE (Minor Alien Good Trait)

One specific environmental force or source of damage has less effect on the alien than it would on a human.

SIZE

Aliens come in all shapes and sizes. Luckily for the Doctor, many of his adversaries are of a relatively similar size to humans but when facing gigantic creatures such as the Beast or the Dalek Emperor, or tiny foes such as the Graske or Cassandra's spider drones, the Gamemaster may wish to include some additional rules to take their size into account. If the creature is larger, they should purchase the Huge Good Alien Trait and if tiny it should take the Small Bad Alien Trait. There are advantages and disadvantages to both but in a combat situation, the benefits of being huge usually outweigh those of being tiny. Taking either of these traits will mean the alien automatically has to take the Alien Appearance trait (see p.49).

HUGE (Minor/Major Good Alien Trait)

This trait means that the alien is larger than human sized. As a Minor Trait, the alien is certainly larger than human, larger than a Judoon. The alien is around the size of a van or an elephant. As a Major Trait, they are even bigger than this - we're getting to the size of a T-Rex or even bigger. Depending upon the level of this trait, the alien will receive a bonus to their Strength and Speed, and modifiers for enemies who try to

shoot at it (see the table). It is not recommended to allow this trait in player characters.

TINY (Minor/Major Bad Alien Trait)

This trait means that the alien is a lot smaller than human sized. As a Minor Trait, the alien is around the size of a Graske, or a very large dog. As a Major Trait, the alien is even smaller, possibly as small as a rat or even smaller! Depending upon the level of the trait, their effective Strength will be reduced but there will be heavy modifiers for anyone trying to attack them, or to even see them (see the table).

SIZE

| | MODIFIER TO EFFECTIVE | | MODIFIER | |
	STRENGTH	SPEED	TO BE HIT	TO BE SEEN
Tiny (Major)	-4	-2	-4	-8
Tiny (Minor)	-2	-1	-2	-4
Human	0	0	0	0
Huge (Minor)	+2	+1	+2	+4
Huge (Major)	+4	+2	+4	+8

As always, if the Gamemaster thinks this rule slows the game down or makes things too complicated, it can be ignored.

Effects: Pick a single element or force, like gunfire, radiation or heat. You halve any damage or effects from that specific source.

SHAPESHIFT
(Minor/Major/Special Good Alien Trait)

Some aliens have the ability to look like something else. This is especially useful if you're a 2 1/2 metre tall green alien with claws, or if you wish to try to mimic someone to gain information. The actual methods of 'shapeshifting' can be as complex as genetic manipulation, or a racial ability, to something as basic (and barbaric) as wearing a suit of human skin.

Effect: As a Minor Good Trait, this means that the alien can disguise itself as a fairly convincing member of another race (usually human). The Slitheen's skin-suit and compression technology is a good example of this, as is the Nestene's tactic of replicating humans. In both of these cases, the disguise was not perfect, and at this level close examination may reveal the truth.

As a Major Good Trait, the alien can physically shapeshift, like the Werewolf, the Krillitane or the Carrionite witches, into a perfect human (or other specified race). The change is so complete that the alien's form cannot be discovered by basic physical examination or observation.

If the alien is able to shapeshift into multiple forms and replicate actual people, like Prisoner Zero, then the trait is a Special Good Trait that costs 4 points.

SPECIAL (Special Good Alien Trait)

Sometimes aliens can do something remarkable and odd, something that none of the other powers and abilities listed here covers. It could be the Weeping Angel's ability to send its victims back through time or the Krillitane's ability to steal the traits and features of the races they conquer. This trait allows the Gamemaster to go wild and create the odd and special powers that can sometimes define the race.

Effect: This is a Special Trait that costs 3 points or more. The more powerful the ability, the more the trait costs. Using other powers as a guide, the Gamemaster can create any power they feel necessary to make a cool alien. This can be around 3-4 points for the Krillitane's ability, to 7-8 points for being able to move faster than you can imagine (when you're not looking) and being able to send your victims back in time. Specific traits for these powers can be created, or the Gamemaster can simply use the Special Trait to cover these.

TELEPORT (Major Good Trait)

It is rare for a creature to be able to teleport, to disappear from one location and appear in another. However, some aliens have developed the technology to do it. Some, particularly scarce creatures can do it without the means of gadgets or gizmos. If, like the Slitheen, they can teleport with a device, then it's simply a Gadget. If they can teleport without a device, appearing wherever is necessary, like the Reapers, who appear where a paradox is evident, then this is an Alien Trait.

Effect: Teleport is a Major Good Trait. The alien will have to make an Awareness + Resolve roll to teleport, and can only 'jump' to places they are familiar with. Most aliens that appear in unfamiliar places have some sort of psychic ability to see the location before teleporting. If they're familiar with the location, the Difficulty is 12, thought the Gamemaster may increase this due to environmental factors. Good or Fantastic results mean a perfect teleport, however a Success means they find themselves weakened and disorientated for a few minutes until they can recover and get their bearings. Failure means the alien doesn't move, though a Disastrous Result teleports the alien into some object or item that will cause D6 levels of damage before their reflexes teleport them to a safer location.

VORTEX (Special Good Alien Trait)

The Alien version of the Vortex trait (see pg.57) costs 8 points. This high level of Vortex means the character can time travel without the need of a ship or device, literally stepping through time.

Effect: The Vortex trait adds +2 to any roll that involves piloting a time travel or Vortex manipulating device. Controlling the TARDIS (or other such time vessels) is so tricky to the unskilled, that it is almost impossible to actually be able to succeed at the task without having the Vortex trait. The Alien level of this trait, that allows time travel without a device and requires an Ingenuity + Resolve roll to use, and the expenditure of two Story Points. The more successful the roll, the more accurate the 'jump' through time.

⚙ BAD ALIEN TRAITS

ALIEN APPEARANCE
(Minor/Major Bad Alien Trait)

While many aliens can pass for human under some circumstances (or low lighting), you have an obviously alien appearance. It could be that you're basically human but green, or have a large head to accommodate the massive brain power or pointy ears, or it might be rather more extreme such as reptilian features or you might look like a big bug or a cat!

Effect: Alien Appearance is a Bad Trait. The more severe the Alien Appearance trait, the more 'alien' the character looks. As a Minor Bad Trait, Alien Appearance means the character is basically humanoid but with a distinctive alien feature. In most cases, when they encounter people who are OK with aliens their reaction will be minimal, however when meeting inhabitants of lower-level planets (see Tech Levels, pg.66) who may not have met aliens before, social rolls will all suffer a -2 penalty (that is if they don't just run away!).

As a Major Bad Trait, the 'alien-ness' of the character is more extreme. The may have tentacles instead of limbs, or a face like a squid – they could look like anything! Again, on advanced planets that are used to aliens this isn't a problem, but if they meet less experienced peoples they will suffer a -4 penalty on social rolls (possibly even become the target of scared locals who assume the alien is hostile).

ENSLAVED (Major Bad Alien Trait)

In a universe of war and hostility, there are many races that are unable to defend themselves, and suffer under the dominion of others. The Enslaved trait can mean that the alien is part of an enslaved race, such as the Ood, or even just a race that has been genetically created to serve others, such as the Pig Slaves that served the Cult of Skaro in Manhattan.

Effect: Enslaved means that the alien is part of a recognisably enslaved race. While the race may have been freed, they may still suffer the social stigma of their past, or they may currently be under the control of a dominant race. On top of being under the control of others, the alien will get a -2 penalty on all social rolls (usually involving their Presence or Resolve) when trying to voice their opinion because of their enforced subservient nature. Even if freed, it will take time to break their submissive attitude. It doesn't mean it is impossible, there have been many occasions of vocal slaves leading a revolution, but they will have to overcome their subservience.

IT'S A ROLLERCOASTER WITH YOU!

✸ HOW TO PLAY A ROLEPLAYING GAME

Hopefully by this point you'll have a good idea of what this roleplaying thing is all about and what a game entails. However, we know that this may be new to a lot of people, so we've dedicated a chapter in this book to show you how a game should work: what you can do as a player to make the game more fun, as well as plenty of advice for the Gamemaster on the daunting task of running a game.

YOUR FIRST GAME

The first game you play may be a little awkward, but don't let it put you off. It's only your first game and it'll take a few goes to get used to how to 'do' things, whether this is how the rules work for performing a task, or just interacting with the other characters. After a few rolls, and a couple of scenes, you'll soon pick it up and we think that after a few games you'll be so confident you probably won't have to look in the rulebook very often unless something tricky occurs.

HELP EACH OTHER

Unlike most games that you may be familiar with, there are no winners or losers in the **Doctor Who Roleplaying Game**. In fact, there are no winners or losers in any roleplaying game; it's all about having fun and telling a great story. With no winners, it means there's no competitive streak coming into play between the players, so they should actually help each other to achieve their goals.

Characters should help each other just as they would do in the actual situation. But it doesn't have to stop there – you can always extend this help to other players, rather than just other characters. If your character is in a different location, and not playing an active part at that moment, there's nothing stopping you from helping if one of the players is stuck or unsure what to do. It may depend upon the situation, of course. If you're going to be helpful, try to think of what the other player's character is like and the situation they're in. Don't just say, "My character is locked in the third cell on the left," if the other player is searching the facility to rescue you. If a player acts on information that their character wouldn't know, there's a special word for it: it's called 'metagaming'. Metagaming is a no-no. It destroys the suspension of disbelief and can ruin the feel of a game. We'll cover that in a moment.

Instead, you could help by aiding the other players in coming up with great and imaginative actions that make great storytelling, ensuring the game rattles along at a great pace.

RULES ARE MEANT TO BE BROKEN

Don't let the rules slow things down. Everything in the game can be accomplished with the same basic rule, from folding an origami bird to rewiring the TARDIS. Most of the time, the Gamemaster will help with these rules and how to use them, but don't worry too much about following everything to the letter. The rules are there to ensure everything runs smoothly, but pausing in the middle of a desperate chase to look something up is going to halt the flow and the suspension of disbelief.

Simply put: don't worry about it. Run with it, and remember, the Gamemaster is there to help you out and to keep things running smooth.

DON'T CHEAT

On the other hand, however, you shouldn't cheat. Cheating takes the fun out of the game. If it's a really crucial moment, and your character is looking like they're gonna get fried by the Judoon as they march into the place, it's not really your place to cheat. Characters die, they get fed up and leave, and you move on – you get a new character who may be even better than your last! If you think you're going to get killed, go out fighting or doing something suitably heroic.

Become the stuff of legend. If you do something memorable and the odds were really against you, the Gamemaster will reward you with Story Points or other cool stuff for your next character.

It doesn't mean that cheating doesn't go on in the game, but this is purely up to the Gamemaster. If a situation is dire, or if you're about to uncover the villain's plot way too early in the story, the Gamemaster may fudge some rolls. They won't tell you about it but any cheating done this way is for the benefit of the whole game. Having the characters killed too early because you've done something silly, or ruining the villain's plot, will spoil the game for everyone, so there may be a little bending of the rules. It won't happen often, and the Gamemaster has the final say, but they're the only ones who should be 'cheating'.

METAGAMING

Metagaming is a fancy word for your character doing something based on information they wouldn't have. There's a difference between what you know as a player, and what your character knows. Sometimes this can be information that's important to the plot. For example, if you as a player have overheard where the villains have taken your fellow time traveller, you may be tempted to act upon this information and say, "I know – they've taken Clara to Holding Cell 7 on the mothership." You have to remember, if your character has no way of knowing this, they shouldn't be acting upon the information. It should be part of the adventure where the characters investigate to uncover their location, and how to attempt a rescue.

The other way you may be tempted to metagame, and almost as bad as the previous example, is having your character know something purely because of the rules. If, for example, Danny is cornered by a Cyberman in the school canteen, he wouldn't know about the Cyberman's weakness to gold. Danny's player may know about the Cyberman's weakness but Danny himself has never encountered a Cyberman before, at least not face to face.

Again, knowing how strong an enemy is from reading through the rulebooks shouldn't influence your character's actions; if you do, it's a great excuse for the Gamemaster to make the villains even more powerful than you were expecting!

PUT THE 'CHARACTER' IN CHARACTER

There's a massive difference between your character being just a bunch of numbers and statistics on a sheet of paper, and them actually being a 'character'. There are a few ways of doing this, and it doesn't take too much work.

First of all, think of who your character is. Imagine you're writing a book. We've already suggested when you put the 'finishing touches' to your character that you think about who they are and what they do, what their family is like, and so on. You can take this a step further and come up with some interesting back-story.

Clara was 'the Impossible Girl', a figure who the Doctor kept meeting in different times and places. She became a mystery for the Doctor to solve, and in doing so Clara joined him on his adventures - until one day she became an irrevocable part of his personal timestream.

Little details like that may seem unimportant when you're first creating your character, but the Gamemaster may take these facts away with her and write something into a future adventure that may relate to your character's history. In Clara's case, her mysterious background became a means to save the Doctor from the Great Intelligence's trap.

Another way to add depth to your character is to actually talk for your character in the game. It doesn't mean you have to put on an accent or anything, though you can if you like. Rather than saying, "My character asks them where they were when the body was found," you could act as your character and say, "Where were you when the body was found?" It'll help.

Of course, you may not want to put on an accent, but you can change the way you speak to be more like the character. If getting into character means doing odd things, go for it if it helps. If you feel more in character if you actually had a Sonic Screwdriver when you're using it in the game, feel free to wave a prop one around at the appropriate moment. It all adds to tone of the game and keeps it fun and exciting.

GET INVOLVED

One of the great traps with roleplaying games is to slip out of the game and start chatting about what was on TV the other night. You're with your friends,

so there are bound to be moments of conversation during the game like this. However, if you're not involved in the game, you're losing out.

Roleplaying games are interactive, and the more you put into the game, the better it'll be. Keep a pencil and paper handy, and make notes if you need to. Most of us do – it makes it better if you can say "Mr. Smiggins, the groundsman, was found killed by a monstrous creature" and you can actually remember his name from earlier, rather than just saying "That guy we met earlier with the accent and the hat... er... what was his name again?" This is especially so if you can't remember the names of the other players' characters!

You'll find that there are scenes when your character isn't doing anything, when the action focuses on other members of the TARDIS crew. There are a couple of ways of looking at this – you could read this book and switch off from listening, thinking "If my character isn't there, I wouldn't know all this is going on, so I shouldn't ruin it!" That's fine, but we don't want you to sit and get bored if there's a particularly long scene that you're not involved in. The other way is to listen to what is going on. As long as you're not acting on any of the information, and you get back 'into character' when you're involved again, there's no problem with paying attention to what other characters are doing, or even offering ideas and suggestions (see above).

Of course, the ultimate way to get involved is to make sure you turn up to the game. There's nothing more frustrating for the Gamemaster than preparing a great and exciting adventure and then not have players show up because they're too busy playing on their games console. It's OK if you're only intending on turning up when you can, if you have commitments, but the Gamemaster may assign you interesting supporting characters rather than a major character that continues from adventure to adventure. You could end up playing someone like Professor Palmer one game, Captain Ferring the following game, or even Vincent Van Gogh the next; characters who don't really continue from one story to the next, but can play an important part in the overall plot. Story Points would continue from one character to the next, depending upon how well you played, but it means you get to stretch yourself and play loads of different people!

DON'T BE AWKWARD

Sometimes, you can have a great idea for a character, and it just doesn't fit in with the rest of the game. Imagine you have a game planned: the characters are a group of friends who all hang out together. They're average older student types who sit around in gloomy bars and wonder why their lives are so grey. They're going to get caught up in a great plot where aliens are invading and brainwashing kids through their MP3 players, turning them into dangerous killers.

The players all generate their characters, work out their backgrounds, and then one of them says, "My character is eight years old, she's a psychic who can break things with her mind and she's escaped from a children's home where they were experimenting on her abilities." Great idea for a character, but as the rest of the group are all sulky students, they're not going to hang around with an 8-year old. It'd be

like the player saying, "my character is a survivor of the battle of Canary Wharf, he was partially cybered when the Cybermen tried converting him, but they all got sucked into the Void. He's a good guy now, though he looks about 80% Cyberman." Interesting choice for a character, but they're going to be a little obvious when they're walking about or trying to sneak into places.

Try to come up with a character that works with the other players, and everyone can get on with. It'll make it more fun for everyone involved.

DON'T HOG IT!

Just because you're playing the Doctor, doesn't mean you have to be the centre of attention all the time. Let the other characters (and players) have their chance to shine. We're going to help the Gamemaster (in the next chapter) to ensure that everyone has their chance to be cool, be the key element in the story, and to prove their worth, so don't try to be the focus of the story when it's obviously not your turn.

For example, when Danny was killed by a car and taken to the Nethersphere, the other characters took centre stage as they tried to save him. When the TARDIS was shrunk by the Boneless, even the Doctor had to take a back seat as Clara tried to save him.

Everyone will have their turn.

WHAT WOULD THE DOCTOR DO?

The greatest bit of advice for any player of the **Doctor Who Roleplaying Game** is to ask yourself this question: "What would the Doctor do?" If trapped in a situation, or facing seemingly unbeatable odds, try to think like the Doctor.

⚙ RECURRING THEMES

There are a few recurring themes in the Doctor's adventures and they're important to the atmosphere of the game. If you can capture these themes in the game, it'll feel more like you're part of one of the Doctor's great adventures.

SENSE OF ADVENTURE

All of the characters in the TARDIS have a real sense of adventure: a desire to see the universe and to experience the sheer wonder of it all.

It may seem hard to imagine, but here's a way of looking at it – have a think about the world you're living in. We're not just talking about the game here, we mean the really real world. Think of yourself, sitting reading this book, then imagine your home, the street you're in, the town or city. Keep thinking further out, the countryside around the city, the county you're in, the country. Imagine how small you are if people in a space station were looking down on you from orbit. Now imagine how small the planet Earth is compared to the other planets in our system. Then imagine how small our solar system is compared to the rest of the galaxy, and that's just a fraction of the universe out there. Instead of thinking how small you are, imagine how big the universe is. It's all out there – sights you'd never imagine in your wildest dreams. The Doctor tells Clara about the planet Obsidian, shrouded in perpetual darkness, and Thedion Four, where it constantly rained acid. How cool would they be to visit?

It's the drive to see new stuff that keeps the characters going. The Doctor has been around for hundreds and hundreds of years, but he keeps travelling, because he has the whole universe and the whole of time to explore. That's an awful lot to see.

The whole of time. Now that's an amazing thought too. Imagine you could see the birth of the planet, or its destruction. The Doctor has witnessed both! You could see the dawn of man, what actually killed off the dinosaurs or the rise of the Roman Empire. Visit the old west, feudal Japan or find out who started the Great Fire of London. Or see the first human colonists launch into space, the first cities on the moon or Mars.

THE GOOD, THE BAD AND THE UGLY

Most of the people who travel with the Doctor are inherently good, facing the evils in the universe. Of course, this evil comes in many shapes and forms, but their actions usually declare their evil intentions, and it is clear early on that they are up to no good.

The Doctor usually takes the 'moral high ground' by refusing to kill or use guns. When it comes to his companions, they are under his watchful eye and encouraged to do the same. Even when they're not under the Doctor's watchful eye, characters are inherently good; those who prove not to be either learn from their mistakes, or the Doctor leaves them where they can do little harm.

Villains usually have a purpose that threatens the stability of the universe, or attack anything that is 'different' to them. The prime examples are the Daleks and the Cybermen. Daleks, if you look back far enough, were originally a race called the Kaleds, battling the Thals on Skaro. The Kaleds looked human, but every shred of humanity was removed as the creatures mutated into the hateful creatures that we're familiar with. Anything that wasn't Dalek was inferior and weak, and considered unworthy of living, fit only for 'extermination'. The same can be said of the Cybermen: they again were once human, but have 'upgraded' like the Daleks. Anything that isn't Cyberman is either converted into a Cyberman or 'deleted' as being unfit.

Most villains want to corrupt or mutate humanity in some way or just to rule it as mankind's master and superior. Some, however, just want to watch the universe burn...

CURIOUSER AND CURIOUSER

Another recurring theme is the sense of mystery: investigating the unexplained, the desire to find out more and to learn. This can be as simple as just learning something new to broaden your horizons a bit, but usually this investigation is down to good old-fashioned detective-work. The characters find out something and rather than leaving it for 'someone else to sort out', they get involved, look into the mystery, and try to uncover the villain's plots.

A good story involves a great mystery that needs to be solved. Why does Clara look like someone the Doctor has met before? Why is there a dinosaur roaming about London? Why is humanity planning to blow up the Moon? Who has wiped their memories and ordered them to rob a bank? Is there such a thing as a 'good' Dalek? Where do people go when they die? All these are great questions that'll get you into the action.

THE 'INDOMITABLE' HUMAN RACE

Humanity survives, and seems to be one of the most enduring species in the universe. From their primitive upbringings, humanity may spend a few millennia as downloads or other forms, but eventually they return to the same basic form – right until the end of the universe.

A recurring theme is what it means to be human, just as the villains are usually no longer human and are trying to destroy or corrupt it. You may be travelling the universe through time and space, but there are times when the basics of humanity – family, children, partnership – seem to be even more important than being able to do all these wondrous things. The Doctor can live for centuries, travel anywhere in history and space, but the chance of marriage, children, and a normal life seems to be something remarkable and out of reach.

On the one hand, having a normal life doesn't seem to be all that exciting. Going to work, going home, eating chips, all sound horribly mundane after seeing the wonders of the universe, but to the Doctor this mundanity must seem like a holiday from the constant peril and danger he finds himself in. Only someone with his endurance can keep travelling through all these dangers, and it is no wonder that his companions often need to leave the TARDIS and return to some form of normality, even if it's just for a short while.

Despite their mundanity, humanity as a whole has this persistent spirit. A drive to keep going through all adversity. This spirit and their innate humanity is so strong that it will last to the end of the universe itself. The human race is amazing, and you should never forget that.

MAKING A DIFFERENCE

The Doctor touches many lives in his travels, and every one he encounters is changed in some way. The Earth would have been destroyed many times over if the Doctor hadn't intervened and on an individual level, many people's lives have even been changed by the Doctor completely.

When playing, don't think purely of self-gain. Think of how you can make a difference. You may have landed on an alien world, but think of its inhabitants. They have every right to be themselves and to live free lives. Just because they're aliens, doesn't mean they don't deserve to be saved from hostile forces.

PACIFISM

This is certainly an area where the **Doctor Who Roleplaying Game** differs. Many games thrive on combat and violence. When faced with an invading species, the usual response is to blast 'em out of the sky, charge in with guns a blazing and send 'em packing! Well, that may be the way Torchwood works, but it's not the way the Doctor does things.

The 'Guns are Bad' section in **Chapter Three: I Can Fight Monsters, I Can't Fight Physics** (see pg.88) gives you some alternatives to fighting, but it may be that you'll have to get used to the idea of giving up and allowing yourself to be captured, or running away, rather than trying to face down the overwhelming force with violence.

It may be hard to find, and it might not always be readily accepted, but there is always an alternative – there is always a choice, and even villains should be given the chance to surrender.

⚙ GAMEMASTERING

All of this advice applies to every player of the **Doctor Who Roleplaying Game**, but one player is going to have to take on a bit more responsibility and be the Gamemaster. As such, we'll dedicate the rest of this chapter to the tricky and rewarding task of Gamemastering.

Being the Gamemaster may seem like a lonely job, but the game is designed to be a collaborative effort between Gamemaster and all of the players. We'll guide you through Gamemastering, give you some help through the tricky bits, and advise you on the ways to get the best out of your players and your game.

But what does a Gamemaster do? It is easier than it all sounds: in the role of Gamemaster you'll be asked to be part storyteller and part referee.

Storyteller

Although you're all making a great adventure together, the Gamemaster has the basic idea of where the plot will go, has certain scenes planned and some cool action worked out and knows the story of the adventure. The players could do something completely unexpected, taking the story into new directions, and the Gamemaster will often have to steer the players in the right direction, develop the story with them and inspire a great adventure.

As a storyteller it's the Gamemaster's job to bring the action to life. It's OK to say, "the spaceship takes off", but if you tell the players, "the spaceship rumbles into action, sending vibrations through the ground before it soars into the purple skies, leaving a trail in its wake," it is going to sound cooler and give the players a better picture of what is going on. The better your descriptions, the more the game will come alive for the players and the better they will be inspired to contribute to the story.

When the characters go into a new place, it'll be up to the Gamemaster to describe the location so the characters get a feel for the area. The better the detail and description, the better the players will be able to picture where they are and what they have to interact with. You'll have to describe the place, the sounds, the smells and the weather. How warm is it, is there a bad feeling in the place that indicates that something has happened? All of this can make the gaming experience more engaging and more exciting.

If the players take your description and run with it, inventing further details as they describe what they are doing, then great! It's a sign that they are really getting into it, so encourage this and reward them for it by developing the story around them and incorporate their ideas into your setting.

Referee

While creating great stories and new adventures for the characters, the **Doctor Who Roleplaying Game** is a game and games need rules. This book provides the rules, but in your role as Gamemaster you'll be asked to make judgement calls and decide the outcome of rolls. Not only that, you'll be expected to know the rules fairly well and so it may be up to you to teach the rest of the gaming group exactly how to play!

WHO SHOULD BE GAMEMASTER?

Almost as difficult a decision as 'who should play the Doctor', trying to decide who should or could be Gamemaster can be a tricky one. Usually, it's the person who has purchased the game as they will have more access to the rules and adventures than the players, giving them a chance to prepare between games. Often, the Gamemaster acts as host for the game, and the players gather at the Gamemaster's place.

Of course it doesn't have to be just one person running the game indefinitely. It could be that a new Gamemaster takes over with the start of a new campaign or adventure. A new Gamemaster can change the feel and tone of the game. It also gives you all a chance to give Gamemastering a go, and gives everyone a chance at playing (and having a break from the Gamemastering duties).

Running a game that everyone enjoys is a hugely satisfying experience. It is more challenging that 'just' being a player, but it also more rewarding and a great chance to indulge your creativity.

WHAT DO YOU NEED TO PLAY?

Before you start actually playing, you'll need a few things. Luckily, you should have most of these already. Some, however, will require a little preparation.

The Rulebook: You have this already! You're reading it right now, so that's one off the list. Told you this was easy!

Dice: You can raid your old copies of Monopoly, Ludo or Risk, or get a handful cheap from most toy and game stores. You can buy them in packs of 36 dice from wargaming stores as well. You may not need that many, though you may want to have a couple of dice each – saves having to share.

Somewhere to play: You really need somewhere to play. This can be almost anywhere, though the most traditional place is a decent-sized dinner table. Make sure everyone's comfortable, you can see each other (especially the Gamemaster), and everyone can hear each other. If you haven't access to a dinner table, just find somewhere you can all sit together.

Paper, Pencils and Character Sheets: We've provided character sheets in the appendix, as well as pre-generated sheets for the Doctor and his companions. You may want to photocopy them, or head to our website where you can download character sheets to print out. You just need some pencils (don't write on the sheets in pen as attributes and other stats will change frequently during the game), erasers and some scrappy bits of paper to make notes, draw diagrams, scribble down names and sketch out maps of locations.

Story Points: You can download a sheet of Story Point counters from the website that you can print out onto thin card and cut out, or you can use anything as counters: jelly babies, buttons, poker chips or pennies.

Added Extras: You have everything you need, but you can add to the experience with a few extras. You could get some snacks – just some sweets, drinks or fruit – you don't need a lot, after all it's hard to game with a full plate of fish and chips in front of you and you don't want to distract from the actual game. However, a few nibbles can keep everyone's attention fired up. You could also add a little mood music, with some soundtrack CDs or moody classical music. You could also have a few props if you think it'll help – sonic screwdrivers, miniatures, all that kinda stuff can help the players to imagine what is going on and get more into character.

Players!: Without players, there's no game. We'd probably recommend a smaller group with three or four players and a Gamemaster. Larger groups can be accommodated, but it's better for a 'team' set up like a UNIT squad or a Torchwood team. We'll look at your players in more detail below.

OTHER RESOURCES

There are fifty years worth of books, audio dramas, video and other media dedicated to the Doctor's universe and his adventures, most of which can be used to inspire your adventures. And, unlike boring academic research, reading, watching or listening to the Doctor's adventures can be a fun activity all on its own!

⚙ BASIC GAMEMASTERING

The Gamemaster is the glue that binds the game together. They are the eyes and ears of the players, as well as the voice behind the creatures and characters they meet. They are the narrator and the storyteller who brings the world to life with descriptions, imagination and stories. The Gamemaster is the arbiter of decisions and makes the final call on disputes, questions and problems.

The Gamemaster does not have a character of their own. Instead the Gamemaster acts as all of the NPCs and everyone the players meet. The Gamemaster is the storyteller who knows all the secrets of the game, and it's their job to be mysterious and dynamic, and to keep the pace of the game as exciting as possible. They know what is going on behind the scenes and they act as referee in battles and when a decision needs making on the rules.

They give the universe the spark of magic that turns a mundane story into a great one. The Gamemaster is the schemer who creates the fantastic stories the players will experience, and it's up to the Gamemaster to keep the players on course during their adventures by giving them sufficient clues and to make sure they don't lose their way or get bored.

The Gamemaster is impartial. They do not take sides and should be fair at all times.

BEING IN THE HOT SEAT
You're in the hot seat now, but don't worry - being the Gamemaster is a lot of fun. You can tell simple stories at first that will ease you gently into the game and give you a feel for Gamemastering. But here's a word of caution: don't let all that power go to your head. You have to use the power you've been given as a Gamemaster responsibly and not abuse it. You're there to act as a guide for the players and for everyone to have exciting adventures – it's never about 'winning'. If you find you're trying to kill off the players' characters then you've missed the point of Gamemastering.

BE PREPARED
Just before the players assemble, or the night before, go through the adventure again and make a few notes to keep it fresh in your mind. Think of the various events in the story, highlight them on the pages if you like, and think of the sequence in which they occur.

Remember, they could happen out of sequence – you don't know where the players will go.

Make notes and do your preparation. It may look like a lot of work being the Gamemaster, but it's very rewarding. A bit of preparation goes a long way and if you listen to your players and look where they're going to be for next week's session, you can prepare.

BE FLEXIBLE

The Gamemaster might be in charge, and what they say goes in a game, but you don't have to think up everything beforehand. By listening to the players you can allow them to create their own adventures. For example, they might be talking about what they are going to do next and by listening to their conversations you can plan ahead to the future.

A good Gamemaster is descriptive, creative, energetic and eager to listen to the players as they work with you to create the story. The plot may not go exactly in the direction you had planned but, with a little improvisation and quick thinking, the story will continue and can easily come back to the plot.

It's important to give the players free reign to do as they please (without being pressured into going in a certain direction) and to give them enough to do without being bored or so much that they feel overwhelmed.

✹ EVERYONE HAS A ROLE TO PLAY

The group should contain a wide range of character types. After all, the TARDIS would get very boring if everyone was exactly like Amy, Rory or River Song. Loads of people have travelled in the TARDIS through the Doctor's long history, and each had their own strengths and weaknesses. It's how they react to a particular situation that makes them great.

Try to avoid too many characters with the same role. For example, you could have one person who is experienced in combat, another who is the scientist, one trained in medicine and another who is an everyday average shop assistant. There are hundreds of personality types in the real world, from nurses to teachers to scientists, so there's plenty of choice to inspire you, and a wide pool of backgrounds and personalities that can get involved in the adventures.

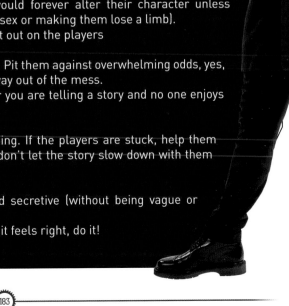

GAMEMASTERING HINTS AND TIPS

- Be creative. There are lots of ways to create atmosphere in a game.
- Remember that the story is everything. You're there to have fun and to tell some amazing stories across time and space.
- Don't let the story you're telling get bogged down in details. Pay attention to the pace and keep things moving.
- Listen to the players – sometimes you can let them create the story for you.
- Don't force them down a path just because you want them to (or because you've worked hard on it) – simply use it at a later date.
- Don't make the players do anything that would forever alter their character unless absolutely necessary (such as changing their sex or making them lose a limb).
- Don't come to a game angry: you'll only take it out on the players
- Be impartial and fair.
- Don't deliberately try to kill off the characters. Pit them against overwhelming odds, yes, but always give them an escape route and a way out of the mess.
- Use the dice rolls to tell the story; remember you are telling a story and no one enjoys needless deaths.
- Don't be afraid to improvise.
- Remember to keep the pace of the game going. If the players are stuck, help them out (maybe at the cost of a Story Point), but don't let the story slow down with them wallowing in confusion.
- Try to avoid clichés.
- Make the game exciting. Be mysterious and secretive (without being vague or frustrating).
- Be spontaneous, go with your gut instincts. If it feels right, do it!
- Remember to have fun!

COMPLEMENTING CHARACTERS

The best groups contain characters that complement each other. A game would be very boring if everyone had the same skills. A group of gung-ho action heroes would make for great battle adventures, but the constant combat would soon get old (and that really isn't what the Doctor stands for). River Song helps with all things technical but can hold her own in a fight, whereas Amy and Rory offered companionship and strength, especially in their bravery and character. They are all very different characters who will react differently to each situation.

A successful group gives each member a unique role. If everyone knows hieroglyphics or how to break the encryption on an alien computer, those skills won't feel so special when they are needed. Everyone should have special skills – they define some of what a character is and make that character feel needed in times of crisis.

Try to ensure the companions have a wide range of skills and abilities and personality types. Not every character should know how to fire a pistol or to perform triage.

GROUP BACKGROUNDS

The big question is "why are these people together?" This is fairly easy when it comes to a standard 'Doctor and Companions' game, after all, the Doctor is accompanied by many different people, and who wouldn't want to experience the adventure of travelling the stars and through time? It gets a little trickier if your game doesn't have the Doctor in it.

Have they all grown up together at the same location? Do they all work together in the same place? Have they all been invited to a certain location for various reasons, like the beginning of a murder-mystery?

Think about how the group acts towards each other. Do any of the characters have particular feelings towards one another? Are they secretly in love with them? Have a jealous rivalry? A lifelong debt after having their life saved? You can spice things up a bit like this quite easily – just look at how the characters are inter-related in popular soap operas... brothers, sisters, friends, enemies, it all makes things more interesting.

The more detailed and interesting the character's background is, the easier it is for the Gamemaster to use elements of their past as plot points in future adventures and make them part of the ongoing story.

⚙ BUILDING ON THE BASICS

Being a Gamemaster is hard work, but it can be exceptionally rewarding as over time, you create a universe of your own. Once you have the basics down, you can get more creative and really bring the universe you're creating to life.

BRINGING NON-PLAYER CHARACTERS TO LIFE

Try to make your NPCs as memorable as possible. Who can forget characters such as Davros or the Master? They are exciting and striking characters with just the right level of wickedness that makes them fantastic villains. It's not just a case of giving your NPCs attributes and skills, try to give them personalities as well. The Master is possibly the most complex of villains in the Doctor's universe, and it's his drives and machinations, and the sheer charisma he exudes, that sets him apart and makes him so memorable.

It's not just the major villains, the minor NPCs should be consistent too. Write things down, especially if you're making up characters as you go. If the characters happen to visit the Metebelis Bar, and you make up a name for the bartender they talk to get some information, make sure that when they travel there the next time you have a note of that name to add some continuity. As the characters build a shared history in the universe you create, they will have a much more personal stake in everything that goes on there. An encounter with a former ally in need or an old adversary bent on revenge can bring a more personal element to an adventure.

BRINGING THE SETTING TO LIFE

Describing the setting and the action is vital, not only for giving the players a sense of location, but also in making sure the players know what is actually going on. You should describe not only the important

elements of the location – where everything is, what it looks like and so on, but also some of the less important details. You don't want to get into the habit of just telling the players what is important – that way they won't actually think for themselves.

For example, if the Gamemaster describes a location like this: "You enter through the wooden door into the study. The chair has been knocked over and there are signs of a struggle. A note is attached to the underside of the chair that says 'Beware the Lake'." They have given the players all of the necessary information and nothing else. The players know what to do next and haven't actually worked it out for themselves.

The scene would be better described as: "The heavy oaken door to the study leads into a scene of violence and struggle. Books and papers are strewn across the floor and the chair has been knocked over behind the huge wooden desk. A fire still burns in the fireplace, and a glass has been tipped over on the desk." The players have a good feel for the place, and you can lead them in, getting them to look for more clues and information. Only if they say they're looking closer at the chair and the desk (very likely in this situation) will the Gamemaster reveal the note (and then they may hide it somewhere a little more interesting).

As well as describing where everything is in the room, you could add some extra details – the heat from the fire, the smell of the spilled whiskey, the sound of the rain outside... things like that. Remember, although the characters are usually **looking** for clues, it doesn't

mean that you should neglect the other senses. The place could smell funny, leave that taste of fresh paint fumes in their mouth, there could be a funny ticking noise, or a cold chill gives them goosebumps as they wander through. You could even use the sixth sense, and they just 'feel' like there is something wrong with the place that needs investigation.

A good description will not only ensure people know what is around them, but in a dramatic scene where there are multiple characters (or villains and NPCs involved) it also helps them understand where everyone is. This is often a good time to draw a little map of the place, so everyone gets it right. If everyone is clear where everyone and everything is, you don't have to worry about people arguing "I thought he was over near the propane tanks?" or "No, I'm over near the door, not close to the fire."On top of that, a good description will help produce the right atmosphere for the game.

ATMOSPHERE

There may be no atmosphere in space, but it doesn't mean that you can't enhance the atmosphere of the game with a few little tricks. In addition to describing the scene and the events well, you can make the game far more atmospheric by changing the mood in the room you're actually in!

Lighting is one way to change the way the game feels. If you're playing a particularly spooky adventure you could dim the lights in the room, draw the curtains, have a few table lamps but keep the place dark with plenty of shadows. Moody lighting helps in most mystery settings, as long as you can read the character sheets, the dice rolls and the rulebook without straining your eyes! Of course, for lighter toned games you can keep the lighting fairly bright, or play outside on a sunny day.

Music can certainly help, with the use of appropriate soundtracks conjuring up the right setting or feel.

Props are another easy way to add to the mood. If the characters discover a scrawled note leading them to the next clue, you could mock up a version of the note – scrawling on a bit of paper, maybe making it a little faded by staining it with old tea. You can have a toy Sonic Screwdriver for the Doctor's player to wave around when the Doctor is using it.

TECHNOBABBLE

There are many alien planets and often they have completely alien words for mundane items in their culture. This goes doubly for their technology, and adding 'technobabble' to your game can add to the atmosphere.

Rather than calling a ray gun simply a 'ray gun', the people of Rotalix 3 could call it a Rotalix Blaster.

It's even more fun to apply technobabble throughout the game. We all know the Doctor can spout technobabble at a vast pace, but the Doctor is a scientific genius and knows what he's talking about. If you get stuck, have a look at the box below and pick some pseudo-scientific gobbledygook you can use in the dialogue to make the science seem clever!

RULES AND WHEN TO BEND THEM

While the rules are there to allow you to play the game, they are not set in stone and a good Gamemaster should know when to bend them.

If there is a rule you're unhappy with in the game, make a new ruling and discuss it with the players before you start to play. Announce at the beginning that you're changing the rules and this will be the

CHAPTER SIX:
IT'S A ROLLERCOASTER WITH YOU!

BABBLING TECHNOBABBLE!

The Doctor will frequently spout some technobabble that'll go completely over the heads of the Doctor's confused companions. You could use the same phrase repeatedly (like "reversing the polarity of the neutron flow") or look at the following list of scientific-sounding words and throw a few together.

Analog, Arc, Array, Auxiliary, Bio-Electric, Breaker, Capacitor, Circuit, Configuration, Continuum, Converter, Dampening, Destabilise, Digital, Dimensional, Energy, Energiser, Extrapolator, Feedback, Field, Fission, Flow, Fluctuation, Fragment, Fusion, Graviton, Gyroscopic, Harmonic, Inertia, Inversion, Kinetic, Link, Loop, Macro-, Manipulator, Matrix, Meta-, Micro-, Modulation, Molecular, Neutrino, Neutron, Nuclear, Oscillator, Particle, Phase, Psychic, Polarity, Projector, Proto-, Pulso, Quantum, Relay, Replicating, Retrogressive, Reversal, Subspace, Sychronise, Temporal, Threshold, Transmission, Vortex, Wavelength, Waveform.

way you're playing. For example, you could say at the beginning of the game, "I want the game to be more cinematic so I'm making everything easier. Instead of 12 being the normal Difficulty for any task, I'm making it 9." Once you've announced the new ruling, stick to it. If it doesn't work, you can scrap it next time, but if you keep changing the rules every five minutes you're going to frustrate and confuse the players.

Likewise if there are bits of the rules you'd like to leave out – Areas of Expertise, say, or the rules for vehicles – then by all means do so. It's your game, after all! Just make sure you tell the players...

Of course, it's not just the rules that sometimes undergo some bending. Often, dice rolls can be tweaked to keep the game going smoothly. As the Gamemaster, you could roll your dice in the middle of the table, just like the players – that way everyone knows that you're being fair and playing the game by the rules. If the dice are unlucky and a character gets exterminated early in the game, it's not your fault as the Gamemaster, it's just those pesky dice. However, it does mean that you may have to get creative to either keep the player alive or to allow a new character to join the group to replace the player's departed character.

Or you could roll your dice out of the sight of the players. Gamemasters sometimes hide behind a screen that protects the adventure details from the prying eyes of the players, and a lot of Gamemasters roll their dice behind the screen. The clatter of dice, and then the sucking air noise that the Gamemaster makes to get the players nervous – a little like when you go to a mechanic and they are about to tell you what's wrong with your car... It means that the dice rolls can be tweaked a little to aid the flow of the story, but be careful it doesn't create distrust from the players.

⚙ DEALING WITH THE PLAYERS

As Gamemaster, you'll be there to guide the players through the creation of their characters (if they're using their own), and moulding the team to the campaign you have in mind.

As you play, you'll discover some players develop certain styles of gaming. Some like to get straight into the action. Others prefer the moody and emotional high stakes, making their character a deep and developed person. Some players just want to know where the aliens are so they can shoot at them, while other players may take more of a back seat, spectating more during the game and enjoying the action as others make the major decisions.

As long as everyone has fun, then that's the key to a good game.

However, there are a few things to look out for that can disrupt or unbalance the game and take some of the fun out of it. Here are a few of the problem players you may encounter.

The Power Gamer

The characters should not be about seeking power for their own ends. At least, not the good guys – there are plenty of forces in the universe trying to do this themselves and it is usually up to our heroes to put a stop to them. However, you may discover a player trying to acquire things for themselves, or using the advanced technology for their own personal gain rather than trying to better the universe.

It could be that you can simply penalise them by not giving them the Story Points that other, less power-hungry players may receive. Maybe not having as many Story Points is enough to fuel a change of heart? However, if they continue in their ways, it may be worth a gentle word off to one side to point out that they may be ruining things for everyone else. It's just not in keeping with the game, and any character who really acted that way would be severely chastised by the Doctor and dropped back to their home time and place, never to be allowed into the TARDIS again.

The Metagamer

Metagaming is when a player uses information that their character wouldn't have. There are a couple of ways this can happen. Usually, it is when the player knows how and where something is happening by listening to the rest of the game in progress. Their character may not be there, but rather than send the player out of the room, they're there and listening in. Normally, this is fine. It's great to listen and find out what everyone else is doing. However, if the player then uses this information to influence their decisions, they're not playing 'in character'. Knowing where the secret plans are, or where one of the other characters is being held prisoner, should come about through investigation and following the clues – not from being told by another player, or overhearing part of the game.

Similarly, if the player acts on information that is out of the game completely, that's another version of metagaming. It could be that they know the weak spot of a particular alien race, or know the next place the aliens will strike, because the player has read it in one of the rulebooks, or knows about it from one of the Doctor's past adventures. Just because the players know to use acetic acid against the Slitheen it doesn't mean that the characters will know.

What do you do if one of the players tries to use information like this? Usually, the easiest way to deal with this is to simply talk to them; ask them "but what would your **character** know?" and try to get them to act on that. If it still doesn't work, you could always change things slightly just to keep them guessing.

The Quiet One
Some people enjoy taking a less active role in the game, whereas others simply cannot get a word in – the other players are so keen to get their intended actions heard that it simply drowns out the great ideas that the quiet player may have.

First of all, ask the player if they're OK. If they're happy taking a back seat and spectating, then that's fine. If they want to be more involved, that's where the Gamemaster really comes in. Give the character an essential role in the story, or an extra cool sub-plot. Bring the player out of the background by making

their character essential to the story. That way, the player has to become more involved, and the others will have to give them a chance to be heard.

The Cheat
The rules are pretty simple in this game, everything being covered by a similar roll. It could be that you have a player who'll roll their dice where no one can see the results, or they come up with some excuse like "Oh, they didn't roll properly, I have to roll them again." It could be that they don't even cheat the rules, but simply manipulate everyone's memory of the game and decide that their character isn't where everyone thought they were, and they may be somewhere else! The best thing to do with this kind of player is to simply keep track of everything. Bring in a firm 'table rule' where everyone has to roll their dice in a clear area in the middle, so everyone can see the results. One roll, no re-rolls.

The Rule-monger
At the other end of the spectrum there's the player who tries to know all of the rules and may try to overrule your decisions by quoting passages from the rulebooks. Luckily, the **Doctor Who Roleplaying Game** only really uses one standard rule, so this rule-mongering should not happen often. However, it is expected that rules will be 'bent' a little to allow for a smooth running game.

As the Gamemaster, you have the final say as the Gamemaster. Whatever you say goes. If you think you may be wrong you should continue on until there is a natural break in the game and you can read through the books to check upon your decisions. If you were wrong, and made a bad decision, you can make it up to the players in other ways – either by giving them Story Points to make up for the bad call, or you could be a little lenient if the bad ruling meant things will become difficult for them later on. Above all, admit your mistake, but explain what happened and how you'll make it up to them. Don't try to hide it, or the players will stop trusting your judgement.

WHAT TO DO WHEN PLAYERS ARE ABSENT

The game doesn't have to stop when a player is absent. You can work them into the story by having them captured, beamed away, or generally give them a reason to be away from the TARDIS. For example, the TARDIS could be in a region of space when one of the companions vanishes in a blaze of light.

This could be the start of an unexpected and exciting new adventure to find out exactly where the companion was taken. Just make sure that if the player returns next session, the character can be easily found or has the opportunity to escape rather than have them sit around idle, otherwise it might put them off coming next time too, and you'll be back to square one!

You could have another player take on the additional role of the missing player's character, literally covering for them, but if they do something that is out of character or that the player wouldn't want them to do, there could be arguments or repercussions later when the player returns. The player should keep the extra character alive and active, but maybe taking a more background role in this session.

✸ EXPERIENCE AND GAIN

Players are generally pretty lucky: not only do they get to play the game, experiencing the thrills of travelling the galaxy and outwitting some of the most dangerous alien foes, but their characters also grow from the experience and gain cool abilities and additional toys that will help them in the future.

The easiest way to reward your players is by allowing the character to grow in some way – usually by increasing their skills, or on rare occasions by increasing their attributes. Usually such increases tie into something the character has done during the adventure – have they used a skill well? Have they shown particular prowess with an attribute? Have they learned something new during the course of the game? All of these are great questions you should ask yourself before dishing out an increase in skill or attribute.

It could be that the character deserves a new trait, or the removal of a Bad Trait that they have struggled with for a while. Are they braver now than they used to be? Does that mean that they should gain the Brave trait, or lose their Cowardly Bad Trait?

Of course, the most common reward will be the restoration of spent Story Points, though on very rare occasions you could allow the character's maximum Story Points to increase so they can keep more Story Points in between adventures.

Skills, attributes, traits and Story Points are not the only way you can reward your players. You could reward your players with some vital information that will lead them onto the next adventure, give them easy access to a secret base, a special Gadget, or item of power, or information that will make a villain pause before acting.

Though most characters will not be as legendary as the Doctor, being able to halt the Vashta Nerada just by his reputation, it could be that successfully accomplishing various tasks and stopping alien invasions gives the character a reputation

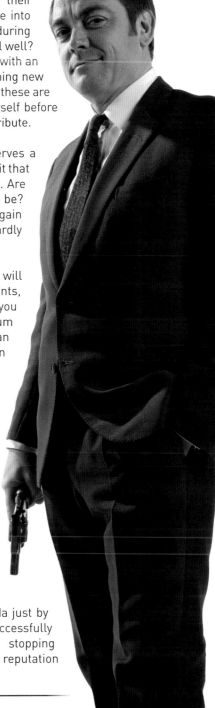

of their own. This could mean that villains will think twice before facing them, or it could mean that they are targeted – surely someone who brings down such a formidable protector of the universe would be even more legendary? Their reputation could get them into places, but they shouldn't fall into the B-list celebrity trap of shouting "Don't you know who I am?" when they don't get their own way!

EVERYTHING HAS ITS TIME...

On the other hand, instead of advancing, the inevitable may happen – one of the characters will die. Not everyone can be gifted with Captain Jack's immortality, but it doesn't have to be the end. No-one wants to see their favourite character killed, but...

It's important to know when to protect the companions from a senseless death. If a character is killed by a stray bullet, it's fine to put steps in place to protect them from leaving the game forever. The 'dead' character could be taken away, only to be regenerated by alien technology, or the aliens could have advanced medical capabilities. A good Gamemaster can heighten suspense by having the character taken away while the other players are unsure whether their companion is alive or dead.

Ideally, the death of a character should be meaningful and heroic. Character death shouldn't be too common in the game – after all, while people do get killed during the frequent alien invasions, it is very rare for one of the Doctor's companions to die. They'll have Story Points to bail them out of an instant extermination, or they could heal by taking a Bad Trait (such as 'Unadventurous') to recover from too many smaller wounds.

If all this doesn't keep the characters alive, the first thing is for the player to know that everyone has been playing fair. If they know the Gamemaster hasn't

been cheating, they should feel better – though a bad dice roll can be pretty harsh, at least they weren't singled out and killed deliberately.

If the character really does die, it's up to the player what they choose to do next. Character death isn't something that should be taken lightly – remember how it is going to affect the Doctor and anyone else involved in the story. It should spur the other players into action to ensure they didn't die in vain while the player creates a new character. Or they could take over one of the more friendly and helpful NPCs in the story until next session – who knows, they may enjoy playing them so much they'll stick with this character and ask to join the TARDIS crew.

⚙ BASICALLY, YOU RULE!

One of the trickiest parts to Gamemastering is being the referee. You should know the rules well and be comfortable making judgement calls when it comes to those odd circumstances not covered by the rules.

The best thing to remember is that the same basic rule can be used for just about anything in the game (Attribute + Skill (+ Trait) + two dice, try to beat the Difficulty). Any problems, make a decision and get on with the story. Try not to stop the game and fumble through the books to find a rule, just run with it. If it's a bad call, you can always make it up to the players in other ways later by being more lenient on them in a crisis or tweaking the course of the adventure so that they gain something as a reward (see above).

There may be times when the players dispute a ruling, and start complaining. It can be difficult, but remember you are in charge. The players should abide by your decisions. If they're unhappy with it, tell them to continue on and not disrupt the game. You can always discuss the decision at the end with the players once the session is over.

HISTORY IS A BURDEN. STORIES CAN MAKE US FLY!

In this chapter, we'll help Gamemasters through the process of running an adventure, how to write their own, and how to make sure everyone has an interesting part to play in the story. On top of that, we'll also discuss story arcs, sub plots, and adventures with a particular theme or special event. Don't worry if some of this sounds confusing, you probably already know this, you just didn't realise it!

⚙ THE STORY

Let's start with the basics. The story is the most important element; without it, there's nothing to say, nothing exciting will happen and it's all going to be a little dull. Have a think about the sort of adventure you'd like to play. You don't have to write anything down, maybe just some key words for the time being to keep the tone of the story in mind. Something like "Orient Express, Space, Mummy" can be all you need to start creating an adventure.

The story told in an adventure is possibly the most important thing to consider. It needs a beginning, a middle and an end, and it needs something exciting to happen. They always say there is no drama without conflict, so there should be a cool villain. If you envision a particular event happening in the game you can make a note of that as well. Characters should grow from the experience, or learn a valuable

lesson. Working out a story for your adventure doesn't mean you need a detailed outline of what you want the characters to do; instead just a basic premise of where the characters will go, and who they will face should be enough.

The players have a lot of control over what they do and where they go. They will have a tendency to stray from a firm path you may lay out for them; unless (or sometimes even if) you make the course of action obvious and clear, they may wander off and do unexpected things. This shouldn't be entirely discouraged, as it can lead to new and exciting avenues that you hadn't planned, but unless you're very good at making things up as you go along, this may be best left for more experienced Gamemasters. You'll soon get the hang of it after a few games though.

Above all, there should be a conflict: good against evil, possibly against overwhelming odds, in which the characters' abilities and spirit should prevail. There will be setbacks, failures and defeat along the way, but in the end good will triumph (at least we hope). This conflict should have some depth to it: it shouldn't be too simple otherwise there will be no investigation or gradual development of plot. You don't want our heroes uncovering the alien plans in the first ten minutes!

THE CONFLICT

Every good story has a conflict in it in some form or another. This can be as simple or obvious a conflict as 'good vs evil' or it can be something as subtle as "I shouldn't fall in love with him, he's an alien." It doesn't have to be a physical conflict, simply a conflict of interests or emotions can be enough to make a great story. A story conflict is when what someone wants and what they actually have is very different: it doesn't matter whether this is the heroes or the antagonists.

What is the conflict about? In most instances it's a pretty simple case of "alien race wants something that doesn't benefit the rest of the universe" – that something might be dominion, control or to upgrade all of humanity.

A race could face a life of slavery, aliens could be on the brink of war with the characters in the middle of the impending bloodshed, a new parasitic race could be controlling the minds of Earth's leaders or the population of a town could go missing. There are loads of possibilities; one of the great things about the Doctor's ability to travel time and space, to go any time or any place, means that there are very few limitations.

THE ANTAGONIST

To have a good conflict, you need a great antagonist. A villain, or someone who simply opposes the actions of the players. In most good stories, the antagonist of a story is unknown to the players, and it is only during the course of the adventure (usually around half way through) that the villain is revealed. Often the villains can become the most iconic part. After all, Davros is quite distinctive, and you'd be hard pushed to find anyone who doesn't know what a Dalek is. A good villain should be seemingly unstoppable, a formidable force to be reckoned with that will require some thought and planning to stop. Charging blindly into a room full of Daleks, guns blazing, is a sure way to find your characters exterminated. Instead, these villains should be almost unbeatable, with a weakness that can be discovered and exploited after some investigation and adventure.

The best villains have a complete personality, a good story behind them and a suitably fiendish plan. Some thought should be given as to their reasoning – why are they evil? What do they hope to achieve? It could be that their intentions are good and it is just that they are going about it in a way that can be perceived as evil.

The Boneless were all out bad: the Doctor gave them a chance, but they continued to be malicious and destructive. The Half-face Man was technically a villain but his intention was good: he wanted to repair his spaceship and follow his programming to reach the Promised Land. Unfortunately, he was willing to sacrifice innocent humans (and dinosaurs) to do so. A bit of complexity to the villain and their motives makes a villain **great**.

Of course, the villain should suit the rest of the story: where it is set, what the story should be about and what is involved.

The antagonist could be anyone or anything. An aggressive warrior race, a group of over-zealous religious types, guerillas, terrorists or rebels, an alien race posing as a huge company or a rich, power-hungry individual who has managed to get his hands on dangerous alien technology.

THE SETTING

Now you have a villain in mind, and an idea of what they are up to, think about where this adventure is going to take place. Is it Earth, at one of the companion's homes? How about another planet? A space station? In an underwater research facility? Deep in a jungle, or underground beneath the city streets. Lost in the desert or drifting in an out-of-control starship. In an alternate universe, or in ours? If you have a great idea about where you'd like the adventure to be set, then go for it – deep underground in the government base in Area 51 or travelling through time in a B52 bomber lost in the Bermuda Triangle, anything is possible!

The Doctor makes frequent stops on Earth, and for a good reason. If Earth is under threat, you feel more emotionally involved in the story than on Planet Zog. Seeing a spaceship crash through the tower at Westminster, demolishing Big Ben,

is more dramatic than seeing a ship crash into a swamp on a distant world.

That said, alien worlds open up a whole new arena of play. The human race spreads to the stars, and a distant colony world where the people have to survive with basic equipment and technology makes an interesting setting. Or a high-tech world with robots and gleaming spires, or a desolate alien world of barren plains and deserts where water is the key to survival. Why stick to planets? Why not a vast space station or starship?

Then, you should also consider when the adventure is going to happen. You could stick to Earth but set it in the distant past, in another country, or the far future. The only thing to remember is that Gallifrey only survived from the Last Great Time War by being locked away in another dimension by the Doctor. Missy somehow escaped it, but until the Doctor finds it again, Gallifrey is one place you cannot visit. Once you have your setting, you can populate it with additional characters. They may be friendly or in trouble and needing your help, or secretly working for the villains. The Doctor and his companions are rarely alone in their adventures, and good NPCs can make things even more interesting.

THE OTHERS

So you know where the story is taking place, but who else is in the story besides the Doctor, his companions

and the villains? There are usually other characters involved, whether collaborators with the villains, innocent villagers, brave survivors or just normal people. They could be the down and outs of the city during the Great Depression, freedom fighters battling against an alien race in a war that has been going on for generations, the companion's friends and family facing the strange and alien, a division of UNIT, a rogue Time Agent, the local press or a race of slaves hoping for freedom.

Often, these 'others' will have as vital a role to play in the story as the antagonist, so having an interesting and fleshed-out idea for these supporting characters is important.

ACTION!

Great drama, explosions and chases can lead to some fantastic action scenes. Thinking up a cool action sequence that takes place in a dramatic or original place, such as a chase along the top of a moving train or a dramatic rescue from a vast galactic prisonship can inspire a great story. For example, you have this idea of the TARDIS being catapulted over a castle wall in the middle of a huge medieval battle. You know you'd like to see that scene in the story, so imagine who's in the castle? Who is attacking? Why would the Doctor be there? Who could be the villain? Would the Cybermen be wandering around, the locals confused thinking they are knights?

Think of something else – you want to see a chase running along the top of a futuristic monorail, travelling over a gleaming city. What city is it? Who are the characters chasing? Often, just coming up with a single scene, answering a few questions about how and why it could happen, and you have the bare bones of an exciting adventure.

When working on the basics of your story, if you have any particular ideas for cool action scenes that would make an exciting and dramatic sequence, pencil it in. The free-form way roleplaying works, it may be that the scene will have to move around in the story structure, so having a few action scenes and locations worked out you'll be prepared no matter where the characters go. Thinking ahead and being prepared means you won't have to force them into your big action finale.

✸ THE ADVENTURE

An adventure tells a story, and all stories have a beginning, a middle and an end. We're not going to get too complicated with this, but most stories can be broken down into the following parts. You probably already know how this works from TV, movies and novels, but may not realise it!

An adventure comprises the following components, though this is just a guide and you can feel free to experiment and try something different:

THE BASIC STORY:

Prologue
The Beginning – Set Up, Investigation
The Middle – Rising Action, Running!
The End – Climax, Resolution
Epilogue – Aftermath

Let's look at this story structure one step at a time and see what happens in each bit.

PROLOGUE

A good way to get everyone interested in the coming story is to have a prologue. It can be a short 5-10 minutes at the beginning of the story that can be used to set the scene, give a rough idea of what's to come, and gets everyone interested. This doesn't need to feature the Doctor or his companions (or your players' characters) at all. It can be used to introduce the threat or other important characters that will be placed in danger.

In the game, a Prologue could involve the players' normal characters, just to set the pace and the scene. Or you could have the players take on the roles of other characters to give the players a sense of what they're about to walk into. This allows them to play new and different characters each adventure, if only for a few minutes, and good storytelling means the reward of Story Points that can be used on their normal characters.

For example, the Gamemaster has an adventure planned around a group of colonists settling down in their new town in the American west. The players could play the town preacher and his wife, investigating the strange noises coming over the ridge at night, and the bizarre lights in the night sky. It would set the location, introduce the threat and some of the themes that the Doctor and his companions will have to deal with in the adventure when they arrive.

Sometimes these prologues are a 'catch-up' of prior events – this can be a great way to remind the players of what happened in the previous session. Anything is possible, as long as it gets the story going, and gets the players interested and intrigued.

INTRODUCTORY BRIEFS

When running a Prologue like this, with the players running different characters for a short section, it pays to write up a separate, brief description of the situation and a little about the background of each character, and hand them to the appropriate players. This gets them into the roles of their temporary character and gives them a small piece of the puzzle to share, if they choose.

THE BEGINNING – THE SET UP, INVESTIGATION

'The Beginning' introduces all of the characters (especially the player characters if they haven't been used before) and gets things moving, revealing the basics of what's going on. If this is the characters' first game, this will set up who's who before something dramatic happens to them to bring them together – an event that will make them want to get involved. This can be anything from a missing friend, a threat to their lives, or something mysterious going on that will pique their interest.

If **Deep Breath** was an adventure in a new game, it has a lot to pack in. The Doctor's companions – Clara, Madame Vastra, Jenny and Strax – might already know one another – but this is their players' first chance to play as them. It is also the opportunity to introduce the latest incarnation of the Doctor, post regeneration.

We see him struggling to recognise his friends and coming to terms with his new characteristics. Post-regeneration confusion is a great way for a new player of the Doctor to try out various ways of portraying him!

There are also plenty for the players to do too, besides getting to know their characters – not only has someone killed a Tyrannosaurus Rex in Victorian London, but humans are being murdered too. The characters can investigate either of these clues, perhaps deducing that their body parts are being harvested by someone – or something.

CHAPTER SEVEN: HISTORY IS A BURDEN. STORIES CAN MAKE US FLY!

196

If they start getting lost or off track, you can have them discover a strange advert in The Times; if they solve the clue, it will lead them to the next part of the adventure: Mancini's Family Restaurant.

Basically, we are introduced to the characters, to the situation they're in, and the reason why they're doing what they are. Something will happen that the characters will have to get involved in. This can be anything from a missing friend, a threat to themselves or the planet, someone needs saving or something mysterious is going on. Once they realise what is happening, the characters will start to investigate...

Investigation is key to a good adventure and now the characters are aware that something is amiss they will look into it a little further. This is when the characters do their investigating, sneaking around, looking for clues, questioning NPCs, and the Gamemaster will give the players bits of information, leading them from one clue to another until they start to work out what is going on. They could discover that someone is messing with the water in a reservoir that supplies the governing powers of the city, or that people they thought were just acting funny are in fact clones working for an invading alien army. The players will discover clues that will lead them on a trail. This trail of breadcrumbs will lead them further and further into the plot.

As the characters get closer and closer to the root of the plot, things are likely to heat up. There may be encounters with henchmen, with alien troops or dangerous situations. It is usually at the end of the beginning section that the villain of the story becomes aware of the character's actions and something happens to our heroes to foil their investigations.

In his first adventure, the Twelfth Doctor and Clara investigate Mancini's Family Restaurant, discovering a new twist to the horror – all the diners are puppets, and the waiter is a Clockwork Robot! Having discovered too much, they wind up on the menu and are captured!

THE MIDDLE – RISING ACTION, RUNNING!!

In the middle of the story, the characters are starting to get the idea of what's going on. They've uncovered the problem and are working on a way to solve it, though they may not be aware of who exactly is behind it. They'll know that their chances are slim, but they'll be ready to face the challenge ahead. However, it is usually at this time that the villains become aware of the characters' 'interfering' and may send out some of their minions or soldiers to try to put a stop to them.

This will spur the characters into further action. They'll become resolute and more determined to stop the villain's plans. The story will become more intense, and it'll usually lead to more investigation, discovery, and a lot more running.

INVESTIGATION AND CLUES

Experienced roleplayers may think it a little odd that the game doesn't have a specific skill for investigating or searching for clues. This is because nothing can throw a good investigation off the rails like missing a clue due to failing a roll. In the game, the characters should find clues if they're looking in the right place, and not have to rely on the roll of the dice.

The Gamemaster, when thinking of the story, should plot a series of clues that'll lead the characters closer and closer to the big reveal. As long as the characters go to the right place and look for the right things, they'll uncover the information they need to lead them to the next clue.

Don't let the game grind to a halt just because they're not looking where they should be – that's what Story Points are for, after all, for either getting a handy pointer from the Gamemaster or even coming up with something clever to add to the story!

Let's look at the middle section, continuing the Doctor, Clara and the Paternoster Gang's adventure facing the Clockwork Robots. Clara and the Doctor have both done some investigating on their own, and the villain (the Half-face Man) knows the Doctor and Clara are trying to interfere. In this part of the story they are captured and come face to (half) face with the villain, discovering his true nature. While the Doctor and Clara try to escape, the rest of the players join the action, as Madame Vastra, Jenny and Strax come to rescue them. By the end of this section, the Clockwork Robots have all activated and are attacking the gang. We're getting close to the climax.

In the latter part of this section, the Gamemaster can reveal a plot twist. Is the villain not the villain at all? Was the plot to take over the world actually a plan to defend it? Usually it is at this moment when one of the characters has a major revelation, just when they are at their lowest ebb and seemingly have no chance of resolving the conflict.

THE END – CLIMAX & RESOLUTION

Everything has been building up to the big finale, the climax of the story, where all the clues have been leading. The characters will stop the villains (though not always, it could all go horribly wrong and lead to another series of adventures where the characters try to set things right!). It could be the big final chase, the destruction of the villain's superweapon, or the big fight when UNIT storm the alien base under the volcano.

After the big finale, everything should be returned to normal, though the characters will have grown from the experience. The Earth should be safe again (at least until the next invasion) and everyone can take a breath.

The big climax is the Half-face Man's showdown with the Doctor, as he tries to escape in a hot air balloon. It ends with the Doctor struggling with the Half-face Man high above London. The Doctor prevails, and the Half-face Man falls to his death – the Clockwork Robots halt, and the Doctor's companions are saved.

EPILOGUE – AFTERMATH

In the final couple of minutes of the story we see the results of the characters' actions. The characters should grow from their encounter, the world should be safe and any loose ends should be tied up. The ending can be as simple as the Doctor's offer of travelling through time and space, or finding a clue that will lead the characters on to the next adventure. If the Gamemaster is plotting an overarching story arc for his campaign (see pg. 200) then they might want to tease this a little, either to the characters or just to the players.

At the end of the adventure, we get to see how Clara and the Doctor's relationship has developed. They get time together in the TARDIS, discussing their history – and their future. We also get a tantalising hint of the campaign's bigger story arc – we see Missy for the first time.

THE FINISHED ADVENTURE

So once you have the basics, and know how the adventure is going to run, you can add some details, expand on your ideas and think about some additional elements. You can add a 'Sub-plot', a secondary storyline that isn't as huge as the main one, but may be more of a personal quest for one of the characters.

You can introduce elements from your campaign story arc (more on those in a moment) so you can foreshadow some of the events that will be major and important in your campaign's finale. This can be something subtle like mentioning that "Silence will Fall" or hints of Trenzalore.

Something else you should consider when constructing your adventure is what happens to the characters during the story and how they will develop. In some cases, it may be worth looking at the characters' backgrounds, their friends and families and seeing if there's a good way to bring them into it. It could be that, even if the family isn't involved, events from their past can be brought up, allowing them to come to terms with things, or to grow.

✪ TWO (AND THREE) PART STORIES

Of course, there are times when the adventure is so big you can't fit it into an evening's gaming. These epic two or three part stories are basically the same as a normal adventure. They have a beginning, middle and end, though many elements will take longer. The set up will probably be around the same, but the investigations that follow may be more elusive, or the trail may be longer. There may be a few plot twists and sudden changes in direction. When the villains discover their interfering, they will try to foil their actions on many occasions, which will lead to one of the most important elements of the two-parter... the Cliffhanger!

CLIFFHANGERS

The term 'Cliffhanger' comes from the old cinema serials, where each episode ended with the hero in some dramatic situation where it looked as if they could not survive. This way, the audience felt that they **had** to return to see the next episode, to find out how their hero could escape. A good two-parter should have the same effect – your players should be left with the need to return to the game.

A great way to end an evening's gaming is with a cliffhanger, leaving the characters in a predicament where it looks like there is no escape. Surrounded by Weeping Angels, or with the Doctor shot by a mysterious astronaut, these are great ways to leave your characters. The players can spend the time between gaming trying to fathom a great way out, and you've left them wanting more.

NEXT TIME...

Do you know what your next adventure is going to be? If you've planned ahead, you could script some little teaser scenes that the players can run through, quickly cutting between the scenes with a bit of dramatic music. It'll bring the players back, intrigued to find out what happens next in the game!

STORY POINTS

In between the parts of a two-part or three-part story, the characters should keep the Story Points they have. If you feel that they have done particularly well in the first part, but may need a little help in order to finish the adventure, you can give them some Story Points back as a little boost, but their totals shouldn't be reset – after all, it's the same story, it just takes a little longer.

THE SECOND PART

Continuing a multi-parter isn't all that different from a normal adventure. Instead of a prologue you'd best have a bit of a recap of what's gone on before. This is especially handy as it gives you and the players a great chance to catch up on what's happened, and it serves as a good reminder for where they all were last time you all met up.

The second part continues as the characters get out of their 'cliffhanger' predicament (hopefully) and continue with their investigations and the rising conflicts and challenges ahead. The end of the adventure will have the same structure, coming to a climax as the villains are defeated. As it's a two- (or three-) parter, the finale should be bigger, grander, and more dramatic than your cliffhanger. Two-parters in the middle of your campaign should hint at events to come in the campaign finale, while the finale itself should be the biggest bang of all. Pull out all the stops!

⚙ CHARACTER STORIES

During the campaign, every character should have their opportunity to shine. The Gamemaster should create adventures that give every player their shot at being the focus, not just following the Doctor.

To do this, the Gamemaster can chat with the player about their character's background. Is there something about the character the player hasn't explored? Events in their past that haven't been detailed could be filled in, or people can resurface in their lives that haven't appeared in the game before. Their focus doesn't have to be the central point of the adventure, you can still have all the action and drama going on as normal, but there can be a sub-plot, a little side story that intertwines with the main plot that revolves around a character, making them just as important (if not more so) than the Doctor.

It could be that the villain is a childhood friend of one of the characters – can they be shown the error of their ways and redeem themselves, or are they lost? Does a romantic interest develop in one of the character's lives? Focusing on each character in turn makes sure that over the course of the game, everyone gets a chance to do something extra special, and their characters can develop and grow.

⚙ CAMPAIGNS

By now you should have your adventure ready to go. This is great if you're just planning on running a one-off game, but the great thing about roleplaying games is that you can keep playing for as long as you like. Some games have been known to continue for many years, with players coming and going, characters leaving or dying, and new and bigger battles to face every time. If you're planning on some form of continuing story – known as a campaign – you may want to consider the structure of it as a whole.

CONSTRUCTING A CAMPAIGN STORY ARC

Creating a campaign arc is just the same as creating an adventure. It has a beginning, a middle and an end, just like any story. Instead of getting all of these elements into a single adventure, you space it out over your campaign, however long that is.

Let's say we're going to run a campaign over thirteen adventures. The story arc is going to revolve around the mystery of the Promised Land. Over the course of the campaign we are going to find out more about it, until we get to the big two-parter where the Promised Land is going to be at the centre of it all.

However, it's not just the Promised Land; we're also going to find out the identity of the enigmatic 'Missy' too. As we haven't encountered Missy before, we're going to have to introduce her somewhere along the way too.

So, starting small, you can add a couple of early references to the Promised Land in early adventures – the Half-face Man mentions it, then the destination of the Robot Knights' spaceship is spotted to be there too. Then we might find out that the Promised Land is where people go when they die – could it really be heaven? We might get a glimpse at Missy too, and find that she is connected to the Promised Land in some way, although no hint as to who she really is. All the clues are there ready for the big ending – all it takes is a tragic death to take the players there...

PERSONAL STORY ARCS

It is not just the campaign storyline that can have a story arc. Characters can have them too. Usually not as prominently, but the characters will grow and develop over time. Danny's a great example of this. He's had his fill of adventure and danger from his time in the army - and is still haunted by a traumatic event in his past. He cares for Clara but worries about her adventures with the Doctor. Although it takes his death - and resurrection - to do so, he comes to terms with his trauma and sacrifices himself to save Clara.

Most of the time you won't have to plan a character's arc too heavily, it'll develop by itself as the game progresses. If you want to develop a character's story, you should discuss the character's background with the player – see if there's anything they'd particularly like to do with the character that'd be cool and exciting.

Then, just like a campaign story arc, you can work in some teaser hints, some little scenes that build the character's arc, before they have their focus adventure. The character's adventure should appear just after the middle point of you campaign arc, so you can build up to it, and yet not have it get in the way of the finale.

OPENING ADVENTURES

So you have your campaign arc and you know where the stories will lead. You may need to consider the first adventure slightly differently. After all, it'll be where the players get used to the characters, set the scene for things to come and learn how the game works if it's your first time playing. As the game progresses, the players will become used to their characters and each other's characters until

they gel as a unit. Until then you may need to run the first adventure or two to really establish who they are, how they know each other and why they're getting involved in the adventures.

Your opening adventure, no matter what setting or story you have planned, should give the players a chance to get the feel for their characters, and to get to know the other characters as well.

'DOCTOR-LITE' ADVENTURES
The Doctor doesn't have to be the prominent element in a story, and 'Doctor-lite' adventures are a great opportunity to try something a little different. You could create all new characters and have a little 'side' story, where you follow a different group of people. The Paternoster Gang are a good example of a set of characters who are not always tied to the main campaign storyline, but make a great change if you want to spice things up a bit, or you could follow Psi and Saibra in a cool adventure of their own.

If a player cannot attend for any reason, it might be a great excuse to run a 'lite' story where their character doesn't get involved. If the player who plays Clara couldn't attend one week, you could run a solo adventure for the Doctor and vice versa – if the Doctor's player can't attend, it's a great opportunity to see what happens when Clara has her own solo adventure (while the Doctor is trapped in his TARDIS, for example).

FINALES
Another special type of adventure is the finale. Usually a two-, sometimes a three-, parter, joined together by a massive cliffhanger that revolves around a disastrous setback as the villains reveal themselves or the catastrophic event reaches a critical point. The finale is always something really big, dramatic and doesn't hold back, and the characters will have to work together, and possibly make a great sacrifice to put things right again.

Fleets of invading Daleks, millions of Cybermen, whole planets being moved and the Earth's population being decimated, all make a great finale – just be careful of doing something so cataclysmic that you make your follow up campaign almost impossible.

Just imagine if Missy had succeeded at taking over the world with her Cybermen - while a whole campaign where most of the Earth's population

(living and dead) have undergone Cyber-conversion might be interesting, it certainly changes the tone of the game! While it would be an exciting series of adventures, you'd need to get back to your original story somehow.

⚙ 'SPECIALS'
Of course, in between these big campaigns you can run one-off adventures. It could be that you have a bit more time to spend on your game – maybe rather than an evening a week, there's an opportunity for an afternoon session where you can play a little longer. The most likely time that you'll find more time on your hands (and your players will be free) will be public holidays, which is a great opportunity to theme your adventure!

Just because it's Christmas, it doesn't mean you can't play a game. Maybe you're bored on Boxing Day, full of Christmas dinner, and have an idea for a game. Why not make it Christmas themed, and throw in Santa and his elves for good measure? Or you could do them on other holidays like Easter, or best of all Halloween!

A special adventure can be simply a slightly longer normal story, with a theme that reflects the time of the year. It needn't be as long a story as a two-parter, but you can do something dramatic, exciting and a bit different with a special, with new companions or characters, without affecting your normal campaign.

Of course, if you've been playing for a while, you could have an anniversary episode, where past characters are reunited. That said, all of this is just advice and guidelines. You should feel free to experiment with the format of your adventures and campaign to settle on a game that you're most happy with. Have fun, and run with it! And who knows, maybe after fifty years of gaming you'll be running a special anniversary adventure of your own!

STORMRISE

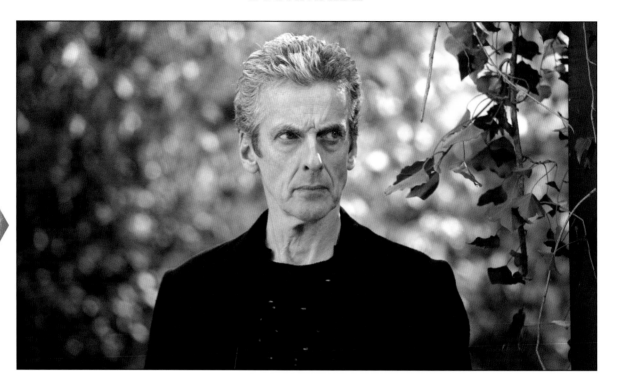

In this adventure the characters visit a coastal village as it is engulfed by a horrific storm. Hiding in the storm is an evil force that seeks control of powerful Time Lord technology. Can the characters hold off disaster?

This adventure is great as a one-off adventure and for games that are already in progress, but it is particularly suited as the starting point for a new campaign. During this adventure a set of disparate characters will be brought together, equipped to adventure through time and space, and given an ongoing mystery to explore – all you need to launch a series of exciting adventures!

✸ ADVENTURE SYNOPSIS

The characters arrive at the seaside village of Batterlee on the third anniversary of a horrific storm. The villagers gather to witness the consecration of a memorial to those lost. Unfortunately, the day is destined for trouble. Another vicious storm strikes, and deadly creatures lurk in the raging winds. The source of the trouble is a piece of malfunctioning Gallifreyan technology called the Vector Key. The characters must locate this object and deactivate it while surviving the storm, escaping predatory beasts and outwitting the malign intelligence that controls them.

HOW THIS ADVENTURE IS ORGANISED

In the sections following, information will be presented about the village, the Vector Key, the storm it creates and the beings that can be found within. Then the memorial ceremony, where the adventure begins, is described. After this point the adventure becomes quite open-ended, so there is discussion of the things that the characters might do and the consequences of their success or failure. Finally, ideas for further adventures in Batterlee are discussed, and using this adventure to start a new campaign.

✸ BATTERLEE

The Vector Key landed on Earth in the vicinity of the village of Batterlee. This is a small coastal village with a fishing fleet, clifftop views, ancient pubs, stone churches and an old lighthouse. There is a stony beach at one end of the village, and a deeper harbour with pier at the other end.

Occasionally tourists stop in at a bed and breakfast here, but mostly the people of Batterlee are left to their own devices, which suits them just fine. There is a rocky island not far offshore. Rough stone juts sharply from the water, posing a danger to unwary ships and boats. The island, which the locals call simply "the Rock", is home only to seabirds.

RECENT HISTORY

Three years ago, the small coastal village was rocked by an unprecedented storm. It tore down power lines, ripped ships from their moorings, and shattered windows. There were no survivors from the three small boats caught in the storm. This horrid storm shocked Batterlee to its core, and the village hopes the ceremony to bless a new memorial will help them put this disaster behind them.

The storm was caused by the Vector Key, which had landed in the water near the Rock. Damaged by its passage, the malfunctioning Key generated an energy surge that opened pinprick holes in the sky, bringing down the storm. The Key is still active and still malfunctioning, and it will soon bring down another storm.

PEOPLE IN BATTERLEE

Gary Spencer, the Eccentric

This grumpy, eccentric fifty-something occasionally visits the Captain's Room pub for a pint, but mostly spends his time beachcombing with his metal detector or in his flat, sorting through piles of found objects. He believes he saw monsters in the storm three years ago. He still has nightmares about them. His only friend is Michael, the voice in his head.

Mark Covacks, the Widower

Mark is in his early thirties and is a single father to Evelyn, who is seven years old. Mark's wife Belinda died in the storm three years ago. Batterlee has united behind Mark, and while he still grieves for his loss, he is optimistic that things are going to turn out all right in the end. However, he is troubled by his daughter, who is badly behaved and distant from him.

Evelyn Covacks, the Daughter

Evelyn is seven years old. She is fidgety, imaginative, sullen, boisterous and all points in between. She is close to fearless. She never leaves the house without her favourite teddy bear strapped into a tiny backpack. She is deeply troubled by her mother's death, and has convinced herself that her father will soon die as well. She doesn't want to talk about these fears, and tries not to think about them.

Lucy Thorp, the Vicar

Lucy Thorp can often be found running along the shoreline, or fixing church windows at the top of very tall ladders. She has been Batterlee's vicar for nearly two years, and despite her youth she has won over almost everyone in the village.

Mrs Millidge, "the Mayor"

Everyone calls Anna Mary Millidge "Mayor", including the village's representatives on the district council. If Mrs Millidge overhears, she'll shush the person and tell them not to be silly, but it's clear she delights in the appellation.

She's in her mid-60s and knows everyone in the village and everything that is happening. She's on every organising committee and knows how to get things done. She always keeps smiling, but everyone knows it's a bad idea to get on the wrong side of Mrs Millidge.

Sinead Inglis, the Young Academic

Sinead is a friendly but awkward postgraduate with a bad habit of saying the wrong thing. She's staying in Batterlee as part of her thesis work on the weather patterns attached to the strange storm and the unusual and unpredictable winds observed here. She believes there is a meteorological phenomenon to be discovered here that could make her career!

LOCATIONS

The Captain's Room

This grimy, dark pub is down near the memorial and will be an obvious place for people to seek refuge when the weather turns. It is reputed to be an old smuggler's pub, with secret passages out back.

Spencer's Home

Spencer's small house is overgrown with weeds and full of junk. The interior of the house is crowded with a hugely elaborate machine apparently made out of junk (this is a psychic resonator). In the living room, where Spencer sleeps on a mat on the floor, is a shrine to an unexploded shell from World War II (this shell is the focal point for the Stormhead, and it talks to Spencer).

The Old Church

The church is on a gentle hill, overlooking the rest of the village. It is old and in need of renovation, which Lucy is working on enthusiastically by herself.

Other Places

- The Happy Bun coffee shop.
- Batterlee Village records office and library.
- Linda's Traditional Sweets.
- The old windmill – so old, it's just a tower now without blades.

THE VECTOR KEY

The Vector Key is a shiny metal ring about the size of dinner plate. It is studded with circuitry and appears rough and unfinished, as if it was made in a hurry (it was). The Key is essentially a modified time vector generator in a circular casing. Time vector generators are used in TARDIS construction to maintain the "bigger on the inside" effect, but they can be used by themselves as rough hand-held time machines and dimensional portals.

The Vector Key has empathic circuits and forms a psychic bond with potential operators. If three (or more) people with these empathic bonds hold on to the ring at the same time, the Key's Vortex circuits activate, allowing travel through time and space.

The Vector Key was engineered by three Time Lords who were trapped in the Time War and wanted to escape. It didn't work as intended. When they activated the Vector Key it broke through the Time Lock and landed on Earth; the Time Lords didn't make it through, their fate is unknown.

The Key was damaged en route and when it reached Earth it created the great storm. It has maintained an empathic link with the area, and now it is reacting to the psychic overload of the memorial ceremony by trying to escape, once again creating a great storm. When the Storm Bats appear, it will sense that the Stormhead is hunting for it, and its fears will increase.

FORMING A PSYCHIC BOND

There are two steps to forming a psychic bond with the Key. First, the character must be noticed by the Vector Key. They can come to its attention in several ways:

- They come into the presence of the Vector Key – even if they aren't aware the Vector Key is there.
- They have a positive interaction with someone who already has a psychic bond, such as by saving them or trying to protect them. (For example, any character who takes care of Evelyn is instantly noticed by the Vector Key, even if the Key is somewhere else.)

- They undertake some dramatic action in the village and the Vector Key happens to notice them. The trigger for attention could be any Story Point expenditure to affect a result, as the additional positive outcome of a Yes, And result, or simply at the Gamemaster's discretion.

Once the Key has noticed them, it will evaluate them for suitability as operators. The Gamemaster should make the decision on behalf of the Key, using the following principles:

- If you're intending to use the scenario to start an ongoing campaign game, the Key will find all the characters worthy; their link through the Key will be the basis for their ongoing relationship.
- If the game is a one-off, or an adventure in an already-existing campaign, look at the character's behaviour towards other people. If they are selfless and generous, the Vector Key will likely approve of them. However, its reasoning could be more idiosyncratic here; it could decide not to bond with a Time Lord, fearing it might be taken back into the Time War or it could decide to pass over a character who uses bad language. At least one character should pass muster, however, or the adventure might end rather badly!

If the Key judges the character as a suitable operator, it will extend a psychic "offer" to the character. Characters with psychic training or abilities will be aware of another presence offering itself for contact; others will only sense a strange but unthreatening disturbance in their perceptions. Even if the character doesn't accept the offer, the Key extends to them all the benefits of the bond, for them to use or ignore as they see fit. If the Key needs to communicate something, it may bring forth a ghost from the character's past.

VECTOR KEY (SPECIAL GADGET)

Traits: Psychic, Restriction (must be held by three operators at once to travel), Teleport, Vortex
Story Points: 6

⚙ THE STORM

The storm is caused by the malfunctioning Vector Key. The Key punches small holes in the fabric of the time-space continuum, and the holes open on some of the greatest storms in the histories of Earth and many other planets besides.

THE STORM RISES

The storm starts swiftly, and gets bigger and bigger. During the storm, the characters will be presented with a range of dangers. It is up to the Gamemaster to decide which challenges occur when and how. Difficulties relate to the intensity of the storm:

- *The storm begins*: no rolls needed at this stage, and no strange events yet.
- *The storm becomes dangerous:* occasional standard challenges, usual difficulty is normal (12). No strange events yet.
- *The storm rages:* regular standard challenges, usual difficulty is tricky (15). Some strange events.
- *Full intensity:* regular standard challenges, usual difficulty is hard (18). Frequent strange events.

STANDARD CHALLENGES

The storm creates a range of 'standard' dangers and challenges:

- Characters who are outside encounter a barrage of flying debris (2/4/6). Characters can protect themselves by diving for cover (Coordination + Athletics) or by any other means they can think of.
- Characters outside have live power lines come down near them. The cables whip back and forth in the storm. Characters might have to turn back to avoid them, or they could try and move past them (Coordination + Athletics). The sparking electricity is very dangerous (4/L/L). Resourceful characters might find other ways to deal with the cables.
- Characters who are on a roof, a cliffside or any other high place threaten to be knocked off by a strong gust of wind. They can hold on using Strength + Athletics or keep safe some other way.
- Characters inside are endangered by a window that shatters after being hit by a flying tree branch. If they have quick enough reactions they might protect themselves with Awareness + Survival from being hurt by shards (1/3/5 damage).

- Characters see another person threatened by any of these. They may choose to help by taking a risk themselves, or they may hold back.

STRANGE EVENTS

This storm is far from ordinary, and those caught within it will encounter some strange events.

- Some strange debris comes hurtling down from the sky: a cannon from a Caribbean pirate ship, a piece of a renowned battleship destroyed in the great storm of 1703, a chunk of solar sail from a Venusian windjammer from the 25th century, a wing from a WWI biplane.
- A rip in reality opens, storm winds rushing through, while on the other side an entirely different time and place is briefly visible.
- A Storm Bat swoops towards the characters, claws gleaming, intent on stealing anything they carry.
- A tornado of time energy ripples towards the characters, and anyone caught in it is given a glimpse of their own past or future. If multiple characters are caught, they can witness each others' past or future moments – you can invite the players to invent their own past or future moments here!
- A village street becomes abruptly overlaid with another time and place, where shiny-suited aliens swiftly tie down their laser harpoons as a storm whips at them.

⚙ CREATURES OF THE STORM

GHOSTS

At the start of the adventure, Evelyn leaves the ceremony in pursuit of the ghost of her mother, Belinda. Belinda appears as she did in life, but strangely out of phase, unable to touch things in the real world, and eerily silent. There may also be other ghosts in the adventure with the same attributes.

Origin of the Ghosts

All these ghosts are time refractions caused by, and to an extent controlled by, the Vector Key. The Key wants to be found and protected by people it views as safe, and when it finds someone appropriate, it forms an empathic bond and communicates with them using a ghostly figure.

The Vector Key has already bonded with Evelyn, judging correctly that she will work hard to protect it. The ghost of her mother works to lead Evelyn to the Key and then to warn her against any further dangers.

Seeing the Ghosts

Most people in Batterlee cannot see the ghosts. For example, Evelyn's father Mark cannot see the ghost of his wife Belinda, no matter how much he might want to. However, the characters will be able to see them if they have any of these:

• An empathic bond to the Vector Key.
• The Feel the Turn of the Universe trait.
• The Vortex trait.

New Ghosts

Ghosts are created when the Vector Key forms an empathic bond with someone during the course of this adventure. After a ghost is created the person will catch glimpses of them and will occasionally see them for longer moments. The ghosts will direct the person to where they need to be to help protect the Vector Key.

When the character sees their ghost for the first time, you should tell the player they are seeing a ghost from their past, someone important to them who has died. Ask the player who it is their character sees. Allow the player to invent someone on the spot, if they wish. If they don't have any ideas then suggest someone – a much-loved grandparent is usually a fairly safe choice.

Are they Real?

Is the dead person actually there, crossing over folds in space and time? Or are the ghosts just visual hallucinations, convenient disguises used by the Vector Key? The truth is unclear, for time refraction technology is very strange indeed. It is up to the Gamemaster to decide what is appropriate if this question ever comes up in play.

STORM BATS

The Storm Bats, known as Trellmargs on their home planet of Optimos, are human-sized winged predators that soar through the lashing rain and howling wind. They are time-sensitive, for on Optimos they hunt rabbit-sized animals who can hop through time to escape predators. They are solitary hunters and avoid larger creatures such as humans.

A character with knowledge of time and space might recognise the Storm Bats and know the above with an Ingenuity + Knowledge roll (Difficulty 21). The creatures are a long way from home, and they are also behaving in a very unusual way during this storm!

The reason for their strange behaviour is a mind parasite calling itself the Stormhead. The Stormhead is driving them to be aggressive to humans and to search the village for something. The Stormhead can even speak through a Storm Bat if it chooses (normally they only bark and shriek). If and when the Stormhead is driven from their minds, the Storm Bats will revert to normal behaviour and will fly back through time holes to their home.

STORM BATS

AWARENESS	3	PRESENCE	2
COORDINATION	3	RESOLVE	2
INGENUITY	1	STRENGTH	3

SKILLS
Athletics 3, Fighting 2, Subterfuge 2, Survival 1.

TRAITS
Alien

Alien Appearance (Major): Storm Bats are human-sized creatures with enormous batlike wings. Their heads and torsos appear vaguely canine, like bull terriers, with lean muscular legs ending in clawed feet.

Alien Senses: Storm Bats are time-sensitive creatures. They can sense artron energy and time technology like the Vector Key. This sense is not strong enough to lead them right to the hidden Vector Key, but as they search they will get closer and closer...

Enslaved: These Storm Bats are in thrall to the psychic parasite known as the Stormhead.

Environmental (Minor): Storm Bats thrive in storms, the stronger the better.

Flight (Major): Storm Bats catch the winds of storms and can fly through them at astonishing speeds.

Natural Weapon (Minor): Storm Bats have sharp claws on their feet for grabbing and tearing (2/5/7).

STORY POINTS: 1

THE STORMHEAD

"The Stormhead" is the name currently used by a psychic parasite that has haunted the Batterlee area for a very long time. It was present during the storm three years ago, and sensed the presence of the Vector Key. It desperately wants to find the Key and has been searching for it ever since.

The Stormhead and Spencer

During this adventure, the Stormhead presence is centred in the home of Spencer the eccentric. The focus for the Stormhead is an unexploded shell that Spencer dug up one cold morning. Spencer has built a shrine around this shell, and it sits in his living room where any other person would have a television.

The Stormhead talks to Spencer, and Spencer listens and does what he's told, more or less. (Spencer believes the Stormhead is the voice of someone he calls "Michael", specifically the Archangel Michael.) Following the Stormhead's instructions, Spencer has built a psychic resonator device out of scrap metal and odd parts. The device has taken over much of his home.

The Stormhead and the Storm Bats

During the storm three years ago, the Stormhead encountered a Storm Bat that had crossed over through one of the openings to other worlds – Spencer also saw this Storm Bat, hence his ranting about seeing monsters in the storm.

The Stormhead knew the Vector Key would create a storm again one day, and he has prepared himself to summon the Storm Bats again to use as servants.

Sure enough, as the storm breaks, the winds activate the psychic resonator, and the Storm Bats come flying through the portal. The Stormhead seizes control of them, one by one, until it has its army. The Stormhead can:

- See and hear through the eyes and ears of any Storm Bat.
- Give any Storm Bat simple instructions like "chase that person" and "destroy that building".
- Possess any Storm Bat, using its body and speaking through its poorly-formed vocal muscles for the duration of the possession.

What does the Stormhead want?

The Stormhead wants the Vector Key so it can become a full-scale time monster, able to move through the Vortex and tear apart the walls of time. If it manages to fuse itself with the key, Batterlee will be destroyed, and perhaps the entire world will follow.

At the beginning of the adventure, Gary Spencer is the Stormhead's only servant. Spencer busily searches the beaches and environs around the village for the lost Vector Key.

Once the storm begins, the Storm Bats come through and the Stormhead largely abandons Spencer for these new servants. It instantly begins a huge search through the village, tearing apart homes and buildings. It will ruin Batterlee entirely if that's what it takes to find the Key.

THE STORMHEAD

AWARENESS	4	PRESENCE	6
COORDINATION	1	RESOLVE	6
INGENUITY	4	STRENGTH	1

SKILLS
Convince 2, Craft 3, Knowledge 2, Transport 2.

TRAITS
Alien
Flight: The Stormhead's energy cloud can fly in any direction.
Possess: The Stormhead can possess any Storm Bat in the flock at any time. Once the Stormhead has taken control of a Storm Bat, it must "drive" it like an airline pilot (Coordination + Transport, difficulty varies). It takes a full turn for the Stormhead to exit a possession and return to its free-floating state.
Psychic
Special (Energy Cloud): The Stormhead's physical form is a diffuse cloud of pulsing silver energy. It can move against the winds of a storm, but only with difficulty, and it can affect physical objects only with great concentration.
Vortex: The Stormhead has travelled through time in the past and would love to regain access to the timestream.
Weakness (Major): The Stormhead's focus is an unexploded shell in Spencer's home, and also in the minds of the Storm Bats. It can be forced from the Storm Bats through psychic battle, and the shell can be detonated. If both these things happen, the Stormhead will be banished.

TECH LEVEL: 8   **STORY POINTS: 10**

⚙ RUNNING THIS ADVENTURE

PACING SUGGESTION
This adventure is fairly complicated. There is a backstory, a mysterious device, storms, monsters, ghosts and a disembodied enemy. A gaming group could easily spend many sessions working through all these elements. However, the recommended speed for this adventure is "fast". In many of the Doctor's adventures, complicated situations are resolved at great pace through grand flourishes.

Allow your game to echo this. In particular, Story Points allow players to leapfrog many obstacles, so embrace this power when they solve a problem by moving on to the next one.

For the players, some of the pleasure of this adventure will be seeing how the disparate elements – ghosts, storms, monsters – come together into one single problem for them to solve using their ingenuity, so keep up the pace and keep moving forward towards the climax.

GETTING THE CHARACTERS INVOLVED
To get involved in this adventure, characters need only be in Batterlee; events will soon drag them into the drama. If they are already looking into Batterlee's strange events, however, it will be even easier to draw characters in. There are many reasons why characters might be in the village:

- They live in the village – Batterlee is their home.
- They lost relatives or friends in the storm and have come to the memorial ceremony to honour them.
- They are independent researchers, investigators or journalists looking into some aspect of the storm, and they are attending the memorial as part of this project.
- They have other business in Batterlee, and stumble on the memorial ceremony by accident.
- If they have advanced technology, they may have detected energy spikes in the area and have come to investigate further.
- They are here to look into the rumoured ghost sightings in the village.
- They are from another time and place entirely, and have just fallen through a pinhole in reality and landed here, wherever "here" is.

If the characters are not already friends or colleagues, then they can be in the village independently, for a variety of reasons. If you are using this adventure with an established group of characters (like the Doctor and friends), then just select one or two reasons – it's a good idea to have both a procedural reason (like detecting energy spikes) and a personal reason (like having relatives affected by the big storm), to engage characters on multiple levels.

If the characters do not know each other at the start of play, everyone will need to co-operate to create connections during play. The Vector Key also provides a direct way to pull characters together.

THE MEMORIAL CEREMONY

Begin the adventure at the memorial ceremony. Many, if not all, of the characters should be in attendance. As this sequence progresses, some characters may move away from the ceremony, but it is likely most will stay until the storm begins.

Setting the Scene

It is Autumn, not long after dawn. Almost the whole village has gathered at the memorial site: a large stone with a brass plate inscribed with the names of those who were lost and the date of the storm. The memorial stone looks across the beach and out to the water, to the treacherous Rock and the open sea beyond. It is a cloudy day with a mild breeze.

Ask the players to describe where they are (up the front? in the back? running late?) and introduce these characters to the scene as well.

- Lucy Thorp, the Vicar, is there to lead the service. She is wearing her robes, waiting for the right time to begin, making polite conversation with those around her.
- Mark Covacks is there with his daughter Evelyn. They are up the front and it is obvious from Mark's demeanour, and from the crowd's solemn support, that he is one of those who lost someone close. Evelyn, his daughter, is restless and distracted.
- Mrs Millidge passes through the crowd. She is handing out carnations to everyone who wants one, smiling gently as she goes. About one person in three will say "thanks Mayor" as they take a carnation, to which she smiles graciously.
- Gary Spencer is on the beach close by. He is ignoring the memorial ceremony and the memorial. With his headphones on, he swings his metal detector back and forth, stomping along the gritty sand. He talks to himself loudly as he goes, "nothing nothing nothing..." To those at the memorial, this intrusion is most unwelcome, but none of them will make the effort to say anything to Spencer (a character might decide to, however).
- Sinead Inglis is near the back. She is clearly interested in every word being spoken, but she is not a local, judging by the way others in the crowd react to her.

The Ceremony Begins

When the time on the village clock marks the minute when the storm began three years ago, the Vicar begins the ceremony. She welcomes everyone and thanks them for coming with words like these:

- "Three years ago, a great storm struck Batterlee and many precious lives were lost. I arrived in Batterlee a year later, when the pain of that storm was still fresh. Since then I have been endlessly impressed by how you have come together to support each other in this time of great trial, and with the way this community has sought out ways to honour the past while moving forward into the future. Today, with great solemnity and care, we mark a significant milestone in that journey, as we bless this memorial stone and the memory of the seven people who died."

The ceremony continues with personal remembrances of each of the seven victims. The first to speak is Mark Covacks, who talks briefly about his wife Belinda and her love of the water and her love of Batterlee.

While he speaks, Evelyn edges away from him and rejoins the crowd, where she is obviously more comfortable. She will shortly slip away.

Spencer Interrupts

Just as Mark is finishing, Gary Spencer appears suddenly at the front, having climbed up from the beach. He is clearly agitated, and hasn't even paused to take off his metal detector headphones. He yells words like these:

- "What's the point of that then? It won't help! It won't change a thing! There's monsters in the winds! What's the point of it, then? Nothing! Nothing!"

He keeps yelling, increasing in volume, until someone intervenes to move him away. If none of the characters get there first, Mrs Millidge is only too happy to do this, frog-marching him out of earshot. He will then walk home.

A character may wish to interact with Spencer now, diverting him from his path or accompanying him. As the storm picks up, he panics, then does his best to force people to leave him alone; he wants to get back to his house and consult with the Stormhead in privacy.

Evelyn is Missing

As calm returns after the interruption from Spencer, Mark looks about, growing increasingly concerned. He can't find Evelyn! A character near the edge of the crowd, or any observant character, might have seen her slip away from the ceremony and disappear into the village's narrow streets. Characters may want to follow Evelyn or help Mark look for her.

Evelyn leaves the ceremony because she has seen a ghost of her mother, beckoning to her. If the characters do not interrupt her then this is what happens with Evelyn:

- Curious and unafraid, she follows these ghostly glimpses of her mother out of the village and along the rocky coast.
- She is led by the ghost to something remarkable: a strange device hidden among the rocks, humming and blinking.
- This, Evelyn decides, is something her mother wanted her to find, and she puts it carefully in the bottom of her backpack.

By this time, however, the storm has picked up, and getting home might not be straightforward.

Sudden Storm

Before the end of the memorial service, the clouds abruptly darken, and rain begins to fall. No one was expecting this; there are no umbrellas to speak of. As the wind picks up, people begin to abandon the memorial ceremony. The village folk decamp to pubs, cafes and other such haunts, where they peer out at the weather with a suspicious eye. They have seen this before. But there are two people who don't seek shelter, both of them newcomers who didn't witness the last storm.

- One is Lucy the Vicar. She decides to stay on to give the ceremony a proper finish. A bit of wind and rain doesn't bother her! But the storm gets worse far quicker than she thought possible, and she finds herself in more trouble than she expected.
- The other is Sinead the Young Academic. She is excited by the rising winds and rushes away to check her instruments and make sure they are working properly. Plenty of people see her go and shout at her to take cover but she doesn't listen. Her instruments could be in any number of dangerous spots: at the top of the cliff path or on the church steeple perhaps.

✖ WHAT NEXT?

The initial sequence of this adventure is a fairly straightforward series of events - the ceremony begins, Spencer interrupts, Evelyn sneaks away, and then the storm starts up. After this, however, the adventure becomes much more open-ended.

Your job as Gamemaster is to let the players take the reins of the adventure from here on in. Let them explore the situation as they like. While they

do this, introduce challenges and complications as the Stormhead gets closer and closer to its goal of finding the Vector Key.

INITIAL PROBLEMS

The characters could look into any of the following things right away:

- Mark is distraught that his daughter Evelyn is missing. Stopping him from doing anything stupid or helping him find her are both valid options.
- There are three people out in the storm who could be in need of help:
  - Lucy the Vicar – out in the storm but close to cover, she is an easy person to rescue.
  - Sinead the Student – out in the storm and heading away from shelter, she will take some persuading to seek cover.
  - Evelyn the little girl – last seen heading off along the rocky shore, she could be in real trouble.
- The Vector Key is looking for new operators and, as soon as it finds them, it will create ghosts to communicate with them; so some of the characters might soon glimpse ghosts out in the rain and wind.
- The strange behaviour of Spencer the eccentric might be worth immediate investigation, depending on the interests and expectations of the characters. Spencer is right now in the service of the Stormhead, but soon the Stormhead will abandon him, and he will be confused and bereft – and might then become a useful ally.
- The storm itself is very unusual, and some characters may try to work out what is happening with it. (See **Understanding the Storm**, opposite.)
- Some characters will simply want to take cover to wait out the storm. This is fine for a while, but no place is safe forever. A Storm Bat or two come barging into their haven and begins tearing people to pieces, and more Storm Bats will gather outside soon enough.

Using Mrs Millidge

Mrs Millidge is not tied to any specific problem. As a busybody she is a wild-card character, and can turn up pretty much anywhere at any time. If you ever have a moment where you're not sure what to do next, have Mrs Millidge walk up to a character and tell them off for doing something wrong, and then have a Storm Bat grab her and start dragging her away.

UNDERSTANDING THE STORM

Characters can use skills, Story Points, Sonic Screwdrivers or other means to uncover some of the storm's secrets. Share this information whenever appropriate; the adventure will run more smoothly if the characters know these things. If none of the characters has the skills or Gadgets to figure this information out, Sinead Inglis will work these things out soon enough.

- The storm began much too quickly for it to be an ordinary weather event.
- The storm is centred over the village. It is not moving, except to grow steadily bigger.
- The storm is increasing in intensity and size and shows no sign of settling down or passing.
- The rate of increase is exponential. If the storm continues along the same curve, then soon the entire landscape as far as the eye can see will be nothing but dust.
- The storm's weather patterns make no sense at all. Winds blow in contrary directions, air pockets form and drop without warning. It is as if there are hundreds of pipes, each pumping kinetic energy directly into the system, which there are.
- If the pipes are closed off, the storm will end. But how on earth can that be accomplished? Perhaps whatever opened them could also close them?

STORM BATS ON THE HUNT

As the storm progresses, the Storm Bats search the village and surrounding area for the Vector Key. They will smash into windows, tear roofs off buildings, scramble through cellars, and kill anyone who gets in their way. The bats will catch traces of its scent as they search, but then lose the trail again. They will not stop and they will not be turned away.

Throughout the adventure, the Storm Bats provide an ongoing source of danger and pressure for the characters. Whenever things slow down or the characters start feeling safe, have Storm Bats swarm down and start wrecking things.

As the adventure progresses, the Storm Bats will form a tighter and tighter cordon around the Vector Key and the characters protecting it. Eventually, it should come down to a standoff, with the Stormhead speaking through a Storm Bat and demanding the Key be handed over to it.

FINDING THE VECTOR KEY

If the characters help Evelyn, they might spot the Key in her bag - that's an easy way to find it! They might also work out there is something out there to find by talking with Spencer, or talking with the Stormhead, or using TARDIS scanners, to name just

three possible routes. If they are looking for the Key, there are several ways they can find it:

- Follow a friendly ghost! The ghosts want good people to defend the Vector Key.
- Use some high-tech detection device! The Sonic Screwdriver, aligned to the right setting, might lead a character right to the Key. Another character might be able to Jiggery-Pokery a Gadget to do the trick.
- A character might just get lucky, or have a flash of inspiration, or make psychic contact with the Key and talk with it – all these and more are possible with a spend of Story Points.

ENDING THE STORM

Once the Vector Key is in hand, it can be used to end the storm. The Key can be repaired mechanically, but the best way to deal with the situation is to communicate with it empathically. Someone with a psychic bond who holds the Key and spends a bit of time trying to understand it will sense the following:

- The Key sensed the community's thoughts of death and loss, and interpreted this as a warning of danger.
- The Key is causing the storm in its frantic efforts to escape through time and space.
- If the Key's panic reaction ends, the storm will likewise end.

Each group of players will have their own ideas of how best to end the storm. Some ways to deal with the Key:

- Explaining the memorial stone to it, so it can understand what it was reacting to.
- Convincing it to bond with Mark, so he can see his wife's ghost and the Key can understand grief and memory.
- Having Evelyn confess her own fears to Mark, so her relief will spread to the Key.
- Deactivating its time circuits so it can't punch holes in time.
- Repair it so it can escape as it wants to.
- And so forth. The expenditure of Story Points could establish many other possible ways to end the storm.

When the characters try to end the storm, you may call for a roll (for example, Ingenuity + Technology to repair the Key, or Presence + Convince to help Evelyn to confess her feelings to her father). Alternatively, you may decide a roll is unnecessary if the solution feels right.

If you call for a roll and it fails, you will need to decide what happens next: does that solution get closed off entirely? Is some additional action or ingredient needed to succeed? Is the solution a successful one, and the failure just means that it doesn't get fixed immediately, forcing the characters to hold out a few more rounds?

Note that some characters with extensive resources (like the Doctor with his TARDIS) might try to close off the storm without using the Key, for example by using time engineering to directly sealing up the holes in the Vortex. That's absolutely fine!

Note also that ending the storm does NOT remove either the Storm Bats or Stormhead from the village. They must be dealt with separately.

DEFEATING THE STORM BATS

The problem of the Storm Bats is dramatic and difficult to resolve. However, characters are resourceful and imaginative, and with Story Points to help they might come up with any number of creative plans to get the Storm Bats out of the way. For example:

- Electrocuting them all by overcharging the storm with energy.
- Widening the vortex holes enough to suck them all through.
- Shooting them with weapons that fell through the storm.
- Luring them away with trails of artron energy.

The simplest way to deal with the Storm Bats, however, is to defeat the Stormhead. When the Stormhead is overcome, the Storm Bats will revert to normal animal behaviour, and using their ability to sense time they'll find their way home through any remaining time holes.

DEFEATING THE STORMHEAD

The Stormhead has two points of focus, and both must be dealt with to drive it away from Batterlee. First, the Stormhead emanates from the unexploded shell in Spencer's living room. If this shell is detonated, then the Stormhead will lose this focus. If the Stormhead loses the Storm Bats, it will retreat to this shell, perhaps biding its time until another opportunity to conquer arises.

Second, the Stormhead exists in the minds of the Storm Bats. If the Storm Bats are driven out of this reality, then they will take the Stormhead with them.

However, that is not easy to do. The Stormhead can, however, be driven out of the minds of the Storm Bats by engaging it in a psychic battle (see below).

Anyone with a psychic bond to the Vector Key might realise this, and Spencer might figure it out as well (in his own idiosyncratic way) and tell the characters to try it.

Psychic Battle

Driving the Stormhead out of the Storm Bats requires a fierce psychic battle. It will probably take a group of characters working together to match the psychic might of the Stormhead! A psychic bond with the Vector Key allows even non-psychic characters to join in this fight.

- The battle is fought with opposed Resolve + Presence rolls.
- If multiple people are involved on one side, choose a leader to make the roll. The other characters are helpers and add +2 to the leader's roll.
- The winning side does damage to the mental attributes of the other side. (Damage is shared out evenly among a group working together.)
- Damage is equal to the leader's Resolve score.

- If the Stormhead's Resolve and Presence is reduced to 0, it is defeated and cast out from the Storm Bats.
- If all the characters have their Resolve and Presence reduced to 0, then they are defeated and the Stormhead can claim the Vector Key!

Describe the psychic battle as an argument: the Stormhead is trying to convince those it contacts that the world is rough and violent and full of unexpected pain, and submitting to its will is the only way to be safe from awful emotions like loss and heartache.

The characters can make any counter-arguments they like in response. This is obviously the time to roll out all the Story Points the characters can bring to bear.

The characters might suggest other appropriate bonuses, for example, having this battle in the presence of the memorial will give a +2 bonus to the roll, as the memorial stone is charged with psychic power from the ceremony.

A particularly striking argument might also be worth a bonus at the Gamemaster's discretion.

IF THE STORMHEAD WINS

If the Stormhead captures the Vortex Key, there is a flash of light as everyone falls unconscious. They wake some time later to find Batterlee wrecked but not entirely ruined. The storm is over, the Storm Bats are gone, and so is the Stormhead.

Over the next few days, the characters all have bad dreams about the Stormhead causing mayhem in other places in other times. They feel a sense of great responsibility. And then Evelyn contacts all of them. She tells them the Vector Key planted a time equation in her head that lets her open doorways. If they want to save the Key and stop the Stormhead, she can show them the way...

⚙ AN ONGOING CAMPAIGN

This adventure provides everything needed to launch a new campaign:

- The characters (who may be a disparate bunch of people) are united by their strange experience and their psychic bond with the Vector Key.
- The Vector Key allows travel through time and space – either accidentally, or deliberately, depending on the type of campaign desired.
- Batterlee itself provides a base of operations. The Vector Key will naturally return here, and Batterlee might well have secrets of its own.
- The Stormhead can be a recurring enemy who will reliably provide problems for the characters whenever it returns.

WHY BATTERLEE?

Of all the places in the universe to go, why did the Vector Key arrive on Earth, in this seaside village? The answer to this question could drive several adventures, or even an entire campaign. Here are some possible answers:

- A Time Lord has already escaped from the Time War and arrived here; the Vector Key was just following the same route. But where is that Time Lord hiding, or as who? And why did he or she come here?
- Batterlee Church is alive. The kindly intelligence within its stones offered sanctuary to the fleeing Vector Key, inviting it to shelter here.
- There was no reason at all. It was just random, and those who seek patterns in the random chaos of the universe are destined to lose their minds...
- The Vector Key was following a trail to another Gallifreyan device that was already in

Batterlee. Sure enough, in the deepest part of the harbour is a blue police box, its blue light shining in the darkness. The Doctor's TARDIS has been down there for centuries - but where is the Doctor? Is he trapped in the past and needing rescue?
- Batterlee right now is a temporal nexus point. Evelyn is an important figure in future history, and the fate of worlds depends on her. All this time energy was irresistible to the Vector Key, which was drawn to her like a moth to a flame.

WHAT IS THE STORMHEAD?

The Stormhead can be a recurring enemy and a source of significant mystery. The true origin and nature of the Stormhead is deliberately left unclear in this adventure so the Gamemaster can develop it for their own campaign. Here are some ideas:

- The Stormhead is actually the Master, trapped between regenerations and causing trouble.
- The Stormhead is some other Time Lord, escaped from the Time War but now without physical body.
- The Stormhead is a future incarnation of one, or all, of the player characters.
- The Stormhead is a fragment of the Great Intelligence.
- The Stormhead is its own independent entity, simply a malicious spirit like the Mara or the Malus.
- On each subsequent appearance, the Stormhead's powers and situation can be changed so players never get too comfortable with it and never know quite what it might be capable of doing.

WHO CREATED THE VECTOR KEY?

Characters examining the Vector Key might inadvertently trigger a holographic message. Three figures, dressed in workroom clothes marked with Gallifreyan insignia. They speak into the recorder:

- "We are trapped in here with this war and we can't cope any more. We're trying to escape. If we don't make it through, know this - the enemy has also been trying to get through the time lock. Their war machines will eat your reality. Whoever gets this message, please, you have to stop them or everything will be for nothing..."

SEEING EYES

This adventure begins with the characters waking up in a strange and dangerous situation with no memory of how they ended up in this predicament. As the characters race to escape, the adventure progresses through a planned sequence of scenes leading to a dramatic climax facing very dangerous foes.

The adventure is particularly suited for groups playing the Doctor and one or two companions, but it easily fits any group of time travellers. For simplicity, it is assumed the characters are roaming through time and space in a TARDIS. If not, tweak the final encounter to remove the TARDIS and replace it with something similar.

This adventure includes many examples of player ideas, and Gamemaster responses. If the players ever get stuck, sharing these suggestions might help them out.

⚙ ADVENTURE SYNOPSIS

The adventure takes place on the *SS Marie-Anne Lavoisier*, a ship staffed by Clockwork Robots. Time energy in the ship's quantum drive attracted a flight of Weeping Angels, who seized the ship and killed the human crew. The Angels are throwing the ship backwards through time to feast on the time energy, but the strain is tearing the ship to pieces.

To repair the damage, the Clockwork Robots are preparing some children's brains to become a replacement computer system.

The following information might come to light through the ship's computer, or a soldier, or a Clockwork Robot, or any other source that seems reasonable.

What exactly happened to create this situation?
Here's the sequence of events:

1. The ship's time engines attracted the attention of a flight of Weeping Angels.
2. The Weeping Angels killed the human crew and used their powers to send the entire ship back through time, feasting on the potential energy released.
3. The first timefall damaged the ship's computer. The malfunctions have spread with each subsequent timefall.
4. The Angels instructed the Clockwork Robots to repair the damaged ship's computer.
5. To do this, the Clockwork Robots began stealing teenagers through time windows.

6. They are teaching the teenagers the knowledge they need to become part of the ship's computer.

7. The characters arrive onboard the ship (see below), unconscious, and are set to become dissection subjects for the teenagers. This is where the adventure starts.

What do the Weeping Angels want?

They want the ship to be stable so they can keep pushing it through time and continue feasting.

What kind of ship is this?

It is the *SS Marie-Anne Lavoisier*, a general-purpose freighter that ran several lines between human colonies before being waylaid by Angels. It is not designed for time travel! The time engines are for faster-than-light travel only. The Angels are misusing the engines!

What is the purpose of the pretend school?

The pupils are being mentally prepared to become the control and memory systems of a new ship's computer, and the Clockwork Robots have decided that a pretend school is the most successful way to teach them.

How do the characters get here?

The TARDIS was sucked into the disturbance created by an unsecured timefall. While the TARDIS recalibrated, it dumped its passengers. The passengers all suffered unconsciousness from the timefall. They were found by the Clockwork Robots and immediately put to use as dissection specimens.

Why do the characters appear as lizards in the first room?

The Clockwork Teachers found that pupils were squeamish about dissecting humans, so they invented this ruse.

Why are they being taught dissection anyway?

Because the Clockwork Robots regard the human body as a prime source of replacement parts for repairs. This is a known habit of Clockwork Robots.

Why is the time window pointing at the early 21st century London?

The time window is aimed at the ship's next timefall destination. Right now the ship is in the late 21st century. One more timefall will put it in the early 21st century, right over London. That would be bad.

⚙ DISSECTION TIME

Begin the adventure by telling the players this: "*you open your eyes*". Then describe what the characters can see, hear, and feel. Go through the points below, taking time to ensure the players fully understand the situation they are in before you move on with the scene.

- You are lying on your back, restrained by strong leather straps around your wrists and ankles.
- About two handspans above your face is a transparent barrier. It looks a lot like plexiglass. In fact, that barrier extends around you on all sides: you are in a box with transparent sides.
- Mounted on the transparent ceiling of the box is a small metal pipe about the size of a pencil. The tip is pointing right at your bellybutton.
- Outside the box is what appears to be a classroom. About two dozen children, aged about fourteen or fifteen, sit at desks watching you. They wear school uniforms like you'd find at any London comprehensive.
- Nearby you can see another box (or several other boxes). It appears identical to yours but it contains a strange horned reptile, wriggling in its restraints.

Standing close by is a teacher straight out of a boarding-school story, a tall severe man wearing black robes and mortarboard, and holding a cane. He speaks, but you can't hear. He writes on the chalkboard: "Goatasaurs: dumb animals, feel no pain." Then: "Task: Dissect the goatasaur and remove three major internal organs."

THE ANATOMY LESSON

Laughing and joking and insulting each other, the class gathers around the boxes. Class leaders take hold of joysticks on the edges of the cases. As they start moving the joysticks, the laser scalpels (the pencil-size pipes) begin to wiggle and warm up...

The characters are inside crates, about to be dissected as a class lesson.

- The pupils cannot see the characters as people – the crates are layered with perception filters that make the characters appear to be 'goatasaurs'. If these are disrupted somehow, the pupils will be shocked and will not carry on with the dissection.
- The crates are soundproof.
- The characters don't have any useful items (such as the Sonic Screwdriver!) in reach. The items might be somewhere on their person, however.

Escape!

It is up the characters to get out of this situation before the laser scalpels start dissecting them! How will they do it? There is no set way to escape. As the players consider their options, you should remind them that they can use Story Points to adjust their situation.

As the players try things out, it is your job to choose the difficulty they face. Don't make escape too hard – the Clockwork Robots didn't think the characters would wake up before dissection time!

Here are some ideas:

- "The Sonic Screwdriver is in my pocket and I can just reach it if I stretch my fingers!" (Spend a Story Point, make a Coordination + Subterfuge roll, Difficulty 9)
- "I'm going to headbutt the box until it cracks open!" (That's a Strength + Athletics roll. It might be Difficulty 18 to crack open the box, but a result below full success might still disrupt the holographic conversion and reveal the characters to the class.)

- "I used this type of medical restraint when I was an intern at Mars Hospital! I'll use the voice commands for emergency release!" (Spend a Story Point, make an Ingenuity + Medicine roll, Difficulty 15)
- "I'll wiggle out of the restraints!" (That's Co-ordination + Subterfuge, probably Difficulty 18, but a lesser result might get one hand or leg free.)
- "I'll take a deep breath, then I'll blow really really hard on the laser so it points at the side of the box and blasts it apart." (That's... probably going to need some Story Points.)

Blinded!

There is one more unpleasant surprise awaiting the characters. When they break out of the crates, after their first round of action they sense something odd about the environment. After their second round free, their eyes begin to water. After the third round free, they are completely blind!

- There is a preserving chemical in the air throughout the ship. It is affecting their eyes.
- The pupils all get a daily injection: "Oh, you didn't get your shots this morning? There's some nanochem in the air, keeps everything clean, but you need your shots or you go blind!"

Once blinded, the characters need to ask the pupils to guide them through the adventure.

THE TEACHER

"I'll perform the dissection myself! Sit down, all of you! Anyone who disobeys will be expelled!"

The teacher is determined to carry out the dissection. The threat of expulsion sends most of the pupils to their seats, but some bravely stay put and argue loudly for the teacher to stop.

IDEAS FOR AND... OR BUT...

- ...the action tears the black robes off the teacher, exposing an array of clockwork mechanisms!

- ...a pupil stumbles into the teacher's path, and is promptly stunned and hurled into the expulsion chamber!

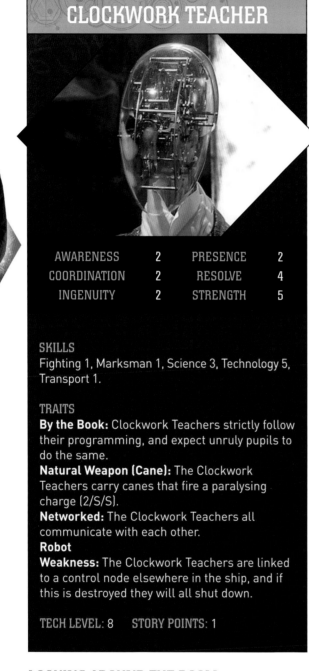

CLOCKWORK TEACHER

AWARENESS	2	PRESENCE	2
COORDINATION	2	RESOLVE	4
INGENUITY	2	STRENGTH	5

SKILLS
Fighting 1, Marksman 1, Science 3, Technology 5, Transport 1.

TRAITS
By the Book: Clockwork Teachers strictly follow their programming, and expect unruly pupils to do the same.
Natural Weapon (Cane): The Clockwork Teachers carry canes that fire a paralysing charge (2/S/S).
Networked: The Clockwork Teachers all communicate with each other.
Robot
Weakness: The Clockwork Teachers are linked to a control node elsewhere in the ship, and if this is destroyed they will all shut down.

TECH LEVEL: 8   STORY POINTS: 1

LOOKING AROUND THE ROOM
When the characters get a chance, they can look around the room. They'll see plenty of school desks and the remnants of the dissection crates. There are three exits: to the expulsion chamber (the pupils are afraid of this one), to the dormitory, and to the rest of the school.

Broken Crates
Characters might grab the perception filters from the cages and carry it with them. (Minor Gadget, Trait: Shapeshift) They might also grab the laser scalpels – they could come in useful too. (Minor Gadget, Trait: Weld)

- "I want to use the laser scalpel as a weapon!" (Spend a Story Point, and you can safely use the laser scalpel as a 3/6/9 weapon for one combat scene.)

Expulsion Chamber
This is an airlock into cold, unforgiving space. When a pupil is expelled, the teacher throws them in this room, closes the door, and they are vented into space. No one comes back from being expelled.

- "I want to come back from being expelled!" (That'll take several Story Points and a clever idea!)

Dormitory
This is a single long hall with a draped curtain dividing into girls' and boys' sections. Apart from attached bathrooms, the room is self-contained with no other exits, not even windows.

The boring little beds are entirely devoid of personal effects. Attached to each is a headset that erases the pupil's memories while they sleep.

- "I'll try and reverse the polarity of the memory headsets so they restore memories instead of removing them!" (Spend a Story Point, and make an Ingenuity + Technology roll, Difficulty 15. Pupils will remember being abducted, and realise all their classes have been about using human body parts for engineering repairs.)

⚙ THE PUPILS
After the teacher is deactivated, the characters will be surrounded by interested, excited pupils. With patience (or a good teacher voice) the following information should come out:

- The pupils don't know where they are, beyond "school".
- None of them are surprised the teacher is a robot: "It makes sense if you think about it."
- "The masters wipe our memories every morning. Helps us focus on the new stuff we're learning. All the old memories grow back overnight!"
- They don't know what else is in the school. They only know about this classroom and their dorm room, and what they have glimpsed in the corridor outside.

Two brave pupils volunteer to help:

- Carole: She has a really exuberant personality, asking lots of questions and not really listening to the answers.
- Elvis: He sometimes stutters. When he does, singing his words helps get them out.

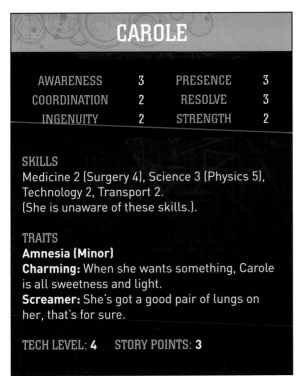

CAROLE

AWARENESS	3	PRESENCE	3
COORDINATION	2	RESOLVE	3
INGENUITY	2	STRENGTH	2

SKILLS
Medicine 2 (Surgery 4), Science 3 (Physics 5), Technology 2, Transport 2.
(She is unaware of these skills.).

TRAITS
Amnesia (Minor)
Charming: When she wants something, Carole is all sweetness and light.
Screamer: She's got a good pair of lungs on her, that's for sure.

TECH LEVEL: 4   **STORY POINTS: 3**

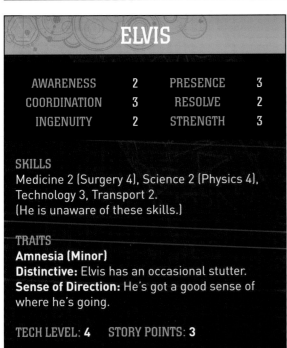

ELVIS

AWARENESS	2	PRESENCE	3
COORDINATION	3	RESOLVE	2
INGENUITY	2	STRENGTH	3

SKILLS
Medicine 2 (Surgery 4), Science 2 (Physics 4), Technology 3, Transport 2.
(He is unaware of these skills.)

TRAITS
Amnesia (Minor)
Distinctive: Elvis has an occasional stutter.
Sense of Direction: He's got a good sense of where he's going.

TECH LEVEL: 4   **STORY POINTS: 3**

✹ THE UNREFINED LEADING THE BLIND

"There's lots of teachers patrol these halls, we see them through the windows in the door. Come on!" The characters are dragged along a hall to a door. "They don't seem to come in here though. Should be safe!"

The characters arrive in Engine Room #1. They can't stay here, for the engines will soon overload and fill the room with molten plasma. They can't go back the way they came either, as squadrons of deadly teachers wait for them there. They must find a way to reach the exit on the far side of the room.

DESCRIBING THE ROOM

It is hot and stinky and sweaty, and noisy with the roaring of great machines and the steady beat of machinery. The pupils can see and describe:

- the room itself – cavernous, high ceiling.
- big vats of something bright orange and bubbling.
- big signs everywhere saying Engine Room #1 (the pupils will invariably say "hashtag one").
- a big window on the wall, currently covered with a metal sheet.
- a computer screen with a flashing red message.
- the only way out, high up – but the stairs and ladders that lead to it are damaged.

The vats contain roiling plasma, superheated to keep the engine coils operational. For any character of at least TL 7, Ingenuity + Knowledge or Transport (Difficulty 12) will know these are warp engines for starships.

THE WINDOW

A winding mechanism is easily found by the window, and it will open the shield. Through the window can be seen outer space! ("Miss! We're in space!") Earth and the moon are visible, with the sun off to the side. It isn't possible to see any more from this window, even when you squish your face hard against it. (Both helpers will try squishing their faces against it.)

THE COMPUTER ALERT

"It just says warning, warning, warning over and over. Boring." This terminal gives access to some of the ship's systems. There is a keyboard, but the computer will convert to voice communication if instructed. If the characters and pupils manage to

use the faulty computer, they can discover some information. Each round of use, roll Ingenuity + Technology (Difficulty 12). For each level of success, they discover one of the following things or some equivalent information.

Much information is unavailable, however (e.g. on failed rolls) – the computer invariably indicates that an override from Engine Room #2 has locked this information down.

- Detail on the warnings: all of the ship's systems are decaying, and engine overload is imminent. Service crew are making ongoing repairs but cannot keep pace.
- Engine room #1 – this room! – will soon flood with molten plasma. This isn't the first time, either. "Yeah, the bottom half of this room does look all cleaned off and a bit melty."
- Engine Room #1 (conventional engines) is paired with Engine Room #2 (time engines). ("Time engines? Cool!").
- The atmospheric composition cannot be altered from this terminal.
- The TARDIS has been removed to Engine Room #2.
- Details on the educational programme for the pupils: high-end physics, engineering, human biology and nothing else.
- Deckplans are available. They show only one classroom, with the expulsion chamber marked "airlock".
- It is not clear why memories are being wiped or where the pupils really belong.

CLIMBING OUT

The exit from this room is hard to reach. ("You're mental if you think I'm going up there!") First, someone needs to climb up a melted, rickety ladder to release an emergency stairwell (Strength + Athletics, Difficulty 15, or 18 if blind but guided, or 21 if just blind).

After this other people can climb up easily. However, everyone will need to swing across a tricky gap to the door (Coordination + Athletics, same Difficulty as before for the first person, then Difficulty 12/15/18 for everyone else).

- "I want to see if there's a mechanism to winch a movable walkway across to make things easier!" (Spend a Story Point, and roll Awareness + Ingenuity, Difficulty 12 – every degree of success reduces the Difficulty of everyone's climb by a step, but failure knocks something loose and increases the Difficulty!)

- "I want to instruct the pupils to treat this as a physics problem and build us a human catapult to safely hurl us up there!" (Spend 3 Story Points, and each catapulted person must make a Coordination + Resolve roll, Difficulty 12 to land without injury...)

IDEAS FOR AND... OR BUT...

- ...a chunk of melted metal breaks off and falls down on a Clockwork Teacher (see below), crushing it! One person is not targeted this round!

- ...a chunk of melted metal breaks off and makes it even harder to climb up! All difficulties are increased by one level!

RISING DANGERS!

The Teachers

"Are you bunking off, children? Open this door at once or you'll get six of the best!" Clockwork teachers start hammering on the door after the characters have been in the room for two rounds. After Round 4 they break in, waving their canes. The teachers are not capable of climbing, however, so in Round 5 they stay on the ground and demand the characters come down.

If the characters refuse, the teachers will launch a fusillade of energy bursts from their canes! In Round 6, target half the characters with a shot, then the other half in Round 7. Any stunned characters who fall will be dragged away to be expelled. In Round 8 the teachers will suddenly and silently leave. The engine is about to overload.

Rescuing a Character from Expulsion

Any character captured by the teachers will be carried to an airlock and then vented into space. Players will have to be creative to rescue them:

- "I'll use this computer terminal to remotely open a locker in the expulsion chamber, revealing the airlock's emergency spacesuit!" (spend a Story Point).
- "I'll re-program this Clockwork Teacher to convince the others the misbehaving student is their fault for being bad teachers and they should eject themselves!" (Presence + Technology, Difficulty 21 – that roll will probably need some Story Points too).

- "I'll find an air-vent that takes me right to the classroom so I can rescue them!" (spend a Story Point, and start a new scene outside the expulsion chamber).

Engine Overload

From the moment the characters arrive, the engines are heading towards overload. Plasma bubbles higher and higher! At the end of round eight, the engines will overflow and the bottom of the room will fill with molten plasma, instant death to anyone (or anything) caught in it.

By the end of round ten the plasma has risen to just below the level of the exit door – and it stops rising there.

"I'll balance on the melting frame of a clockwork teacher and float up to the exit!" (Spend 2 Story Points. Maybe 3.)

⚙ CRY ME A RIVER

"Where are we now? I can hardly see anything, there aren't many lights here and they keep flickering!"

The upper exit from the engine room puts the characters right into another dangerous situation. Lurking in the shadows here is a Weeping Angel, and the only exit is blocked. Help is on the way, if the characters can only hold out long enough...

DESCRIBING THE ROOM

It is cool thanks to a steady breeze of cold air. Every footstep echoes on the metal floor. The pupils will see and describe some obvious things right away:

- The gallery is wide and divided into three aisles by a series of columns.
- The middle aisle has working lights but the others are in shadows.
- Even the working lights are flickering. ("Like at a disco!").
- There's something down the middle there that doesn't look like the columns. It's kind of person-shaped.
- There is an exit door at the other end of the hall – directly behind the person-shaped thing.

A few more details are noticeable:

- The squared-off columns are constructed of the same translucent plastic used for the dissection boxes. They appear to be full of cables and pipes running floor to ceiling.

("But there could be lizard people in there or anything, right?").
- On the wall beside the entryway is a computer terminal. To use it you have to turn your back on the whole room, of course.
- There are some air vents high on the side walls, where the breeze is coming from.

THE PERSON-SHAPED THING

"Yeah, I see it better now. It's a statue! It's a person with wings on them. And its hands are over its eyes. It's an angel I guess? I don't know, it's a bit hard to see clearly because the lights keep flickering."

This Weeping Angel wants to play. It will use its incredible speed to herd these intruders back and forth, striking at will to wound and panic. The flickering lights protect the Angel from being quantum locked in one place. Every round, it waits for a flicker then moves behind a different person and slashes at them, deliberately doing no more than 2 damage. Only after everyone has been slashed will it try to kill or time-devour someone.

Stats for the Weeping Angel can be found on pg. 163. It has 6 Story Points.

THE COLUMNS

As TL 7 people may know (Ingenuity + Knowledge or Transport, Difficulty 12), each column is a stabilisation vane for the ship's warp drive. They are an integral part of the ship's ability to move beyond the speed of light.

If the plastic casing can be opened (any Gadget with the Weld trait, or Strength + Technology Difficulty 15 to force open a weak spot), the vanes can be manipulated:

- "I'll use the Sonic Screwdriver and figure out what's going on with the ship!" (Ingenuity + Technology, Difficulty 12, to discover the ship is in the middle of a series of unsafe time jumps.)

- "I'll use them to zap the Weeping Angel with anti-time!" (Spend a Story Point, cables can bypass quantum locking to stun the Angel for 1/2/3 turns).
- "I'll try and stall the ship's next jump through time!" (Ingenuity + Technology, Difficulty 18, to delay the next jump.)

THE COMPUTER SCREEN

Alternatively, they can spend the round attempting something with the computer. Just finding information is the same as before: roll Ingenuity + Technology (Difficulty 12) and learn one thing for each level of success:

- "I want to turn on all the lights in the shadowy sides of the room!" (Ingenuity + Technology, Difficulty 12.)
- "I want to access the atmosphere controls and change them so we can see again!" (Ingenuity + Technology, Difficulty 18.)

There is a danger hidden in the computer, however. It has been colonised by the Weeping Angels. On the second round the characters spend on the computer, the screen will start flickering. This will worsen in the third round. If the computer is used during the fourth round or subsequently, the screen will suddenly be replaced by the face of an Angel, fangs out and grinning!

Everyone looking at the screen will have to resist infection (Resolve + Strength, Difficulty 12; on a Bad or Disastrous result they are infected). Infected people must make the check again the following round, losing a level of Resolve for each level of failure. At Resolve 0, they turn into an Angel.

THE EXIT DOOR

This door is completely sealed. It has been locked and welded shut. Before long the door will be opened from the other side, but until then:

- "We use the computer to open the locks!" (Ingenuity + Technology, Difficulty 12.) "Then we smash the welding points!" (Strength + Athletics, Difficulty 18.)
- "I try and melt it using the energy cables from the columns!" (Spend a Story Point, and roll Ingenuity + Technology, Difficulty 15.)
- "I trick the Weeping Angel into tearing open the door! (You'll need a more specific plan than that. And probably a few Story Points will be needed to pull it off!)

- "Forget the door! I climb into the air vents!" (Strength + Athletics, Difficulty 9, to get into the air vents. It's not entirely safe in there however...)

SOLDIERS!

Soon after the characters arrive in the room, probably while they are trying desperately to evade the Weeping Angel, the door starts being cut open from the other side. The bright flare of a laser cutter illuminates that end of the room, and even blinded characters will see this intense light.

Two rounds later, the cut door topples and a group of soldiers come charging through.

- The soldiers immediately form a defensive perimeter around the door. They are all armed and ready for trouble. The characters and pupils are ordered to hit the floor.
- If they see the Weeping Angel, and they probably can, they fix it with the spotlights on their guns. It doesn't drop to the floor, of course. One soldier scans the Angel and says "this is charged up with weird energy!"
- The Sergeant then orders the squad to carry the Angel back to their ship. Unless the characters intervene, this is exactly what will happen.

The soldiers, led by Sgt Shachi Phadke, are from the Indian Space Forces. They were on a patrol mission and detected strange energy signals from the ship, and they've come aboard to secure the vessel. They want to take the Weeping Angel back to their ship so they can examine it and work out what happened here. Sgt Phadke is quite clear about her orders, and if the characters don't persuade her otherwise, back it goes...

The soldiers also intend to take the characters back to their ship, at gunpoint if necessary.

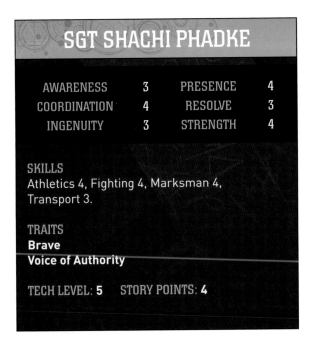

SGT SHACHI PHADKE

AWARENESS	3	PRESENCE	4
COORDINATION	4	RESOLVE	3
INGENUITY	3	STRENGTH	4

SKILLS
Athletics 4, Fighting 4, Marksman 4, Transport 3.

TRAITS
Brave
Voice of Authority

TECH LEVEL: 5   STORY POINTS: 4

RIFLEMAN, INDIAN SPACE FORCES

AWARENESS	3	PRESENCE	2
COORDINATION	3	RESOLVE	3
INGENUITY	3	STRENGTH	4

SKILLS
Athletics 3, Fighting 3, Marksman 3, Transport 3.

TRAITS
Brave

TECH LEVEL: 5   STORY POINTS: 1

⚙ A SIT-DOWN AND A NICE CUP OF TEA

The soldiers hustle everyone down corridors to the ship's docking station. The soldiers boarded here, and their shuttle is currently clamped to the side of the ship. The shuttle is too small to be comfortable as a base of operations, so the soldiers have set up in the docking rooms.

On arrival the soldiers give blinded characters some retinal equalisers to clear up their vision. Then they offer cups of tea, because they aren't barbarians.

DESTINATION: ENGINE ROOM #2

During this scene the characters will realise they need to go to Engine Room #2. As the interaction with the soldiers unfolds, share some or all of these reasons:

- The ISF isn't ready for time technology! They'll break the future, or maybe all of time!
- The ship can't simply be destroyed – an uncontrolled time engine explosion could upset the entire Solar System.
- The ship can't be left to the Weeping Angels either, they'll cause an explosion!
- The TARDIS is there!

LIEUTENANT PATEL, ONSCREEN

Sgt Phadke activates a holographic projector that puts a new person in the room. This is Lieutenant Sonal Patel. She is managing the mission remotely from the ISF Patrol Ship. Very politely, but with increasing vehemence, holographic Lt Patel lays down the law:

- The other schoolchildren will be rescued immediately – there is an airlock by their classroom so this will be easy.
- The characters are to be confined to the shuttle until everything is resolved.
- Basically, enjoy your cups of tea and stay here while we handle it.

Lt Patel does have a mission here: ISF sensors have detected the time energy and want to seize this technology to analyse it. Patel doesn't volunteer this information, but the capture of the Weeping Angel does hint that this isn't a simple rescue mission.

Her intent is to remote pilot the shuttle to rescue the schoolchildren while ordering her soldiers to go to Engine Room #2 and steal the time core.

How the interaction proceeds is very open-ended. Allow the characters Presence + Convince rolls against Lt Patel's Resolve + Convince whenever they try to persuade her of something. Perhaps the characters ally with the soldiers, perhaps they agree (or pretend) to do as they're told, perhaps they talk the Lieutenant around, perhaps they cause so much trouble the soldiers tie them up to keep them quiet and out of the way. Before the interaction can develop too far, however, it will be rudely interrupted...

LT SONAL PATEL

AWARENESS	4	PRESENCE	4
COORDINATION	4	RESOLVE	3
INGENUITY	4	STRENGTH	3

SKILLS
Athletics 3, Convince 3, Fighting 2, Knowledge 2, Marksman 3, Transport 2.

TRAITS
Brave
Voice of Authority

TECH LEVEL: 5   STORY POINTS: 4

⚙ DOUBLE DOSE OF TROUBLE

A Weeping Angel strikes unexpectedly, and the Clockwork Robots chase the characters to the final confrontation!

FIRST: ANGEL FACE

The communication signal to Lt Patel is invaded by the virtual Angel seen earlier. The intrusion will only be visible to Lt Patel. She will say something like: "You're breaking up... The signal is cutting in and out... Wait, there's something else coming through..." If the characters are quick they might cut off communications. Otherwise, Lt Patel is doomed. They watch her hologram and hear her words as she sees the Angel: "Sergeant, if you can hear me, I have another face interfering with the signal... You trying to scare me? Your fangs don't bother me!"

Then, as people watch, her holographic form will transform into a Weeping Angel. This is bad news, but the characters have other things to worry about...

SECOND: COMING OUT OF THE GOSH-DARNED WALLS

The other trouble comes through a steady escalation of warning signs:

- At about the same time as Lt Patel starts to notice the signal interruption, one of the troopers will sound off a perimeter warning. A sensor has picked up something approaching. Sgt Phadke orders troops into a defensive formation...
- Another sensor goes off, closer. Then another... Any moment now they'll be hammering at the door...
- But nothing comes at the door. What is out there? Are they waiting outside? Preparing something? What could it be?
- Then – perhaps just at the moment Lt Patel begins to transform into an Angel – the source of movement is revealed. Clockwork Robots drop through the ceilings to attack!

The Clockwork Robots have approached through ventilation shafts! The robots rapidly fill the room, their ragged and torn black robes giving them the aspect of giant crows or sinister grim reapers. They start stunning everybody in sight, and they just keep coming! Every round select one character at random and target them for a blast from a teacher's cane.

LET'S GET OUT OF HERE!

Soldiers and Clockwork Teachers are engaged in a pitched battle, and the Teachers have the advantage of numbers. It's time to head for Engine Room #2.

Racing through the Ship
The characters could try to find their way through the corridors and vents of the ship. (Roll Awareness and Ingenuity, Difficulty 12, repeat every round.) Count up levels of success: Success gives one level,

Good Success is two levels, Fantastic Success is three levels, but Failure results indicate the characters lose their way and the total is reduced in the same way.

After accumulating eight levels of success (or five if the characters have seen a deckplan), the characters reach Engine Room #2.

As they run they are pursued by Clockwork Robots. Assume there is one for each character. Run this as a chase sequence, using the standard chase rules on pg.98. The characters start with a lead of only 1 Area. The Clockwork Robots are slow so they will push to go faster each round (roll Coordination + Athletics, Difficulty 12).

Walking on the Outside

Characters could exit the ship and use spacesuits to walk across the exterior. This will avoid the Clockwork Robots, who will not exit the ship, but finding spacesuits for everyone is hard (Awareness + Transport, Difficulty 18). Compounding matters, the Weeping Angel from the warp stabilisation room will try to pursue the characters.

Commandeering the Shuttle

Characters might jump into the military shuttle (TL 5) and steer it directly to the engine room (Ingenuity + Transport, Difficulty 15). There is no dock at the Engine Room #2 end, but the shuttle could blast a hole and dock with that.

Sgt Phadke is going to be very unimpressed by characters trying to steal her shuttle.

⚙ TIME ENGINES

This is the centre of all the trouble. In Engine Room #2, the Angels have overloaded the ship's time engines to feast on leaking energy and they are preparing for the delights of another timefall. The TARDIS is also here, as is a time portal to a school playground in London in the early 21st century. The master of ceremonies, so to speak, is a Clockwork Robot who has been rebuilt around a Weeping Angel.

LOOKING AROUND

The characters might reach this room from a number of directions. Regardless, they will encounter the same scene:

- The time engine is about the size of a coffee table. It sits in a mount at the very centre of the room. Huge spindly cables rise out of it and reach the ceiling, where they spread out and drop back down to the floor like water streams from a giant fountain. The engine constantly vibrates and hums and groans, and a nimbus of reddish energy plays angrily across its surface, while blue pulses of light rush along the cables.
- Scattered around the room, all facing towards the time engine, are eight Weeping Angels. Their hands are over their eyes, but they are smiling.
- Only one thing in the room is moving. It is large – about the size of a police box, in fact. It walks with an ungainly motion. Its silhouette is strange and hard to interpret.
- On the far side of the room, dimly lit, is the TARDIS. Beside it is a glowing doorway.

THE FIXATED ANGELS

There are indeed eight Weeping Angels in the room, all fixated on the time engine. They will ignore the characters unless provoked. These Angels might simply be avoided, or they could be dealt with by rewiring a time portal and tipping them all in, or by sending the ship on a warp jump into the sun, or by some other dramatic means. The characters are left to devise their own way of dealing with this deadly threat.

THE CLOCKWORK ANGEL

The large moving object is another Weeping Angel wrapped up in a Clockwork Robot frame. Whenever the characters get close to it, they will see:

- A bulky, squared-off frame covered with tattered black cloth.
- A multitude of bent and twisted Clockwork Robot parts jut out from the frame, including four legs and four arms. There is one head, which slides around the front of the frame.

CLOCKWORK ANGEL

AWARENESS	4	PRESENCE	3
COORDINATION	4	RESOLVE	4
INGENUITY	2	STRENGTH	5

SKILLS
Fighting 4, Knowledge 4, Marksman 1, Science 3, Subterfuge 4, Technology 5, Transport 1.

TRAITS
Alien
Alien Appearance
Alien Senses (Blind-sense)
Armour (5)
Immortal
Natural Weapons: Electrified Whip, (3/S/S)
Networked: The Clockwork Angel is the control node for the Clockwork Robots.
Robot
Scan
Slow
Special (Lights out)
Special (Quantum Locking)
Special (Time Eater)

STORY POINTS: 8

- Within the frame, visible through the tattered cloth, is a Weeping Angel. The Angel has its arms and wings spread wide, and its face is locked in a fanged grin. The clockworks are entangled and embedded in the Angel like a body-horror Escher drawing. These creatures have become one horrific combined entity.

The Clockwork Angel is completely controlled by the Angel's consciousness. The Angel can speak through the Clockwork Robot's face, and it will ask intruders what they want, and mock their inability to drink from the well of time.

It offers them freedom: they can take the TARDIS or use the time portal, and go.

The Angels only want to be left alone with their time engine. The Clockwork Angel will allow the characters to leave in the TARDIS or use the time portal, as long as they do so immediately. Any delay will be met with lethal force...

The Clockwork Angel is the final threat in this adventure. The characters must defeat it if they want to do much of anything in this room, for it will brutally stop them otherwise.

THE TIME ENGINE

The time engine is, of course, the centre of attention for the Angels and the source of all the trouble unfolding on this ship.

Extracting the Time Engine

This isn't too difficult – two Ingenuity + Technology rolls (Difficulty 12) can remove the clamps. They can even be done on the same round if two people work together. The time engine is heavy, and it takes two people to lift, one at each end. Both need to make Strength + Athletics rolls (Difficulty 9). A success means they can only move at half speed while they carry the engine.

Ultimately, however, extracting the time engine is not particularly difficult. The trouble, of course, is what comes next – a room full of Weeping Angels who are very unimpressed with anyone trying to steal their engine.

Destroying the Time Engine

This isn't too difficult either, which is a definite problem. Anyone causing 4 levels of damage to the time engine in a single round will send it into crisis mode. While in crisis, the engine can be stabilised with Ingenuity + Technology (Difficulty 18).

If it takes a further 4 levels of damage in a single round while in crisis mode, it immediately begins to meltdown.

Meltdown takes three rounds. The time engine can be stabilised as above, but the task is much harder (Difficulty 24). At the end of the third round, it will explode, enveloping the entire ship in a time warp field that will destroy everything by folding it into null-time. (Story points spent here can change the outcome of the meltdown drastically, however.)

De-powering the Time Engine

This is a bit trickier. The time engine is designed to be self-sustaining, requiring no maintenance or power inputs. That means turning it off is very tricky indeed. It will take two Ingenuity + Technology rolls (Difficulty 18), and the first one will immediately slow the engine, enraging the Weeping Angels. However, success on both checks will deactivate the time engine. It cannot be reactivated except in the heart of a quantum furnace.

THE TARDIS AND THE TIME PORTAL

The time portal and the TARDIS are close together on the far side of the engine room. They are unlikely to be at the centre of activity during this climax; the Weeping Angels and the Clockwork Robots are uninterested in them, at present.

However, they might form part of any number of plans by the characters, and they are both of obvious use in ending the adventure.

⚙ ENDING THE ADVENTURE

The adventure ends when the Weeping Angels are dealt with and the time engine is brought under some kind of control – or when the characters flee, but that isn't terribly heroic.

* The characters can reunite with the TARDIS.
* The pupils can simply be sent back through the time portal to arrive back home.
* The soldiers, if any survive, can be delivered back to their patrol ship, unless Lt Patel has been turned into an Angel, in which case things get trickier. Whatever solution the characters come up with for this problem is likely to work without complication.

Once these loose ends are tied up, the characters can press on to their next adventure!

DOCTOR WHO
ROLEPLAYING GAME

THE DOCTOR

BIODATA

PERSONAL GOAL
To find out if he is a good man.

PERSONALITY
The twelfth incarnation of the Doctor is intimidating, insulting and difficult to like. A darker side of his personality has emerged with this regeneration, and he now speaks his mind bluntly with little care for the feelings of others. And yet those who pay attention will see that this Doctor is just as genuine and heartfelt as any who came before, he just buries these feelings beneath fearsome eyebrows and constant demands that the pudding-brains around him shut up, shut up, shuttety up.

BACKGROUND
This Doctor is the first incarnation in a new cycle of regenerations. This life is one the Doctor never expected to have, and it has forced change on him, made him question himself and his most fundamental nature. Nevertheless, he remains the Doctor – champion of the innocent, protector of Earth, and one of the last of the Time Lords (at least until he can track down Gallifrey).

SKILLS

④ ATHLETICS	③ MEDICINE
④ CONVINCE	⑤ SCIENCE
② CRAFT	③ SUBTERFUGE
④ FIGHTING	④ SURVIVAL
⑥ KNOWLEDGE	⑤ TECHNOLOGY
② MARKSMAN	④ TRANSPORT

STUFF

Sonic Screwdriver
Spoon (for duelling)
Psychic Paper
TARDIS

⬡ 10

Timelord

ATTRIBUTES

④ AWARENESS	○○○
⑤ COORDINATION	○○○○
⑨ INGENUITY	○○○○○○○○○
④ PRESENCE	○○○○
⑤ RESOLVE	○○○○○
③ STRENGTH	○○○

TRAITS

Boffin
Feel the Turn of the Universe
Friends (Major, UNIT)
Indomitable
Keen Senses
Quick Reflexes
Psychic
Run For Your Life!
Technically Adept
Telepathy
Time Lord
Experienced Time Lord x12

Time Traveller (All)
Voice of Authority
Vortex

Adversary (Major: Too Many To List)
Code of Conduct
Distinctive
Eccentric (blunt and inconsiderate)
Insatiable Curiosity
Obsession

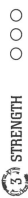

DOCTOR WHO
ROLEPLAYING GAME

CLARA

ATTRIBUTES

AWARENESS (3) ○ ○ ○

COORDINATION (3) ○ ○ ○

INGENUITY (4) ○ ○ ○ ○

PRESENCE (3) ○ ○ ○

RESOLVE (4) ○ ○ ○ ○

STRENGTH (2) ○ ○

TRAITS

Attractive
Brave
Friends (Major, The Doctor)
Lucky
Psychic Training
Technically Adept

Eccentric (Minor, Control Freak)
Insatiable Curiosity
Obligation (Major, Coal Hill School)

SKILLS

〈3〉 **ATHLETICS**

〈4〉 **CONVINCE**

〈1〉 **CRAFT**

〈2〉 **FIGHTING**

〈4〉 **KNOWLEDGE**
(History +2)

〈2〉 **MARKSMAN**

〈0〉 **MEDICINE**

〈3〉 **SCIENCE**

〈4〉 **SUBTERFUGE**

〈1〉 **SURVIVAL**

〈3〉 **TECHNOLOGY**
(Computers +2)

〈3〉 **TRANSPORT**

STUFF

None

〈5〉

BIODATA

PERSONAL GOAL

To see the universe and help innocent people in trouble.

PERSONALITY

Clara is happy, energetic and whip-smart. She is forthright and likes to take control of any situation. She considers the Doctor her most trusted friend, and would sacrifice herself to save him. (She's already done it once.) She has matured and become more confident through her travels with the Doctor, and senses the value of maintaining a strong grounded ordinary life rather than disappearing entirely into the Doctor's world. However, as she learns from the Doctor, she also becomes more like him – and sometimes that isn't a good feeling, because there is a lot of darkness in Clara.

BACKGROUND

Clara always wanted to travel, but ended up looking after two children after their mother died. When the Doctor offered her all the travel she could want, she insisted on always returning to her responsibilities, an insistence she kept up after changing jobs to become a schoolteacher. She cares deeply for the Doctor, although it took her a while to warm to the new, older version. As she cautiously builds a relationship with fellow teacher Danny Pink, she struggles to balance ordinary life and the wilds of time and space.

DOCTOR WHO
ROLEPLAYING GAME

DANNY PINK

ATTRIBUTES

 AWARENESS ○ ○ ○ ○ — 4

COORDINATION ○ ○ ○ ○ — 4

INGENUITY ○ ○ ○ ○ — 4

PRESENCE ○ ○ ○ ○ — 4

RESOLVE ○ ○ ○ ○ — 4

STRENGTH ○ ○ ○ ○ — 4

TRAITS

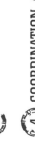

Attractive
Brave
Sense of Direction
Tough
Voice of Authority

Code of Conduct (Minor)
Dark Secret (Accidentally shot a child)
Obligation (Major, Coal Hill School)
Unadventurous

SKILLS

3 ATHLETICS   0 MEDICINE

2 CONVINCE   3 SCIENCE
               (Mathematics +2)

0 CRAFT   0 SUBTERFUGE

2 FIGHTING   1 SURVIVAL

2 KNOWLEDGE   3 TECHNOLOGY

3 MARKSMAN   1 TRANSPORT

STUFF

None

5

BIODATA

PERSONAL GOAL

To see what's in front of him more clearly.

PERSONALITY

Danny is calm and self-possessed, two handy attributes when trying to keep a handle on an unruly classroom. He keeps his head even in unusual circumstances, although his attempts to connect with the kids sometimes fall flat. Two exceptions to his fortitude, however: when someone reminds him of the awful event that pushed him out of the Army he can freeze up with guilt, and when he's trying to impress Clara, he's prone to saying all the wrong things.

BACKGROUND

Danny's life got more complicated after he met Clara Oswald, but it wasn't exactly simple before. As a soldier on the ground in Afghanistan, he entered combat zones and faced life-threatening danger. The wound he carried home wasn't to his body, but to his soul. Danny became a maths teacher at London's Coal Hill School, where he met and fell for fellow teacher Clara Oswald. Through her, he soon found himself exposed to a much more complicated world full of alien robots, unexpected forests and, of course, Clara's mysterious, frustrating friend, the Doctor.

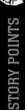

DOCTOR WHO
ROLEPLAYING GAME

MADAME VASTRA

ATTRIBUTES

- (4) AWARENESS ○○○○
- (4) COORDINATION ○○○○
- (5) INGENUITY ○○○○○
- (4) PRESENCE ○○○○
- (4) RESOLVE ○○○○
- (4) STRENGTH ○○○○

TRAITS

Alien
Armour [Minor, 5]
Environmental: Extreme heat
Friends [Major, The Doctor]
Friends [Minor, Paternoster Gang]
Friends [Major, Scotland Yard]
Quick Reflexes

Special – Tongue Attack*
Telepathy (with Jenny only)

Alien Appearance [Major]
Code of Conduct
Dark Secret [Eats People]
Last of My Kind
Weakness [Minor, Cold]

*Range 3m, S/S/S or mutation venom [Strength + Resolve, diff. 12, every hour or mutate]

SKILLS

- (3) ATHLETICS
- (3) CONVINCE
- (0) CRAFT
- (4) FIGHTING
- (3) KNOWLEDGE
- (3) MARKSMAN [Tongue +2]
- (2) MEDICINE
- (3) SCIENCE
- (3) SUBTERFUGE [Disguise +2]
- (3) SURVIVAL
- (3) TECHNOLOGY
- (1) TRANSPORT

STUFF

Mask or veil
Katana (4/8/12)

⑥

BIODATA

PERSONAL GOAL

To solve mysteries, uncover secrets, and stand against all dangers.

PERSONALITY

Vastra is a mighty warrior, but her chief weapon is her mind. She is a skilled and insightful detective and draws great satisfaction from her successes. She is open-minded and delights in defying convention, and she has even found love for a human. Nevertheless, she is a reptile, not a mammal, and she has a streak of ruthlessness that she does not keep hidden.

BACKGROUND

Vastra awoke from hibernation in the early 1880s and in a rage she killed several Underground workers in vengeance for the deaths of her sisters. The Doctor put her on a new path, protectress of London and humanity. Vastra set up house at 13 Paternoster Row, making herself available to aid Scotland Yard and also private individuals facing vexing mysteries. Her maidservant Jenny Flint became her investigative companion, then her lover, then her wife, giving clear proof of how far her views on humanity had changed since she awoke. Vastra has repaid the Doctor many times over, helping him at Demon's Run and protecting him when he was in hiding or in a state of post-regenerative confusion.

JENNY FLINT

ATTRIBUTES

AWARENESS (3) ○ ○ ○

COORDINATION (4) ○ ○ ○ ○

INGENUITY (4) ○ ○ ○ ○

PRESENCE (3) ○ ○ ○

RESOLVE (5) ○ ○ ○ ○ ○

STRENGTH (3) ○ ○ ○

TRAITS

Brave
Empathic
Friends (Major, The Doctor)
Friends (Minor, Paternoster Gang)
Keen Senses (Major, All senses)
Telepathy (with Vastra only)

Obligation (Major, Protect Madame Vastra)

SKILLS

(3) **ATHLETICS**   (2) **MEDICINE**

(3) **CONVINCE**   (2) **SCIENCE**

(2) **CRAFT**   (4) **SUBTERFUGE**

(4) **FIGHTING**   (2) **SURVIVAL**

(3) **KNOWLEDGE**   (2) **TECHNOLOGY**

(2) **MARKSMAN**   (2) **TRANSPORT**

STUFF

Leather fighting uniform (Armour 1)
Sword (2/5/7)
Scanner glove (Minor gadget, Trait: Scan,
Story Points: 1)

⬡ 4

BIODATA

PERSONAL GOAL
To protect the vulnerable and root out evil wherever it may hide. All in a day's work!

PERSONALITY
Jenny is quiet and reserved, but she has a fiercely open mind and a taste for adventure that defies both her sex and her class. Also, she married another woman, and a reptilian one at that. Jenny understands the importance of keeping up appearances but will not allow conventional expectations to limit her life or her choices.

BACKGROUND
Born in London's East End to an impoverished school teacher, Jenny became the trusted companion of the mysterious consulting detective Madame Vastra. Her life became full of adventure and wonder. She rose to every challenge put before her and won Vastra's respect and admiration, and eventually her love. She and Vastra are married, although Jenny still plays housemaid in their daily life.

DOCTOR WHO
ROLEPLAYING GAME

STRAX

BIODATA

PERSONAL GOAL
Strax always does his duty, especially when his duty involves his enormous skill at warfare.

PERSONALITY
Strax is driven to excel in battle, and where that fails he'll do his best to be a good butler, or cab driver, or nurse. His experiences have made him a very unusual Sontaran, and he feels something like friendship for his current commanding officer Madame Vastra and the human scum who serve with him. He now positively enjoys protecting weaklings who would die quickly in any proper war.

BACKGROUND
After his clone batch was defeated by the Doctor, Strax pledged to regain his honour by becoming a nurse. Eventually the Doctor asked him to help in the battle at Demon's Run, where he met Madame Vastra and Jenny Flint. After they saved his life, he joined them as their butler, coach driver and chief military adviser. He has followed their orders, and offered plenty of much-needed tactical advice, ever since.

ATTRIBUTES

- (3) AWARENESS ○○○
- (4) COORDINATION ○○○○
- (3) INGENUITY ○○○
- (4) PRESENCE ○○○○
- (6) RESOLVE ○○○○○○
- (6) STRENGTH ○○○○○○

SKILLS

- (3) ATHLETICS
- (1) CONVINCE
- (0) CRAFT
- (5) FIGHTING
- (3) KNOWLEDGE
- (5) MARKSMAN
- (4) MEDICINE
- (3) SCIENCE
- (3) SUBTERFUGE
- (4) SURVIVAL
- (3) TECHNOLOGY
- (3) TRANSPORT

TRAITS

Alien
Brave
Friends (Major): The Doctor
Friends (Minor): Paternoster Gang
Tough

Alien Appearance (Minor)
By the Book
Eccentric
Obligation (Major): The Doctor
Special – Probic Vent (a hit to the vent will stun Strax; -4 penalty on attempts to target the vent)
Weakness (Major, Coronic Acid)

STUFF

Sontaran Rifle (4/L/L)
Shock Staff (S/S/S)
Battle armour (5)
Medical scanner (Minor gadget; Trait: Scan,
Story Points: 1)

7

BBC DOCTOR WHO
ROLEPLAYING GAME

KATE STEWART

ATTRIBUTES

- (2) AWARENESS ○○
- (2) COORDINATION ○○
- (4) INGENUITY ○○○○
- (4) PRESENCE ○○○○
- (4) RESOLVE ○○○○
- (2) STRENGTH ○○

SKILLS

- ⟨1⟩ ATHLETICS   ⟨2⟩ MEDICINE
- ⟨3⟩ CONVINCE   ⟨4⟩ SCIENCE
- ⟨0⟩ CRAFT   ⟨1⟩ SUBTERFUGE
- ⟨0⟩ FIGHTING   ⟨1⟩ SURVIVAL
- ⟨3⟩ KNOWLEDGE   ⟨4⟩ TECHNOLOGY
- ⟨1⟩ MARKSMAN   ⟨1⟩ TRANSPORT

BIODATA

PERSONAL GOAL
Defend the Earth.

PERSONALITY
Kate Stewart is cool, collected and efficient. She is extremely savvy and strong-willed and she knows how to work an institution. That's how she managed to transform UNIT into its current sophisticated and successful form. She makes big decisions swiftly and with confidence, even with the fate of the world at stake. She is a skilled leader, and part of that is knowing when she needs help. The Doctor gives the kind of help she can't get anywhere else.

BACKGROUND
After some time doing other things with her life, Kate fell back into the orbit of her father, Alastair Gordon Lethbridge-Stewart. She joined UNIT but followed a scientific path rather than her father's military one. As she advanced in the hierarchy she dragged UNIT towards a greater emphasis on science. She is now UNIT's Head of Scientific Research, which makes her one of the most powerful women in the world.

TRAITS

Brave
Friends [Major, UNIT]
Friends [Major, The Doctor]
Indomitable
Technically Adept
Voice of Authority

By the Book
Obligation [Major, UNIT]

STUFF

None

⬡ 5

DOCTOR WHO
ROLEPLAYING GAME

OSGOOD

ATTRIBUTES

(4) AWARENESS ○○○○

(2) COORDINATION ○○

(6) INGENUITY ○○○○○○

(2) PRESENCE ○○

(3) RESOLVE ○○○

(2) STRENGTH ○○

SKILLS

0	ATHLETICS	0	MEDICINE
0	CONVINCE	6	SCIENCE
1	CRAFT	0	SUBTERFUGE
0	FIGHTING	0	SURVIVAL
4	KNOWLEDGE	5	TECHNOLOGY
0	MARKSMAN	0	TRANSPORT

TRAITS

Boffin
Friends (Major, UNIT)
Run for your Life!
Technically Adept

Clumsy
Dependency (Minor, Asthma Inhaler)
Distinctive
Impaired Senses (Minor, Needs Glasses)
Obligation (Major, UNIT)
Obsession (Minor, The Doctor)

BIODATA

PERSONAL GOAL
To travel in the TARDIS.

PERSONALITY
Osgood is a *huge* fan of the Doctor, almost to the point of hero worship. She even takes inspiration from his varied dress sense. She is very intelligent and always the first to work out what's really going on. She does lack confidence in herself, because she was always overshadowed by her prettier sister.

BACKGROUND
Osgood was a scientist working for UNIT under Kate Stewart, trusted with both access to the Black Archive and with knowledge of the Doctor. She assisted in the attempted Zygon invasion, although she was duplicated in the process and subsequently had her memory wiped by the Doctor to assist in the negotiations – she alone worked out whether she was Zygon or human. She later helped capture Missy during her invasion of London, but became another one of the Time Lord's victims.

STUFF

None

5

DOCTOR WHO
ROLEPLAYING GAME

SAIBRA

ATTRIBUTES

- (5) AWARENESS ○○○○○
- (3) COORDINATION ○○○
- (3) INGENUITY ○○○
- (3) PRESENCE ○○○
- (3) RESOLVE ○○○
- (3) STRENGTH ○○○

TRAITS

Empathic
Friends (Minor, The Doctor and Clara)
Shapeshift (Major)

Outcast

SKILLS

- (2) ATHLETICS
- (5) CONVINCE
- (0) CRAFT
- (1) FIGHTING
- (3) KNOWLEDGE
- (1) MARKSMAN
- (0) MEDICINE
- (0) SCIENCE
- (3) SUBTERFUGE
- (1) SURVIVAL
- (2) TECHNOLOGY
- (0) TRANSPORT

STUFF

Hologram Shell (Minor Gadget; Trait: Shapeshift; this provides the illusion of changed clothing when Saibra uses her power; Story Points: 1)

(7)

BIODATA

PERSONAL GOAL
To connect with good people.

PERSONALITY
Saibra is smart, friendly and very perceptive. These attributes meant she knew very well the impact her shapechanging power had on those around her, and it made her reserved and isolated and lonely. Now that her power is under control, her natural generosity of spirit is reasserting itself and she is looking forward to building some genuine friendships.

BACKGROUND
Saibra is a mutant human, and for most of her life her mutation caused her huge problems. Whenever she touched someone, she would change shape to replicate them perfectly. She couldn't control this power, and it meant people didn't like being around her. After the Doctor recruited her to help break into the Bank of Karabraxos, she acquired a gene suppressant that allowed her to control when her mutant power worked. Delighted, she embarked on a new stage of her life where human connections would not be forever beyond her reach.

BBC DOCTOR WHO
ROLEPLAYING GAME

PSI

ATTRIBUTES

- **AWARENESS** (4) ○ ○ ○ ○
- **COORDINATION** (3) ○ ○ ○
- **INGENUITY** (4) ○ ○ ○ ○
- **PRESENCE** (3) ○ ○ ○
- **RESOLVE** (3) ○ ○ ○
- **STRENGTH** (3) ○ ○ ○

SKILLS

- (1) **ATHLETICS**
- (2) **CONVINCE**
- (2) **CRAFT**
- (0) **FIGHTING**
- (2) **KNOWLEDGE**
- (1) **MARKSMAN**
- (0) **MEDICINE**
- (1) **SCIENCE**
- (4) **SUBTERFUGE**
- (0) **SURVIVAL**
- (4) **TECHNOLOGY** (Computers +2)
- (0) **TRANSPORT**

TRAITS

Cyborg
Friends (Minor, The Doctor and Clara)
Keen Senses
Open/Close
Photographic Memory
Quick Reactions
Technically Adept

Dark Secret (Minor, Criminal Record)
Weakness (Minor, Occasional Drive Glitch)

STUFF

None

7

BIODATA

PERSONAL GOAL
To open closed doors, for reward or simply for the challenge of it.

PERSONALITY
For a criminal, Psi was remarkably compassionate and generous: when the raid on the Bank of Karabraxos went wrong, he willingly sacrificed his life to save Clara's. When he survived anyway and got what he wanted, he went back into the deadly bank to help Clara and the Doctor find what they were looking for. He's basically a hero, despite his unorthodox and criminal methods.

BACKGROUND
Psi was a bank robber and hacker who deleted his memories of his family and friends to ensure he didn't betray them under interrogation. This loss left him bereft and isolated. He enhanced his cybernetic capabilities, but the absence of human connection gnawed at him. When the Doctor asked him to help in a raid on the Bank of Karabraxos, he was promised the reward of a neophyte circuit that restored his lost memories. The bank heist gave him this reward, but also strong new friendships in the form of Saibra, the Doctor and, especially, Clara.

DOCTOR WHO
ROLEPLAYING GAME

COURTNEY WOODS

ATTRIBUTES

(3) AWARENESS ○ ○ ○

(3) COORDINATION ○ ○ ○

(3) INGENUITY ○ ○ ○

(3) PRESENCE ○ ○ ○

(2) RESOLVE ○ ○

(2) STRENGTH ○ ○

TRAITS

Empathic
Face in the Crowd
Indomitable
Owed Favour (The Doctor)
Run for your Life!
Screamer!

Argumentative
Inexperienced
Insatiable Curiosity
Obligation (Still at school)
Weakness (Travel/Space sickness)

SKILLS

2 ATHLETICS   0 MEDICINE

3 CONVINCE   0 SCIENCE

0 CRAFT   3 SUBTERFUGE

1 FIGHTING   1 SURVIVAL

1 KNOWLEDGE   1 TECHNOLOGY

0 MARKSMAN   0 TRANSPORT

STUFF

None

5

BIODATA

PERSONAL GOAL
To prove people wrong when they doubt her.

PERSONALITY
Courtney is a disruptive influence. Plenty of teachers have said so, and the headmaster too, and her parents despair. But what can you do? There's true things that need saying out loud and that's all there is to it. Also, doors that are closed should be open. People keep all sorts of strange secrets, and there's nothing Courtney likes better than figuring them out.

BACKGROUND
Courtney is a Year 10 pupil at Coal Hill School, and she's usually in trouble for something or other. She did figure out that the new caretaker was an alien, though, and went into space with him in his police box, and borrowed his psychic paper to use as fake ID. And he took her to the moon so she could be the first woman on the moon, but then the moon ended up hatching out a sort of space dragon, but then it laid another moon so it was OK in the end (That was in the future). Also she totally was right that Miss Oswald and Mr Pink were in love.

DOCTOR WHO
ROLEPLAYING GAME

RIGSY

ATTRIBUTES

- (4) AWARENESS ○○○○
- (4) COORDINATION ○○○○
- (4) INGENUITY ○○○○
- (3) PRESENCE ○○○
- (3) RESOLVE ○○○
- (3) STRENGTH ○○○

TRAITS

Charming
Face in the Crowd
Sense of Direction

Obligation (Minor, Community Service)

SKILLS

- (2) ATHLETICS
- (2) CONVINCE
- (4) CRAFT [Street Art +2]
- (2) FIGHTING
- (2) KNOWLEDGE
- (0) MARKSMAN
- (0) MEDICINE
- (0) SCIENCE
- (3) SUBTERFUGE
- (1) SURVIVAL
- (1) TECHNOLOGY
- (2) TRANSPORT

STUFF

None

5

BIODATA

PERSONAL GOAL
To make good art, and fight any aliens that turn up.

PERSONALITY
Rigsy's heart is in the right place, although he doesn't have much time for rules and those who enforce them. He's smart, friendly, charming and capable of amazing things. He was brave enough to attempt a heroic sacrifice, but also humble enough to get talked out of this drastic action, and later to laugh about his own foolishness.

BACKGROUND
Rigsy is a young man from a Bristol housing estate. He's a talented artist, but he's been in trouble for graffiti. He's close to his mum, but his aunt was one of a number of strange disappearances from the estate that were caused by extra-dimensional entities. A chance conversation with a woman in the street dragged him into a desperate fight against these aliens, where he witnessed up close the heroics of Clara Oswald and her alien friend the Doctor.

DOCTOR WHO

ROLEPLAYING GAME

ROBIN HOOD

STORY POINTS 12

ATTRIBUTES

- ③ AWARENESS ○○○
- ⑤ COORDINATION ○○○○○
- ② INGENUITY ○○
- ④ PRESENCE ○○○○
- ③ RESOLVE ○○○
- ④ STRENGTH ○○○○

SKILLS

② ATHLETICS	◇	◇ 0 MEDICINE
② CONVINCE	◇	◇ 0 SCIENCE
0 CRAFT	◇	◇ 2 SUBTERFUGE
3 FIGHTING	◇	◇ 2 SURVIVAL
0 KNOWLEDGE	◇	◇ 0 TECHNOLOGY
5 MARKSMAN	◇	◇ 0 TRANSPORT

BIODATA

PERSONAL GOAL
To do right and inspire others.

PERSONALITY
Cheerful and merry, but serious and sober when he needs to be.

BACKGROUND
Robin Hood's story is similar to the fictional one; he is a landowner that was forced to become an outlaw by a corrupt sheriff in order to protect the weak and less fortunate. This has made him an outlaw and a thief, as he is forced to do so in order to aid the downtrodden.

As his main nemesis, the Sheriff of Nottingham, was aided by alien robots, so Robin is not dismissive of such things. He refuses to give up even when the odds are stacked against him.

TRAITS

Brave
Charming
Keen Senses (Sight)
Quick Reflexes
Voice of Authority

Adversary (The Sheriff of Nottingham)
Impulsive

STUFF

Longbow (5/7/9)
Sword (4/6/8)

2

DOCTOR WHO
ROLEPLAYING GAME

JOURNEY BLUE

ATTRIBUTES

- **AWARENESS** 4 ○○○○
- **COORDINATION** 5 ○○○○○
- **INGENUITY** 3 ○○○
- **PRESENCE** 3 ○○○
- **RESOLVE** 4 ○○○○
- **STRENGTH** 3 ○○○

SKILLS

- **ATHLETICS** 4
- **CONVINCE** 1
- **CRAFT** 0
- **FIGHTING** 3
- **KNOWLEDGE** 0
- **MARKSMAN** 3
- **MEDICINE** 0
- **SCIENCE** 0
- **SUBTERFUGE** 0
- **SURVIVAL** 0
- **TECHNOLOGY** 2
- **TRANSPORT** 5

TRAITS

Brave
Friends (Major, Combined Galactic Resistance)
Quick Reflexes
Tough

Adversary – Daleks
Argumentative

STUFF

Laser Pistol (4/L/L)

7

BIODATA

PERSONAL GOAL
To avenge her brother.

PERSONALITY
Journey Blue has a lot of anger and sorrow in her life. All she has known is war, and loss, fighting in the resistance against the Daleks. When the Doctor rescued her, she threatened him with her gun, but her adventure with him gave her a glimpse at another life, a life she could have had were it not for the war. Although she was brave, she was still a soldier and for that reason the Doctor refused to take her with him.

BACKGROUND
Lieutenant Journey Blue was a pilot who fought for the Combined Galactic Resistance against the Daleks, answering to the call sign Wasp Delta. She was rescued by the Doctor when her ship received a direct hit – an attack in which her brother, Kai, died. When he took her back to the command ship Aristotle, she convinced its commander – her Uncle Morgan Blue – that the Doctor might prove useful. She accompanied the Doctor and Clara on their expedition inside a malfunctioning Dalek, but he would not take her on the TARDIS as she was still a soldier.

DOCTOR WHO
ROLEPLAYING GAME

UNIT SOLDIER

BIODATA

NAME:

PERSONAL GOAL
To serve the United Intelligence Taskforce, defending the Earth from alien and terrestrial threats.

MILITARY OPERATIONAL SPECIALITY
You recieved advanced training in one skill. Add +1 to one of your Skill Ratings.

DESCRIPTION:

SKILLS

◇ 1	MEDICINE	◇ 2	ATHLETICS
◇ 0	SCIENCE	◇ 1	CONVINCE
◇ 2	SUBTERFUGE	◇ 0	CRAFT
◇ 3	SURVIVAL	◇ 3	FIGHTING
◇ 1	TECHNOLOGY	◇ 0	KNOWLEDGE
◇ 1	TRANSPORT	◇ 3	MARKSMAN

STUFF

5

Flak Jacket
9mm Pistol (Dmg 5)
Mobile Phone

ATTRIBUTES

- (3) AWARENESS ○ ○ ○
- (4) COORDINATION ○ ○ ○ ○
- (3) INGENUITY ○ ○ ○
- (3) PRESENCE ○ ○ ○
- (4) RESOLVE ○ ○ ○ ○
- (4) STRENGTH ○ ○ ○ ○

TRAITS

Brave
Friends (Major – UNIT)
Quick Reflexes
Tough
Voice of Authourity

Code of Conduct (Minor – Military Code)
Obligation (Major – UNIT)

DOCTOR WHO
ROLEPLAYING GAME

SCIENTIST

ATTRIBUTES

AWARENESS (4) ○○○○

COORDINATION (2) ○○

INGENUITY (5) ○○○○○

PRESENCE (3) ○○○

RESOLVE (4) ○○○○

STRENGTH (2) ○○

TRAITS

Boffin
Photographic Memory
Technically Adept,
Resourceful Pockets

Eccentric (Minor - Choose a Behaviour)
Insatiable Curiosity

SKILLS

ATHLETICS ◇ 0

CONVINCE ◇ 2

CRAFT ◇ 2

FIGHTING ◇ 0

KNOWLEDGE ◇ 3

MARKSMAN ◇ 0

MEDICINE ◇ 1

SCIENCE ◇ 4

SUBTERFUGE ◇ 0

SURVIVAL ◇ 0

TECHNOLOGY ◇ 3

TRANSPORT ◇ 2

STUFF

Lab Coat
Pencil
Notebook
Smart Phone

〔5〕

BIODATA

NAME:

PERSONAL GOAL
To discover the unknown and push back the boundaries of science.

DOCTORATE
Although you have a keen interest in all areas of science, you recieved your Doctorate in one particular area of expertise (Physics, Biology, Geology, etc., choose one). You recieve a +2 when making Science Skill rolls in the field of:

DESCRIPTION:

DOCTOR WHO
ROLEPLAYING GAME

ROCK STAR

ATTRIBUTES

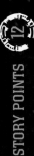

AWARENESS ○○○○ (4)

COORDINATION ○○○○ (4)

INGENUITY ○○○ (3)

PRESENCE ○○○○○ (5)

RESOLVE ○○ (2)

STRENGTH ○○○ (3)

TRAITS

Attractive
Charming
Lucky
Quick Reflexes

Eccentric (Minor - Choose a Behaviour)
Distinctive
Impulsive
Selfish

SKILLS

(1) ATHLETICS   (0) MEDICINE

(5) CONVINCE   (0) SCIENCE

(5) CRAFT   (2) SUBTERFUGE

(2) FIGHTING   (0) SURVIVAL

(0) KNOWLEDGE   (1) TECHNOLOGY

(0) MARKSMAN   (1) TRANSPORT

STUFF

Musical Instrument (Choose one)
Stage Costume
Flippin' Great Wads of Cash (Earth TL5 only)

(5)

BIODATA

NAME:

PERSONAL GOAL
You rose from homeless street thief to the top of the charts, but Earthly fame isn't enough. You want your music to ring out across time and space.

VIRTUOSO
You are a virtual musical polymath, but there is one instrument for which you are world renowned. Pick a single musical instrument or your voice. You recieve a +2 when making Craft Skill rolls to use it:

_____

DESCRIPTION:

DOCTOR WHO
ROLEPLAYING GAME

ADVENTURING ARCHAEOLOGIST

BIODATA

NAME:

PERSONAL GOAL
To explore the ruins of ancient civilizations, learn everything you can about them and then return their artefacts to a museum so others can learn about them as well.

PROFESSOR OF ARCHEOLOGY
You recieve a +2 when making Knowledge rolls pertaining to Earth History or Science rolls pertaining to Archaeology.

DESCRIPTION:

ATTRIBUTES

AWARENESS ○○○○
COORDINATION ○○○○
INGENUITY ○○○○
PRESENCE ○○○○
RESOLVE ○○○○
STRENGTH ○○○○

SKILLS

ATHLETICS ⟨1⟩   MEDICINE ⟨1⟩
CONVINCE ⟨1⟩   SCIENCE ⟨2⟩
CRAFT ⟨0⟩   SUBTERFUGE ⟨2⟩
FIGHTING ⟨2⟩   SURVIVAL ⟨1⟩
KNOWLEDGE ⟨2⟩   TECHNOLOGY ⟨1⟩
MARKSMAN ⟨2⟩   TRANSPORT ⟨1⟩

STUFF

⬡ 4

Fedora
Leather Satchel
Bullwhip
Pistol
Notebook
Portable Archaeology Kit

TRAITS

Lucky
Quick Reflexes
Run For Your Life!
Tough

Code of Conduct (Minor)
Impulsive, Insatiable
Curiosity
Obsession (Minor - Explore Ancient Ruins)

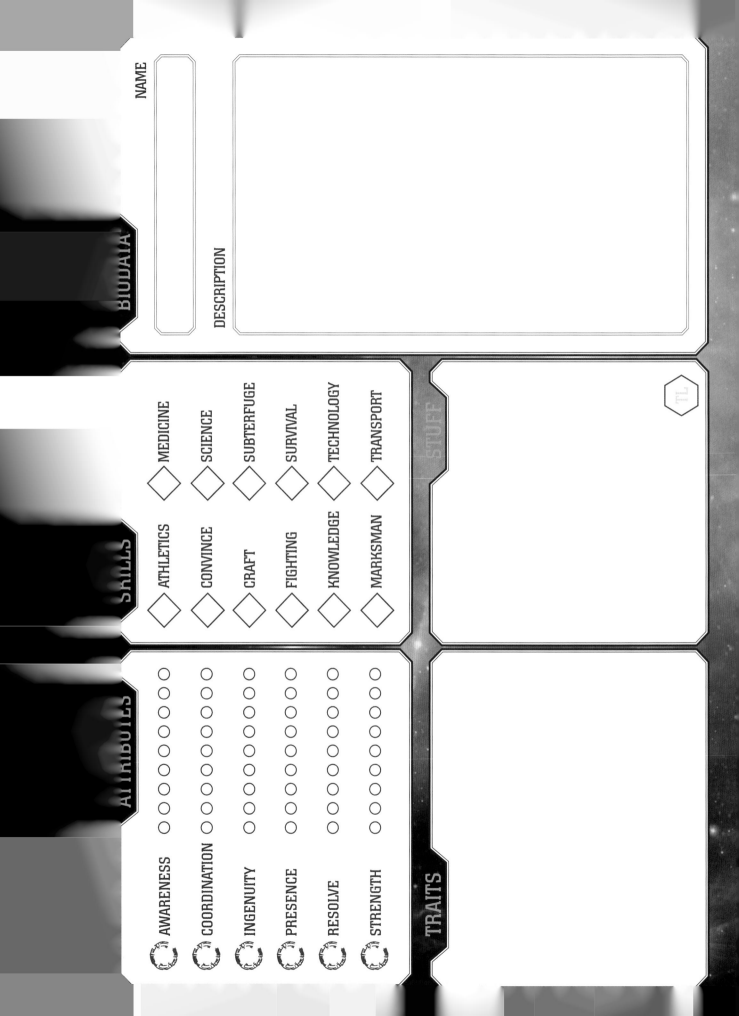

BIODATA

NAME

DESCRIPTION

SKILLS

MEDICINE
SCIENCE
SUBTERFUGE
SURVIVAL
TECHNOLOGY
TRANSPORT

ATHLETICS
CONVINCE
CRAFT
FIGHTING
KNOWLEDGE
MARKSMAN

ATTRIBUTES

AWARENESS
COORDINATION
INGENUITY
PRESENCE
RESOLVE
STRENGTH

STUFF

TRAITS

DOCTOR WHO
ROLEPLAYING GAME

PLAYER NAME

CHARACTER NAME

ATTRIBUTE + SKILL (+TRAIT) + TWO SIX SIDED DICE = RESULT
(TRY TO MATCH OR BEAT THE DIFFICULTY OF THE TASK)

LEVELS OF SUCCESS

ROLL	RESULT	DID YOU SUCCEED?	DAMAGE
9+ above	Fantastic!	Yes AND good things happen.	x1.5
4-8 above	Good	Yes.	x1
0-3 above	Success	Yes, BUT it's not all good.	x1/2
1-3 below	Failure	No, BUT it's not all bad.	x1/2
4-8 below	Bad	No.	x1
9+ below	Disastrous!	No AND bad things happen.	x1.5

EXTENDED ACTION SUMMARY

1. ESTABLISH THE SCENE
Where is everyone and what is the environment like?

2. ESTABLISH INTENT
What is everyone (including the NPCs) planning to do?

3. TAKE ACTIONS
Everyone gets their action (including the NPCs), in order of what they're planning on doing:

a) **Talkers** – any people who are just going to speak? Now's their time to talk.

b) **Runners** – people who are just moving? Here's when they go!

c) **Doers** – non-combat actions. Need to fix something, now's the time to act!

d) **Fighters** – combat actions go last.

Remember, actions directed at another character can be resisted as they occur.

4. DO IT ALL AGAIN
If the conflict isn't resolved, go back to Step 2 and decide what everyone is going to do next.

USING STORY POINTS

STORY USE	COST (SP)
"I dunno… I'm stumped…" The Gamemaster gives you a subtle clue or some event occurs that nudges you in the right direction.	1
"We only get one shot at this." Buy extra dice to add to your roll before you make it. The first SP spent earns 2 extra dice, each additional SP after that earns a single die.	1
"That was close, nearly didn't make it!" Bump your Level of Success of Failure up by one for each SP spent. Levels of Failure can only be bumped up to an ordinary Success.	1/Level
"It was just a scratch." Restore half (round up) of your Attribute levels that have been lost due to injury or losing a conflict.	1
"Like this, Doctor?" After being instructed, use a skill you don't have for a single scene ignoring unskilled penalties and roll using your Attribute + the Skill rating of the person who instructs you. You may not score higher than a Success on this roll.	1
"What's that you're building?" Build a Gadget or use an existing Gadget's Story Points to use it in non-standard ways.	Variable
"Hang on, I have an idea!" Make a minor change to the plot or story for your temporary advantage. Gamemaster approval required.	1
"You can do it, I know you can." Donate some of your Story Points to another character in some manner, from a dramatic and rousing speech, to a word of encouragement or even a kiss.	Variable
"Doing something remarkable." Do the impossible, like create a beneficial paradox, bring someone back to life or reboot the universe. Gamemaster approval required.	Variable

DOCTOR WHO · THE CARD GAME

DALEKS! CYBERMEN! SONTARANS!

The list of threats is endless and no place in the universe is ever truly safe from danger. But there's one man who's made it his mission to defend the defenceless, help the helpless, and save everyone he can. The Doctor!

Doctor Who: The Card Game is by internationally renowned designer Martin Wallace, and has been designed for both seasoned timetravelling gamers and newly regenerated players.

In **Doctor Who: The Card Game** you:

- Defend the universe with the Doctor and his companions.
- Exterminate your opponents with Daleks, Cybermen and other enemies.
- Control locations through time and space to win.
- Use Jammy Dodgers, Sonic Screwdrivers and other clever plans to save the day.

The new, second edition of **Doctor Who: The Card Game** features the same great game as the first edition, but with loads of new cards, including the Ninth, Tenth and Twelfth Doctors, companions such as Clara and Rose, new locations and enemies, and a set of variant rules for playing with two players!

The game contains everything you need to play: a set of English rules, 132 cards, a set of counters and a player aid card.

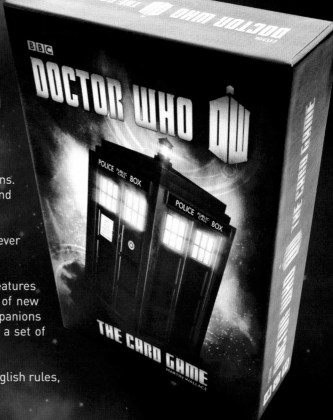

www.cubicle7.co.uk

CB72105 $29.99
ISBN: 978-0-85744-241-3